Science and the Precautionary Principle in International Courts and Tribunals

By canvassing a range of international scientific disputes, including the *EC – Biotech* and *EC – Hormones* disputes in the WTO, the *Case concerning Pulp Mills* and the *Gabčíkovo-Nagymaros* case in the International Court of Justice, and the *Mox Plant* and *Land Reclamation* cases dealt with under the United Nations Convention on the Law of the Sea, Caroline Foster examines how the precautionary principle can be accommodated within the rules about proof and evidence and advises on the boundary emerging between the roles of experts and tribunals. Breaking new ground, this book seeks to advance international adjudicatory practice by contextualising developments in the taking of expert evidence and analysing the justification of and potential techniques for a precautionary reversal of the burden of proof, as well as methods for dealing with important scientific discoveries subsequent to judgments and awards. A new form of reassessment proceedings for use in exceptional cases is proposed.

CAROLINE E. FOSTER is a senior lecturer in the Faculty of Law at the University of Auckland, New Zealand. She also advises governments and NGOs on matters relating to disputes before international courts and tribunals and issues arising in public international law more generally.

Science and the Precautionary Principle in International Courts and Tribunals

Expert Evidence, Burden of Proof and Finality

Caroline E. Foster

CAMBRIDGE
UNIVERSITY PRESS

CAMBRIDGE UNIVERSITY PRESS
Cambridge, New York, Melbourne, Madrid, Cape Town,
Singapore, São Paulo, Delhi, Mexico City

Cambridge University Press
The Edinburgh Building, Cambridge CB2 8RU, UK

Published in the United States of America by Cambridge University Press, New York

www.cambridge.org
Information on this title: www.cambridge.org/9780521513265

First published 2011

A catalogue record for this publication is available from the British Library

Library of Congress Cataloguing in Publication Data
Foster, Caroline E., 1969–
Science and the precautionary principle in international courts expert
evidence, burden of proof and finality / Caroline E. Foster.
p. cm.
Includes bibliographical references and index.
ISBN 978-0-521-51326-5
1. Environmental law, International. 2. International courts.
3. Evidence (Law) 4. Precautionary principle. I. Title.
K3585.F67 2011
344.04′6–dc22
2010034229

ISBN 978-0-521-51326-5 Hardback

For Annie

'As science begins to change the social world, great transformations of factual inquiry lie ahead for all justice systems.'

Damaška, Mirjan *Evidence Law Adrift* (New Haven: Yale University Press, 1997), p. 151

'science *n.* 1. the intellectual and practical activity encompassing the systematic study of the structure and behaviour of the physical and natural world through observation and experiment.'

The Concise Oxford Dictionary, 12th edn (Oxford Reference Online, 2010)

Contents

Preface

Cases involving scientific knowledge and the risk of future harm raise a host of new problems in connection with evidence, proof and the finality of adjudicatory decision-making. Indeed, international rules relating to evidence and proof in international courts and tribunals are evolving as a result of the increasingly high incidence of such disputes. Increased use is being made of different methods for the taking of expert evidence; the rules on the allocation of the burden of proof are coming under scrutiny; and the rules ensuring the finality of international adjudication require consideration. This book explores and evaluates the procedural developments that are taking place and assesses further steps to be taken, particularly with a view to recognising and accommodating the precautionary principle.

According to the precautionary principle, action to counter a serious threat to human health or the environment should not be delayed merely because of scientific uncertainty. The need to protect human life or health and the environment should be assumed, once certain thresholds are crossed. Proving that harm will occur is not required. This approach sits awkwardly with the usual precepts of adjudication, which revolve around the proof of fact. The challenge is for adjudicators to make reasoned decisions that pay due heed to the harm that is threatened in every dispute, despite the absence of perfect knowledge.

The topics of international scientific disputes are greatly varied. They have included subjects as diverse as fish stock conservation, radioactive pollution of the rivers and of the oceans and the air, global warming, coastal erosion, ecological damage, nuclear weapons trials, the release of carcinogens in pulp and paper processing, protection of sea turtles, the harmfulness of white asbestos, use of growth-promotion hormones in beef production, sanitary and phytosanitary risks to salmon and to horticultural production, and the safety of genetically modified organisms in the food chain and the biosphere. Science does not provide conclusive and comprehensive answers to all the questions that arise in such fields in a physically and economically interdependent world.

Scientific disputes are characterised by diverging views on the science, and frequently revolve around identifiable scientific uncertainties.

Members of international courts and tribunals must endeavour to the fullest extent possible to reach a cogent understanding of relevant scientific points. In part, they will depend on counsel's skill in crossing the disciplinary divide. International lawyers dealing with the type of case discussed in this book must therefore be able to come to terms with the salient points of conflicting scientific advice. The advocate's primary aim in a dispute involving scientific uncertainty must be to present the content of applicable science in a clear and logical way. The science must be put forward in a form that is readily digestible by a court or tribunal composed of individuals whose qualifications and experience lie in the field of law rather than science. This may involve many hours' preparation by a litigating team, where counsel work closely with the team's scientific advisers in order to identify how the existing scientific research may strengthen a party's legal arguments, and how aspects of the science being advanced by the other party require to be tested. Yet neither counsel nor judges can expect to become expert biologists or physicists fully capable of addressing scientific issues in the context of those disciplines. Nor should an advocate's understanding of the way that the law may operate be expected from individuals whose expertise lies in the sciences.

What then are the best methods for facilitating a process that enables conflicts and inconsistencies in the scientific evidence to be worked through intelligibly to all those involved? The existing adversarial approach may provide a good starting point. Parties' confrontations of one another through the adversarial process will help to flush out the technical issues, and to increase the overall intensity with which the evidence is scrutinised. There is also a trend towards investigative procedures. Scientific disputes appear to be prompting a gradual evolution in international judicial practice in relation to evidence and proof, even as developments in civil procedure have been taking place in many jurisdictions at the national level. International courts and tribunals are increasingly likely to take steps to investigate scientific disputes themselves, including site visits, consultation with international organisations, and the appointment of independent experts. International law offers an invaluable laboratory in which the trammels of domestic debate over the respective merits of adversarial and inquisitorial procedures are readily escaped and a fresh interplay in the field of evidence and proof may be experienced. Eclecticism is permissible, and provides scope for practical experimentation with different options, including new procedures for the taking of expert evidence, as seen in the World Trade Organization (WTO) dispute resolution process.

Certain problems do arise in the course of such developments, particularly in relation to international courts' and tribunals' reliance on expert evidence. The role of an expert appointed by a court or tribunal is formally limited to assisting a tribunal in the establishment or elucidation of matters of fact, but in practice how easy is it to identify a dividing line between questions and issues on which expert comment may appropriately be made and those in respect of which this may be less appropriate? Law and fact often run closely together in the type of case that is under consideration in the book. Experts will sometimes have genuinely helpful insights to offer not only into solely scientific questions, but also into interpretative aspects of the legal questions before a court. Is this advice a positive feature of the adjudication of international disputes involving scientific uncertainty? Associated with the central matter of how to accommodate the precautionary principle in international adjudication is the question of the best way to deal with independent experts' beliefs about the degree of precaution that would be appropriate in a case. For example, a marine biologist may be able to advise a court on the importance of precautionary approaches and of urgent action in stock management. Does international tribunals' receipt of such advice raise cause for concern? Or is it a welcome element of the adjudication of international disputes involving scientific uncertainty, in that the receiving of expert testimony may enable a tribunal to gain a fuller appreciation of the need for precaution in the circumstances of the case? The view taken in this book is to accept that experts' advice will impact closely on judicial appreciation of questions arising in scientific disputes, while continuing to require international tribunals to take full responsibility for their decisions. Transparency in relation to the reliance placed on expert evidence is important at all stages of the proceedings, and will help ensure that parties have the opportunity to contradict evidence with which they disagree.

A related question is the extent to which expert testimony may be used to discharge the burden of proof that is usually shouldered by a litigant. A tribunal's reliance on experts' input will naturally alleviate the load carried by disputants. Is this objectionable in principle, or is it simply part of the reality of the international litigation of scientific disputes? Do the same principles apply in relation to scientific and technical information provided by international organisations? Surely it is artificial to maintain the view that the evidence that goes to discharge the burden of proof is strictly limited to that submitted by the parties?

Despite the trend towards greater use of investigative mechanisms, the allocation of the burden of proof may remain a potentially decisive factor in a dispute's adjudication. One of the central issues addressed in this book is that, where there is an established situation of scientific uncertainty, it may be unfair to make findings against a party for failure to discharge the burden of proof. The usual rules on burden of proof may require modification. Can the precautionary principle reverse the burden of proof in international adjudication? Arguably there is indeed scope for international courts and tribunals to reverse the burden in the exercise of their inherent powers. From a technical point of view, the best method for reversing the adjudicative burden of proof in order to give effect to the need for precaution would be by introducing a partial reversal through the application of a precautionary prima facie case approach. Where it was proven as a matter of fact that a particular risk was sufficiently serious, scientific certainty about the dimensions of the risk should not be necessary. For example, this would help a complainant more easily make out a case that a respondent was engaging illegally in hazardous polluting activities or unsustainable resource extraction. Similarly a precautionary prima facie case approach would help a respondent to protect itself against health and environmental risks under exceptions within the free-trade regime and similar regional rules. In all cases the justification for applying a prima facie case approach would need to be assessed carefully. The blend of law and fact in the applicable legal rules will vary, and the appropriate outcome will vary.

Coming to the question of the finality of international adjudication, it is clear that there will sometimes be discontent with decisions that have been handed down in scientific cases, especially where these disputes centre around issues that are particularly contentious at the domestic level. This discontent may be articulated with reference to developments in the scientific knowledge in the period after the decision is handed down, and indeed in some instances there may be subsequent scientific developments that do affect the basis of a previous judgment or award. To put themselves in a position where their pronouncements could be undermined by subsequent scientific developments will be unappealing to international courts and tribunals. What can be done?

The law on revision of international judicial decisions is, appropriately, limited in its scope. Would the doctrine of nullity assist in a case where scientific developments reveal that an adjudicatory decision has been based on a significant misapprehension of the facts? What will happen if a party previously found to be out of compliance with its international obligations declares that scientific research has revealed new information and as a result this party is now in compliance with its international legal obligations? If there are new proceedings, which party will bear the burden of proof? Should expert advice be sought from the same sources as in the previous proceedings, and will relevant scientific issues require to be canvassed *de novo*? How will the principle of res judicata operate in this context?

This book advances three recommendations in relation to how the precautionary principle is to be accommodated within international adjudicatory process. The first recommendation is that we should welcome the precautionary influence wielded through expert scientific evidence - whether this be scientific evidence from the parties and their appointed experts, or evidence from experts appointed and consulted directly by international courts and tribunals. The second recommendation is that international courts and tribunals give consideration to modifying the way they apply the rules on burden of proof in order to accommodate the precautionary principle in exceptional cases. As mentioned above, this could be achieved through the exercise of courts' and tribunals' inherent powers, and would best take the form of a precautionary prima facie case approach. The third recommendation is that provision be made by individual courts and tribunals within their decisions, or institutionally in the case of ad hoc tribunals, for the reassessment of cases where it is asserted that subsequent scientific developments affect the basis of a decision.

The book addresses a wide range of disputes. International courts and tribunals are being called upon to deal with disputes involving alleged risks to human health and the environment under bilateral and multilateral treaties, as well as under general international law. A central characteristic of such disputes is that they look to the future. Disputants come to an impasse not over a past injury, with illegality, causation and harm requiring to be proved and compensation duly granted. Rather, disputes are arising over the risk of future harm to human health or the environment that could be produced by a particular activity. These disputes concern 'live' policy decisions. Usually, a claimant's desired outcome is a change of conduct by the respondent.

The subject matter of these disputes, already alluded to above, has been diverse. There have been disputes relating to the use and development of watercourses, as in the *Case concerning the Gabčíkovo-Nagymaros Project (Hungary/Slovakia)* and the *Case concerning Pulp Mills (Argentina* v. *Uruguay)*, both heard before the International Court of Justice. There have been disputes concerning the protection of marine resources and the marine environment, as in the *Southern Bluefin Tuna case (Australia and New Zealand* v. *Japan)*, the *MOX Plant case (Ireland* v. *United Kingdom)*, and the *Case concerning Land Reclamation (Malaysia* v. *Singapore)*. All three of these cases were dealt with under the dispute settlement provisions of the United Nations Convention on the Law of the Sea. Disputes have arisen relating to nuclear testing, as in the *Nuclear Tests cases (Australia* v. *France) (New Zealand* v. *France)* and the related proceedings in *Request for an Examination of the Situation*, both heard by the International Court of Justice, or the construction of hazardous waste facilities, as in the investment dispute *Metalclad Corporation* v. *United Mexican States*, which arose under the North American Free Trade Agreement and was decided under the Additional Facility Rules of the International Centre for Settlement of Investment Disputes (ICSID). There has also been a significant series of cases involving scientific uncertainty under the multilateral agreements of the WTO. The cases *United States – Import Prohibition of Certain Shrimp and Shrimp Products* and *European Communities – Measures Affecting Asbestos and Asbestos-Containing Products* concerned trade-restrictive measures adopted under environmental and health exceptions to the General Agreement on Tariffs and Trade (GATT), while the cases *European Communities – Measures Concerning Meat and Meat Products*, *Australia – Measures Affecting Importation of Salmon* and *European Communities – Approval and Marketing of Biotech Products* are examples of cases assessing similar measures for the protection of human, animal and plant life and health adopted under the WTO Agreement on Sanitary and Phytosanitary Measures (SPS Agreement).

The decisions of the various different international courts and tribunals will be considered in the book, including the decisions of the International Court of Justice, its predecessor the Permanent Court of International Justice, the International Tribunal for the Law of the Sea and arbitral tribunals operating under the United Nations Convention for the Law of the Sea, the United Nations Human Rights Committee, dispute settlement panels established under the WTO, the WTO Appellate Body, the Permanent Court of Arbitration and other arbitral tribunals, including tribunals operating under the auspices of the ICSID.

Occasional reference is made to the practice of international administrative tribunals and claims commissions, the European Court of Human Rights, the Inter-American Court of Human Rights, the Court of Justice of the European Committees, the Court of First Instance of the European Communities and the Court of the European Free Trade Area. Although reference is made to the practice of the European courts, the book concerns disputes under public international law. The specific focus in the book is on international disputes where there is an alleged breach of international law and questions of state responsibility are raised. Boundary disputes and forensic disputes in international criminal law are not addressed, as they do not raise the same problems of prospective harm. Nor does the book examine determination of the quantum of damages due to an injured party.

For ease of reference, the term 'adjudication' is used to refer to the decision-making both of international courts and international arbitral tribunals. The terms 'adversarial' and 'investigative' are used to refer to trends in civil procedure, rather than the alternative terms 'accusatorial' and 'inquisitorial' that are often used respectively by civil lawyers and common lawyers in discussions about the distinctions between the civil and common law systems. The aim is to move away from a perspective that incorrectly views the civil and common law traditions as mutually exclusive, and to use the descriptors 'adversarial' and 'investigative' in their own right as ways to describe developments in international law. In making reference to national legal systems, indulgence is sought for a predominance of reference to English, French and occasionally Spanish civil procedure from among the civil law systems; and equally for the restriction of comparative work largely to the common law and the civil law. This is largely due to the author's background, as well as the availability of resources.

A word might also be said about the inclusion of WTO dispute settlement bodies in the category of international courts and tribunals. The highly developed dispute-settlement mechanisms of the WTO, established in 1995 under the WTO Understanding on Rules and Procedures governing the Settlement of Disputes, have provided a framework for the thorough judicial investigation by WTO panels of a considerable number of disputes where scientific uncertainties lie close to the heart of the issues dividing the parties. Many of these disputes have fallen under the SPS Agreement. Sanitary and phytosanitary measures are measures applied to protect human, animal and plant life and health against risks from pests and diseases, as well as additives or contaminants in food. A number of the disputes have also been decided under the environmental and health exceptions found in Article XX(b) and (g) of the GATT. In most of these cases there has been an appeal to the WTO Appellate Body, usually in relation to a broad range of issues, both substantive and procedural. The result is a sophisticated set of panel and Appellate Body reports that give close consideration to many of the issues addressed in this book.

Acknowledgements

This book has its genesis in issues I dealt with in the legal division of the New Zealand Ministry of Foreign Affairs and Trade, particularly the relationship between the Cartagena Protocol on Biosafety (which we negotiated during that time) and the law of the World Trade Organization. Following my time at the Ministry, I was fortunate to carry out my doctoral work at the University of Cambridge on scientific uncertainty in international adjudication, under the supervision of Daniel Bethlehem, QC, now Legal Adviser to the Foreign and Commonwealth Office. During the last seven years since the completion of that thesis, much has taken place in the fields of science and precaution in international courts and tribunals. The jurisprudence is growing thickly around us, and arbitral and adjudicatory practice continues to advance in an effort to deal with the new challenges posed. In the interim, my perspectives on the procedural aspects of the adjudication of international scientific disputes have developed further and I have been able to consult widely with individuals working in the field. As a result, I have many people to thank for their help in producing this book.

The Lauterpacht Research Centre for International Law has always opened its doors to me when I have had the opportunity to carry out focused work on this project in the quiet and beautiful environs of Cambridge. During the book's gestation I have been fortunate to meet with many people with more direct, first-hand insights than me into the problems dealt with in this book. At an early stage, a number of individuals helped in the evolution of my thinking on the problems of scientific evidence, including Professor Thomas Cottier, Theofanis Christoforou, Professor Peter Van Den Bossche, Valerie Hughes, Professor Don McCrae, Torsten Ström, Olivier Lalande, Professor

Michael Hart, Professor Michael Trebilcock, Amelia Porges, Professor John Jackson, Ted Thompson and Professor Joost Pauwelyn. All of these individuals participated in work that I carried out as part of the British Institute for International and Comparative Law's pilot project on Evidence Before International Courts and Tribunals, funded by the Leverhulme Trust and focusing on the topic of scientific evidence. I have also benefited greatly from discussions with Professor James Crawford, Professor Vaughan Lowe, Samuel Wordsworth, Sir Eli Lauterpacht, Sir Franklin Berman, Professor John Bell and Professor Andrew Sterling. In Geneva I have received unfailingly kind and constructive responses from staff at the Secretariat of the World Trade Organization, including Gabrielle Marceau, Gretchen Stanton, Mireille Cossy, João Magalhães, Bruce Wilson, Reto Malacrida, Kerry Allebeury, Werner Zdouc, Yves Renouf and Marie Isabelle Pelan. In Washington I talked with Canadian Kevin Thompson and with US government staff Laurel Celeste, Dr Eric Flamm and Dan Brinza. All of these individuals were helpful and generous with their time and insights. My thanks also to the organisers of the workshop on Science in International Law convened in Helsinki, Finland, in 2009 by the European Society of International Law and the American Society of International Law. Special thanks to Jorge Viñuales, Céline Lévesque and Elizabeth Fisher, with whom I enjoyed discussions at the workshop and who were generous in their subsequent correspondence. I should like also to mention Judges Bruno Simma and Al-Khasawneh of the International Court of Justice, whose reasoning in their Joint Dissenting Opinion in the *Case concerning Pulp Mills on the River Uruguay* interweaves with many of the arguments in the book dealing with expert evidence.

As the project has neared its completion, Professor David Williams QC, Rodney Neufeld of the Canadian Department of Foreign Affairs and International Trade, and Kitt Littlejohn have helpfully reviewed excerpts and provided comments. Professor Ivan Shearer of the University of Sydney has very kindly read through the full manuscript for me. Throughout this period I have had a supportive work environment here in the Faculty of Law at the University of Auckland in New Zealand, for which I thank my colleagues and also my mentor, Professor Bruce Harris. The University of Auckland's New Staff Research Grant and provisions for research leave have also assisted greatly. In preparing the final chapters of the book I received valuable research assistance from Deirdre Bourke, and many others have helped me throughout the project with typing and finding references.

For financial and academic support in the early years, my major debts of gratitude are to Gonville and Caius College, my home in Cambridge during my doctoral studies, and the College's W. M. Tapp Scholarship. I owe special thanks to Dr Pippa Rogerson for her support as Director of Studies in Law at the College. I am grateful also to the New Zealand Vice-Chancellor's Committee for the award of a Gordon Watson Scholarship which facilitated my studies. In Cambridge I came to know Daniel Bethlehem, who became an essential source of support and enthusiasm in his role as my doctoral supervisor and met with me for lengthy discussions about my work. To my colleagues on the doctoral programme at Cambridge, for whom I have a special fondness, thank you also. My particular thanks to those of you who carefully read through a number of the chapters of my thesis as they were written, Associate Professor Chester Brown, Matthew Conaglen, and Ben Olbourne. Professor Scott Davidson, formerly of the University of Canterbury in New Zealand where I completed my undergraduate studies, graciously read over my thesis before its submission, as did my colleague Barbara von Tigerstrom, now Associate Professor at the University of Saskatoon. Professor James Crawford and Professor Alan Boyle provided extremely helpful feedback in their examiners' reports, which laid the foundations for a broader approach to the topic as I wrote this book.

My warmest and deepest thanks go to my husband Rob Stock, whose constancy and determination to give practical effect to our decisions to take equal responsibility in the home have enabled us to maintain a two-career household and at the same time to produce and begin to raise our two wonderful young girls, Catherine and Zoe, during the period this book was being written. Finally, I must also mention my father Richard and my mother Virginia who have always been supportive of my plans and projects and from whom I am continuing to learn many of life's most important lessons.

PART I

Context and theory

1 Introduction

International adjudication

There is increasing commonality in the procedural rules that international courts and tribunals apply in relation to matters of proof and procedure.[1] This commonality may be explicable largely on the basis that international courts and tribunals essentially perform the same function as one another, but it is also due to the powerful intrinsic reasons for common practice, such as the perceived fairness and utility of the rules.[2] As reciprocal relationships among international courts and tribunals deepen and formalise, we are moving towards a time when they may potentially be viewed as forming part of the same court system.[3] The development of rules for the allocation of jurisdiction between tribunals may be the most important contributing factor.[4] However, increasing coherence in the handling of procedural matters indicates that informal relationships among courts are already building up at a systemic level.[5] Though there is no formal doctrine of precedent in international adjudication, courts and tribunals do look to one another's decisions for insight – on both substantive and procedural matters.[6] A 'community of international courts' is gradually forming.[7]

In this developing community, the impartial, reasoned and fair disposition of public international legal disputes has long been regarded as requiring considerable freedom for international courts and tribunals in relation to matters of evidence. An overarching emphasis has been placed on finding the 'truth' lying at the heart of an international

[1] Brown, *A Common Law*, p. 13. [2] *Ibid.*, p. 233.
[3] Shany, *The Competing Jurisdictions*, p. 106. [4] *Ibid.*, pp. 106–10
[5] Brown, *A Common Law*, p. 258. [6] Shahabuddeen, *Precedent*, p. 6.
[7] Brown, *A Common Law*, p. 258, noting Slaughter, 'A global community'.

dispute.[8] For this reason, international law knows little restriction on the admissibility of evidence, and the concept of the court's free evaluation of the evidence also prevails.[9] Accordingly, the focus of the discussions in this book lies more on matters associated with proof, rather than evidence as the field is known in the common law.

Little distinction need be made between the practice of international courts and the practice of international arbitral tribunals for the purposes of these studies, although a higher degree of technical specialisation amongst tribunal members is possible in the case of arbitration.[10] Perhaps the most relevant point of difference in regard to arbitral tribunals is that disputants usually have greater control over the procedure that is applied in an arbitration. The parties may therefore be more likely to take the initiative regarding decisions about such matters as the choice of procedures for putting expert evidence before the tribunal. The parties' level of control over the proceedings may also generate a different tone. However, the arguments and proposals canvassed in the chapters that follow generally apply equally to the practice of both judicial and arbitral tribunals. The challenges faced in dealing with science are similar, and the need to accommodate the precautionary principle should be recognised equally in either forum.

The cases discussed in the pages that follow present issues from a wide range of fields, revealing the contestability of scientific knowledge across different scientific specialisations, such as marine biology, nuclear technology, coastal geomorphology and endocrinology, to name only a few. They include cases where a disputant objects to another actor's activity because of the risks associated with the activity, and cases where a disputant objects to measures taken by another actor to protect itself against particular risks. For example, in resource-related disputes arising under the law of the sea complainants insist upon legal limitations to respondents' freedom to engage in

[8] Amerasinghe, *Evidence*; Sandifer, *Evidence*; Witenberg, '*Onus probandi*'; Brown, *A Common Law*, pp. 83, 85.

[9] Sandifer, *Evidence*, Chs. 1 and 4; Highet, 'Evidence and proof of facts', 358. See Iran–United States Claims Tribunal Final Rules of Procedure, 3 May 1983, 1 Iran–US CTR 57, Article 25(6); United Nations Commission on International Trade Law (UNCITRAL) Arbitration Rules 1976, www.uncitral.org, Article 25; ICSID Rules of Procedure for Arbitration Proceedings, *ICSID Convention, Regulations and Rules* (Washington: International Centre for the Settlement of Investment Disputes, 2006), Rule 33(1).

[10] Rosenne, *The Law and Practice*, p. 12. For wider discussion, *ibid.*, pp. 9–14.

disputed activities. In contrast, in the trade arena cases are lodged to defend exporters' freedom to engage in international trade, with arguments put forward insisting that there are no applicable legal limitations in relation to the exports in question. The arguments that will be made in the course of the book apply equally to both forms of dispute.

The rationalist tradition

The notion that it is a court or tribunal's task to apply the law to the facts forms part of what has been characterised in the West as the 'rationalist' tradition.[11] This tradition originated in the Enlightenment period, following the discrediting of the mediaeval method of trial by ordeal as a legal institution for determining the truth of a matter.[12] A rationalist approach to adjudication has sat well with the traditions of different domestic legal systems and is compatible both with standard liberal and socialist theories of law.[13] In the rationalist conception, fact and law are approached as distinct and separate. Rules governing evidence and procedure serve to help bring about 'rectitude of decision' through the 'correct application of valid law to true facts'.[14] Basic assumptions of the rationalist tradition view procedural law as facilitating this determination of true past facts as accurately as possible.[15] However, it is accepted that this may not always be possible, and rationalism is best understood as aspirationalist. The expectation of being able to determine the facts is the guiding principle.[16]

In disputes involving scientific uncertainty and potential future harm, international courts and tribunals are called upon to make judicial decisions in circumstances where potentially decisive facts about

[11] Twining, *Rethinking Evidence.* [12] *Ibid.*; Taylor, 'A comparative study', 185.

[13] Twining, *Rethinking Evidence*, pp. 199–200.

[14] Bentham, *Rationale*; Twining, *Rethinking Evidence*, p. 41; see also p. 423 on the empiricist tradition initiated by Bentham, Bacon, Mill, Jevons and Sidgwick. Bentham's work on the theory of adjudication has been described as the only sustained English-language attempt to produce a philosophical account of procedural law, with the exception of Fuller's work. Postema, 'The principle of utility and the law of procedure', 1393, citing Jeremy Bentham, 'The Principles of Judicial Procedure' in *Works of Jeremy Bentham*, II, pp. 1, 6. See also p. 1415. See also Anderson *et al.*, *Analysis of Evidence* pp. 78–84. Additionally, Jolowicz, *On Civil Procedure*, pp. 59, 86, 396; Stein, *Foundations of Evidence Law*, pp. 10, 56, 113 and 219–20; Fuller, 'The forms and limits'.

[15] Twining, *Rethinking Evidence*, p. 447.

[16] Often, rationalist theories about proof are concerned with the establishment of the approximate truth as a matter of probability. Twining, *Rethinking Evidence*, p. 76, point 4 and p. 273, point 12.

future events clearly cannot be obtained at the time of adjudication. While it may be disingenuous in other kinds of dispute to approach the rationalist tradition by interpreting its aspiration for certainty literally,[17] the situation is somewhat different in relation to a category of cases where the facts needed to decide a case are clearly unavailable. Here the concept of 'certainty' is to be taken literally: an absence of certainty has to be accepted from the start. This raises various tensions within the rationalist tradition.

Naturally, international legal rules are often crafted with scientific uncertainties already in mind, and as a result many international scientific disputes are governed by legal provisions involving mixed questions of scientific fact and law. For example, parties may be obligated to take all 'reasonable' measures to preserve the environment. Experts with detailed scientific knowledge will help adjudicators determine what can be considered 'reasonable'. In these cases, the usual rationalist distinction between fact and law may no longer so clearly prevail, and a clear-cut distinction between the role of an adjudicatory body and the role of experts advising a court or tribunal cannot be fully maintained. The scientific expert participates in the interpretative process carried out by the court or tribunal. Further, it becomes clear that the rules on burden of proof are not merely procedural in nature and can affect the outcome of a case. The application of the usual rules on burden of proof can lead to significant unfairness in a situation where scientific knowledge is simply not available. Additionally, the usual conclusive character of rationalist adjudication comes into question: if the science can change, how final should an adjudicatory decision actually be? In relation to all three of these sites of challenge within the rationalist tradition – expert evidence, burden of proof and the finality of adjudication – the degree of tension will depend partly on the specific legal rules at issue, especially the extent to which they have been designed to accommodate scientific uncertainty.

Proceduralisation and harmonisation in international law

In all of this, adjudication must be seen in a proper perpective. Adjudication is a tool for use in selected situations, and it is a highly

[17] *Ibid.*, p. 104.

rigid process that will not necessarily deal well with all aspects of scientific disputes. The substantive law governing international actors' relations with one another in relation to risks of potential future harm is gradually evolving in ways that take the emphasis off substantive determinations of rights through international adjudication. Increasingly, the international legal community deals with the need to mitigate risks and prevent environmental harm through a sophisticated network of international procedural obligations, found for the most part in multilateral environmental agreements.[18]

These obligations include requirements to obtain advance informed agreement or prior informed consent, such as in relation to transport of hazardous substances;[19] and requirements of prior notification, consultation and negotiation, such as in relation to shared watercourses.[20] By way of example, in one of the most well-known disputes, the *Lac Lanoux* case, the Arbitral Tribunal held that France was required to notify Spain of its intention to carry out work affecting the river's flow and to hear Spanish views.[21] Also included in the category of procedural obligations are general duties of co-operation, such as in respect of biodiversity[22] and under the United Nations Convention on the Law of the Sea (LOSC),[23] as well as general duties of consultation.

The requirements for risk assessment that dominate international trade law dealing with sanitary and phytosanitary risks also exemplify this growing focus on procedural obligations. Provisions requiring environmental impact assessments are central. Requirements to use the best available technology[24] or to design measures using the best

[18] On procedural obligations in customary international law, see Birnie *et al.*, *International Law*, pp. 126f, 559; Okowa, 'Procedural obligations', 317 f.

[19] For example, see the Cartagena Protocol on Biosafety to the Convention on Biological Diversity, Cartagena, 29 January 2000, in force 11 September 2003, 39 ILM 1027; the Convention on the Control of Transboundary Movements of Hazardous Wastes and their Disposal, Basel, 22 March 1989, in force 24 May 1992, 28 ILM 657; and the Convention on the Prior Informed Consent Procedure for Certain Hazardous Chemicals and Pesticides in International Trade, Rotterdam, 1988, in force 24 February 2004, 38 ILM 1.

[20] See the Convention on the Law of the Non-Navigational Uses of International Watercourses, New York, 21 May 1997, 36 ILM 719.

[21] *Affaire de Lac Lanoux* (Spain/France) XII UNIRAA 281 at 308.

[22] See the Convention on Biological Diversity, Rio de Janeiro, 5 June 1992, in force 29 December 1993, 31 ILM 818.

[23] United Nations Convention on the Law of the Sea, Montego Bay, 10 December 1982, in force 16 November 1994, 21 ILM 1261.

[24] For example, see the Convention on Long-Range Transboundary Air Pollution, Geneva, 13 November 1979, in force 16 March 1983, 18 ILM 1442.

scientific evidence available[25] may similarly be regarded as at least partly procedural. Obligations to comply with standards of due diligence and duties to prevent harm to other actors from hazardous activities[26] could also be considered to belong to the same family, although their substantive content remains apparent. Increased attention is being paid to the importance of public consultation, both in a state where a risk-generating activity is to take place and in an affected state.[27] Indeed, contemporary commentary on the precautionary principle emphasises that decision-making processes should involve public participation and deliberation.[28] The importance of collective consent to decision-making, and public trust in the responsible institutions has been emphasised.[29]

Procedural obligations form a vital part of international legal structures aimed at substantive outcomes, such as prevention and reduction of damage,[30] and their legal status is no less than that of substantive obligations: they are binding. It might be suggested that procedural obligations help fill the void in international risk regulation that corresponds to the activity of relevant executive and administrative bodies in domestic legal systems, by 'systemati[sing] co-operation'[31] between states. Procedural obligations enable situations of risk to be regulated with a degree of flexibility, over time, on the basis of ongoing interaction between international actors. As states devote more attention to fulfilling their procedural obligations, the likelihood and intensity of international litigation of disputes over potential future harm may diminish.[32]

25 See LOSC, Article 119(1)(c). 26 Birnie *et al.*, *International Law*, pp. 137–50.

27 For example, see Articles 2(2), 2(6), and 3(8) of the Convention on Environmental Impact Assessment in a Transboundary Context, Espoo, 25 February 1991, in force 27 June 1997, 30 ILM 802; Convention on Access to Information, Public Participation in Decision-Making and Access to Justice in Environmental Matters, Aarhus, 25 June 1998, in force 30 October 2001, 38 ILM 517.

28 Fisher and Harding, 'The precautionary principle', 290; Cameron, 'The precautionary principle: Core meaning', 56.

29 McDonell, 'Risk management', 190, 203; Wynne, 'Risk and environmental issues'.

30 For example, Okowa observes the vital role of procedural obligations as practical underpinnings of 'aspirational and programmatic' principles of less clear legal status. Okowa, 'Procedural obligations', 334.

31 *Ibid.*, 334.

32 For further discussion, Stephens, *International Courts*, pp. 98–100. At the same time it has to be acknowledged that an emphasis on procedural obligations does not address the values at issue, and the need for normative criteria to resolve international environmental disputes appropriately in many instances. Koskenniemi, 'Peaceful settlement of environmental disputes'.

Proceduralisation operates in counterpoint with harmonisation, and both operate together with the precautionary principle.[33] Prominent among agreements emphasising harmonisation is the World Trade Organization (WTO) Agreement on Sanitary and Phytosanitary Measures (SPS Agreement).[34] The SPS Agreement offers a definition of harmonisation, as well as specifying that the international standards, guidelines and recommendations referred to in the Agreement are those of the Codex Alimentarius Commission, the International Office of Epizootics and those developed under the International Plant Protection Convention.[35] Harmonisation is not a phenomenon limited to the trade field. Reference might be made to the development of 'standards' of international environmental protection through multilateral agreements.[36] Standards emanating from the private sector may also have an effect within international law. For example, industry standards were used as a benchmark in assessing the production technology used at the Orion mill in the *Case concerning Pulp Mills on the River Uruguay (Argentina* v. *Uruguay)*.[37] From time to time actors will seek a higher level of protection than that offered by international standards. The difficulty with keeping international standards up to date with scientific developments has been recognised.[38] There may also be issues due to the fact that

[33] Obligations relating to consultation, the conduct of environmental impact assessments, and the sharing of information have been described by commentators as companion obligations to the precautionary principle. Handl, 'Environmental security', 76.

[34] Agreement on the Application of Sanitary and Phytosanitary Measures, WTO, *The Legal Texts: The results of the Uruguay round of multilateral trade negotiations*, p. 59. See also the Agreement on Technical Barriers to Trade, *ibid.*, p. 121.

[35] SPS Agreement, Annex A paras. 2 and 3. For background, Victor, 'The SPS Agreement'.

[36] For example, see *United States – Import Prohibition of Certain Shrimp and Shrimp Products*, Complaint by India (WT/DS58), Complaint by Malaysia (WT/DS58), Complaint by Pakistan (WT/DS58), Complaint by Thailand (WT/DS58), Report of the Panel DSR 1998: VII, 2821, paras. 7.52, 7.55.

[37] *Case concerning Pulp Mills on the River Uruguay (Argentina* v. *Uruguay)*, Judgment of 20 April 2010, ICJ Reports 2010 paras. 223–5.

[38] See *EC – Asbestos* where the EC argued that advances in science could 'render an international standard ineffective or inappropriate'. *European Communities – Measures Affecting Asbestos and Asbestos-Containing Products*, Complaint by Canada (WT/DS135), Report of the Panel DSR 2001: VIII, 3305 paras. 3.374, 3.375. The EC noted that the North American Free Trade Agreement (NAFTA) allowed specifically for this. NAFTA Article 905(1): 'Each party shall use, as a basis for its standards-related measures, relevant international standards or international standards whose completion is imminent, except where such standards would be an ineffective or inappropriate means to fulfil its legitimate objectives, for example because of fundamental climatic, geographical, technological or infrastructural factors, *scientific justification* or the level of protection that the party considers appropriate.' Emphasis added. *Ibid.*, para. 3.374.

international standards are not always equally applicable in all environments.[39] However, generally, increased harmonisation over time can, like the greater use of procedural obligations, be expected to reduce the scope for disputes over risk-response measures.

In tandem with these trends, increasing international acceptance of the precautionary principle as an appropriate and justifiable basis for decisions in situations of risk and scientific uncertainty will also reduce friction between international actors over activities involving risks. Despite these positive trends, however, it is clear that the adjudication of international disputes will continue to require international courts and tribunals to grapple with the hard science.

The nature of scientific knowledge

Scientific disputes must be adjudicated in the knowledge that all scientific assertions are subject to the possibility of being discarded should they prove to be false.[40] This dedication to empiricism is a signature feature of scientific method. Today's 'minority science' could become tomorrow's 'mainstream science'.[41] Further, science is profoundly social.[42] What we know as an 'invulnerable core of scientific knowledge' ultimately consists of scientific claims that no scientist any longer challenges.[43] This is important in the context of scientific disputes. The interface between science and law generates changes in the dynamics of what will pass for scientific knowledge and expertise. All involved need to be aware of the social and legal construction of scientific knowledge and scientific expertise, as well as their fragility in sceptical legal contexts.[44]

The 'systematic and formulated knowledge' on which we rely to interpret the natural world is recognised within the discipline in which it is developed as contingent. Scientific hypotheses and assertions are formulated and adopted in the light of focused observations, measurements and modelling. The design and execution of the studies on which they are based, and the quality of their analyses, are subject to vigorous peer review. These hypotheses and assertions are then permitted to prevail, based on their merits and the understanding that they could later be superceded by alternative hypotheses and assertions. However,

[39] See below, Ch. 4.

[40] Popper, *The Logic of Scientific Discovery*. See also Popper, *The Myth of the Framework*.

[41] Kuhn, *The Structure of Scientific Revolutions*. [42] *Ibid.*

[43] Jasanoff, 'What judges should know', 349. [44] Smith and Wynne, 'Introduction', 12.

differences of view among scientists as to the validity of hypotheses and assertions can be expected to remain indefinitely in varying degrees. Differences may be due to numerous specific factors, such as the ways in which samples are selected, variables chosen, methods of measurement employed, models adopted and causal inferences drawn.[45]

As in other fields of research, the scientific mainstream has an inherent pull. Prevailing perspectives influence the scope of contemporary scientific research, as well as scientific methodology and working assumptions.[46] Research funding structures and constraints are among the more overt determinants of the parameters of scientific development, but less obvious influences must also be taken into account. There are disciplinary efficiencies in according ready acknowledgement to work carried out by known and respected researchers, or within the frameworks that have been established by their work. New work, or radical assertions and hypotheses, will be subject to more intense review, and publication may be more difficult.[47] Yet recognising the potential value of new science is important. On various occasions in recent history, developments in technical and scientific understanding have revealed fatal and pernicious errors in relation to the safety of particular products and practices. Well-known examples include the use of asbestos, thalidomide and ozone-depleting substances.[48]

Scientific uncertainties permeate the evidence in the type of case under study in this book. It is the task of international courts and tribunals to come to terms with the science in order to dispose appropriately of the cases that come before them. For the purposes of the discussions that follow, we can say that there is 'scientific uncertainty' where reputable scientists agree that further research needs to be carried out on a particular question, or their disagreement on issues germane to a dispute makes it clear this is so.[49]

[45] Fraiberg and Trebilcock, 'Risk regulation'; Hickey and Walker, 'Refining the precautionary principle', 408.

[46] Kuhn, *The Structure of Scientific Revolutions*.

[47] Peel, *The Precautionary Principle*, p. 131.

[48] Harremoës *et al.*, 'Twelve late lessons', 185 - 215.

[49] Wynne, 'Uncertainty and environmental learning', 111-27. Alternatively, see von Schomberg, 'The precautionary principle', 29. See also Stirling, 'The precautionary principle', 80. It is important also to acknowledge potential ignorance, where 'we do not know what we do not know'. Wynne, 'Uncertainty and environmental learning', 111-27; See also Harremoës *et al.*, 'Twelve late lessons', 187; McDonell, 'Risk management', 190.

The admissibility of scientific evidence

The courts in the United States have wrestled for some time with the question of what constitutes good or reliable science. This debate became popularised, with an emphasis on the potential for distortion and abuse of the scientific discipline in the courtroom.[50] Since, there has been a move away from determining the admissibility of scientific evidence purely through reliance on the general acceptance of scientific views within the scientific community. Citing influential philosophers of science, Karl Popper and Carl Hempel,[51] the US Supreme Court found that the admissibility of scientific evidence in United States' courts should depend on a broad concept of 'scientific validity'.[52] To meet this test, scientific knowledge must be derived by scientific method, and indicators of its validity include its testability or falsifiability, subjection to peer review, publication, the error rate in the techniques used, as well as the broader acceptance of the opinion in the scientific community.[53]

In international adjudication the free admissibility of evidence is the guiding principle[54] and there is therefore no call for a direct parallel to the US approach.[55] Further, very few international disputes actually come to adjudication. When they do, assistance is sought from scientists who are, as a general rule, highly qualified and internationally respected. The challenge in many cases is not to determine what constitutes good or reliable science, but to reach a well-informed view of the existing science and the boundaries of the relevant scientific knowledge sufficient to assess whether there has been compliance with applicable international legal obligations.

The issue of the acceptability of scientific evidence has arisen from time to time in the international cases. In the case *Japan – Measures affecting the Importation of Apples*, Japan argued unsuccessfully that the

50 See e.g. Huber, *Galileo's Revenge*, p. 24.

51 Citing Popper, K. *Conjectures and Refutations: The Growth of Scientific Knowledge*, 5th edn (London; New York: Routledge, 1989); and Hempel, Carl G. *Philosophy of Natural Science* (Englewood Cliffs, NJ: Prentice-Hall, 1966).

52 *Daubert* v. *Merrill Dow Pharmaceuticals, Inc.* 113 S. Ct. 2786 (1993) 483, applying the 1995 Federal Rules of Evidence. See also *General Electric Co.* v. *Joiner*, 522 US 136 (1997), and *Kumho Tire Co.* v. *Carmichael*, 526 US 137 (1999). Mueller and Kirkpatrick, *Evidence*, pp. 651–61.

53 For discussion, see Foster and Huber, *Judging Science*.

54 See above, p. 4.

55 Although see below, Ch. 4, pp. 178–81, on issues connected with the quality of scientific evidence.

World Trade Organization (WTO) panel hearing the case should consider only peer-reviewed evidence and publicly available information. The Panel declined to take a position on the issue.[56] The US argued in the same case that scientific evidence should be considered only where it was valid according to objective principles of scientific method.[57] The Panel indicated in response that it favoured relying on scientifically produced evidence, and that this excluded 'insufficiently substantiated information' and material such as 'non-demonstrated hypotheses'.[58] However, the issue to which US argument was directed was not the admissibility, or even the weight, of the scientific evidence that could be put before a WTO panel. Rather, it was the substantive legal question of what might constitute 'scientific evidence' under Article 2.2 of the WTO Agreement on the Application of Sanitary and Phytosanitary Measures (the SPS Agreement).[59] The US argued that Japan was maintaining measures 'without sufficient scientific evidence' and was in breach of Article 2.2.

In the *Continued Suspension of Obligations* cases[60] in the long-running transatlantic dispute over the use of growth-promotion hormones in beef production, the WTO Appellate Body indicated that a risk assessment as required under Article 5.1 of the SPS Agreement[61] had to be 'supported by coherent reasoning and respectable scientific evidence and [be], in this sense, objectively justified'.[62] The Appellate Body found that the scientific basis for a risk assessment had to have 'the necessary scientific and methodological rigor to be considered reputable

56 *Japan - Measures Affecting the Importation of Apples*, Complaint by the United States (WT/DS245), Report of the Panel DSR 2003: IX, 4481, para. 8.47.

57 *Ibid.*, para. 8.90. 58 *Ibid.*, paras. 8.93–8.95.

59 Article 2.2 of the SPS Agreement reads: 'Members shall ensure that any sanitary or phytosanitary measure is applied only to the extent necessary to protect human, animal or plant life or health, is based on scientific principles and is not maintained without sufficient scientific evidence, except as provided for in paragraph 7 of Article 5.'

60 *Canada - Continued Suspension of Obligations in the EC - Hormones Dispute*, Complaint by the EC (WT/DS321) Report of the Panel, Report of the Appellate Body, adopted 14 November 2008; *United States - Continued Suspension of Obligations in the EC - Hormones Dispute*, Complaint by the EC (WT/DS320) Report of the Panel, Report of the Appellate Body, adopted 14 November 2008 (hereafter respectively *Canada - Continued Suspension* PR, *United States - Continued Suspension* PR, and, to refer to the identical paragraphs of the two Appellate Body reports, *Continued Suspension* ABR).

61 Article 5.1 of the SPS Agreement reads: 'Members shall ensure that their sanitary or phytosanitary measures are based on an assessment, as appropriate to the circumstances, of the risks to human, animal or plant life or health, taking into account risk assessment techniques developed by the relevant international organizations.'

62 *Continued Suspension* ABR paras. 278, 315–16, 581, 590.

science'.[63] Although the views in the risk assessment did not have to represent the majority view of the broader scientific community, they 'must be considered to be legitimate science according to the standards of the relevant scientific community'.[64] However, like the US arguments in *Japan – Apples*, the Appellate Body was here dealing with the interpretation of the specific requirements of the SPS Agreement, rather than addressing in general terms the admissibility of scientific evidence.

The standard of review

Findings like those of the Appellate Body in the *Continued Suspension of Obligations* cases are sometimes understood to infer a 'standard of review', establishing a level of deference that is to be shown towards the national level decision-making of sovereign states. The standard of review is a concept drawn from administrative law at the national level that does not apply in any formal sense in disputes over compliance with public international law[65] but has been of considerable political importance and interest to scholars in the trade context.[66] Standard of review is taken to refer to the intensity of international judicial scrutiny of states' activities.[67] There has been strong advocacy for standards of review that incorporate a significant level of deference towards national-level decision-making.[68]

The push for deference is partly a response to the difficulties of requiring international adjudicators who are inexperienced in the sciences to make decisions requiring a close engagement with scientific issues. More profoundly, it is due to sensitivities about the loss of

63 *Ibid.*, para. 591. 64 *Ibid.*, para. 591.

65 Except of course where specified in the applicable legal obligations. For example, see Article 17.6 of the WTO Anti-Dumping Agreement, Agreement on Implementation of Article VI of the General Agreement on Tariffs and Trade, WTO *The Legal Texts: The results of the Uruguay round of multilateral trade negotiations*, p. 147. See also Article 1904, Chapter 19, of the North American Free Trade Agreement, under which parties may seek binational panel review of national determinations on anti-dumping measures and countervailing duties. North American Free Trade Agreement, San Antonio, 17 December 1992, in force 1 January 1994, 32 ILM 289. National 'investigating authorities' are identified under NAFTA, and national legislation is specified as the standard for the review of their decisions. Annex 19(11). For commentary, Croley and Jackson, 'WTO dispute procedures', 194–5.

66 See e.g. Oesch, *Standards of Review*. 67 *Ibid.*, p. 15.

68 Wirth, 'The role of science'. See also Button, *The Power to Protect*, advocating that a concept of the 'reasonable regulator' would appropriately articulate the appropriate standard of review in the health context.

sovereignty associated with subscribing to the multilateral free trade regime, even though it is clear under WTO law that all WTO members are free to apply their own standards of protection against health and environmental risks. Discussion often focuses on the question of how to sustain democratic decision-making about risk.[69] Perhaps more importantly, though, it has been asked whether rules like those in the SPS Agreement are suitable tools to regulate international risks, and whether the adjudicative framework is truly an appropriate substitute for administrative decision-making in disputes in this field.[70] The debate over standards of review underlines that the potentially far-reaching social and cultural dimensions of risk require greater recognition,[71] as does the politicised nature of decision-making about risk.[72] Pending further institutional and legal developments, matters such as the need to permit states to act on the basis of minority science[73] are often to be resolved through the interpretation of the relevant legal rules, as seen in the WTO.[74] The same point has been made in the investment context.[75]

The difficulty with deference may be illustrated with reference to attempts to introduce the concept of standards of review or judicial deference to national decision-making into scientific disputes in contexts beyond the WTO. In the *Southern Bluefin Tuna case (Australia and New Zealand* v. *Japan)* Japan argued that deference should be shown to Japan's decisions with respect to its disputed pilot programme of experimental fishing for southern bluefin tuna. According to Japan,

[69] See the argument of Howse that, contrary to what some might say, democratic process is enhanced by requiring a rational and public process of scrutiny and evaluation of measures like the EC growth-promotion hormones ban through a mechanism such as WTO dispute settlement. Howse, 'Democracy', See also Peel's suggestion that an absence of deference reinforces transboundary democracy, as this encourages national authorities to be more aware of the effects of their actions on those in other jurisdictions. Peel, 'International law', 371.

[70] Fisher, *Risk Regulation and Administrative Constitutionalism*, Ch. 5.

[71] Beck, *Risk Society*. [72] Beck, 'Risk society revisited', 226–7.

[73] *European Communities – Measures Concerning Meat and Meat Products (Hormones)*, Complaint by Canada (WT/DS48), Complaint by the United States (WT/DS26), Report of the Appellate Body DSR 1998: I, para. 135.

[74] Pauwelyn, 'Expert advice', 255.

[75] *Glamis Gold Ltd* v. *United States of America*, Award of 8 June 2009, paras. 23 and 617, where the Tribunal makes clear its disagreement with the view that 'domestic deference in national court systems is necessarily applicable to international tribunals, particularly where a measure of deference is already present in the standard to be applied'. *Glamis Gold Ltd* v. *United States of America*, Award of 8 June 2009, NAFTA (UNCITRAL), para. 23, decision available at http://ita.law.uvic.ca

international tribunals generally respected national determinations in such matters unless they could be shown to be irrational, patently disproportionate, or otherwise fundamentally flawed.[76] Japan believed the subject of dispute involved scientific opinion, inference and prediction, and, drawing on the jurisprudence of the European Court of Human Rights, argued that measures lying within a 'margin of appreciation' should be permitted.[77] Australia and New Zealand observed in response that 'standard of review' was a matter which could only 'be considered in relation to the precise content and meaning of the obligations' in question, and was an issue for the merits.[78] The question of deference to Japan's scientific views or decisions was not addressed by the International Tribunal for the Law of the Sea, and nor did the Arbitral Tribunal, established under Annex VII of the LOSC to deal with the merits, make a finding on this point. Applying the concept of deference in a context like the circumstances of the *Southern Bluefin Tuna* case would leave international resources relatively unprotected and would leave without recourse the populations of states affected by others' decisions.[79] Arguably, the process of international adjudication under public international law would also be undermined.

A general adoption of 'standards of review' that can be adjusted in order to allow greater respect for states' own scientific assessments

[76] *Southern Bluefin Tuna case (Australia and New Zealand* v. *Japan)* Award on Jurisdiction and Admissibility, 4 August 2000, 119 ILR 509 (hereafter *Southern Bluefin Tuna (Jurisdiction and Admissibility)*), Memorial on Jurisdiction of Japan, para. 165.

[77] *Ibid.*, para. 172.

[78] Reply on Jurisdiction of Australia and New Zealand, paras. 172, 183.

[79] See also the *MOX OSPAR* proceedings, where the United Kingdom argued that *de novo* review of its decision to withhold certain information from Ireland in connection with the commissioning of MOX production at Sellafield was inappropriate. The United Kingdom referred to the application of the margin of appreciation doctrine by the European Court of Human Rights, standards of objective assessment of national acts applied by WTO panels and standards of review applied under the North American Free Trade Agreement. *Dispute concerning Access to Information under Article 9 of the OSPAR Convention (Ireland* v. *United Kingdom of Great Britain and Northern Ireland)*, Award of 2 July 2003, 42 ILM 1118. Counter-Memorial of the United Kingdom, para. 1.6; Oral Submissions Day 2, 106 f; Day 3, 4 f. Ireland objected that the Tribunal should not be prevented from carrying out its function of determining the case before it on the merits of the applicable law. The Tribunal was perfectly entitled to substitute its view for the view of the United Kingdom on the question whether the information withheld by the United Kingdom could be considered commercially confidential. Reply of Ireland, para. 18 *et seq.*; Oral Submissions, Day 1, 33 line 11 *et seq.*, and p. 64 line 20 *et seq.*.

or policy choices would openly introduce a broad discretion for adjudicators. The adjudication of disputes under public international law ought to involve the straightforward application by an international court or tribunal of the relevant legal rules in the circumstances before it, without any presupposition that one disputant or the other deserves particular deference. The WTO Appellate Body has held fast to the mast, finding in *European Communities – Measures Concerning Meat and Meat Products (Hormones)* that neither *de novo* review nor full deference is required from a panel assessing the legality of a member's trade measures. As the Appellate Body has pointed out, the appropriate 'standard of review' is reflected in the requirement in Article 11 of the WTO Dispute Settlement Understanding that a panel make 'an objective assessment of the matter before it'.[80] Reducing international adjudication to a form of judicial review, especially to purely procedural review,[81] would be fundamentally inconsistent with maintaining an effective system of substantive international legal rules designed to regulate a balance of interests at the international level.[82]

Debate will need to be ongoing over the appropriate content and institutional framework for rules dealing with risk regulation decisions at the international level.[83] There may even be a need for new rules.[84] In the process, there may be welcome scope for encouraging public participation and decisions about risks at the national level.[85] However, unless and until the relevant rules and institutions are amended, WTO panels and other international adjudicatory bodies will continue to have to engage in the science of the various disputes coming before them in order to determine members' compliance with existing legal obligations, including their substantive elements.

80 *European Communities – Measures Concerning Meat and Meat Products (Hormones)*, Complaint by Canada (WT/DS48), Complaint by the United States (WT/DS26), Report of the Appellate Body, DSR 1998: I, 135, paras. 116–19.

81 As advocated by, for instance, Walker, 'Keeping the WTO from becoming the "World Trans-Science Organisation"', 279: 'In short, the primary issue of fact before a panel should be whether there is any reasonable scientific basis for a member's sanitary measures.'

82 As Croley and Jackson observe, WTO members are 'interested parties whose own (national) interests may not always sustain a necessary fidelity to the terms of international agreements'. Croley and Jackson, 'WTO dispute procedures', 209.

83 Peel, 'International law', 379.

84 Peel discusses the relative normative vacuum under the SPS Agreement and the need for greater global debate over the acceptability of health and environmental risks. Peel, 'Risk regulation'.

85 Peel 'International law'; Foster, 'Public opinion'.

The precautionary principle

The role to be played by the precautionary principle within the application of the rules on the burden of proof is quite a different matter to the notion of a standard of review, or of deference to national decision-making. Nor is it designed to deal with all the problems to which the concept of a standard of review responds in the debate over multilateral trade and risk response. Depending on how the precautionary principle is accommodated within the rules on burden of proof, it is true that international courts and tribunals may claim new licence to defer to national level decisions in certain cases. However, the thresholds for the invocation of the precautionary principle are generically defined, and a reversal of the burden of proof as discussed later in this book would be applicable only in cases involving a specific category of subject matter. Further, the thresholds of the precautionary principle are high, and will be crossed only in exceptional cases.

The precautionary principle is understood to involve a move away from the 'primacy of scientific proof'.[86] The emphasis falls instead on the limitations of scientific prediction,[87] and the need for decision-making that errs on the side of allowing for worst-case scenarios. Under the precautionary principle, the idea that it is better to ascertain the facts before taking action is reversed, and it is recognised that it may be better to act first and then set about ascertaining the facts more closely. While preventive action involves intervention prior to the occurrence of damage in relation to known risks, precaution involves a preparedness by public authorities to intervene in advance in relation to potential, uncertain or hypothetical threats.[88] If the risk is sufficiently serious in character, precaution may posit intervention even where a risk is simply suspected, conjectured, or feared.[89]

Accordingly, it is commonly understood that precaution requires actors wishing to engage in activities potentially involving risk of serious harm to bear the burden of proving the safety of the proposed activities before the activities are permitted to proceed. This is often

[86] Hohmann, *Precautionary Legal Duties*, pp. 334–5; Gündling, 'The status', 26. See also Birnie *et al. International Law*, p. 154; Sands, *Principles*, pp. 6–8, 268.

[87] Freestone and Hey, 'Origins and development of the precautionary principle', 12.

[88] de Sadeleer, *Environmental Principles*, p. 91.

[89] *Ibid.*, p. 91.

described as a reversal of the burden of proof,[90] though sometimes also as a lowering of the standard of proof.[91] The key point is that a lack in evidence of harm does not provide a basis for reaching the conclusion that there is no threat of harm.[92]

Originating in decisions adopted at the North Sea Ministerial Conferences in the 1980s,[93] the precautionary principle has become interwoven with international environmental law at large, and now appears in institutional contexts and in a variety of instruments regulating the use of the oceans and of international watercourses, controlling air pollution and climate change, and relating to the conservation of endangered species and biological diversity more broadly, as well as trade in hazardous waste.[94] Global recognition of the importance attaching to the precautionary concept came in 1992 at the Earth Summit in Rio de Janeiro, in a proposal put forward by the European Union and supported by the US.[95] Principle 15 of the Rio Declaration exhorted states not to postpone environmental action on the basis of lack of full scientific certainty:[96]

> In order to protect the environment, the precautionary approach shall be widely applied by States according to their capabilities. Where there are threats of serious or irreversible damage, lack of full scientific certainty shall not be used as a reason for postponing cost-effective measures to prevent environmental degradation.

The Rio Summit's Plan of Action, Agenda 21, described the need for a precautionary and anticipatory approach to protecting the marine environment.[97] Also adopted at Rio, the Convention on Biological

[90] *Ibid.*, pp. 202–7; Sands, *Principles*, p. 273; Birnie *et al.*, *International Law*, pp. 154–9. Peel, *The Precautionary Principle*, p. 154; Hohmann, *Precautionary Legal Duties*, p. 334; Wynne, 'Uncertainty and environmental learning', 123; Cameron, 'The precautionary principle in international law', 120. See also the EC Communication on the Precautionary Principle, Communication from the Commission on the Precautionary Principle, Commission of the European Community Brussels 02.02.2000 Com (2000) 1, para. 6.4.

[91] Birnie *et al.*, *International Law*, p. 157.

[92] Fisher, 'Is the precautionary principle justiciable?', 319; Peel, *The Precautionary Principle*, p. 48.

[93] de Sadeleer, *Environmental Principles*, p. 94.

[94] *Ibid.*, pp. 94–9; Birnie *et al.*, *International Law*, pp. 154–64.

[95] Birnie *et al.*, *International Law*, p. 154, citing UN Doc. A/CONF. 151/PC/WG.111/L.8/Rev.1 (1991), containing the EU proposal.

[96] Declaration of the UN Conference on Environment and Development, adopted by the UN Conference on Environment and Development at Rio de Janeiro, 14 June 1992, UN Doc. A/ CONF.48/14, 11 ILM 1416, Principle 15.

[97] Agenda 21, Report of the United Nations Conference on Environment and Development, Rio de Janeiro, 3–14 June 1992, UN Doc. A/CONF.151/26/Rev.1 (1992), para. 17.21.

Diversity[98] and the United Nations Framework Convention on Climate Change[99] reflected the precautionary principle, complementing the principle's prior explicit expression in the 1987 Montreal Protocol on Substances that Deplete the Ozone Layer.[100] Both the Montreal Protocol and the subsequently negotiated 1995 United Nations Agreement on Straddling Fish Stocks and Highly Migratory Fish Stocks state expressly that states are to be more cautious when information is uncertain, unreliable or inadequate, and that the absence of adequate scientific information shall not be used as a reason for postponing or failing to take conservation and management measures.[101] The Cartagena Protocol on Biosafety allows for states to refuse imports of modified organisms in circumstances where scientific certainty is lacking, in order to avoid or minimise their adverse effects.[102]

A primary role of the precautionary principle in international law has thus been to catalyse multilateral action in the face of serious threats, encouraging states to take action in response to the early warning signs of such threats even though science cannot reveal for certain whether or not they will eventuate. In the field of climate change especially, political endeavours continue towards achieving the best possible application of the principle. In the European Union, the precautionary principle has been recognised as central to environmental law and to Union policy.[103] In 2000, the European Commission issued its Communication on the Precautionary Principle.[104] The Commission sought to help build a common understanding on the assessment, appraisal and

[98] Convention on Biological Diversity, Rio de Janeiro, 5 June 1992, in force 29 December 1993, 31 ILM 818, preamble.

[99] Framework Convention on Climate Change, Rio de Janeiro, 9 May 1992, in force 21 March 1994, 31 ILM 851, Article 3(3).

[100] Montreal Protocol Protocol on Substances that Deplete the Ozone Layer, 16 September 1987, in force 1 January 1989, 26 ILM 1550, preamble and Article 6(2).

[101] Article 6 of the United Nations Agreement on Straddling Fish Stocks and Highly Migratory Fish Stocks, 4 December 1995, in force 11 December 2001, 34 ILM 1542. See also Stockholm Convention on Persistent Organic Pollutants, Stockholm, 22 May 2001, in force 17 May 2004, 40 ILM 532, Article 4, and also Article 8(7)(a) and (e) on the listing of chemicals in Annexes A, B or C to the Convention.

[102] Cartagena Protocol on Biosafety, Montreal, 29 January 2000, in force 11 September 2003, 39 ILM 1027, Articles 10(6) and 11(6), 39 ILM 1027.

[103] See Article 191(2) of the Consolidated Version of the Treaty on the Functioning of the European Union, 09.05.2008, OJ C 115/47. See also the Bergen Ministerial Declaration on Sustainable Development in the European Commission for Europe (ECE) (May 1990), Reprinted in (1990) 1 *Yearbook of International Environmental Law* 431.

[104] Communication from the Commission on the Precautionary Principle Commission of the European Community, Brussels 02.02.2000 Com (2000) 1.

management of risks that science is not yet able to evaluate fully in order to explain its own approach and to facilitate better decision-making and higher levels of public confidence in related fields.[105] As a matter of rhetoric, the US preference is for reference to the more flexible and possibly less restrictive notion of a 'precautionary approach', while the EU prefers to speak of the 'precautionary principle'. However the distinction has been considered essentially semantic.[106]

The importance of precautionary action has been recognised implicitly in the decisions of international courts and tribunals, particularly those of the International Tribunal for the Law of the Sea. As discussed further in Chapter 6, the precautionary principle has not been recognised as a rule of customary international law, yet it is a powerful tool in the development of new international legal instruments and is frequently cited in argument in international legal disputes. A close evaluation of the influence of the precautionary principle within international adjudicatory procedure reveals that the principle exerts a force requiring recognition and open discussion.

For the purposes of this book, the most obvious question in connection with applying the precautionary principle relates to the potential reversal of the adjudicatory burden of proof to accommodate scientific uncertainty. Complementing this enquiry are important issues connected with the precautionary influence wielded by scientific experts assisting an international court or tribunal. The precautionary principle is here to stay. Trends towards more investigative procedures and increased judicial encouragement for direct technical co-operation between the parties take some of the emphasis away from the need to consider reversing the burden of proof, but precaution will always enter in, often through the views of the experts consulted by the parties and by the court or tribunal.

Directions for procedural development in international scientific disputes

An adversarial form of adjudication comes naturally in international law. Central and planned regulation is absent, the law develops mainly

[105] Press Release, Commission adopts Communication on Precautionary Principle, IP/00/96 Brussels, 2 February 2000.

[106] De Sadeleer, *Environmental Principles*, p. 92; Hey, 'The precautionary concept', 304; Birnie *et al.*, *International Law*, p. 155.

through negotiation between sovereign actors (as well as their practice), and the jurisdiction of courts and tribunals is essentially non-compulsory.[107] Disputing parties must voluntarily agree to submit to the jurisdiction of a court or tribunal, and in doing so they will expect to remain more or less in charge of the presentation of the case. The absence of appeal mechanisms in most international courts and tribunals accentuates the importance of the outcome for the parties, re-inforcing their desire for control over the case. Respect for the sovereignty of the parties remains a check on international courts' and tribunals' development of their procedures.[108]

The adversarial nature of international procedure is partly due also to the common law influence in the design of international courts' and tribunals' working procedures, resulting from the part played by the English-speaking world in structuring international legal proceedings in the mid-twentieth century.[109] There have been some recent limited changes in civil procedure in England.[110] In the US the use of party-appointed experts is still the norm,[111] although US judges have the power to appoint court experts where the parties have not produced evidence of clear probative value on complex or technical issues.[112]

Various theorists have proposed changes in the rules and procedures relating to proof at the national level in order to deal with the difficulties posed by scientific disputes. Common law scholars have identified the need for a shift from the adversarial towards the investigative in cases raising matters of policy generally[113] and specifically in cases involving scientific opinion.[114] Judges are considered to be too

[107] For the typology from which these observations are drawn, see Damaška, *The Faces of Justice and State Authority*; Twining, *Rethinking Evidence*, pp. 194–6. See also Twining, *Theories of Evidence*, p. 25, referring to the view of Jeremy Bentham that the theory underpinning rules relating to evidence and proof sits within an understanding of the role of adjudication, which itself forms part of a wider theory of government within the relevant legal system.

[108] Riddell and Plant, *Evidence*, pp. 20–1. [109] *Ibid.*, p. 312. [110] See, below, pp. 27–8.

[111] See Federal Rules of Evidence, Rules 702–5. For commentary, Mueller and Kirkpatrick, *Evidence*, pp. 615–48.

[112] See Federal Rules of Evidence, Rule 706. Also Mueller and Kirkpatrick, *Evidence*, pp. 648–51. Encouraging the use of court-appointed experts in scientific cases, see the *Reference Manual on Scientific Evidence* (Federal Judicial Centre, 2001), pp. 1–8.

[113] Calling for a move from adversarial to inquisitorial judicial procedure in public law cases, Griffith, 'Judicial decision-making', 564 and 582. Allison, *A Continental Distinction*, pp. 190–206. For an historical comparative study on the active role of the judge, see Cappelletti and Jolowicz, *Public Interest Parties*.

[114] Jasanoff, 'What judges should know', 358.

restricted by adversarial philosophies and procedures such as the allocation of a burden of proof and the absence of a judicial responsibility to pose questions, seek answers, and ensure that the material before them is complete.[115] Civil lawyers working within the common law have also underlined the appropriateness of blended adversarial and investigative procedures in disputes involving science at the national level.[116] Adversarial process has its advantages, and can help to reveal weaknesses and deficiencies in scientific evidence,[117] but a system of party control over the gathering and presentation of evidence may not meet all the needs of good adjudication. There is a danger that in a system of partisan scientific experts the dynamics of the proceedings will magnify their differences of opinion.[118] Additionally, there may be a loss of focus: even if it is possible to examine expert witnesses back-to-back, this will not afford the opportunity for consideration of scientific issues one by one sequentially. Yet so far as developments in civil procedure at the national level are concerned, different governmental traditions and deep-seated cultural differences between continental and English-speaking countries may inhibit far-reaching adjustment to adversarial procedures for taking expert evidence in common law countries.[119]

In international law there is greater scope for faster change. Tradition is less of a tie, because it is accepted that international procedure will be influenced by a combination of methodologies from different traditions. Promising new evidentiary procedures are easier to introduce than in the national courts, particularly for international courts and tribunals operating in new institutional contexts. It is in 'wandering between worlds'[120] that the international system derives its uniqueness as a testing ground for new procedures in proof and evidence. International judges and arbitrators, as well as counsel, enjoy differing legal backgrounds and this contributes to the melange of approaches to

[115] Griffith, 'Judicial decision-making', 500 quoting from Devlin, Patrick *The Judge* (Oxford University Press, 1979) pp. 54 and 584.
[116] Damaška, *Evidence Law Adrift*, pp. 143–52.
[117] Peel, *The Precautionary Principle in Practice*, p. 223.
[118] Damaška, *Evidence Law Adrift*, p. 145.
[119] *Ibid.*, pp. 149–50. Accordingly, it is to the gradual development of the existing adversarial common law system that Damaška turns for an accommodation in English-speaking countries of the challenges posed by disputes involving scientific and technological questions.
[120] Arnold, Mathew 'Stanzas from the Grande Chartreuse' in *Poems* (London, 1903), I, 286, quoted in Damaška, *Evidence Law Adrift*, Epilogue, p. 152.

procedural issues found in international courts and tribunals.[121] A contrast might be drawn with the procedure and practice of the European Court of Justice, a court operating within a relatively homogeneous community, where continental legal procedure is followed. In the European Court, overtones of the civil law are apparent in the expectation that the parties will be motivated by a relatively strong sense of duty to the Court in bringing forward their evidence, and that the Court will take an active, 'semi-inquisitorial' role in seeking out what further information it may need in order to attain *'la verité juridique'*.[122]

Generally, scientific disputes within the European Union are much less likely to give rise to mixed questions of fact and law than in international law.[123] As highlighted in the cases concerning the bovine spongiform encephalopathy (BSE) episode in the United Kingdom in the 1990s, EU institutions are empowered to take protective measures without having to wait for the reality and seriousness of risks to become apparent.[124] There will be occasional instances where the ECJ must take a position on scientific points. For example, in case C-157/96 the ECJ stated that the new information contained in British announcements on BSE meant that the link between BSE and Creuzfeldt-Jacob disease (CJD) had ceased to be a theoretical hypothesis and had become a possibility.[125] The Court also characterised the information as having established a probable link between BSE and

[121] Judges will be influenced both by their national legal traditions and the traditions of the jurisdictions in which they have trained. Riddell and Plant, *Evidence*, pp. 36–7.

[122] MacLennan, 'Evidence, standard and burden of proof', 265–88, 268; Lasok, *The European Court*, pp. 422, 423.

[123] Wirth wrote in 1994 that 'The case law in the European Union is noteworthy precisely because it does not address the role of scientific evidence'. Wirth, 'The role of science', 849.

[124] See Case C-180/96, *United Kingdom of Great Britain and Northern Ireland* v. *Commission of the European Communities* [1998] ECR I-02265. In this case the Court rejected the United Kingdom's complaints about the European Commission's actions in response to the BSE crisis. See also the decision on the application for interim relief in this case, Case C-180/96 R, *United Kingdom of Great Britain and Northern Ireland* v. *Commission of the European Communities* [1996] ECR I-03903; and the reference for a preliminary ruling from the High Court in Case C-157/96, *The Queen* v. *Ministry of Agriculture, Fisheries and Food, Commissioners of Customs & Excise, ex p. National Farmers' Union, David Burnett and Sons Ltd, R. S. and E. Wright Ltd, Anglo Beef Processors Ltd, United Kingdom Genetics, Wyjac Calves Ltd, International Traders Ferry Ltd, MFP International Ltd* [1998] ECR I-02211. Additionally, see the judgment of the Court of First Instance in Case T-13/99, *Pfizer Animal Health* v. *Council of the EU* [2002] ECR II-305, para. 170. This case concerned the validity of a regulation withdrawing authorisation for the use of the antibiotic virginiamycin in feedstuffs.

[125] Case C-157/96, para. 31; Case C-180/96, para. 52.

CJD.[126] However, tasks involving scientific assessment are delegated within the Union's apparatus to specific scientific committees, and this will frequently preclude the need for close judicial consideration of scientific matters.[127] Cases may also turn on whether proper procedures have been followed where a Member State disagrees with a central decision,[128] or where a Member State wishes to follow its own policies instead.[129] International courts and tribunals must more frequently deal directly with scientific disputes.

Scientific disputes under public international law are often by their nature polycentric.[130] Both the science and the policies at issue will be in a fluid state. A multiplicity of parties will have an interest in the outcome, including public and private actors at the international and

[126] Case C-157/96, para. 40; Case C-180/96, para. 61. See also, for example, the Court's assessment of the evidence in *Sweden* v. *Commission* Case T-229/04, European Court of Justice, 11 July 2007, [2007] ECR I-2437, paras. 172–91, 229–61. In this case Sweden successfully sought annulment of the European Commission's decision to list paraquat under a directive regulating the marketing of plant protection products.

[127] See e.g. Case C-236/01, *Monsanto Agricoltura Italia SpA and others and Presidenza del Consiglio dei Ministri and others* [2003] ECR I-8105; and Joined Cases C-439/05P C-454/05P, *Land Oberösterreich and Republic of Austria* v. *Commission of the European Communities* [2007] ECR I-7441. In this decision the Court dismissed an appeal challenging a decision of the Commission rejecting an Austrian ban on genetically modified organisms within a specified Austrian province because it did not fulfil the criteria in the EC Treaty for diverting from harmonised measures. See also, concerning the use of bergamot essence in sun oils, Case T-199/96, *Laboratoires Pharmaceutiques Bergaderm SA and Jean-Jacques Goupil* v. *Commission of the European Communities* [1998] ECR II-02805, and, on appeal, Case C-352/98 P, *Laboratoires Pharmaceutiques Bergaderm SA and Jean-Jacques Goupil* v. *Commission of the European Communities*, [2000] ECR I-5291. Also Case C-286/02, *Bellio F.lli Srl* v. *Prefettura di Treviso* [2004] EC I-3465. This case involved a reference for a preliminary ruling during the BSE episode, dealing with the accidental presence in a consignment of fish flour from Norway of fragments of mammalian bone.

[128] See, also arising out of the BSE episode, Case C-1/00, *Commission of the European Communities* v. *French Republic* [2001] ECR I-09989; C-241/01, *National Farmers' Union* v. *Secrétariat Général du Gouvernement* [2002] ECR I-907; C-514/99, *Commission of the European Communities* v. *France* [2000] ECR I-4705; Case C-393/01, *French Republic* v. *Commission of the European Communities* [2003] ECR I-05405.

[129] See Case C-236/01, the *Monsanto* case, in which the Court found that the relevant provision in the applicable EC Regulation allowed Italy to have recourse to a safeguard procedure permitting restriction or suspension of trade by a Member State where, by virtue of new information or a reassessment of existing information, the Member State had detailed grounds for considering that the use of a particular food or food product endangered human health or the environment.

[130] A term adopted by Lon Fuller, derived from the economic work of Polyani. See Polyani, M. *The Logic of Liberty: Reflections and rejoinders* (London: Routledge and Kegan Paul, 1951), pp. 170 ff. See also Stephens, *International Courts*, pp. 95–7.

national level.[131] The metaphor of a spider's web is helpful: 'a pull of one strand will distribute tensions after a complicated pattern throughout the web as a whole'.[132] Lon Fuller himself flagged that the French approach to adjudication, in which a rapporteur makes a preliminary study of a case, could be seen as a 'special form' of adjudication that 'might accommodate a greater degree of polycentricity'.[133] Building on Fuller's work, a conception of adjudication as 'collaborative expert investigation' has been identified as a practical response to problems of polycentric disputes.[134] In this conception, adjudication is characterised both by party participation and by an active role for adjudicators, who may have to complement the parties' proofs, and even their arguments, in considering the ramifications of a decision.[135]

Alternatively, a combination of forms of social ordering is possible, for example combining adjudication and collaborative expert investigation, potentially producing even 'obligations to negotiate under the threat of an exercise of adjudicative powers'.[136] Here, the adjudicatory phase of a dispute may no longer be a self-contained event. Phases of adjudicatory process may be interspersed with periods of negotiation or mediation. Relief may be complex and ongoing.[137] The judge may take on a new role in guiding the processes related to the case, including through the appointment of other individuals in capacities that will assist the judge in his or her decision-making, such as masters and experts. At the national level, in recent decades US judges have made increasing use of investigatory mechanisms, including appointing special masters and independent experts, making use of panels and

[131] There are echoes here of US arguments in the jurisdictional phase of the *Nicaragua* case where it was asserted unsuccessfully that a judgment of the International Court of Justice while the parties were still involved in combat would be irrelevant if not impossible. Franck, *Fairness in International Law and Institutions*, p. 339. See also 'Fact finding by the International Court with particular regard to "fluid" situations' (1987) *American Society of International Law Proceedings* 484–501.

[132] Fuller, 'The forms and limits', 127–8.

[133] Allison, *A Continental Distinction*, p. 205; and Allison 'The procedural reason', p. 467, citing Note, Box No. 10, Folder No. 12, Lon Luvois Fuller Papers, Harvard Law School Library. See also Allison, 'The procedural reason,' p. 456 citing Letter to W. Gellhorn, 23 October 1959, Lon Luvois Fuller Papers, Harvard Law School Library.

[134] Allison, 'Fuller's analysis', 381. See also Allison, *A Continental Distinction*, pp. 205–6.

[135] Allison, 'Fuller's analysis', 381.

[136] Fuller,'The forms and limits', 406.

[137] Chayes, 'The role of the judge', 1282–84; see also 1302.

advisory committees, and receiving briefs and materials from amici curiae.[138]

Movement in many of these directions is taking place in the way that international scientific disputes are handled. Judicially mandated technical co-operation between the parties has proved valuable, as discussed in Chapter 2. This is seen most clearly in the *Case concerning Land Reclamation by Singapore in and around the Straits of Johor (Malaysia* v. *Singapore)*[139] and also in its antecedent the *Trail Smelter Arbitration (US* v. *Canada)*.[140] New procedures for taking expert evidence have also been developed, mainly in some of the more recently established adjudicatory bodies. The submission of briefs by amici curiae is also a growing feature of the international adjudicatory process, particularly in disputes concerning threats to human health and the environment and primarily in WTO dispute settlement and investment arbitration.[141] As seen for example in *European Communities – Measures Affecting the Approval and Marketing of Biotech Products*,[142] international courts and tribunals may be wary of formally acknowledging reliance on information contained in briefs submitted by amici curiae.[143] Amici are a step further removed than experts from the adjudicatory process, are self-selecting, and in international cases they are not involved in the oral hearings.[144] At the same time, the material contained in amicus briefs may draw the attention of an international court or tribunal to important aspects of a case, and deepen its understanding of the context in which the case has arisen.[145]

In the interim, there is a hint of movement towards convergence within national legal systems. Arguably English procedure is moving

[138] Allison, 'The procedural reason', 468, citing Chayes, 'The role of the judge'. 'Mass tort litigation' has posed particular problems in the US which have affected the way that the courts deal with their need for expert advice. There has been an increasing use of court-appointed expert panels, for example in litigation over artificial breast implants, and asbestos. Erichson, 'Mass tort litigation'; Hooper *et al.*, 'Assessing causation'.

[139] *Case concerning Land Reclamation by Singapore in and around the Straits of Johor (Malaysia* v. *Singapore)* (Provisional Measures), Order of 8 October 2003 (hereafter *Land Reclamation* (Provisional Measures)), decision available at www.itlos.org. See the discussion of this case below in Ch. 2, pp. 36–7.

[140] *Trail Smelter Arbitration (US* v. *Canada)* 16 April 1938, 11 March 1941, 3 UNRIAA 1905.

[141] Pauwelyn, 'Expert advice', at 238 and 239–40.

[142] *European Communities – Measures Affecting the Approval and Marketing of Biotech Products*, Complaint by United States, Canada, Argentina (WT/DS291, WT/DS292, WT/DS293), Report of the Panel DSR 2006: III, 847.

[143] See e.g. the amicus brief submitted by five individuals in *EC – Biotech*. Winickoff *et al.*, 'Adjudicating the GM food wars'.

[144] Foster, 'Social science experts'. [145] *Ibid.*

towards becoming more investigative, while French procedure is urged to become more adversarial.[146] Under English civil procedure reforms,[147] court control over parties' expert evidence has become extensive,[148] although critics of the reforms suggest that they have not gone far enough[149] and that a more mixed system of party appointment and court appointment of experts may be necessary.[150] Yet there is still a long-standing reluctance to move towards greater use of independent, court-appointed experts,[151] stemming not least, perhaps, from the awareness that this would be a 'Continental solution'.[152] Within the US the system of party-appointed experts also remains the mainstay, but scholars have suggested that the US would do well to borrow from Continental procedure and increase the judge's responsibility for fact-finding.[153] Meanwhile, scope has been identified for evolution within French civil procedure in the direction of greater party involvement in matters relating to evidence,[154] although at present the parties have no right to bring expert evidence before the court themselves[155] and the French judge continues to play an important and often active role in the civil process, especially in relation to evidence.[156]

Reorientation of international judicial practice in relation to evidence and proof takes place against the backdrop of these developments and critiques within civil procedure at the national level. At the same time,

[146] Jolowicz, *On Civil Procedure*, pp. 386–97.

[147] See the Civil Procedure Act 1997 (UK) and the Civil Procedure Rules adopted under the Act.

[148] Zuckerman, *Civil Procedure*, p. 724. For details of the rules governing expert evidence today, see also Loughlin and Gerlis, *Civil Procedure*.

[149] Jolowicz, *On Civil Procedure* pp. 240–2. [150] *Ibid.*, 240–2.

[151] See Lord Woolf's discussion of the reception given to the recommendations concerning experts in his interim report. Right Hon. Lord Woolf MR, *Access to Justice*. On the Woolf enquiry and subsequent reforms generally, Jolowicz, *On Civil Procedure*, Ch. 19.

[152] Jolowicz, *On Civil Procedure*, p. 239.

[153] Damaška, 'The uncertain fate'; Langbein, 'The German advantage'; Reitz, 'Why we probably cannot adopt the German advantage'; Bohlander, 'The German advantage revisited'; Sward, 'Values'.

[154] Garapon, 'Incertitude et expertise', 10; Matet, 'Propositions du Groupe de Travail', 5. A powerful historical tradition lies behind the use of the expert in France. Taylor, 'A comparative study', 190; see also Jolowicz, *On Civil Procedure*, p. 227. For details of the rules governing expert evidence today, see also Bell *et al.*, *Principles of French Law*; Ngwasiri, 'Some problems'; Ngwasiri, 'The role of the judge'; Garapon, 'Incertitude et expertise'. For an account of the development of inquisitorial judicial procedure, and the specific procedures of the Conseil d'État, see Allison, *A Continental Distinction*, pp. 207–16.

[155] Bell *et al.*, *Principles of French Law*, p. 96.

[156] *Ibid.*, p. 80; Ngwasiri, 'The role of the judge'. This has been important in the absence of a process for pre-trial discovery as seen in the common law.

there is a new 'forward looking' approach in the International Court of Justice since the turn of the century.[157] The trend is away from a general judicial deference towards sovereign states and in the direction of greater procedural control over cases.[158] There appears to be a feeling within the Court that the bench may need to become more interactive, although this remains coupled with a care to retain order in the courtroom. Certainly, there is scope for fuller use of the procedures available to the Court, including the use of experts and assessors.[159] Commentators have emphasised the pervasive importance of factual and technical issues in environmental disputes especially and have urged the Court to consider adopting 'more radical' approaches such as the use of assessors and special masters, and even of procedures allowing other tribunals who may be more suited to fact-finding sometimes to 'state a case' for the Court to determine.[160]

Conclusion

Even when the science says that an important issue is not subject to conclusive proof either way, an international court or tribunal must nevertheless proceed to apply the legal rules. Expert evidence will cast considerable light on the situation, especially if experts' input is obtained through interactive processes. Independent expert advice may be particularly helpful, combined with other investigative procedures such as site visits where this will assist the court or tribunal. International adherence to a model of adjudication that is predominantly adversarial is being tempered with gradual steps towards increased use of procedural approaches incorporating investigative elements. Increasingly it is recognised that the adjudicatory phase of a dispute may be twinned with other phases involving expert investigation. This will ideally take place through the co-operation of the parties. Accordingly, Chapter 2 will address the co-operation of the parties as a central element in the resolution of international disputes involving scientific uncertainty.

Chapters 3 and 4 address the ways in which international adjudicatory procedure is developing, and the issues that this raises in

157 Rosenne, *The Law and Practice*, p. 1338.
158 *Ibid.*, Higgins, 'Respecting sovereign states'.
159 As recommended by Jenks as long ago as 1964. See Jenks, *The Prospects*, p. 151.
160 Fitzmaurice, 'Equipping the court', 415–16; Brown Weiss, Edith, *In Fairness to Future Generations: International law, commmon patrimony and international equity* (Hotei Publishing, 1989), p. 625. See the discussion in Ch. 4, below, pp. 158–65.

connection with the retention of legal decision-making authority by international courts and tribunals. As foreshadowed above, a central problem is that expertise in both fact and law is often needed in order to interpret and apply the applicable legal provisions. Mixed questions of fact and law produce an intertwining in the roles of adjudicators and experts. International courts and tribunals must rely on expert assistance, yet it is not the role of the expert or experts to decide a case. A diminution in rationalist expectations of international adjudication will have to be accepted, as fact and law can no longer be regarded as altogether distinct. To deal with the change, international courts and tribunals must continue to assume responsibility for decision-making and make a renewed commitment to transparency in relation to experts' input and their reliance on expertise. These points will be of especial importance where experts espouse precautionary approaches to cases, which inevitably they will do on many occasions, with the potential to influence the outcomes of these cases. Provided there is clarity about the experts' views on the need for precaution, this may provide a valuable new dimension to international adjudicatory decision-making in disputes involving scientific uncertainties.

Chapters 5 and 6 explore the pressures that come to bear on the rules relating to allocation of the burden of proof in disputes involving scientific uncertainty, and the potential for a reversal of the burden of proof. Chapter 5 investigates the sources, content and rationale of the rules on burden of proof in international adjudication. This topic has been neglected somewhat in doctrine in recent years and the general analyses in Chapter 5 provide a starting point for the discussions that follow in Chapter 6. Chapter 6 contemplates the possibility of the reversal of the burden of proof to accommodate the precautionary principle. A reversal of the burden of proof would relieve the unfairness and potential prejudice to substantive interests involved in seeking to apply a narrower conception of rationalist adjudication in a context of scientific uncertainty. A precautionary prima facie case approach is proposed for application in exceptional cases where the high thresholds of the precautionary principle are crossed.

Chapters 7 and 8 consider the implications for the finality of adjudication of the ongoing development of scientific knowledge. These chapters focus on an assessment of the different procedural options for challenge to an adjudicatory decision in the light of subsequent scientific advances. Protecting the finality of adjudication is fundamental to preserving the authority of international law, but at the same time it is important to identify workable processes for adjusting decisions that may otherwise remain unimplemented. These chapters evaluate the scope of the rules regarding revision, the doctrine of nullity, and the potential for righting the balance through appropriately designed forms of reassessment proceedings. Specific issues arising under the doctrine of res judicata are discussed.

The overall picture of international adjudication resulting from these investigations is of an international dispute-settlement mechanism that continues to be serviceable in scientific disputes. However, allegiance to traditional practices based on a strict conception of rationalist adjudication may not enable adjudicators to get to the heart of disputes, nor on occasion to accommodate pressing precautionary needs. A measure of evolution in the procedures of international courts and tribunals will facilitate satisfactory dispute resolution in scientific cases and help ensure the integrity and authority of international adjudication.

2 Co-operation between disputing parties

The importance of co-operation between disputing parties

Co-operation between the disputing parties will often be key to the successful resolution of a scientific or technical dispute, and may also allow for a calibrated application of the precautionary principle that may not be as achievable through adjudicatory dispute settlement. Whether or not disputants ultimately do co-operate effectively cannot by any means be guaranteed, but judicial prompting may assist. The two awards in the well-known *Trail Smelter Arbitration (US* v. *Canada)* provide an early demonstration of how helpful it may be to allow time for co-operative study of how to address or ameliorate a problem, here the distribution of sulphur dioxide from the Canadian smelter at Trail through cross-border currents in the upper air. In its first award the Tribunal decided that three consultants would be appointed for the gathering of meteorological observations, and prescribed a temporary emissions limitations regime. In its second award the Tribunal was then in a position to lay down a detailed and permanent regime.[1]

Adjudicatory proceedings may be just one of the stages through which a dispute proceeds, and it is part of the function of an international court or tribunal to take this into account in deciding how to deal with a case.[2] The practical significance of scientific and administrative co-operation is apparent upon considering the various high-profile international disputes involving scientific uncertainties introduced in the pages that follow. This introduction to selected decisions is intended

[1] *Trail Smelter Arbitration (US* v. *Canada)* 16 April 1938, 11 March 1941, 9 ILR 315. For an overview, Stephens, *International Courts*, pp. 125–36.

[2] Rosenne, *The Law and Practice*, p. 208; Reisman, *Nullity*, p. 627.

also to provide insights into the scientific issues in these cases that are not conveyed in reports of the cases in the growing body of literature analysing the disputes, nor readily apparent from a direct consultation of the judgments themselves. The cases will form the subject of thematic discussion throughout the book, and a familiarity with the relationships between the science and the law in the various disputes will assist the reader. The decisions presented have been chosen as a representative selection; additional cases will be introduced in the course of the book.

Applications for provisional measures feature frequently in the cases. Depending on the case, lodging a prompt request for provisional measures could be the only way to gain proper protection for the environment. Prompt action may also be important to prevent irremediable harm, and a speedy resolution of a dispute may be necessary as a matter of commercial reality - particularly where construction projects are concerned. For example, proceedings in the *Case concerning Land Reclamation by Singapore in and around the Straits of Johor (Malaysia* v. *Singapore)* were brought just in time to permit adjustment to the design of the Singaporean project.[3] Provisional measures have been sought under the United Nations Convention on the Law of the Sea (LOSC)[4] also in the *Southern Bluefin Tuna cases (New Zealand* v. *Japan; Australia* v. *Japan)*,[5] and the *Dispute concerning the MOX Plant, International Movements of Radioactive Materials and the Protection of the Marine Environment of the Irish Sea (Ireland* v. *United Kingdom)*.[6] The International Court of Justice has handled requests for provisional measures in the *Nuclear Tests cases*

[3] *Case concerning Land Reclamation by Singapore in and around the Straits of Johor (Malaysia* v. *Singapore) (Provisional Measures)*, Order of 8 October 2003 (hereafter *Land Reclamation (Provisional Measures)*), decision available at www.itlos.org.

[4] United Nations Convention on the Law of the Sea, Montego Bay, 10 December 1982, in force 16 November 1994, 21 ILM 1261.

[5] *Southern Bluefin Tuna cases (New Zealand* v. *Japan; Australia* v. *Japan) (Provisional Measures)*, Order of 27 August 1999, 38 ILM 1624 (hereafter *Southern Bluefin Tuna (Provisional Measures)*).

[6] *Dispute concerning the MOX Plant, International Movements of Radioactive Materials and the Protection of the Marine Environment of the Irish Sea (Ireland* v. *United Kingdom) Request for Provisional Measures*, Order of 3 December 2001, 41 ILM 405 (hereafter *MOX Plant (Provisional Measures)*). See also the reaffirmation of the Tribunal's measure by the Tribunal constituted under Annex VII of the LOSC to hear the merits of the case, in *Mox Plant case (Ireland* v. *United Kingdom) (Suspension of Proceedings on Jurisdiction and Merits and Request for Further Provisional Measures)*, Order of 24 June 2003, 42 ILM 1187 (hereafter *Mox Plant case (Suspension of Proceedings on Jurisdiction and Merits and Request for Further Provisional Measures)*.

(Australia v. *France) (New Zealand* v. *France)*[7] and in the *Case concerning Pulp Mills on the River Uruguay (Argentina* v. *Uruguay).*[8] The *Case concerning the Gabčíkovo-Nagymaros Project (Hungary/Slovakia)* is a rare example of environmental litigation that has reached the stage of the merits.[9] Provisional measures were not requested in this case. The parties' Special Agreement incorporated a clause precluding the lodging by either party of a request for interim measures.[10] The contribution that provisional measures applications, hearings and orders may make to the peaceful resolution of these disputes is apparent particularly from the *Southern Bluefin Tuna* case and the *Land Reclamation* case. In some instances, a provisional measures order is the best and most timely vehicle for encouraging co-operation between the parties.[11]

The question whether the encouragement of co-operation may usefully extend to directing the parties to negotiate a settlement is more difficult. Judicially directed negotiation does have a history of endorsement in the international jurisprudence.[12] The International Court of Justice in one

[7] *Nuclear Tests case (Australia* v. *France) Request for the Indication of Interim Measures of Protection*, Order of 22 June 1973, ICJ Reports 1973 99 (hereafter *Nuclear Tests case (Australia* v. *France) (Interim Measures)*); *Nuclear Tests case (New Zealand* v. *France) Request for the Indication of Interim Measures of Protection*, Order of 22 June 1973, ICJ Reports 1973 135 (hereafter *Nuclear Tests case (New Zealand* v. *France) (Interim Measures)*). Interim measures were sought also in *Request for an Examination of the Situation in Accordance with Paragraph 63 of the Court's Judgment of 20 December 1974 in the Nuclear Tests case (New Zealand* v. *France)*, Judgment of 22 September 1995 ICJ Reports 1995 288 (hereafter *Request for an Examination of the Situation*).

[8] *Case concerning Pulp Mills on the River Uruguay (Argentina* v. *Uruguay), Request for the Indication of Provisional Measures*, Order of 15 July 2006 (hereafter *Case concerning Pulp Mills (Provisional Measures)*) ICJ Reports 2006.

[9] *Case concerning the Gabčíkovo-Nagymaros Project (Hungary/Slovakia)*, Judgment of 25 September 1997 ICJ Reports 1997 7 (hereafter *Gabčíkovo-Nagymaros* case).

[10] Article 4(2) of the Special Agreement signed on 7 April 1993 in Brussels. If either party believed its rights were endangered, that party was entitled to request immediate consultation and reference to experts (including the Commissioner of the European Communities) with a view to protecting those rights.

[11] Mansfield, 'The *Southern Bluefin Tuna* Arbitration', 362; Mansfield, 'Compulsory dispute settlement', 271.

[12] Note in particular the case of *Passage through the Great Belt (Finland* v. *Denmark) (Provisional Measures)*, Order of 29 July 1991, ICJ Reports 1991 12, 20, citing the remarks of the Permanent Court of International Justice that 'the judicial settlement of international disputes, with a view to which the Court has been established, is simply an alternative to the direct and friendly settlement of such disputes between the Parties; as consequently it is for the Court to facilitate, so far as is compatible with its Statute, such direct and friendly settlement ...' (*Free Zones of Upper Savoy and the District of Gex*, PCIJ Series A No. 22, 13. The dispute in *Passage through the Great Belt* was settled. See also *Case concerning Legality of the Use of Force (Yugoslavia* v. *Belgium) (Provisional Measures)*, Order of 2 June 1999, Dissenting Opinion of Judge Weeramantry, 196–9; *Case concerning the*

case took the view that directed negotiation may be particularly appropriate where obligations to negotiate derive naturally from the character of the rights in question. In the *Fisheries Jurisdiction case (United Kingdom of Great Britain and Northern Ireland* v. *Iceland) (Federal Republic of Germany* v. *Iceland)* the Court considered that because an obligation to negotiate flowed from the very nature of the respective rights of the parties it was a proper exercise of the judicial function to order them to negotiate.[13] The Court also considered the parties better equipped than itself with the scientific knowledge of the fisheries needed for a precise adjustment of the exercise of the parties' rights.[14] As events transpired, the preference of the litigants, and of the international community, was instead to move towards negotiations on the law of the sea regime as a whole, ultimately producing the United Nations Convention on the Law of the Sea.[15] Thus in the circumstances of the *Fisheries Jurisdiction case* effective bilateral negotiations did not result. Yet the underlying principles of co-operation remain important and have been shown to work since. One writer has referred to 'the tendency towards a facilitative approach'.[16]

Encouraging co-operation between disputing parties goes wider than the notion of judicially directed negotiation and is consistent with broader trends in international environmental law. Indeed, working towards achieving the right balance between development and environmental protection has in general required the international community to focus on international co-operation rather than on state responsibility.[17] The Court has continued to emphasise the value and importance of co-operation between the parties in environmental disputes, where appropriate through international institutions, as seen in the *Case concerning Pulp Mills on the River Uruguay (Argentina* v. *Uruguay)*.[18]

Application of the Convention on the Prevention and Punishment of the Crime of Genocide (Bosnia and Herzogovina v. *Serbia and Montenegro) (Provisional Measures)*, Order of 13 September 1993, ICJ Reports 1993 325, Dissenting Opinion of Judge Tarassov, 451–2.

13 *Fisheries Jurisdiction case (United Kingdom of Great Britain and Northern Ireland* v. *Iceland)* Judgment of 25 July 1974 ICJ Reports 1974 1, 32–4; *Fisheries Jurisdiction case (Federal Republic of Germany* v. *Iceland)*, Judgment of 25 July 1974 ICJ Reports 1974 175, 201–2, 205.

14 *Ibid. (UK* v. *Iceland)* para. 73; *(FRG* v. *Iceland)* para. 65.

15 Stephens, *International Courts*, p. 97.

16 *Ibid.*, pp. 100–101.

17 Shaw, *International Law*, p. 845. Consider for example the emphasis placed on international negotiations in *US – Shrimp. United States – Import Prohibition of Certain Shrimp and Shrimp Products* Complaint by India (WT/DS58); Complaint by Malaysia (WT/DS58); Complaint by Pakistan (WT/DS58); Complaint by Thailand (WT/DS58), Report of the Appellate Body, DSR 1998: VII, 2755, para. 166.

18 *Case concerning Pulp Mills on the River Uruguay (Argentina* v. *Uruguay)*, Judgment of 20 April 2010, ICJ Reports 2010 (hereafter *Case concerning Pulp Mills*), paras. 266, 281.

Case concerning Land Reclamation (Malaysia v. *Singapore)*

The *Case concerning Land Reclamation* represents a high-water mark in the co-operative settlement of international disputes involving scientific uncertainty. The *Land Reclamation* case involved complaints by Malaysia about the increase in ocean currents and sedimentary transportation caused by a land reclamation project being implemented by Singapore.[19] Malaysia asserted that the results of Singapore's reclamation works included changes in the transportation and deposit of sediment by the ocean currents in the vicinity, changes in the salinity of estuary waters and coastal erosion. As well as affecting the environment these changes threatened aquaculture and the interests of local fishermen, navigation and the stability of jetties.[20] Malaysia was concerned that questions about these changes could not be answered with confidence in the absence of a calibrated, validated, sufficiently long-term geomorphological hydro-environmental study.[21] Flow-on effects could include changes in tidal and flood elevations, the wave climate, the long-term sea-bed level and oxygen and pollution levels in the water. Seagrass, coral and mangrove forests were potentially subject to destruction, and a major impact on inter-tidal habitats and the aquatic ecosystem as a whole could be projected.[22] Singapore had prepared no full Environmental Impact Assessment for the project, and had given insufficient attention to the project's design. At the same time, a complicating factor that was not closely addressed in the evidence was the Malaysian contribution to environmental degradation through deforestation, the reclaiming of mangrove forests, exploitation of inshore fisheries, non-biodegradable pollution, refinery discharges and the dumping of sewage.[23] Malaysia argued that Singapore had breached obligations owed to Malaysia under the LOSC and general international law.

[19] For an overview of the case, Stephens, *International Courts*, pp. 240–2.

[20] Request for Provisional Measures, 4 September 2003, paras. 5 and 17.

[21] *Ibid.*, para. 5, citing Malaysia's Note to Singapore of 25 August 2003. See also the evidence of Malaysia's independent expert Professor Falconer, Verbatim Record, Thursday 25 September 2003, 10.00 am, 34, lines 42 *et seq.*

[22] Evidence presented by Malaysian expert Professor Sharifah Mastura and by Malaysian independent expert Professor Falconer, Verbatim Record, Thursday 25 September 2003, 10.00 am, 26–34.

[23] See cross-examination of Malaysian Technical Adviser, Professor Sharifah, by Mr Reisman for Singapore, Verbatim Record, Thursday 25 September 2003, 10.00 am, 31–2; see also Verbatim Record, Friday 26 September 2003, 10.00 am, 9; and Verbatim Record, Friday 26 September 2003, 3.00 pm, 16, lines 46–50, and 24, lines 6–9.

On application by Malaysia, the International Tribunal for the Law of the Sea made a provisional measures order requiring the parties to enter into consultations to establish promptly a group of independent experts with a mandate to conduct a study over a period of one year to determine the effects of Singapore's land reclamation and to propose measures to deal with any adverse effects.[24] The following year a conference was held at The Hague at the parties' request, at which they presented to the Annex VII Arbitral Tribunal established under the LOSC to hear the merits of the case an overview of the joint study and informed the Tribunal that they had agreed on a draft settlement agreement. On 1 September 2005, the Tribunal made an award on agreed terms at the parties' request, including provision for ongoing technical co-operation between the parties.[25] Thus, the dispute was brought to an end by the parties as a result of the technical work that had been carried out and without the need for a hearing on the merits.

In this case, Malaysia had previously stated that it would propose such a study and Singapore had said that it agreed to such a study.[26] The experts carrying out the work were chosen by the parties. Singapore and Malaysia each appointed two members of the group, who were in fact the same experts who had appeared for the two parties respectively in the proceedings before the International Tribunal for the Law of the Sea. The major task of the group was to oversee a study based on a simulation of the works that Singapore was intending to carry out and to reach agreement on an appropriate reconfiguration of Singapore's project. Liaison with the parties' legal teams was maintained throughout the period during which the work took place.

Case concerning the Gabčíkovo-Nagymaros Project (Hungary/Slovakia)

The International Court of Justice also placed great emphasis on co-operation in the *Gabčíkovo-Nagymaros* case.[27] This was consistent with the tenets of international law relating to international

[24] *Land Reclamation (Provisional Measures)*, para. 106(1)(a)(i).

[25] *Case concerning Land Reclamation by Singapore in and around the Straits of Johor (Malaysia* v. *Singapore)*, Award on Agreed Terms, 1 September 2005, XXVII UNRIAA 133 (hereafter *Land Reclamation)*.

[26] *Ibid.*, para. 86.

[27] For a fuller overview of the case, Stephens, *International Courts*, pp. 174–86.

watercourses.[28] This case arose out of a change in attitude by Hungary towards the completion of a construction programme to build a series of reservoirs, dams and locks on the River Danube for the generation of hydroelectricity in accordance with a treaty concluded in 1977 between Hungary and Czechoslavakia (the Treaty).[29] Under the Treaty, two hydroelectric plants were to be built, one upstream at Gabčíkovo in Slovakia and one downstream at Nagymaros in Hungary. Hungary had experienced dramatic political transformations over the period from 1989–90. A growing climate of concern and opposition had developed in Hungary within a sector of public opinion and in some scientific circles about the project's economic viability and as to the environmental guarantees that were considered necessary.[30] Hungary had eventually abandoned work under the joint programme, contending that the completion of the project would have produced a range of adverse environmental effects. Slovakia proceeded unilaterally. The Danube was dammed and diverted by putting into operation a dam at Cunovo, in Slovak territory.

The position adopted by Hungary was that unacceptable ecological risks would have been associated with peak-mode operation of the new power plant at Gabčíkovo, which would have discharged high volumes of water into the Danube downstream of the project. The significant daily variations in water level that resulted would threaten aquatic habitats.[31] The upstream section of the river would be seriously affected by the project, too. Diverting the river was going to affect both surface and groundwater in the ecologically valuable area of Hungary known as the Szigetkőz. The quality of the groundwater would seriously diminish as its level dropped. Surface water would become subject to risks of eutrophication. Flora and fauna in the area would face extinction. The same was going to be the case for the fluvial flora and fauna that had inhabited the abandoned riverbed of the old Danube. What would be left was a river choked with sand, with only a trickle of water. Hungary also raised serious concerns about the effects of construction and operation of the Nagymaros dam on the water supply to Budapest. The yield of the bank-filtered wells that provided two-thirds of

[28] See e.g. the Verbatim Record in the *Gabčíkovo-Nagymaros* case, Monday 3 March 1997, translation, remarks of Slovakia, 13, and of Hungary, 42; also of Tuesday 15 April 1997, translation, 37 and 43–7.

[29] By the time of the proceedings the Slovak Republic had become party to the Treaty as a successor state to Czechoslovakia. *Gabčíkovo-Nagymaros* case, para. 123.

[30] *Ibid.*, para. 32. [31] *Ibid.*, para. 40.

the Budapest supply was going to be affected.[32] Siltation following the dam's construction would also have produced a deterioration in the water quality of bank-filtered wells in the upstream sector.[33]

A distinguishing feature of the *Gabčíkovo-Nagymaros* case was the commitment made by the parties in Article 5(2) of their Special Agreement promptly to carry out negotiations on the implementation of the Court's judgment. In this case the obligation to negotiate had come about through the prior agreement of the parties and did not need to be drawn from the intrinsic nature of the rights at issue. When the parties' obligations regarding protection of water quality, nature and fishing interests under Articles 15, 19 and 20 of their 1977 Treaty were also taken into account, their responsibility to negotiate the future of the *Gabčíkovo-Nagymaros* project became clear. The Court's judgment pointed the parties towards such negotiations as the way forward in dealing with their dispute,[34] finding that the Treaty was still in force, that Hungary had not been entitled to suspend and abandon work at Nagymaros and that Slovakia had not been entitled to proceed to put the Čunovo dam into operation.[35]

The Court declined to rely on the precautionary principle in relation to Hungary's invocation of the doctrine of ecological necessity to justify non-compliance with its treaty obligations. The Court was keenly aware of the uncertainty in the relevant factual evidence, quoting from the report produced by the ad hoc Committee of the Hungarian Academy of Sciences on 23 June 1989:

> The measuring results of an at least five-year monitoring period following the completion of the Gabčíkovo construction are indispensable to the trustworthy prognosis of the ecological impacts of the barrage system. There is undoubtedly a need for the establishment and regular operation of a comprehensive monitoring system, which must be more developed than at present. The examination of biological indicator objects that can sensitively indicate the changes happening in the environment, neglected til today, have to be included.[36]

However, in the Court's view, the threshold for the invocation of the doctrine of ecological necessity was a high one, and did not

[32] *Ibid.*, para. 40.

[33] The scientific complexity of these key points is conveyed in the advocacy for Hungary of scientists Professor Gábor Vida and Dr Roland Carbiener, Verbatim Record, Monday 3 March 1997, 47 ff and translation 67 ff, as well as those of Dr Klaus Kern and Dr Howard Wheater on Tuesday 4 March, 20 ff.

[34] *Gabčíkovo-Nagymaros* case, paras. 132–47.

[35] *Ibid.*, para. 125.

[36] *Ibid.*, para. 56.

incorporate a great tolerance for such uncertainty in the relevant factual evidence.[37]

As the Court recognised, by the time of the Court's judgment there was little point in building the plant at Nagymaros, due to what was, effectively, agreement between the parties not to pursue the peak-mode option for the project. Further, the plant at Gabčíkovo had been in operation for some five years and was fed via the dam constructed at Čunovo.[38] The Court noted that the parties themselves had demonstrated that they considered the explicit terms of the Treaty to be negotiable; an example was their willingness to agree to discard the option of peak-mode operation.[39] The Court did observe that despite the often contradictory conclusions of the numerous scientific reports presented by the parties, these reports provided abundant evidence that the project did involve a considerable impact on the environment. This impact and its implications were to be a key issue for the parties to consider in their negotiations under Article 5.[40] There was a growing international awareness of the risks of unconsidered interventions in the environment, and vigilance and protection were required in light of the often irreversible character of damage. The parties were to find an agreed solution, to be 'pursued in a joint and integrated way',[41] and to restore to the project the character of a joint regime that was a basic element of their original Treaty.[42] The Court provided a degree of substantive direction. In the Court's view, it would be appropriate for the works at Čunovo to become a jointly operated unit, as the Čunovo dam had taken over the role envisaged for the works at Dunakiliti under the Treaty, and the status quo should be transformed into the new joint regime that was to be sought by the parties.[43]

The negotiations to be conducted by Hungary and Slovakia did not run as smoothly as had been hoped. Following the transmission of the Court's judgment, the parties duly commissioned expert groups and entered into negotiations. They initialled a draft Framework Agreement, but the negotiations faltered with the change of government in Hungary in 1998.[44] Consistent with Article 5 of the Special Agreement, Slovakia requested an additional judgment determining

[37] For an analysis see Foster, 'Necessity and precaution'. See also, inter alia, Bostian, 'Flushing the Danube', 425, suggesting that the precautionary principle 'might have offset the need for "imminence"'.

[38] *Gabčíkovo-Nagymaros* case, para. 134.

[39] *Ibid.*, para. 138. [40] *Ibid.*, para. 140. [41] *Ibid.*, para. 141. [42] *Ibid.*, para. 144.

[43] *Ibid.*, para. 146. [44] Szabó, 'The implementation of the judgment of the ICJ'.

the modalities for executing the original judgment.[45] Hungary objected to the Slovak request.[46] Negotiations continued.[47] In 2006 a water-management working group successfully completed work on the future of the project. However, the product was a list of the points on which the parties disagreed.[48] Should the Strategic Environmental Assessment that was due to be concluded in December 2009 fail to produce movement forwards, the case may come before the International Court of Justice again.[49]

Southern Bluefin Tuna case (Australia and New Zealand v. *Japan)*

Provisional measures orders will often incorporate a direction to the parties to co-operate. In the *Southern Bluefin Tuna* case, provisional measures were prescribed by the International Tribunal for the Law of the Sea under Article 290(5) of the LOSC, requiring all three parties to abide by their fishing quotas[50] and to refrain from conducting experimental programmes which caught additional tuna.[51] The Tribunal considered that although it was not possible conclusively to assess the parties' scientific evidence, measures should be taken as a matter of urgency to preserve the parties' rights and to avert further deterioration of the southern bluefin tuna stock.[52] In basing its provisional measures order on the existing quota allocations agreed by the parties, the Tribunal effectively emphasised existing co-operative mechanisms as the appropriate method for resolution of the parties' scientific differences. In addition, the Tribunal specifically ordered the parties to resume negotiations with one another without delay on conservation and management measures for southern bluefin tuna.[53] As well, the parties were to

[45] Request for an Additional Judgment, filed by the government of Slovakia 3 September 1998.

[46] Written Statement of the Republic of Hungary, 7 December 1998.

[47] Report of the International Court of Justice to the 59th session of the General Assembly, UN Doc A/59/4, paras. 139–47.

[48] Szabó, 'The implementation of the judgment of the ICJ'. [49] *Ibid.*

[50] *Southern Bluefin Tuna*, Provisional Measures Order, para. 90. These quotas were to be modified for 1999 and 2000 to take account of fish caught in Japan's 1999 experimental fishing programmes.

[51] *Ibid.*, para. 90. For an overview of the case, Stephens, *International Courts*, p. 220–8. See also for interest Foster, 'The "real dispute" in the *Southern Bluefin Tuna* case: A scientific dispute?' (2001) 16(4) *International Journal of Marine and Coastal Law* 571–601.

[52] *Ibid.*, para. 80. [53] *Ibid.*, para. 90.

make further efforts in their negotiations with other fishing states and entities.[54] The Tribunal required a report from the parties within just a few weeks.[55]

The dispute in this case arose after several years' unsuccessful discussions under the 1993 Convention for the Conservation of Southern Bluefin Tuna[56] on a possible experimental fishing programme for southern bluefin tuna. In the absence of such a programme, Japan had unilaterally undertaken a 'pilot programme' of experimental fishing in 1998, without the agreement of Australia and New Zealand. This 'pilot programme' took 1,464 tonnes of fish over and above Japan's total allowable catch (TAC) allocation of 6,065 tonnes. In 1999 Japan had announced its intentions to begin a full experimental fishing programme imminently.

Fishing quotas for southern bluefin tuna had begun to be put in place in the 1980s, when studies revealed the parental stock level of the tuna to have been reduced to only 23–30 per cent of its 1960 level.[57] The Scientific Committee established under the 1993 Convention to assist the Commission for the Conservation of Southern Bluefin Tuna later identified the 1980 parental biomass level as the threshold for a biologically safe population. At the time of the proceedings, recent Scientific Committee assessments had found the current size of the spawning stock was still only 25–53 per cent of the 1980 level. Given these conditions, the threat posed to the stock was the possibility of an abrupt decline in breeding numbers and a collapse of the fishery. The issue was whether the spawning stock or 'parental biomass' of the tuna was still declining, or whether it was on the road to recovery. Estimates of the probability of recovery varied from <14 per cent (Australia's and New Zealand's scientists) to 76–87 per cent (Japan's scientists).[58]

To work out whether the parental biomass of southern bluefin tuna was still in decline required an estimate of the age at which the tuna reached maturity and could reproduce. A figure of eight years of age was

[54] *Ibid.*, para. 90. [55] *Ibid.*, para. 90.

[56] Convention for the Conservation of Southern Bluefin Tuna, Canberra, 10 May 1993, in force 20 May 1994, 1819 UNTS 360.

[57] *Southern Bluefin Tuna cases (Australia and New Zealand* v. *Japan) Jurisdiction and Admissibility*, 4 August 2000 (hereafter *Southern Bluefin Tuna (Jurisdiction and Admissibility))*, 39 ILM 1359, 12.

[58] Opinion of Australian scientists, Dr T. Polacheck and Ms A. Preece, p. 6, presented in evidence by Australia and New Zealand, citing the report of the 1998 Commission for the Conservation of Southern Bluefin Tuna Scientific Committee Meeting.

sometimes used, but some scientists said this should be not less than twelve years of age, and maybe older. The difference was significant:

> If the average age at sexual maturity is as low as age eight, evidence is mixed on what the trend in the spawning stock biomass ... has been since 1994 ... However, for average ages at a maturity of ten or greater, all assessments show a continuing decline in the spawning stock.[59]

There was also uncertainty about natural mortality rates and susceptibility to catch, and about unreported catches and discarding of fish, as well as uncertainty about environmental factors which might affect the state of the fish stocks.

A key issue in interpreting catch data for the purposes of virtual population analysis was how to estimate the fish that were present in areas that had been fished previously but were not being fished in a particular year. Accordingly, a focus in Japan's scientific assessments had been to estimate the ratio of the mean density of fish in unfished areas to that in fished areas.[60] One approach was based on the assumption that there were no fish in the areas not being fished. This approach indicated stability or a continued decline in southern bluefin tuna stocks in the 1990s.[61] Another approach was based on an alternative assumption that the density of fish in the unfished areas was the same as in the areas being fished. This approach indicated stability or increases in the stock in the 1990s.[62] The Japanese assumption was that the density of fish in the unfished areas was the same as in the areas being fished, and Australia and New Zealand considered this to be producing inaccurate models of the fish population.

A related difference of opinion was a debate about the targeting of fish by Japan's fleets. Had the fleets been redirected by industry, which recognised that the future of the fishery was best protected by fishing in areas where larger, older and fattier fish were found rather than where increasing proportions of younger fish were being caught?[63] Or should the fishing fleets be assumed to be targeting the areas where fish density was highest in order to maximise their returns?[64] Japan's programme

[59] Opinion of Professor Sir John Beddington, presented in evidence by Australia and New Zealand, para. 28. Comments on the issues raised by T. Polacheck and A. Preece, 'A scientific overview of the status of the southern bluefin tuna stock' and by Talbot Murray's 'Comment' on that overview (hereafter Opinion of Professor Sir John Beddington).

[60] *Ibid.*, para. 48. [61] *Ibid.*, para. 48. [62] *Ibid.*, para. 48.

[63] Views of Dr Sachiko Tsuji, presented in evidence by Japan, para. 35.

[64] Opinion of Professor Sir John Beddington, para. 50.

was further criticised because its design was based on tracts of ocean some 220,000 km^2 in area, a very large area in relation to which it is difficult to be precise – it was observed that the presence of just one longliner could result in classification of a square as fished rather than unfished.[65] If fishing vessels did not take samples from unfished areas then it was very difficult to estimate the ratio of the mean density of fish in unfished areas to that in fished areas, in comparison with standard statistical survey techniques using pre-selected random sampling locations.[66]

Australia and New Zealand alleged that Japan was breaching obligations of co-operation and conservation in respect of the living resources of the high seas under the LOSC.[67] Japan was not a willing participant in the proceedings taken by Australia and New Zealand, and the Tribunal that was constituted under Annex VII of the LOSC to deal with the merits upheld Japan's arguments that there was no jurisdiction over the dispute under the LOSC.[68] Thus the case did not progress beyond the provisional measures stage. Although the provisional measures order made by the Tribunal was important in reinforcing commitment to a co-operative approach,[69] there have been ongoing difficulties since.[70] In 2006, marketing figures from Japan showed a large over-catch of about 1,500 tonnes, and the Japanese government agreed to take a corresponding cut in its quota for 2007.[71]

The MOX Plant cases (Ireland v. *United Kingdom)*

In the *Mox Plant* case, the provisional measures order issued by the International Tribunal for the Law of the Sea focused directly on co-operation between the parties.[72] The *MOX Plant* case concerned the commissioning of mixed oxide (MOX) fuel production by British

[65] *Ibid.*, para. 49. [66] *Ibid.*, paras. 50–1. [67] Articles 64 and 116–19.

[68] The Annex VII tribunal found that the terms of the 1993 Convention established that the parties had opted for non-compulsory forms of dispute settlement in relation to disputes to which the 1993 Convention applied, and therefore compulsory jurisdiction under the LOSC was excluded. *Southern Bluefin Tuna (Jurisdiction and Admissibility)*, paras. 56–8; see also Separate Opinion of Sir Kenneth Keith; also Memorial on Jurisdiction of Japan, paras. 38–48; Reply on Jurisdiction of Australia and New Zealand, para. 139.

[69] Mansfield, 'Compulsory dispute settlement'. [70] Stephens, 'The limits'.

[71] 'Bluefin tuna plundering catches up with Japan,' 16 October 2006, ABC News Online.

[72] *MOX Plant (Provisional Measures)*. Further detail is to be found in the written and oral proceedings submitted on the merits in the proceedings before the Annex VII Tribunal, below. For an overview of the case, Stephens, *International Courts*, p. 232–40.

Nuclear Fuels Limited (BNFL) at the nuclear plant at Sellafield in Cumbria, north-west England. The closest point in Ireland lies only 112 miles away on the other side of the Irish Sea. MOX fuel is a mixture of plutonium dioxide and uranium dioxide.[73] Producing MOX fuel is a way of recycling the plutonium that is generated as a waste product by nuclear reactors running on enriched uranium oxide. MOX manufacturing therefore reduces the volume of plutonium that requires to be stored long term.[74] None of the British reactors run on MOX. The plant was set up in order to reprocess and re-export fuel from abroad, including Japan.

Ireland expressed concerns about the production of radioactive waste at the MOX plant in solid, liquid and gaseous form. Ireland was anxious that such wastes would be discharged into the Irish Sea or into the atmosphere.[75] Particular characteristics of MOX fuel were cited, including its automated production, its reliance on powder technology (which is known for reliability concerns), the potential seriousness of lapses in the quality of inspections and the relatively low temperature at which exposed MOX pellets will give off respirable particles following relatively short exposure periods.[76] Ireland described how cylindrical pellets of reprocessed fuel would be produced at the MOX plant, made from a granulated powder produced by grinding, milling and blending uranium dioxide and plutonium dioxide.[77]

The United Kingdom argued that the doses of radioactivity from MOX production were of negligible radiological significance. According to the United Kingdom, the impact from gaseous discharges from the MOX plant was estimated as amounting to 0.002 microsieverts per year (two-thousandths of a millionth of a sievert), while the estimated dose from liquid discharges was estimated at 0.000003 microsieverts per year (three-millionths of a millionth of a sievert). A radiation dose of 1 whole microsievert corresponded with a risk of a 1 in 20 million chance of contracting a fatal cancer. One microsievert per year was the level which the International Commission on Radiological Protection had recommended be placed on human exposure to anthropogenic

[73] Churchill and Scott, 'The MOX Plant litigation', 644.

[74] Written Response of the United Kingdom, Request for Provisional Measures (hereafter UK Written Response), paras. 28–9. On the production of MOX fuel, see also Statement of Case of Ireland, Ireland's Request for Provisional Measures (hereafter Request for Provisional Measures), paras. 7 and 8.

[75] *Ibid.*, para. 32. [76] *Ibid.*, para. 32. [77] *Ibid.*, para. 30.

sources of radiation, as reflected in Directive 96/29/Euratom of 13 May 1996 laying down basic safety standards.[78]

Ireland contended that the authorisation and operation of the MOX plant would be inconsistent with a number of the United Kingdom's obligations under the LOSC relating to co-operation to protect the marine environment,[79] environmental impact assessment[80] and the protection and preservation of the marine environment from intended, accidental and unexpected terrorist releases of radioactive materials or wastes from the MOX plant and/or ships travelling to and from the plant.[81] Pending the constitution of an Arbitral Tribunal to hear the merits of the case, constituted under Annex VII of the LOSC, Ireland requested that the International Tribunal for the Law of the Sea prescribe measures compelling the United Kingdom immediately to suspend authorisation of the MOX plant and prevent its operation, and that the United Kingdom ensure there were no movements of radioactive substances into or out of its maritime zones in connection with the plant.

The United Kingdom emphasised its commitment to reducing concentrations of radiation in the marine environment to historic levels.[82] The United Kingdom also informed the Tribunal that the issuance of a provisional measure restraining authorisation for the plant's commissioning would be likely to result in the loss of the plant's first customer, at a cost of £10 million minimum, while direct costs to the United Kingdom also included approximately £385,000 per week for maintaining the plant in a state of operational readiness. Loss of a further two customers was also possible, and there would be damage to BNFL's competitive position.[83] The United Kingdom considered that Ireland's case was based solely on uncertainty as to the effects of low-dose radioactive discharges on non-human biota. While the United Kingdom conceded that further research was desirable on these points, the current lack of knowledge did not call into question existing standards of radiological protection.

The lack of evidence adduced by Ireland to support its request for provisional measures was emphasised by the United Kingdom throughout written and oral submissions.[84] For its part, Ireland submitted that the precautionary principle informed the conditions under which the

[78] UK Written Response, para. 35. [79] LOSC, Articles 123 and 197.
[80] *Ibid.*, Article 206. [81] *Ibid.*, Articles 192–4, 207, 211 and 213.
[82] Verbatim Record, Tuesday 20 November 2001, 3.15 pm.
[83] UK Written Response, 19–22 and 49–58.
[84] For example, *ibid.*, paras. 1(4), 134, 224, 227–30.

International Tribunal for the Law of the Sea should approach the question of urgency and the prima facie merits of the Irish case.[85] However, the United Kingdom also argued that, for provisional measures to be awarded, there must be a real risk of harm, and not a purely hypothetical one. The United Kingdom referred to the *Southern Bluefin Tuna* case as an example where evidence was provided to the Tribunal supporting the claim of a real risk of harm.[86] Further, the United Kingdom considered that harm must be imminent.[87] For its part, Ireland sought to rely on the precedent of the *Southern Bluefin Tuna* case, submitting that the 'prudence and caution' referred to by the Tribunal in that case were similarly appropriate in the *MOX Plant* case.[88] The United Kingdom countered that precautionary dictates could not be relied upon as a substitute for a basic foundation of evidence.[89]

The International Tribunal for the Law of the Sea did not find the urgency of the situation to require the prescription of the provisional measures requested in the short period before the constitution of the Annex VII Tribunal.[90] However, the Tribunal considered that prudence and caution required that Ireland and the United Kingdom should co-operate in exchanging information about the risks or effects of operating the MOX plant and in devising ways to deal with them as appropriate. Accordingly Ireland and the UK were to co-operate and to enter into consultations forthwith in order to exchange further information on possible consequences for the Irish Sea from commissioning of the plant, to monitor risks or effects of the operation of the plant in relation to the Irish Sea and to devise such measures as might be appropriate to prevent pollution of the marine environment resulting from the plant's operation.[91] This provisional measure did result in improved co-operation between the parties, and was of some benefit.[92]

[85] Ireland's Request for Provisional Measures, paras. 97 and 101.

[86] UK Written Response, paras. 142, 147, 149 and 157; Verbatim Record, Tuesday 20 November 2001, 9.30 am, 16 and 27.

[87] UK Written Response, para. 148, citing the *Case concerning Passage through the Great Belt (Finland* v. *Denmark) (Provisional Measures)*, Order of 29 July 1991, International Court of Justice Reports 1991, 12 at paras. 24 and 27; Verbatim Record, Tuesday, 20 November 2001, 9.30 am, 11, line 40 and 27, line 15, where the United Kingdom took the view that imminence is presupposed by the criterion of urgency.

[88] Ireland's Request for Provisional Measures, para. 100; Verbatim Record, Monday, 19 November 2001, 10.00 am, 13, line 45.

[89] UK Written Response, para. 150.

[90] *MOX Plant (Provisional Measures)*, para. 81.

[91] *Ibid.*, para. 89(1).

[92] Churchill and Scott, 'The MOX Plant litigation', 675.

The Annex VII Tribunal was duly constituted some two months later. However, following the exchange of written proceedings, the Tribunal became concerned that, in order to address the merits of the case, the Tribunal might find itself pronouncing on questions lying within the jurisdiction of the European Court of Justice. Desirous of avoiding a situation where the Tribunal and the Court issued potentially diverging decisions, the Tribunal communicated that it had decided to suspend proceedings and indicated its willingness to consider a further request for provisional measures from either party.[93] Ireland made such a request for provisional measures, and, in suspending proceedings, the Annex VII Tribunal affirmed the provisional measure that had been prescribed by the International Tribunal for the Law of the Sea as well as requiring the parties to submit reports on their compliance with the provisional measures.[94] In considering Ireland's request, the Tribunal expressed concern that, although co-operation between the parties had increased, co-operation and consultation might not have been always as effective or timely as it could have been.[95] Accordingly, the Tribunal recommended that the parties should seek to establish intergovernmental arrangements for co-ordination of all the various agencies and bodies involved, and review their system of intergovernmental notification and co-ordination.[96]

Following the institution of proceedings against Ireland by the Commission of the European Communities in the European Court of Justice four months later, the Annex VII Tribunal further suspended its proceedings until the Court had given judgment,[97] and extended the provisional measures it had ordered in June 2003. As a result of the Court's eventual judgment against Ireland in 2006, the Annex VII Tribunal did not proceed to consider the merits of Ireland's case.[98]

Aspects of the *Mox Plant* case were also considered in another forum. Ireland had originally begun litigation against the United Kingdom internationally by instituting proceedings in June 2001 under the Convention for the Protection of the Marine Environment of the

[93] Statement of the President of the Tribunal, 13 June 2003.

[94] *Mox Plant case (Suspension of Proceedings on Jurisdiction and Merits and Request for Further Provisional Measures)*.

[95] *Ibid.*, para. 66. [96] *Ibid.*, paras. 64–7.

[97] Or until the Tribunal otherwise determined. *Mox Plant case (Further Suspension of Proceedings on Jurisdiction and Merits)*, Order No. 4 of 14 November 2003.

[98] Case C-459/03, *Commission of the European Communities* v. *Ireland* [2006] ECR I-4635.

North-East Atlantic 1992 (the OSPAR Convention)[99] for non-production of unedited copies of two reports concerning the commissioning of the Mox Plant.[100] The tribunal of the Permanent Court of Arbitration dealing with this dispute found against the Irish complaint.[101] The *MOX OSPAR* case is of particular interest because of the approach taken to scientific uncertainty in the Dissenting Opinion of arbitrator Gavan Griffith QC, discussed further in Chapter 6 below.[102]

Case concerning Pulp Mills on the River Uruguay (Argentina v. *Uruguay)*

In the *Case concerning Pulp Mills*, Argentina requested provisional measures requiring Uruguay to suspend the authorisation, construction and commissioning of two mills on the River Uruguay.[103] The International Court of Justice declined the request.[104] The Court was unpersuaded that Argentina's rights would no longer be capable of protection if its request for provisional measures was declined.[105] Nor did the Court consider there were grounds for making an Order for improved co-operation between the parties, taking into account that Uruguay had already offered to conduct continuous joint monitoring of the projects' effects with Argentina.[106]

The first of the mills, which may be referred to as the CMB mill, was to be built by Celulosas de M'Bopicua S.A. The CMB mill was originally to be situated near the Uruguayan town of Fray Bentos, with a population of approximately 23,000, some 25 km from the Argentine tourist resort

[99] Convention for the Protection of the Marine Environment of the North-East Atlantic, Paris, 22 September 1992, in force 25 March 1998, 32 ILM 1069, Article 32.

[100] The first was a report prepared for BNFL by the PA Consulting Group, a 1997 edited copy of which was released to the public. The second report was a business case analysis by Arthur D. Little, also provided to BNFL, and made public in 2001 in edited form.

[101] *Dispute concerning Access to Information under Article 9 of the OSPAR Convention (Ireland* v. *United Kingdom of Great Britain and Northern Ireland)*, Award of 2 July 2003, 42 ILM 1116.

[102] See below, Chapter 6, p. 260.

[103] For an overview of the case, Stephens, *International Courts*, pp. 187–90.

[104] *Case concerning Pulp Mills (Provisional Measures)*. [105] *Ibid.*, para. 76.

[106] *Ibid.*, paras. 83–4. Uruguay also submitted an unsuccessful request to the Court for provisional measures. In Uruguay's case, the request was an attempt to bring an end to Argentinian citizens' blockades impeding transit across the General San Martin Bridge over the River Uruguay. *Case concerning Pulp Mills on the River Uruguay (Argentina* v. *Uruguay), Request for the Indication of Provisional Measures*, Order of 23 January 2007, ICJ Reports 2007.

of Gualeguaychú, with about 80,000 residents. The second mill, which may be referred to as the Orion mill, was located within some 7 km of the CMB plant, and a purpose-built port was to be attached to the mill. By the time that the case reached the merits stage, the construction of the CMB Plant had been relocated, and so the proceedings on the merits concerned only the Orion Mill, to be built by the Finnish company Botnia.

As Argentina put it, there was no doubt that worldwide pollution by pulp mills was immense, and they did have serious adverse impacts. The scientific opinion was consistent on this. The timescales involved ranged from days to decades, although evidence of short-term impacts was 'timely warning of long-term damage to come'.[107] Argentina considered that the wrong site had been chosen for the Botnia Mill, taking into account the tidal character of the river, including the phenomena of low flow and reverse flow. Stagnation could lead to eutrophication and there had been an instance in early 2009 of a large toxic algal bloom which Argentina attributed to the operation of the Botnia Mill, with particular reference to the levels of nutrients in the river, especially phosphorus.[108] According to Argentina, the Botnia Mill would not be permitted at a comparable site in Europe, and key indicators all suggested it should have been situated elsewhere.[109] Argentina emphasised also the already polluted quality of the receiving waters, the detection of nonylphenols (a substance banned in twenty-seven European Union Member States that was commonly used as an industrial cleaner in pulp plants) and the unpleasant sulphurous air pollution experienced since the plant had been in operation.[110]

Uruguay countered that the choice of site for the Botnia Mill was excellent, not only because of its accessibility, the availability of raw materials and water and manpower, but also because it would not cause significant harm to site the mill there.[111] Uruguay was well aware of flow reversal in tidal rivers,[112] and the River Uruguay was a huge river with a high volume of water capable of absorbing what substances might be discharged by the mill.[113] Uruguay believed the

[107] Verbatim Record, Monday 14 September 2009, 52–4.

[108] *Ibid.*, 40, 44, 45. See also Verbatim Record, Monday 28 September 2009, 44–7.

[109] Verbatim Record, Monday 14 September 2009, 57–9. [110] *Ibid.*, 41–50.

[111] Verbatim Record, Tuesday 15 September 2009, translation, 11–13.

[112] Verbatim Record, Tuesday 22 September 2009, 39–40.

[113] Verbatim Record, Monday 21 September 2009, 21.

origins of the algal bloom in February 2009 to have been upriver of the mill.[114]

The Uruguayan mill was to produce air-dried pulp for the manufacture of paper, using a process known as Elemental Chlorine Free Technology (ECF). ECF relies on the use of chlorine dioxide, and produces the harmful pollutants technically referred to as polychlorinated dibenzo-pi-dioxins and dibenzofurans, more commonly known as 'dioxins' and 'furans'. Argentina placed particular emphasis on these substances at the stage of its request for provisional measures, citing Canadian research in support of its concerns.[115] Dioxins and furans have become well known as toxins by reason of their traits as compounds that persist and accumulate in the environment. These are carcinogenic substances, and Argentina listed their potential effects on the body as including reproductive, immunological, endocrinological, respiratory and cardiovascular effects.[116] As explained by counsel for Argentina, pulp is produced from the wood of eucalyptus tees, stripped of its bark and chipped. Using a production process called the Kraft process, the wood chips are cooked in chemicals including caustic sodium hydroxide and sodium sulphide in order to separate out the pulp, which is initially brown in colour but is then bleached. The substance that remains goes by the name of 'black liquor'. The economic efficiency of the Kraft process involves reuse of the inorganic chemicals in the black liquor for the cooking of further wood chips. To recover those chemicals from the black liquor requires combustion of the liquor, and it is at this stage that dioxins and furans are produced.[117]

Argentina also argued at the provisional measures stage that Uruguay had given insufficient consideration to the impact of the pulp mills on tourism and investment,[118] as well as on small-scale fisheries and terrestrial and aquatic fauna.[119] Gas emissions were expected to include nitrogen oxides and sulphur dioxide as well as particulate matter, odorous total reduced sulphur and volatile organic compounds.[120] The prevailing winds would carry these substances along the Argentine coast of the river.[121] Liquid effluents were expected to incorporate high levels of toxic substances and to consume oxygen from the water of the river, affecting the various fish species of the River Uruguay.

[114] Verbatim Record, Tuesday 22 September 2009, 17; Verbatim Record, Friday 2 October 2009, 26–31.

[115] Verbatim Record, Thursday 8 June 2006, 10.00 am, 34. [116] *Ibid.*, 25. [117] *Ibid.*, 33–4.

[118] *Ibid.*, translation, 38. [119] *Ibid.*, 65–6. [120] *Ibid.*, 32. [121] *Ibid.*, 24.

These substances included not only dioxins and furans but also mercury, phosphorus and cyanide.[122] Argentina identified that the river was home to more than 150 species, and observed that two of these species were listed as endangered by the International Union for the Conservation of Nature. Fish population density was exceptionally high downstream of Fray Bentos, and in the spring and summer this density increased at the feeding grounds below the pulp plant sites. The liquid effluent from the plants could be expected irreversibly to affect the metabolism and reproductive capacity of fish and other species.[123] Specific concerns also arose about the fish populations where the port for the Orion site was being built.[124]

For Uruguay, a provisional measures order to suspend construction of the plants would have had a serious economic effect. When operational, the plants were expected to have an economic impact of more than $350 million per annum, amounting to 2 per cent of Uruguay's GDP. The Court declined to order provisional measures.[125] Nothing in the record indicated that an imminent threat of irreparable damage flowed from the authorisation of the plants.[126] Nor had Argentina persuaded the Court that construction presented irreparable environmental damage or a present threat of irreparable economic and social damage.[127] So far as the commissioning of the mills was concerned, the Court reasoned at the provisional measures stage that there could be no imminent threat of pollution as the Orion plant was not expected to be operational before August 2007 and the CMB plant was not expected to be operational before June 2008. Nor did the evidence provided by Argentina suggest that the mills would cause irreparable damage to the river.[128]

The Court's response to Argentina's request for provisional measures was to recall the joint machinery established under the 1975 Statute of the River Uruguay, including a comprehensive and progressive regime allied with the establishment of the Executive Commission of the River Uruguay.[129] The Court stressed the necessity for the parties to implement in good faith the Statute's procedures for consultation and co-operation.[130] Additionally, the Court recalled that, at the conclusion of the provisional measures hearings, the Agent of Uruguay had reiterated Uruguay's offer to conduct continuous joint monitoring with the

[122] *Ibid.*, 25. [123] *Ibid.*, 25. [124] *Ibid.*, 31.
[125] *Case concerning Pulp Mills (Provisional Measures).* [126] *Ibid.*, para. 73. [127] *Ibid.*, para. 74.
[128] *Ibid.*, para. 75. [129] Order of 13 July 2006, para. 81. [130] *Ibid.*, para. 82.

Argentine Republic.[131] This offer by Uruguay was reminiscent of the offers made by Singapore immediately before the close of proceedings in the *Land Reclamation* case. It was in taking note in particular of these commitments as affirmed before the Court that the Court considered there were not the grounds for it to indicate the provisional measures Argentina had requested in relation to co-operation between the parties.

The merits of the complaint lodged by Argentina concerned allegations that Uruguay was in breach of its obligations under the 1975 Statute and other rules of international law, including the international law of watercourses. These included procedural obligations of prior notification to the Executive Commission of the River Uruguay, and to Argentina, under Article 7, and associated requirements under Articles 7–12. They also included substantive obligations, most notably under Article 41 of the Statute which required the parties to 'protect and preserve the aquatic environment and, in particular, to prevent its pollution'. Argentina viewed this obligation as incorporating an obligation to protect biodiversity and fisheries, including by preparing a full and objective environmental impact study. Argentina also invoked an obligation to take all necessary measures for the optimum and rational utilisation of the river, consistent with the objective of the Statute of the River Uruguay as referred to in Article 1 of the Statute. Additionally Argentina invoked an obligation to co-operate in the prevention of pollution and the protection of biodiversity and fisheries.[132]

The Court found that Uruguay had breached its procedural obligations under Articles 7–12 of the Statute of the River Uruguay, but that Uruguay had not breached its substantive obligations under the Statute.[133] The Court emphasised the parties' long-standing tradition of co-operation and co-ordination through the Executive Commission of the River Uruguay, through which they had established a real community of interest in the management of the river and its environment.[134] The obligation to co-operate encompassed the ongoing monitoring of an industrial facility such as the Botnia Mill.[135]

131 *Ibid.*, para. 83.

132 Application Instituting Proceedings of 4 May 2006, *Case concerning Pulp Mills (Provisional Measures)*, 11.

133 *Case concerning Pulp Mills*, para. 282. 134 *Ibid.*, para. 281. 135 *Ibid.*, para. 281.

Nuclear Tests cases (Australia v. *France) (New Zealand* v. *France)*

The International Court of Justice did order provisional measures in 1973 in the proceedings taken against France by Australia and New Zealand in respect of atmospheric nuclear testing in the Pacific in the *Nuclear Tests* cases.[136] The Court has been called upon twice to consider the legality of nuclear testing in the Pacific by France. In 1973 Australia and New Zealand respectively instituted proceedings in relation to atmospheric testing,[137] while in 1995 New Zealand asked the Court to re-examine the situation in relation to France's underground nuclear testing in *Request for an Examination of the Situation in Accordance with Paragraph 63 of the Court's Judgment of 20 December 1974 in the Nuclear Tests (New Zealand* v. *France)*.[138]

Atmospheric tests, initially at Mururoa Atoll in the Tuamotu Archipelago, were carried out in 1966, 1967, 1968, 1970, 1971 and 1972. Australia's and New Zealand's primary concern in the 1973–4 cases was the radioactive fallout, or *retombées*, resulting from the tests. The two complaints by Australia and New Zealand were very similar.[139] The discussion that follows draws on the New Zealand complaint. Mururoa Atoll is approximately 2,500 nautical miles from the nearest point of New Zealand's North Island and 1,050 nautical miles from the nearest point in the Cook Islands, a self-governing state in free association with New Zealand.[140]

New Zealand complained that the nuclear tests produced both tropospheric and stratospheric fallout. Tropospheric fallout consists of radionuclides in the lower atmosphere, generally entering the human food chain through their deposit in pastures consumed by cattle producing

[136] *Nuclear Tests case (Australia* v. *France) (Interim Measures)*; *Nuclear Tests case (New Zealand* v. *France) (Interim Measures))*. For an overview of cases see Stephens, *International Courts*, pp. 137–45.

[137] *Nuclear Tests case (Australia* v. *France)*, 20 December 1974, ICJ Reports 1974 253 (hereafter *Nuclear Tests case (Australia* v. *France))*; *Nuclear Tests case (New Zealand* v. *France)*, 20 December 1974, ICJ Reports 1974 457 (hereafter *Nuclear Tests case (New Zealand* v. *France))*.

[138] *Request for an Examination of the Situation in Accordance with Paragraph 63 of the Court's Judgment of 20 December 1974 in the Nuclear Tests case (New Zealand* v. *France)*, Judgment of 22 September 1995, ICJ Reports 1995 288 (hereafter *Request for an Examination of the Situation*).

[139] For differences between the cases, see Stephens, *International Courts*, pp. 139–45.

[140] *Nuclear Tests case (New Zealand* v. *France)*, para. 17.

milk for human consumption. The substance in question, iodine-131, has a short half-life of eight days. Stratospheric fallout in the upper atmosphere produces strontium-90 and caesium-137, which enter the human body through food and have longer half-lives, of approximately twenty-eight and thirty years respectively. Strontium-90 is deposited with calcium in human bone, while caesium-137 tends to be found in muscle tissue. Stratospheric fallout would take several years to drop down into the troposphere and then tends to be deposited in the mid-latitudes, where New Zealand is situated. In contrast, tropospheric fall-out would be deposited within two to three weeks, after being borne around the globe on easterly winds, or alternatively might be deposited within two to three days in Pacific Island countries due to 'blow back' in westward anticyclonic eddies. On occasion, fresh fission products may be deposited by rain, and may be found in drinking water.[141] Fallout may affect the natural resources of the oceans, especially fish and plankton, and will have an effect on the food chain. The deposit of fission products in the human body may produce leukaemia, other malignant diseases and skin diseases, cataracts, fertility impairment and ageing, as well as genetic effects.[142]

The Court responded to the Australian and New Zealand requests for provisional measures in an order requiring France to avoid nuclear tests causing the deposit of fallout on their territory.[143] The Court did not engage in a substantive analysis of the facts,[144] considering that for the purposes of the provisional measures proceedings:

> It suffices to observe that the information submitted to the Court ... does not exclude the possibility that damage to New Zealand might be shown to be caused by the deposit on New Zealand territory of radioactive fall-out resulting from such tests and to be irreparable.[145]

[141] *Nuclear Tests case (New Zealand* v. *France)*, Application Instituting Proceedings, 9 May 1973, paras. 12–15; Request by New Zealand for Interim Measures of Protection 14 May 1973 (Request by New Zealand for Interim Measures of Protection), Annex VII 'Effects of French Nuclear Testing on Radiation Levels in New Zealand', paras. 6–20, *ibid.*, 53.

[142] *Nuclear Tests case (New Zealand* v. *France)*, Application Instituting Proceedings, para. 16; Request by New Zealand for Interim Measures of Protection, Annex VII, para. 16. See also graphs attached to Annex VII.

[143] *Nuclear Tests case (Australia* v. *France) (Interim Measures)*, para. 35; *Nuclear Tests case (New Zealand* v. *France) (Interim Measures)*, para. 36.

[144] As noted by Stephens, *International Courts*, p. 141.

[145] *Nuclear Tests case (New Zealand* v. *France) (Interim Measures)*, para. 30. See also *Nuclear Tests case (Australia* v. *France) (Interim Measures)*, para. 29.

At the stage of the merits the Court subsequently rejected the cases brought by Australia and New Zealand on the basis that their claims no longer had any object[146] as the President and Minister of Defence of France had made statements to the effect that French atmospheric testing was to come to an end.[147] The Court did note that the United Nations Scientific Committee on the Effects of Atomic Radiation (UNSCAER) had recorded measurable quantities of radioactive matter from nuclear testing around the world. However, the Court also noted the French contention that radioactive matter produced from French testing had been infinitesimal and any fallout in New Zealand had never involved danger to the population's health. The Court refrained expressly from giving its view on these points, stating that this was necessary because they were matters that went to the merits of the case.[148]

In its judgments in the *Nuclear Test* cases the Court added that if the basis of its judgments were to be affected, the applicants could request an examination of the situation.[149] New Zealand relied upon this part of the Court's judgment in submitting a request for an examination of the situation in 1995 in *Request for an Examination of the Situation*.[150] Although atmospheric testing had ceased, between 1974 and 1992 France had conducted underground nuclear tests at Mururoa and also at Fangataufa atolls, detonating approximately 134 nuclear devices.[151] A moratorium on underground testing was then instituted by France, and it was the abandonment of this moratorium and the announcement of a final series of a further eight underground tests that prompted New Zealand's request in 1995.[152]

In *Request for an Examination of the Situation* in 1995, New Zealand expressed strong concerns about the ability of Mururoa and Fangataufa

146 *Nuclear Tests case (Australia* v. *France)*, para. 62; *Nuclear Tests case (New Zealand* v. *France)*, para. 65.

147 *Nuclear Tests case (Australia* v. *France)*, paras. 47–60; *Nuclear Tests case (New Zealand* v. *France)*, paras. 36–62.

148 *Nuclear Tests case (Australia* v. *France)*, para. 18; *Nuclear Tests case (New Zealand* v. *France)*, para. 18.

149 *Nuclear Tests case (Australia* v. *France)*, para. 60; *Nuclear Tests case (New Zealand* v. *France)*, para. 63.

150 *Request for an Examination of the Situation*. For an overview of cases see Stephens, *International Courts*, pp. 145–9.

151 *Request for an Examination of the Situation*, Application Instituting Proceedings, 21 August 1995, para. 21.

152 *Ibid.*, para. 1.

atolls to withstand underground testing. New Zealand argued that there was a growing body of scientific evidence questioning the safety of underground testing at Mururoa and Fangataufa atolls, including the danger that consecutive tests had weakened the structure of Mururoa atoll, creating a risk that it might split open or disintegrate and discharge the accumulated radioactive waste contained within it.[153] Additionally, New Zealand was concerned about the leakage of radioactive contamination from the atolls via groundwater. Both New Zealand and France provided descriptions of the structure of atolls, and specifically of Mururoa atoll. Atolls have a volcanic base topped with a limestone and coral crown.[154] The submarine foundation of an atoll has very low permeability, due to the weathering of the original materials making up the volcanic lava of which it is composed. However, this basalt foundation does possess a hydro-geological system in which water circulates, while the calcareous structures in the crown of the atoll also have a hydro–geological system. Water rises through the atoll at a speed of approximately a metre per year and is replaced at the base of the atoll by cold water coming in from the ocean.[155]

When a nuclear test is conducted, a shaft is drilled down into the atoll, of about 1½ m in width. Into the shaft is lowered a cylindrical container in which is placed a nuclear bomb of about 60 cm in diameter. The canister may be up to 14 m high, while the weapon inside will be only approximately a metre high. The rest of the canister contains electronic equipment which relays back to the surface information about the explosion in the microsecond before it is destroyed by the blast of the bomb. After the device has been lowered into the shaft, the shaft is packed tight with a special kind of concrete and other materials to block the escape of radioactive material at the time of the explosion. When the explosion takes place, a ball shaped chamber or cavity is blasted or melted into the surrounding rock, of between 50 and 120 m in diameter depending on the size of the explosion. Cracks and fractures are also created, with the roof of the vitrified cavity collapsing upwards

153 *Request for an Examination of the Situation*, para. 33.

154 Argument by Mr Elihu Lauterpacht for New Zealand, Verbatim Record, Monday 11 September 1995, 54, para. 23.

155 Opening argument of M. Marc Perrin de Brichambaut for France, Verbatim Record, Tuesday 12 September 1995, 10.00 am, 47, translated in Watts, *New Zealand at the International Court*, p. 195 at 199. See also Dissenting Opinion of Judge Weeramantry, at p. 351, citing the expert studies by the MacEwan and Atkinson teams, as referred to below.

and forming what is known as a chimney, filled with pieces of rock to about the height of five times the radius of the cavity. The cavity and the chimney will rapidly fill with water. The blast will also cause an earthquake shock registering between four and six on the Richter scale, with effects on the surface of the atoll including fracturing of the atoll's limestone layer, submarine landslides and tsunamis.[156]

The Court considered New Zealand's request for an examination of the situation together with its request for further provisional measures, and dismissed both requests on the basis that the request for an examination did not fall within paragraph 63 of the Court's 1974 judgment.[157] The Court reasoned that the basis of the judgment delivered by the Court in 1974 was that the object of New Zealand's original case was to seek a halt to atmospheric nuclear testing.[158] It was not open to the Court to go beyond the framework of that judgment.[159]

Complaints were also lodged in the 1990s with international human rights bodies about underground nuclear testing by France in the Pacific. Both the European Commission on Human Rights and the United Nations Human Rights Committee appear, in effect, to have rejected the admissibility of the complaints before them for failure to sustain the burden of proof. In the 1995 case of *Noël Narvii Tauira and eighteen others* v. *France*,[160] the applicants complained to the European Commission on Human Rights about leakage of radiation from the underground tests conducted by France on Mururoa atoll in French Polynesia, and the effects on the health of people living in the area. The applicants complained that the French authorities had not done comprehensive studies ruling out the risk that Mururoa atoll might fracture. They observed that a 1987 mission to the region by Jacques Cousteau had noted major fractures and fissures in the atoll from an incident in 1979 when a device was detonated at 400 m underground instead of the intended depth of 800 m.[161] France said it had proved the consequences of testing asserted by the applicants highly unlikely and that it had no duty to prove the tests to be entirely risk free.[162] The

[156] Argument by Mr Elihu Lauterpacht for New Zealand, Verbatim Record, Monday 11 September 1995, 56–60. For the comments of France, see Opening Argument of M. Marc Perrin de Brichambaut, Verbatim Record, Tuesday 12 September 1995, 10.00 am, 51–3, translated in Watts, *New Zealand at the International Court*, pp. 201–2.

[157] *Request for an Examination*, para. 68. [158] *Ibid.*, para. 62. [159] *Ibid.*, para. 59.

[160] *Noël Narvii Tauira and eighteen others* v. *France*, Application No. 28204/95 4 December 1995 3 IELR 774.

[161] *Ibid.*, 787. [162] *Ibid.*, 792f.

French government consistently maintained, as it did in *Request for an Examination*, that the heat and pressure of the underground blasts (tens of millions of degrees and several millions of atmospheres) had melted the surrounding basalt rock into a glass-like material, trapping radioactive wastes and preventing the escape of radioactivity.[163] The European Commission on Human Rights concluded that the applicants' allegations were not sufficiently substantiated to found a conclusion that prima facie they could claim to be victims under the Convention, and rejected the case on the basis it was inadmissible. The Commission said an applicant had to produce reasonable and convincing evidence of the likelihood that events contemplated would occur, and that mere suspicion or conjecture was not enough.[164]

In *Bordes, Tauira and Temeharo* the United Nations Human Rights Committee also ruled, the following year, on a complaint by French citizens living in French Polynesia about France's underground nuclear testing at Mururoa, including in relation to contamination of the food chain, the lagoon, the ecosystem, the marine environment and the atmosphere.[165] In reasoning similar to that of the European Commission, the Human Rights Committee likewise rejected the complainants' communication on the basis of inadmissibility. The Committee found that no 'real threat' or violation had been established in respect of the authors' rights under the ICCPR,[166] despite their arguments that the risks they faced clearly exceeded the purely hypothetical.[167] The Committee also said it was not possible for it to ascertain the validity or correctness of the authors' contention that testing would cause further deterioration and fissures in the atolls, and described the contention as 'highly controversial even in concerned scientific circles'.[168]

[163] *Ibid.*, 783.

[164] *Ibid.*, 797. See also *Balmer-Schafroth and others* v. *Switzerland*, Judgment of 26 August 1997, 25 EHRR 598, 615, where a complaint concerning the operation of a nuclear power station was ruled inadmissible for failure to establish that the complainants were personally exposed to a serious, specific and, above all, imminent danger.

[165] *Bordes, Tauira and Temeharo* v. *France*, 30 July 1996, [1996] UNHRC 28.

[166] *Ibid.*, para. 5.5.

[167] *Ibid.*, para. 4.4, citing the Committee's own decision in *EW and others* v. *Netherlands*, 8 April 1993, [1993] UNHRC 12.

[168] *Ibid.*, para. 5.6.

European Communities - Measures Affecting Asbestos and Asbestos-Containing Products

Under the World Trade Organization (WTO) Dispute Settlement Understanding there is no provisional measures jurisdiction, and less scope for a judicial emphasis on co-operation. Once adjudicatory proceedings have been initiated, clear findings will usually follow on whether a WTO member is in compliance with its legal obligations. The *European Communities - Measures Affecting Asbestos and Asbestos-Containing Products* case provides an example.[169] This case concerned Canada's challenge to a decree adopted by the French government in 1996 prohibiting manufacture, processing, sale, import and marketing of all forms of asbestos and products containing asbestos. Asbestos fibres are minute bundles of fibrils, with unique properties of mechanical resistance and resistance to heat and chemicals that have resulted in the widespread use of asbestos in the building industry and industrial manufacturing, in shipbuilding and in the chemical, petrochemical, aeronautical and nuclear industries.[170] Asbestos is now known to be responsible for a number of diseases, in particular: mesothelioma, a cancer of the pleura, which is the thin membrane enveloping the lungs; cancer of the lung; and asbestosis.[171] However, the realisation that chrysotile (white asbestos) was of concern to human health came later than it did for the non-serpentine kinds of asbestos, or amphiboles, of which there are five types: amosite (brown asbestos), crocidolite (blue asbestos), anthophyllite, actinolite and tremolite. As the non-serpentine forms of asbestos had already been prohibited, the practical effect of the French decree was to ban chrysotile.

Canada was concerned about the effect of the French ban on the chrysotile mining industry in Quebec. Canada argued that there was 'no credible scientific information supporting a total ban on asbestos'.[172] In 1995 the French government had commissioned a report on the effects of asbestos from France's Institut National de la Recherche Médicale (INSERM),[173] but Canada disagreed that the INSERM report provided a sufficient basis for a complete ban on all forms of asbestos. According to Canada, physical differences between amphiboles and

[169] *European Communities - Measures Affecting Asbestos and Asbestos-Containing Products*, Complaint by Canada (WT/DS135), Report of the Panel DSR 2001: VIII, 3305, Report of the Appellate Body DSR 2001: VII, 3243 (hereafter *EC - Asbestos* ABR).

[170] *Ibid.*, paras. 3.430, 3.428. [171] *Ibid.*, paras. 3.66, 3.430.

[172] *Ibid.*, para. 3.394. [173] *Ibid.*, para. 3.11.

serpentine asbestos rendered amphiboles more pathogenic than chrysotile (by more than a magnitude of ten with respect to mesothelioma).[174] Chrysotile fibres were 'curly' and 'downy' compared with amphibole fibres, which were 'straight and rigid like needles' and 'reported to be associated with greater penetration to the terminal bronchioles', being less easily removed by the natural mucociliary processes of the breathing tract. Amphibole fibres were also more resistant to the acidic medium of the lungs.[175] According to Canada, the half-life of amphibole fibres appeared to be decades, but chrysotile's half-life might be only a few months.[176]

Estimating the risk posed by chrysotile was difficult because of inadequate data on exposure-response and uncertainties associated with relying on animal studies.[177] There had also been some significant differences between the results of studies on the effect of exposure to chrysotile. For example, experts disputed whether mesotheliomas among Quebec chrysotile miners and millers might not be due to tremolite, an amphibole that generally comprised about 1 per cent of Quebec asbestos samples.[178] One study, considered 'complex and sophisticated', found that there was a greater incidence of mesothelioma among Quebec chrysotile miners at Thetford, the mine where there was the greatest concentration of tremolite. Canada also emphasised the 'latency period' in the effects of asbestos on human health, which introduced further uncertainty into the epidemiology of asbestos-related diseases, as observed effects dated back to exposure twenty or thirty years previously.[179]

The Panel's investigations revealed that it was generally accepted by scientists that there was 'a direct and linear relationship between the relative risk of lung cancer and cumulative exposure to asbestos'.[180] An outstanding area of uncertainty, however, was whether there was a minimum exposure threshold below which this relationship did not exist.[181] Data on mesothelioma incidence at low levels of exposure was lacking.[182] Under a solely linear model of carcinogenicity, there would be some risk of cancer at even the lowest level of exposure to asbestos.[183] Canada preferred a threshold model. This model supported Canadian arguments that chrysotile asbestos was relatively safe because

[174] *Ibid.*, para. 3.86. [175] *Ibid.*, para. 3.92. [176] *Ibid.*, para. 3.88.
[177] *Ibid.*, paras. 5.166–5.168. On *in vitro* studies see paras. 5.169–5.170.
[178] *Ibid.*, para. 5.106 *et seq.* [179] *Ibid.*, paras. 2.123, 3.96, 3.157, 3.286.
[180] *Ibid.*, para. 5.147. [181] *Ibid.*, para. 5.152.
[182] *Ibid.*, para. 5.92. [183] *Ibid.*, para. 3.100.

it was used in products where it was 'encapsulated' in cement (such as water pipes, roof tiles, cladding and guttering),[184] and that 'controlled use' could alleviate effectively risks associated with chrysotile asbestos. In defence of the French measure, the EC countered that encapsulation of asbestos in cement did not prevent harm, because chrysotile products still produced dust when sanded, crushed or sawn.[185] The EC also contended that the Canadian analysis disregarded the exposure to asbestos of tradespeople like plumbers and electricians, do-it-yourself enthusiasts, and a huge group of 'secondary users' carrying out servicing and maintenance, who might not be aware they were working with asbestos and who might generate dust levels above those considered safe.[186]

Canada also argued that there had not been any comparative study establishing beyond doubt that products which could be used as substitutes for asbestos-containing products were harmless or were less harmful than chrysotile asbestos.[187] According to Canada, there were more than 150 substitute fibres for chrysotile, the most common being aramid fibres (including Kevlar), polyvinyl alcohol (PVA) fibres, cellulose fibres, glass fibres, ceramic fibres, rock wool and wollastonite.[188] The INSERM report had not addressed the question of the safety of substitute fibres, but considered that research should be done as a matter of urgency before use of substitute fibres became a general practice.[189] The EC argued that products used as substitutes for asbestos products were less dangerous than asbestos, and were chemically different.[190] Therefore the EC was entitled to use those products in substitution for asbestos and would not be in violation of the prohibition in the General Agreement on Tariffs and Trade (GATT) on discrimination against 'like products'.

The Panel found that the French decree treated 'like products' differently, and there was discrimination between asbestos and substitute products.[191] Accordingly, there was a violation of Article III: 4 of GATT.[192] However, the French measure was justified under the exception in Article XX(b) of GATT which allowed for measures to protect human, animal or plant life or health.[193] The Appellate Body reversed the Panel's finding of inconsistency with Article III: 4 of

184 *Ibid.*, para. 3.381. 185 *Ibid.*, paras. 3.132, 3.61. 186 *Ibid.*, paras. 3.63, 8.196.
187 *Ibid.*, para. 3.386. 188 *Ibid.*, paras. 3.173, 3.211.
189 *Ibid.*, para. 3.173. See also paras. 3.325, 3.352. 190 *Ibid.*, para. 3.19.
191 *Ibid.*, paras. 3.414 *et seq.*, 8.157. 192 *Ibid.*, paras. 8.158, 8.159, 9.1(c).
193 *Ibid.*, paras. 9.1(d), 8.241.

GATT,[194] emphasising that Canada bore the burden of proving the likeness of asbestos fibres and asbestos-cement products with substitute fibres and cement products. Canada had not discharged this burden.[195] The Appellate Body found that consideration of consumers' tastes and habits, omitted by the Panel, was indispensable to an analysis of 'likeness' and that it was likely the presence of a known carcinogen would have an influence on consumers' tastes and habits.[196] Canada had failed sufficiently to discharge the burden of showing the 'likeness' of asbestos and substitute products. The Appellate Body upheld the Panel's finding on the application of Article XX.[197]

European Communities - Measures Concerning Meat and Meat Products (Hormones)

Certain WTO disputes concerning human health and the environment have involved particular intransigence on the part of the WTO members involved. The dimensions of the long-running trans-Atlantic dispute in *European Communities - Measures Concerning Meat and Meat Products (Hormones)* were such that they fed into the negotiation and adoption of the SPS Agreement in 1995 at the close of the Uruguay Round of multilateral trade negotiations.[198] The foundations of this dispute lay in the directive adopted in the 1980s and 1990s prohibiting administration to farm animals of substances having a hormonal or thyrostatic action, and prohibiting the placing on the market of meat and meat products from animals to which such substances had been administered, whether this meat was domestically produced or imported. According to the EC there was 'overwhelming' scientific evidence that the use of growth-promotion hormones was 'potentially very dangerous to public and animal health'.[199] The US and Canada lodged a complaint about the directives with the WTO in the mid 1990s.[200]

[194] *EC - Asbestos* ABR, para. 192(e). [195] *Ibid.*, paras. 193(c) and (d).
[196] *Ibid.*, paras. 130, 139. [197] *Ibid.*, para. 193(f).
[198] Agreement on the Application of Sanitary and Phytosanitary Measures, WTO *The Legal Texts: The results of the Uruguay round of multilateral trade negotiations*, p. 59.
[199] *Ibid.*, para. 4.57.
[200] *European Communities - Measures Concerning Meat and Meat Products (Hormones)*, Complaint by Canada (WT/DS48), Complaint by the United States (WT/DS26). Two identically constituted WTO dispute settlement Panels (the Panel) circulated parallel reports in this case: Report of the Panel (Canada) DSR 1998: II, 235 (hereafter *EC - Hormones*, Complaint by Canada, PR), Report of the Panel (United States) DSR 1998: III, 699,

The scientific uncertainties in the *Hormones* case included whether studies on growth-promotion hormones had been conducted over a sufficiently long period of time,[201] the reliability of extrapolation for human beings from studies conducted on animals,[202] and the key question of whether hormones could be genotoxic, i.e. have a direct effect in causing mutations in DNA (or whether their carcinogenicity was due solely to their hormonal effect on the reproductive rate of cells that had already mutated).[203] Finally, there were concerns about the synergies between hormones.[204] In addition, social aspects of growth-promotion hormone use were hard to predict reliably, in particular the extent to which people would follow recommended procedures for the use of growth-promotion hormones. A double dose might be applied in the hope of a better response. In France, farmers had been found to administer a second dose half way through the withdrawal period.[205] Farmers might also try to obtain a faster effect by intramuscular injection rather than implants in the ear,[206] although implantation in the ear was recommended so that implants were detectable by palpation of the ear and residues were unlikely to enter the food supply.

In *EC – Hormones*, the Panel found the EC ban on meat from cattle treated with growth-promotion hormones to be inconsistent with Articles 3.1, 5.1 and 5.5 of the WTO Agreement on Sanitary and

(hereafter *EC – Hormones*, Complaint by the US, PR). See also the Report of the Appellate Body DSR 1998: I, 135 (hereafter *EC – Hormones* ABR).

201 See also Annex, Transcript of the Joint Meeting with Experts, attached to the panel reports in both the complaint by Canada and the complaint by the US (hereafter *EC – Hormones* JM).

202 *EC – Hormones*, Complaint by Canada PR, para. 6.86; Complaint by the US PR, para. 6.87.

203 According to one report, '(p)rogesterone is not carcinogenic per se, but acts via an epigenetic mechanism associated with its endocrine activity, ie its ability to cause a hyperproliferative effect at cellular levels mediated by steroid-hormone receptor interaction'. *Ibid.*, Complaint by Canada PR, para. 6.55; Complaint by the US PR, para. 6.56; citing a Report presented to the Joint Expert Committee on Food Additives of the Food and Agriculture Organization of the United Nations and the World Health Organization (JECFA), para. 9. The Joint Expert Committee is a committee of independent scientists that advises the Codex Alimentarius Commission. For further information on the Codex Alimentarius Commission, see below, p. 103.

204 *EC – Hormones*, Complaint by Canada PR, paras. 6.16, 6.73, 6.164; Complaint by the US PR, paras. 6.17, 6.74, 6.165. One expert gave an example of the complexities, saying that while oestrogen and progesterone seemed to synergise and together produce a heightened risk of breast cancer, they actually antagonised each other for uterine cancer risk.

205 *EC – Hormones*, Complaint by Canada PR, paras. 6.147, 6.148; Complaint by the US PR, paras. 6.146, 6.149.

206 *Ibid.*, Complaint by Canada PR, para. 6.175; Complaint by the US PR, para. 6.176.

Phytosanitary Measures (SPS Agreement).[207] Article 3.1 of the SPS Agreement requires that members are to base their measures on international standards, guidelines or recommendations except as otherwise provided for in the Agreement.[208] The Appellate Body reversed the Panel's finding of inconsistency with Article 3.1.[209] However, the Appellate Body agreed that as the EC measures were not based on a risk assessment the EC had acted inconsistently with Article 5.1, even though the burden of proof under Article 5.1 would correctly have fallen on the complainants.[210] The Appellate Body reversed the Panel's finding that there had been a breach of Article 5.5, as discrimination or a disguised restriction on international trade had not been established by the complainants.[211]

The dispute continued after the adoption of the Appellate Body's report by the WTO Dispute Settlement Body (DSB), with Canada and the US in due course suspending trade concessions against the EC, with DSB approval, in order to pressure the EC to come into compliance with the SPS Agreement. The EC decided to take action to challenge this suspension of concessions. By this time, circumstances had changed. The EC sought to rely on new scientific evidence that was claimed to cast fresh doubt on the safety of using growth-promotion hormones in beef production. Scientific uncertainties invoked by the EC related to the effects of the hormones on prepubertal sectors of the population, latency periods and the effects of the hormones on the immune system and on growth and reproduction. The EC had accordingly replaced its prior measure with a provisional ban covering five of the six hormones. Such a provisional ban was asserted to be justified under the exemption found in Article 5.7 of the SPS Agreement.[212] In relation to the sixth

[207] See above, Introduction, p. 9. [208] *Ibid.*

[209] *EC – Hormones* ABR, para. 253(h).

[210] The Appellate Body modified the Panel's interpretation of Article 5.1, but upheld the finding that the EC had been in breach. Article 5.1 required only that the results of a risk assessment must have a rational relationship with the SPS measure at stake, i.e. a risk assessment must 'sufficiently warrant' or 'reasonably support' an SPS measure. *EC – Hormones* ABR, paras. 193, 253(l).

[211] *Ibid.*, para. 246.

[212] Article 5.7 of the SPS agreement reads: 'In cases where scientific evidence is insufficient, a Member may provisionally adopt sanitary or phytosanitary measures on the basis of available pertinent information, including that from the relevant international organizations as well as from sanitary or phytosanitary measures applied by other Members. In such circumstances, Members shall seek to obtain the additional information necessary for a more objective assessment of risk and review the sanitary or phytosanitary measure accordingly within a reasonable period of time.'

hormone, oestradiol 17ß, the EC considered that all the evidence now available supported a permanent ban.

Following consultations, the EC launched two sets of proceedings, leading to parallel panel reports in the cases *Canada - Continued Suspension of Obligations in the EC - Hormones Dispute*, and *United States - Continued Suspension of Obligations in the EC - Hormones Dispute*.[213] In its main claims in the *Continued Suspension of Obligations* cases, the EC did not directly assert its own compliance with the SPS Agreement. Rather, the EC claimed that the US and Canada had breached the WTO Dispute Settlement Understanding in a number of ways. An understanding of the claims is helpful for discussion in later chapters, particularly Chapter 8. A simplified version of the claims is presented here.[214] First, the EC asserted that Canada and the US had breached the requirement in Article 23.2(a) of the Dispute Settlement Understanding (DSU) that WTO members 'not make a determination to the effect that a violation has occurred ... except through recourse to dispute settlement in accordance with the rules and procedures of this Understanding'.[215] The Panel upheld this first claim,[216] suggesting that Canada and the US should have recourse to the rules and the procedures of the DSU without delay.[217] The Appellate Body disagreed that a 'determination' had been made within the meaning of Article 23.2(a) and revoked the Panel's finding.[218]

Secondly, the EC asserted that Canada and the US were in breach of Article 23.1 of the DSU, which requires that 'When Members seek the redress of a violation of obligations . . . they should have recourse to, and abide by, the rules and procedures of this Understanding.' The EC argued in this second claim that Article 23.1 had been breached through a violation of Article 22.8, which provides that 'The suspension of

[213] *Canada - Continued Suspension of Obligations in the EC - Hormones Dispute*, Complaint by the EC (WT/DS321) Report of the Panel, Report of the Appellate Body, adopted 14 November 2008; *US - Continued Suspension of Obligations in the EC - Hormones Dispute*, Complaint by the EC (WT/DS320) Report of the Panel, Report of the Appellate Body, adopted 14 November 2008 (hereafter respectively *Canada - Continued Suspension* PR, *US - Continued Suspension* PR, and, referring to the identical paragraphs of the two Appellate Body reports, *Continued Suspension* ABR).

[214] For fuller details, see First Written Submission by the European Communities, Geneva, 11 July 2005.

[215] EC main claim, first series.

[216] *Canada - Continued Suspension* PR, para. 7.841(b); *US - Continued Suspension* PR, para. 7.856(b).

[217] *Canada - Continued Suspension* PR, para. 8.3; *US - Continued Suspension* PR, para. 8.3.

[218] *Continued Suspension* ABR, para. 736(a)(v).

concessions or other obligations shall be temporary and shall only be applied until such time as the measure found to be inconsistent with a covered agreement has been removed …'.[219] The EC said that it had notified its implementing measure, and compliance with its obligations under the SPS Agreement should therefore be presumed. The Panel did not accept this argument and determined that the EC was still in breach of Article 5.1 of the SPS Agreement and that the EC could not rely on Article 5.7 of the Agreement.[220] The Appellate Body reversed the Panel's findings in relation to Articles 5.1 and 5.7 of the SPS Agreement[221] for various errors relating in the main to the allocation of the burden of proof[222] and the use of expert evidence.[223] However the Appellate Body upheld the Panel's finding that, given the EC had failed to establish that it had removed its offending measure, there could be no violation of Article 23.1 as a result of a breach of Article 22.8.[224]

The EC additionally made an alternative, conditional claim for consideration in the event no breach of Article 23 were found.[225] The EC asserted that it was in actual compliance, not just presumed compliance, with its SPS obligations and claimed that therefore Canada and the US were in breach of Article 22.8. The Panel did not rule on this claim.

The Appellate Body recommended that the DSB should request Canada, the US, and the EC to initiate proceedings under Article 21.5 of the DSU without delay in order for a determination to be made as to whether the EC had removed the measure found in *EC – Hormones* to be inconsistent with the SPS Agreement and whether the Canadian and US

[219] EC main claim, second series.

[220] *Canada – Continued Suspension* PR, paras. 7.541, 7.548, 7.549. 7.817–7.823; *US – Continued Suspension* PR, paras. 7.573, 7.578, 7.579, 7.831–7.837. The Panel was not convinced that it had jurisdiction to make such findings under the SPS Agreement, and limited its conclusion on this claim to statements that to the extent the EC had not removed its offending measure Canada and the US had not breached Article 22.8 of the DSU and to the extent that Article 22.8 had not been breached neither had Article 23.1, at least as a result of a breach of Article 22.8. *Canada – Continued Suspension* PR, paras. 7.842(a) and (b), 8.3. *US – Continued Suspension* PR, para. 7.857(a) and (b), 8.3.

[221] See *Continued Suspension* ABR, paras. 736(c)(iv), (v), (vi); 736(d)(i), (ii), (iii), (iv), (vi).

[222] See below, Chapter 8, p. 332.

[223] See below, Chapter 4, pp. 174–5.

[224] *Continued Suspension* ABR, para. 736(a)(iii). The Appellate Body reversed a separate finding by the Panel that Canada and the US had violated Article 23.1 directly, not merely through an alleged violation of Article 22.8. *Canada – Continued Suspension* PR, para. 7.841(a); *US – Continued Suspension* PR, para. 856(a); *Continued Suspension* ABR, para. 736(iv).

[225] EC Conditional Claim, First Written Submission by the European Communities, Geneva, 11 July 2005.

suspensions of concessions remained legally valid.[226] Following the adoption of the Appellate Body's report, a provisional settlement of the growth-promotion hormones dispute was reached between the US and the EC in May 2009.[227] No settlement has been reached between Canada and the EC.

European Communities - Approval and Marketing of Biotech Products

The dispute in *European Communities - Approval and Marketing of Biotech Products* concerned an EC moratorium on imports of 'biotech products' or genetically modified organisms (that is to say, plants and the products thereof developed through the use of recombinant DNA techniques).[228] In the light of prolonged delays in EC approval processes for biotech products, the US, Canada and Argentina had initiated WTO dispute settlement proceedings against the EC in 2003. The issues at stake attracted considerable and emotive domestic attention. Global interest in the use of genetic technology in agriculture and food production has also been high, and the environmental movement had high expectations of the outcome in this case. Unspoken economic and cultural dimensions to the dispute included the ramifications of genetic modification for the structure of agricultural production and the rural way of life in Europe. Scientific research on the negative effects of genetically modified crops is still in its early stages.

The Panel's report in *EC - Biotech* largely did not address the EC's compliance with any of the substantive disciplines that apply to sanitary and phytosanitary measures under the SPS Agreement, turning away from these disciplines and focusing instead on the unacceptable level of procedural delay in the processing of import applications for biotech products.[229] There was no appeal in the *EC - Biotech* case and so

[226] *Continued Suspension* ABR, para. 737. For further discussion of the provision in Article 21.5 for determining members' compliance with WTO obligations, see below, Chapter 8.

[227] *European Communities - Measures Concerning Meat and Meat Products (Hormones) Joint Communication from the European Communities and the United States*, 30 September 2009, WT/DS26/28. See also Bridges Weekly Trade News Digest, 13 May 2009, vol. 13, No. 17, 3.

[228] *European Communities - Measures Affecting the Approval and Marketing of Biotech Products*, Complaint by United States, Canada, Argentina (WT/DS291, WT/DS292, WT/DS293), Report of the Panel DSR 2006: III, 847 (hereafter *EC - Biotech* PR), para. 7.1.

[229] For a critical analysis of the Panel's approach, see Foster, 'Prior approval systems'.

the WTO Appellate Body did not have the opportunity to give its views on the Panel's approach.

There were significant scientific uncertainties associated with biotech products, both in relation to their effects on biodiversity, and in relation to food safety. Many ecological questions about genetically modified crops were only just starting to be addressed in the period 1998–2003, and indeed some of the early assumptions in the field had come under challenge.[230] Ecological-scale questions could seldom be answered through the routine agronomic trials carried out by biotech companies,[231] as rigorous ecological research required multiple teams of researchers operating over periods of years.[232] Commercial growing of genetically modified organisms had begun only in 1996–7.[233] There had been no reports of clear environmental problems arising from the cultivation of genetically modified soy bean, cotton and maize in the United States, but there had not been much documentation of the positive and negative effects of this cultivation.[234] However, in Canada, problems from herbicide-resistant volunteers had arisen as a result of growing genetically modified oil seed rape (canola).[235]

The most widely used transgenes are Bt (insecticidal) transgenes, and transgenes that confer resistance to the herbicide glyphosate.[236] Both these forms of genetic modification confer important benefits, improving farm workers' health and working environments through reducing the use of insecticides and allowing the use of glyphosate herbicides in place of methods that would leave longer-lasting residues or produce greater erosion and siltation through tillage.[237] However, the development of resistance to these insecticides and herbicides in target pests was problematic. Target-organism resistance to Bt insecticides had been found in field conditions, for example in diamondback moth on cabbage in Hawaii, Japan and the Philippines.[238] Strategies to try and deal with Bt-resistant target organisms were under development but differences of views continued on their design. The most widely used strategy was to use a high dose of toxin while providing a refuge where the pest could produce a viable population of non-resistant gene stock.[239]

[230] *EC – Biotech* PR, Annex H, Replies by the Scientific Experts to Questions posed by the Panel, 4, para. 13, Dr Snow.
[231] *Ibid.*, 4, para. 14, Dr Snow.
[232] *Ibid.*, 3, para. 12, Dr Snow.
[233] *Ibid.*, 6, para. 19, Dr Snow.
[234] *Ibid.*, 6, paras. 18–19, Dr Snow.
[235] *Ibid.*, 6, para. 18, Dr Snow.
[236] *Ibid.*, 6, para. 20, Dr Snow.
[237] *Ibid.*, 7, para. 23, Dr Snow.
[238] *Ibid.*, 30, para. 91, Dr Andow.
[239] *Ibid.*, 30, para. 98, Dr Andow.

Resistance should become functionally recessive, although it then became difficult to measure the presence of the genes conferring resistance.[240]

Concerns arose also about the effects of biotech crops on non-target organisms, including competitors, prey, hosts, symbionts, predators, parasites and pathogens. Studies detailing evidence of possible risks to lacewings, earthworms, soil organisms and butterflies had been carried out.[241] It was clear that no 'immediate catastrophic adverse effects' had occurred for non-target species, but at the same time it was important to note that 'virtually no monitoring for such adverse effects' had been carried out.[242] Effects within the food chain also required further study, including human food safety issues. There was a concern that widespread consumption of varieties of biotech plants containing antibiotic-resistant marker genes, used in biotech processes, could lead to the development of antibiotic-resistant strains of bacteria,[243] although this seemed unlikely.[244] There were also concerns about allergic and toxic reactions from animals and humans consuming biotech products,[245] and about the increased pesticide residues that would be left by the widespread use of pesticide encouraged by biotechnology that confers pesticide resistance. During the proceedings the issue also arose of the effects of biotech crops on biogeochemical cycles, especially carbon and nitrogen recycling. However, the most fundamental and overarching concern remained the possibility that genetically modified plants could become persistent and invasive in natural habitats as a result of their genetic advantages.

The circumstances leading to the *EC – Biotech* case involved a declaration on the part of five EC Member States – Denmark, Greece, France, Italy, Luxembourg (the G5) – in 1999 that they would take steps to have any new authorisations for the growing and placing on the market of genetically modified organisms suspended, pending EC adoption of rules dealing with the traceability and labelling of genetically modified organisms.[246] The G5 remained unsatisfied with EC action in relation to traceability and labelling, and in 2001 the declaration was affirmed with Austria joining the group.[247] The G5 together had the numbers to block

240 *Ibid.*, 31, para. 98 and note 32, Dr Andow. 241 *Ibid.*, 23–6, paras. 60–8, Dr Andow.
242 *Ibid.*, 26, para. 70, Dr Andow. 243 *EC – Biotech* PR, para. 7.177.
244 Replies by the Scientific Experts, 21–2, paras. 57–9, Dr Nutti.
245 *EC – Biotech* PR, para. 7.177. 246 *Ibid.*, paras. 7.474–7.475.
247 *Ibid.*, para. 7.480, footnote 579.

progress of approval procedures for biotech products within the EC system, and appeared to have been doing so.[248]

The *EC – Biotech* Panel found there to be a general de facto moratorium on approval of genetically modified products in the EC, as well as inaction in relation to specific products. Both these forms of conduct on the part of the EC amounted to 'undue delay' in breach of the EC's obligations under Article 8 and Annex C(1)(a) of the SPS Agreement. The Panel did not consider this conduct to amount to a substantive trade ban and therefore made no findings under Articles 2.2, 5.1, 5.5 and 5.6 of the SPS Agreement.

The Panel did find that individual safeguard measures adopted by Austria, Greece, France, Germany, Italy and Luxembourg to ban genetically modified products were found to be in breach of Article 5.1 of the SPS Agreement on the grounds that they were not based on risk assessments. Although various studies were cited by the EC, the safeguard measures were inconsistent with the reviews carried out by the EC's own internal scientific committees. Nor was Article 5.7 of the SPS Agreement applicable, as the scientific committees had considered there to be sufficient scientific evidence for a risk assessment in every case.[249]

This dispute has been settled as between the Canada and the EC,[250] and as between Argentina and the EC,[251] with the EC agreeing to bilateral dialogues to discuss issues relating to genetically modified products.[252] Within the EU, difficulties are ongoing. The European Food Safety Authority (EFSA) has continued generally to provide positive risk assessments for biotech products, and the central EC authorisation process has been functioning. However the European Commission is having to take decisions through a default process,

[248] *Ibid.*, para. 7.1268.

[249] Regarding the application of Articles 5.1 and 5.7 in *EC – Biotech*, see Foster, 'Precaution, scientific development and scientific uncertainty'. However, note that the Panel wrote a letter to the parties following receipt of their comments on its interim report, making it clear that the Panel's findings left room for the possibility that even if at one point in time the evidence was sufficient for a risk assessment to have been conducted, at a later point in time it was possible that the evidence could become insufficient, and if so then members might need to reassess the risks expeditiously. *EC – Biotech* PR, Annex K.

[250] For further information, www.wto.org.

[251] For further information, www.wto.org.

[252] 'Canada and EU resolve trade dispute on GMOs', Bridges Weekly Trade News Digest vol. 13, No. 27, 22 July 2009, International Centre for Trade and Sustainable Development.

because the Council is not doing so within the prescribed time-frames.[253] The Commission has sought further EFSA opinions where the Commission considers that a Member State's observation raises important new scientific questions not properly or completely addressed by an EFSA opinion, and this has led to legal challenges against the Commission's decision-making by biotech firms.[254] In the meantime, individual safeguard measures have been maintained by the relevant EC Member States, with new measures adopted in some instances, including in Hungary. The Council is allowing these measures to continue, despite action by the Commission to require their repeal.[255]

There will also be scope for challenge in the WTO to national regulations adopted as a result of the instruments on traceability and labelling within the EU.[256] Under these EU instruments, Member States may not prohibit, restrict or avoid the marketing of GMOs, but Member States are permitted to establish measures to avoid the unintended presence of GMOs in other products. Efforts have been undertaken to promote the harmonisation of measures among EC Member States,[257] but in some instances national regulations may offend against WTO disciplines on free trade.[258] It is significant that the *EC – Biotech* panel found that the SPS Agreement applied to labelling requirements under the EC's deliberate-release directives, as this lays the groundwork for disputes over labelling potentially to be addressed under this Agreement. The Panel reasoned that labelling was directed towards the protection of human health and the environment, and could be presumed to lead to better reporting of unanticipated adverse effects so that steps could be taken to mitigate them.[259] Therefore, labeling could be considered a sanitary or phytosanitary measure.

[253] Poli, 'Continuity and change in the EU Regulatory Framework on Genetically Modified Organisms'.

[254] *Ibid.* [255] *Ibid.*

[256] Directive 2001/18/EC of the European Parliament and of the Council of 12 March 2001 on the deliberate release into the environment of genetically modified organisms and repealing Council Directive 90/220/EEC OJ L 106, 17.04.2001, 1–39; and Regulation (EC) No. 1829/2003 of the European Parliament and of the Council of 22 September 2003 on genetically modified food and feed OJ 18.10.2003 L 268, 1–23.

[257] Commission Recommendation of 23 July 2003 on guidelines for the development of national strategies and best practices to ensure the coexistence of genetically modified crops with conventional and organic farming (notified under document number C (2003) 2624) OJ L 189, 29.07.2003, 36–47.

[258] Corti Varela, 'The EU "coexistence" policy'. [259] *EC – Biotech* PR, paras. 7.384–7.389.

Conclusion

The scientific issues arising in international courts and tribunals today are often complex and involve multiple uncertainties. They require an interweaving of legal process with knowledge and expertise drawn from a broad range of disciplines. There is an increasing number of calls for international courts and tribunals to exercise their power to order provisional measures, even where the science is uncertain. There is also an increasing recognition of the need to reinforce the parties' commitment to resolving their disputes and manage their ongoing relationships through technical as well as political co-operation. However, there continue to be cases that reach the stage of adjudication on the merits. This may place considerable pressure on the international adjudicatory process.

PART II

Expert evidence

3 Methods for taking expert evidence in scientific disputes[1]

Sound decision-making is essential in an international legal system where submission to jurisdiction is voluntary and many of the interests at stake are important, sensitive and complex.[2] International courts and tribunals must carry out their functions thoroughly and on the basis of a full understanding of the facts. They must ensure that they are in a position to appreciate the disputed policy choices made by the states appearing before them, and to perform their role wisely with a view to the stability and development of the law, as well as to the importance of ongoing relations between the parties. The task of the international adjudicator today is not simply to choose between two competing conceptions of the facts presented in adversarial fashion.[3]

As a result of the closeness of law and fact in the type of dispute that is the subject of this book, international adjudication is changing. Most obvious and most fundamental is the shift in the role of expert witnesses. The complexity of the science requires heavy consultation with experts, and considerable reliance on their testimony. Inevitably, it seems, experts will be drawn into questions of legal interpretation through their involvement in the application of legal terms. The insights offered by a scientific expert will help determine the application of a legal concept such as 'necessity' or 'reasonableness' in the case at hand - and in the course of this process the scientific expert's advice will also come to shape the development of the conventions and usages on which the established meaning of the legal concept of 'necessity' or 'reasonableness' in the context of the provision in question will be

[1] Selected elements of this chapter and the subsequent chapter are to be published in Foster, C. E. 'The consultation of independent experts by international courts and tribunals in health and environment cases' (2010) *Finnish Yearbook of International Law*.

[2] Riddell and Plant, *Evidence*, p. 3. [3] Damaška, *Evidence Law Adrift*, p. 100.

based.[4] Experts' individual commitments to precautionary approaches to risk will have a direct bearing. These dynamics will be at their most intense where expert evidence is provided by independent experts appointed by a court or tribunal itself.

Even the best efforts to prevent expert engagement in legal aspects of a case will not always be effective.[5] For example, in World Trade Organization (WTO) dispute settlement, panels are increasingly careful in crafting the questions they put to the experts. In addition, the experts' instructions clearly request them to refrain, in their written comments, from expressing views on the legal issues before the panel. This request is repeated at the beginning of the joint meeting with experts.[6] Yet analysis indicates that the experts' scientific input often goes closely to the legal questions.

Concern can be ameliorated to some extent by working to ensure transparent and fair reasoning and processes. However, ultimately international courts' and tribunals' adjudication of disputes involving scientific uncertainty is unlikely to involve a very pure form of adjudication with a guaranteed strict separation between fact and law. We may have to accept a degree of tension within the rationalist model of adjudication, according to which 'operative distinctions have to be maintained between questions of fact and questions of law, questions of fact and questions of value, and questions of fact and questions of opinion'.[7]

[4] As Salmon observes, the interpretation of a legal rule does not always precede its application. Rather, there is a dialectic movement between the two processes. Salmon, 'Le Fait', 343.

[5] '[I]n some circumstances the expert cannot avoid making some assumptions about the value of certain facts in presenting their opinion . . .', Riddell and Plant, *Evidence*, p. 329.

[6] *Canada – Continued Suspension of Obligations in the EC – Hormones Dispute*, Complaint by the EC (WT/DS321); Report of the Panel, Report of the Appellate Body, adopted 14 November 2008; *US – Continued Suspension of Obligations in the EC – Hormones Dispute*, Complaint by the EC (WT/DS320); Report of the Panel, Report of the Appellate Body, adopted 14 November 2008; (hereafter respectively *Canada – Continued Suspension* PR, *US – Continued Suspension* PR, and, referring to the identical paragraphs of the two Appellate Body reports, *Continued Suspension* ABR). For the Chair's instructions see *Canada – Continued Suspension* PR and *US – Continued Suspension* PR, Annex G, Transcript of the Joint Meeting with Experts (hereafter *Continued Suspension* JM), para. 666. Note also US objections to EC questioning of the experts directly on the matter of the 'insufficiency' of scientific evidence, a legal issue arising under Article 5.7 of the SPS Agreement. *Continued Suspension* JM, para. 370. See the subsequent US rephrasing of the issue, asking the experts whether the EC had put forward scientific evidence supporting the conclusion that previous data was no longer sufficient for a risk assessment.

[7] Articulating the traditional approach, see Twining, *Rethinking Evidence*, pp. 75–80; Anderson *et al.*, *Analysis of Evidence*; Jolowicz, *On Civil Procedure*, p. 212. See above, Chapter 1, p. 5.

This chapter considers and compares the various ways in which expert evidence is obtained by international courts and tribunals in scientific cases. International courts and tribunals may still be relatively content with traditional approaches that allow the parties to present countervailing scientific evidence, through expert reports, affidavits, advocacy and the appearance and examination of the parties' own expert witnesses. Much can be learnt this way, as avenues of proof are explored and tested by counsel working with their experts. The process of cross-examination is most valuable in testing the strength of propositions relied upon by the parties. This basic model of adjudication is not to be discarded. The parties may prefer this type of approach, as it allows them to retain more control over their case. Lawyers from common law backgrounds may derive a particular advantage, as they are more used to presenting evidence and engaging in the cross-examination of opposing expert witnesses than lawyers from other legal traditions.

However, there may be also advantages to an active judicial handling of a case. For example, from the point of view of a judge or arbitrator the most practical approach in disputes that are not excessively complex may be to direct the parties' expert witnesses to meet together before the hearing.[8] The experts can be required to discuss the reports they have each prepared without prejudice to the proceedings. They may be asked to provide a joint report summarising their positions and setting out their points of agreement and any points of disagreement. Yet procedures like these may be less likely to offer all that is needed in a large, interstate scientific dispute, where fact and law run closely together. As the studies in this chapter demonstrate, adjudicators' direct and moderately informal consultation of independent experts, along the lines of the procedure seen in the WTO, may be especially helpful in complex scientific cases involving multiple scientific uncertainties.

Accordingly, we should endorse a move towards processes for consultation of experts that draw on a blend of investigative and adversarial procedures. In dealing with issues generated by the closeness of fact and law in scientific disputes, the continued protection of fairness in international adjudicatory procedure will be important, especially through measures to enhance transparency. A helpful starting point may be to

8 See e.g. the practice under the IBA Rules on the Taking of Evidence in International Commercial Arbitration 1999 (London: International Bar Association, 2010) (hereafter the IBA Rules), Article 5.4. This procedure is also used in common law jurisdictions as a way to reduce the volume of issues coming before a court or tribunal.

hold an 'organisational conference' at the outset of proceedings in order to clarify expectations and requests regarding the procedures to be followed in relation to evidence and proof.[9] The existing, limited form of pre-trial conference held by the ICJ could be expanded.[10] Alternatively, the court or tribunal will need direct communication with the parties regarding any issues of this nature requiring to be addressed in advance.

Scientific evidence from the parties

International disputants will generally want to bear primary responsibility for mustering the evidence in support of their cases and presenting it to an international court. They will be wanting an international court to apply the law to the facts in particular ways and to interpret the law in a way that is friendly to their respective causes. The parties may also be seeking to advance their systemic and defensive interests in the interpretation of legal provisions. This may be the case particularly in a multilateral framework, and where subsequent disputes relating to the same provisions are likely, which is the case especially for WTO disputes and for disputes under the United Nations Convention on the Law of the Sea (LOSC). Further, the parties will derive a general sense of fairness from the opportunity to present their cases as they see fit and the control they wield over the presentation of the case. However, for an international court or tribunal the evaluation of a very large volume of partisan evidence will always be a challenge. The court must sift out the scientific issues, assess the quality and reliability of the evidence relevant to each issue and seek to reach findings accurately reflecting the state of current scientific knowledge.

An example from the *Dispute concerning the MOX Plant, International Movements of Radioactive Materials and the Protection of the Marine Environment of the Irish Sea (Ireland* v. *United Kingdom)* demonstrates how evidence on technical matters may not always directly support a case, and may be the subject of controversy.[11] Ireland referred to a 2001

[9] In international arbitration it has been suggested that it is preferable for a tribunal to hold an organisational conference rather than to find later that the parties have developed 'truckloads of evidence'. Holtzmann, 'Streamlining arbitral proceedings'. See also Bishop *et al.*, *Foreign Investment Disputes*, pp. 1402–13.

[10] Rosenne, 'Fact-finding', 247.

[11] *Dispute concerning the MOX Plant, International Movements of Radioactive Materials and the Protection of the Marine Environment of the Irish Sea (Ireland* v. *United Kingdom)*, Request for Provisional Measures, Order of 3 December 2001, 41 ILM 405 (hereafter *MOX Plant (Provisional Measures)*). See above, Chapter 2, pp. 44–9.

report commissioned by the European Parliament's Directorate-General for Research, prepared by ten independent experts.[12] The report recorded that the deposit of plutonium within 20 km of Sellafield from aerial emissions had been estimated at two or three times the plutonium fallout from all atmospheric nuclear weapons testing, and that reprocessing of nuclear fuel at Sellafield and La Hague had led to the largest man-made release of radioactivity anywhere in the world.[13] The report also addressed the potential consequences of an accidental atmospheric release from Sellafield's high-level radioactive waste tanks, which would be far greater than the consequences of the Chernobyl accident in 1986.[14] The United Kingdom noted that the report was said in a leading Irish newspaper to have been characterised as 'unscientific' by leading scientists.[15] Nor did the report address the specific question of the risks that might arise from the MOX plant which was the subject of the dispute. Ireland then presented to the Tribunal the press release on the basis of which the relevant newspaper article had been published, to show that in fact the press release did not criticise or seek to discredit the report.[16]

For its part, the United Kingdom brought considerable evidence to bear in the *MOX Plant* case. Among the documents relied on by the United Kingdom was a 1997 European Commission Opinion, prepared through the consultation of a 'Group of Experts' comprising scientific experts appointed by the Scientific and Technical Committee under Article 31 of the Treaty establishing the European Atomic Energy Community of 1957.[17] The Commission noted that discharge of liquid and gaseous effluence would be in small fractions of the authorised limits and produce only a negligible exposure of the population in Ireland. Nor would doses received in the event of unplanned discharges in case of an

[12] Possible Toxic Effects from the Nuclear Reprocessing Plants at Sellafield (United Kingdom) and Cap de La Hague (France)', produced under the auspices of the Directorate-General's Panel on Scientific and Technological Office Assessment, by the World Informational Service on Energy.

[13] Statement of Case of Ireland, Request for Provisional Measures (hereafter Ireland's request), para. 10.

[14] *Ibid.*, para. 11.

[15] Written Response of the United Kingdom, Request for Provisional Measures (hereafter UK Written Response), paras. 102 and 204.

[16] Verbatim Record, Tuesday 20 November 2001, 3.15 pm, 5, line 33.

[17] Verbatim Record, Monday 19 November 2001, 3.00 pm, 35, line 13. For an overview of the Opinion similar to that seen in the United Kingdom Written Response, see the Verbatim Record, Monday 19 November 2001, 3.00 pm, line 36. For a repetition of the general conclusion, Verbatim Record, Tuesday 20 November 2001, 9.30 am, 35, line 12.

accident be significant.[18] The United Kingdom also cited the view of the Radiological Protection Institute of Ireland, in its Annual Report for 1999, that the significance of doses resulting from Sellafield discharges did not pose a significant health risk to people living in Ireland.[19]

The case of *Request for an Examination of the Situation in Accordance with Paragraph 63 of the Court's Judgment of 20 December 1974 in the Nuclear Tests (New Zealand* v. *France)* also demonstrates the detailed nature of scientific evidence presented by the parties as well as how this evidence may conflict.[20] According to New Zealand, it was well established that the underground tests released radioactive material even in the short term. New Zealand cited a 1983 study led by Hugh Atkinson, Director of the New Zealand National Radiation Laboratory, which found evidence of venting,[21] as well as a 1982 study led by the noted French vulcanologist M. Tazieff, in which the venting of radioactive products had not been excluded.[22] New Zealand also reported that the Atkinson mission had concluded during an aerial inspection of Mururoa atoll that the integrity of the atoll's crown had been impaired by the underground nuclear tests conducted by France. This was acknowledged by France, although it was believed that the risk of further collapse of parts of the atoll's outer rim had been countered by moving tests in from the outer rim of the atoll to the area under the lagoon. New Zealand additionally cited the work of Professor Pierre Vincent, another noted French vulcanologist, who described the situation as 'high risk'.[23] If destabilisation took place, the immediate result would be a sudden spill out of the radioactive 'stockpile' contained within the atoll and a tsunami that would threaten those living in Mururoa and neighbouring archipelagos. Work by Dr Colin Summerhayes, Director of the Institute of Oceanographic Sciences in the United Kingdom, was also cited in relation to the inherently unstable character of volcanic islands and the

[18] UK Written Response, para. 36.

[19] *Ibid.*, para. 101; Verbatim Record, Tuesday 20 November 2001, 9.30 am, 6, line 19; and 3.15 pm, 21, line 20.

[20] *Request for an Examination of the Situation in Accordance with Paragraph 63 of the Court's Judgment of 20 December 1974 in the Nuclear Tests case (New Zealand* v. *France)*, Judgment of 22 September 1995 ICJ Reports 1995 288 (hereafter *Request for an Examination of the Situation*).

[21] 'Report of a New Zealand, Australian and Papua New Guinea Scientific Mission to the Mururoa Atoll' (Wellington, New Zealand: Ministry of Foreign Affairs, 1984).

[22] *Request for an Examination of the Situation*, Application Instituting Proceedings, 21 August 1995, para. 33.

[23] *Ibid.*, Annex V.

effects of landslides caused by triggers such as earthquakes or explosions.[24] France countered the New Zealand argument with reference to the work of M. Tazieff, who held the view that Professor Vincent 'clearly has little knowledge of the resistence of the materials involved in the underground explosions at Mururoa … His statements are born of ignorance.'[25]

In addition to expressing serious concern about the integrity of the atolls where underground French nuclear testing was taking place, New Zealand argued that scientific studies showed a likelihood of both short- and long-term radioactive leakage via groundwater. New Zealand asserted that all the independent scientific missions that had visited Mururoa agreed that long-term leakage from the atoll would occur.[26] M. Tazieff had advised that a systematic study conducted over a number of years was necessary to assess the mobility of radionuclides in groundwater, while the Atkinson report observed that mechanisms did exist for the transfer of the contaminated water into the biosphere and that much depended on the depth of placement of the French explosive devices, which was unknown. An investigation by scientific and film teams led by Jacques Cousteau in 1987 estimated that leakage could occur within 100–300 years. Cousteau's team had carried out underwater filming that revealed fissures and collapses of the rock in the outer part of the atoll. In addition, New Zealand referred to a position taken in the European Commission in 1995, in which it was observed that access to detailed data about the geological structure and movement within the atoll was necessary in order to reach conclusions both in relation to a possible long-term leakage of radioactivity and in relation to the potential for a sudden rupturing of the atoll.[27]

[24] *Request for an Examination of the Situation*, Application Instituting Proceedings, 21 August 1995, paras. 41–4; Opening argument for New Zealand by Hon. Paul East, Verbatim Record, Monday 11 September 1995, 28–9, paras. 69–73.

[25] Translation by the Registry, Opening argument for France by M. Marc Perrin de Brichambaut, Verbatim Record, Tuesday 12 September 1995, 10.00 am, 53. See also translation of the pleadings of M. Brichambaut in Watts, *New Zealand at the International Court*, pp. 201–3.

[26] *Request for an Examination of the Situation*, Application Instituting Proceedings, 21 August 1995, paras. 36–40.

[27] Argument by Mr Elihu Lauterpacht for New Zealand, Verbatim Record, Monday 11 September 1995, 64–5, paras. 55–6. On submarine landslides etc., see *Request for an Examination of the Situation*, Application Instituting Proceedings, 21 August 1995, para. 42. On the structure of atolls and rising of groundwater, *ibid.*, paras. 45–52.

The French position remained that the radioactive impact of testing was infinitesimal and that local radiation levels were still below those in European locations where there had been no testing. Measured in micrograys, the level at Mururoa was 262, while in the Netherlands, for example, it was 280 and in New Zealand it was 900. In the lagoon at Mururoa, plutonium was the only radionuclide with a reading above that observed in the ocean, with a reading of 0.3 becquerels per cubic metre compared with 0.03 becquerels per cubic metre in the ocean. Radioactivity had not been detected in the ocean outside the coral reefs by either French or New Zealand scientists. Nor had any effect on fish been recorded at the laboratory in Papeete or the laboratory at Orsay in France in the most recent measurements. France therefore regarded it as proven that the nuclear tests conducted for the last thirty years at Mururoa and Fangataufa had had no repercussions on the aerial or marine environment. Further, France considered it would be rash to deduce that radionuclides within the atoll would inevitably rise to the surface with the movement of ground water in the atoll. France cited in support the comments of Professor MacEwan, a New Zealand scientist.[28]

Thus, it can be seen, an international court or tribunal may have a challenging job on its hands in measuring the value of conflicting scientific evidence brought forward by the parties and evaluating its relevance in terms of the legal obligations between them. In addition, even where a party seeks to portray its experts as independent or neutral, it will be important for an international court or tribunal to consider any allegiances held by parties' experts, and their background, more generally. For example, in the high-profile investment dispute under the North American Free Trade Agreement, *Methanex Corp.* v. *United States of America*,[29] the United States put the view that 'a long-time consultant to the MTBE industry is neither independent or neutral',[30] for example where an expert or experts, or their firms, had previously been on a retainer from Methanex.[31]

[28] Opening argument by M. Marc Perrin de Brichambaut of France, Verbatim Record, Tuesday 12 September 1995, 10.00 am, 44–9, translated in Watts, *New Zealand at the International Court*, pp. 198–200.

[29] *Methanex Corp.* v. *United States of America*, 3 August 2005 (hereafter *Methanex*), decision available at http.//ita.law.uvic.ca.

[30] Rejoinder of the Respondent, United States of America (hereafter US Rejoinder), 23 April 2004, 38, para. 92, footnote 109.

[31] US Rejoinder, 40, para. 97.

Among the benefits of party control over a large part of the scientific evidence that comes before an international court is the degree to which this may prompt the conduct of new and useful research and the assimilated analysis of existing studies. Governments may make funding available for scientific studies that are important but would otherwise have lacked the political profile to attract support. Such further research will not necessarily produce conclusive or consistent outcomes, but is likely to help illuminate the situation at issue. For example, the dispute in the *Case concerning Pulp Mills on the River Uruguay (Argentina* v. *Uruguay)*[32] led to an Argentine study known as the Uruguay River Environmental Surveillance Programme.[33] The quality of the Argentinian Uruguay River Environmental Surveillance Programme was convincingly endorsed by one of the experts appearing as an advocate for Argentina: 'I would like to record the fact, that, in my opinion, and to the best of my knowledge, the highest principles of scientific integrity have been applied to the Argentinian Science Programme: data have been fully and honestly recorded, whether or not they support Argentina's case.'[34] Nevertheless, as pointed out by Uruguay, it remained the case that this scientific project had been carried out in order to produce evidence for the proceedings.[35] In the past, the Court had indicated that it would treat any such material with caution.[36]

Likewise, when Hungary suspended works at Nagymaros on 13 May 1989, the Hungarian government ordered the ministers concerned to commission further studies during the period of suspension in order to put the Council of Ministers in a position to advise the Parliament on how to deal with the bilateral treaty.[37] An ad hoc Committee of the Hungarian Academy of Sciences recommended further thorough environmental

[32] *Case concerning Pulp Mills on the River Uruguay (Argentina* v. *Uruguay), Request for the Indication of Provisional Measures*, Order of 13 July 2006 (hereafter *Case concerning Pulp Mills (Provisional Measures)*) ICJ Reports 2006.

[33] For an overview of this study see Verbatim Record, Wednesday, 16 September 2009, 37–53, and translation p. 25.

[34] Verbatim Record, Monday, 28 September 2009, 60.

[35] Verbatim Record, Thursday, 24 September 2009, 35.

[36] Verbatim Record, Thursday, 24 September 2009, 36, citing *Armed Activities on the Territory of the Congo (Democratic Republic of the Congo* v. *Uganda)*, ICJ Reports 2005 201, para. 61; *Application of the Convention on the Prevention and Punishment of the Crime of Genocide (Bosnia and Herzegovina* v. *Serbia and Montenegro)*, Judgment of 26 February 2007, ICJ Reports 2007 (hereafter *Application of the Convention on the Prevention and Punishment of the Crime of Genocide*), para. 213.

[37] *Case concerning the Gabčíkovo-Nagymaros Project (Hungary/Slovakia)* Judgment of 25 September 1997 ICJ Reports 1997 (hereafter *Gabčíkovo-Nagymaros* case), para. 33.

and ecological studies.[38] When Hungary extended the suspension of the works at Nagymaros in July 1989, it invited 'international scientific institutions [and] foreign scientific institutes and experts' to co-operate with Hungarian and Czech experts and institutes with a view to assessing the project's ecological impact, as well as developing and implementing a system for guaranteeing water quality.[39] The European Community had also commissioned work including a report developed with the co-operation of Slovakia, described as presenting a 'reliable, integrated modelling system for analysing the environmental impact of alternative management regimes in the Danubian lowland area and for predicting changes in water quality as well as conditions in the river, the reservoir, the soil and agriculture'.[40] According to this report, changes in the ecosystem could not be considered irreversible. Further, based on comprehensive modelling predicting impacts for periods of up to one hundred years, the report concluded that no problems were to be expected in relation to groundwater quality. Hungary had commissioned two international expert reviews which were critical of the EC report.[41]

In addition to documentary evidence annexed to their written pleadings,[42] and audiovisual materials, photographs, models and satellite imagery, the parties may produce affidavits from their experts, or may decide to present their experts in court.[43] Oral testimony from a well-qualified expert may be relatively influential.[44] Historically it has been understood that an expert will speak from his or her special knowledge, providing what is viewed as an opinion on the topic under discussion. An expert will usually be required to make a solemn declaration that he or she will speak in accordance with the expert's sincere belief.[45] In contrast, other non-expert witnesses are brought in to speak based on their direct experience of a matter, and their evidence is considered to go to the facts rather than to be opinion. The boundary between the expert and the witness has been recognised as fragile,[46] and in the

[38] *Ibid.*, para. 35. [39] *Ibid.*, para. 35.
[40] *Ibid.*, Separate Opinion of Judge Abdul G. Koroma.
[41] Verbatim Record, Friday 11 April, 15–20; and see Slovakia's response, Verbatim Record, Tuesday 15 April, 36 ff.
[42] On documentary evidence before the International Court of Justice, see Rosenne, *The Law and Practice*, pp. 1242–7.
[43] For discussion on the practice in the International Court of Justice, *ibid.*, pp. 1305–21.
[44] Lalive, 'Quelques remarques', 101.
[45] For example, on practice in the International Court of Justice, see Rosenne, *The Law and Practice*, pp. 1137–9. Rules of Court of the International Court of Justice, Article 64(b).
[46] Riddell and Plant, *Evidence*, p. 321; Rosenne, *The Law and Practice*, pp. 1137–9 and 1316.

International Court of Justice individuals giving testimony have made dual declarations under Article 64(a) and (b) of the Court's Rules of Procedure, thus serving both as experts and as witnesses. This took place as early as the *Corfu Channel case (United Kingdom of Great Britain and Northern Ireland v. Albania)*.[47] Where scientific experts speak directly from their own empirical research it may be particularly appropriate to accept testimony from them as witnesses as well as experts.

The procedure for oral testimony in the International Court of Justice is now reasonably well established, although it is not frequently used. The usual procedure will involve an examination in chief by the party for whom the witness is appearing, followed by cross-examination and re-examination, with any questions by the judges subsequently.[48] The Court may also have questions for the parties, which may be particularly important if there are no independent expert witnesses or no questions for the parties' own witnesses. Article 61 of the Rules of Court includes provision for the Court to indicate issues on which it considers there has been sufficient argument or which it would like the parties specifically to address, and may question or request explanations from the agents, counsel and advocates.[49] The agents, counsel and advocates may answer immediately or within timeframes fixed by the President of the Court.[50] Questions will be put to the parties at the end of the first round of oral pleadings.[51] The judges' questions may be answered orally or in writing.

Attempts may be made to prompt identification of the commonalities between the evidence of the experts from the disputing parties.[52]

[47] Riddell and Plant, *Evidence*, p. 321; *The Corfu Channel case (United Kingdom v. Albania)* Order of 17 December 1948, ICJ Reports 1947–1948 124; Judgment of 9 April 1949, ICJ Reports 1949 2.

[48] Riddell and Plant, *Evidence*, p. 312; Rosenne, *The Law and Practice*, pp. 1309–21. On witness examination in another context, see e.g. Rule 35 of the ICSID Arbitration Rules, which governs the examination of witnesses and experts before ICSID tribunals. This may even take place otherwise than before a tribunal itself, under Rule 36(b). ICSID Rules of Procedure for Arbitration Proceedings, *ISCID Convention, Regulations and Rules* (Washington: International Centre for the Settlement of Investment Disputes 2006) (hereafter ICSID Arbitration Rules). United Nations Commission on International Trade Law (UNCITRAL) Arbitration Rules 1976, www.uncitral.org (hereafter UNCITRAL Arbitration Rules), Articles 24 and 25(2).

[49] Rules of Court of the International Court of Justice, www.icj-cij.org, Article 61.

[50] Rosenne, *The Law and Practice*, pp. 1298–9.

[51] *Ibid.*, p. 1299. See also pp. 1303–4. Riddell and Plant, *Evidence*, p. 312, see also pp. 60–1, 308–11, 340–3.

[52] Rosenne, *The Law and Practice*, p. 1312.

Questions put by the judges may indicate problems that could arise during the Court's deliberations, and may also call attention to issues that may produce modifications in parties' submissions.[53] At present, practice in the Court is limited to the posing of only occasional questions by individual judges during the oral pleadings, as seen, for example, in the *Case concerning Pulp Mills*.[54] In contrast, a WTO dispute-settlement panel may put lengthy written questions to the parties. A good example is provided in the case *Brazil – Measures Affecting Imports of Retreaded Tyres*, where both Brazil and the European Communities replied to many detailed questions.[55] These included questions concerning the compatibility with the General Agreement on Tariffs and Trade (GATT) of Brazil's import ban on retreaded tyres and its justification under Article XX(b) as a measure to protect human health and the environment against risks arising from the accumulation of waste tyres. With existing volumes of waste tyres in Brazil amounting to over 40 million tyres each year, there were serious environmental and human health concerns.[56] These risks included the problem of an increased incidence of mosquito-borne disease, including dengue fever, yellow fever and malaria, as well as the adverse effects known to be associated with tyre fires and toxic leeching from waste tyres. The Panel was able to pursue the development of a thorough understanding of all aspects of the case by means of specific, direct questions to the parties after each of the oral hearings, or substantive meetings with the parties.

Advocates presenting the science

In a number of cases in different international adjudicatory fora the parties have adopted the strategy of asking their scientists to act as

[53] *Ibid.*, p. 1304.

[54] Verbatim Record, Thursday, 17 September 2009, 67; Verbatim Record, Tuesday, 22 September 2009, 43; Verbatim Record, Tuesday, 29 September 2009, 61.

[55] *Brazil – Measures Affecting Import of Retreaded Tyres*, Complaint by the European Communities (WT/DS332), Report of the Appellate Body DSR 2007: IV, 1527, Report of the Panel DSR 2007: V, 1649 (hereafter *Brazil – Tyres* PR), Annex 1. By way of additional example, it may be noted that in the *EC – Biotech* case questioning by the Panel was particularly intensive, with the parties also commenting on one another's replies and responding to questions from one another after the first substantive hearing, and third parties responding also to questions from the Panel and the parties. *European Communities – Measures Affecting the Approval and Marketing of Biotech Products*, Complaint by United States, Canada, Argentina (WT/DS291, WT/DS292, WT/DS293), Report of the Panel DSR 2006: III, 847 (hereafter *EC – Biotech* PR), Annexes C, D, E, F, G.

[56] *Brazil – Tyres* PR, para. 7.180.

advocates.[57] In the *Gabčíkovo-Nagymaros* case, Hungary had its four scientists appear as 'advocates' while Slovakia had its two scientists appear as 'counsel and experts'. Counsel for Hungary made a point of clarifying that Slovakia's scientists, like Hungary's scientists, appeared as advocates.[58] In the *Case concerning Pulp Mills*, both parties included six delegation members as 'scientific advisors and experts'. Correspondence between the parties clarified that these representatives were speaking in the capacity of advocates rather than expert witnesses.[59]

Where a disputing party decides to adopt this approach, the scientist will generally neither be examined by another member of the party's legal team nor subjected to cross-examination by the opposition.[60] Nor will he or she be required to make the solemn declaration of an expert.[61] It is to be expected that the weight to be given to the information the scientist presents may differ from the weight attached to information from expert witnesses.[62] This strategy could work well for a party if its scientists rank highly in credibility and if their science continues to appear strong in the face of competing science put forward by the opposition. Certainly, the effect of a personal appearance before a court or tribunal may exceed the persuasive quality of written communications.[63] For example, in the *Gabčíkovo-Nagymaros* case the participation of experts as advocates had considerable effect, although the adoption of this same procedure by both litigating parties meant that a 'battle of the experts' was reproduced in a new procedural form.[64]

Strong teamwork within the litigating party will be important where this strategy is adopted. The lines of argument that will be presented must be planned out thoroughly by the team as a whole before the oral proceedings, to ensure that the scientists' input will be deployed to the best effect. Where the scientist is included in the team of advocates, he or she will receive the support of the team in assessing the significance of the scientific aspects of the case in a legal context and calibrating the content of the scientist's submissions to align with the rest of the submissions that make up the party's case. This contrasts with the situation where the scientist is instead employed as an expert who takes the stand,

[57] On the hearing of witnesses as party representatives in the Iran–US Claims Tribunal see Kazazi, *Burden of Proof*, p. 105; Amerasinghe, *Evidence*, p. 387.

[58] Verbatim Record, Tuesday 25 March 1997, 10.00 am, 39

[59] Verbatim Record, Tuesday 22 September 2009, translation, 2.

[60] Bowett, D. *et al.*, *The International Court*, p. 17. [61] Rosenne, *The Law and Practice*, pp. 1137–9.

[62] Amerasinghe, *Evidence*, pp. 387–8. [63] Rosenne, *The Law and Practice*, p. 1297.

[64] See e.g. the Verbatim Record, Friday 11 April and of Tuesday 15 April.

presents his or her view on the facts of a case, and responds to questions. If the scientist takes the stand, it is usually left to the advocate to attempt to convey how the expert's evidence fits into the party's case. Fact and law are kept separate in an attempt to bolster the perceived objectivity of the factual presentation. There are risks here that, because the expert is presenting only his or her evidence, and not the party's case as such, the expert may place a different emphasis on the relative significance of different assertions of fact and could potentially convey the relationships between these assertions in ways that cut across a party's case. Bringing science and the law closer together, as in the *Gabčíkovo-Nagymaros* case, may be a more appealing strategy.

Depending on the tolerance of the international court or tribunal, there may be scope for experts to continue to serve as counsel but to be cross-examined. An international court or tribunal will not necessarily favour this course, however. The International Court of Justice indicated in the case concerning *Pulp Mills on the River Uruguay (Argentina* v. *Uruguay)* that 'those persons who provide evidence before the Court based on their scientific or technical knowledge and on their personal experience should testify before the Court as experts, witnesses or in some cases in both capacities, rather than counsel, so that they may be submitted to questioning by the other party as well as by the Court'.[65] The matter was addressed further by Judge Greenwood in his separate opinion, underlining that the Court had 'unequivocally indicated' that the practice of presentation of scientific expertise by experts appearing as counsel should not be repeated in future cases.[66] Judge Greenwood noted the vital distinction between evidence and advocacy.[67] The judge pointed out that a witness or expert owes a duty to the court, as reflected in the declaration required of such an individual, whereas the duties of counsel are quite different. The problems associated with experts appearing as counsel were particularly acute where, as in this case, they had been 'actively and closely involved in the preparation of scientific reports which were part of the evidence before the Court'.[68]

[65] *Case concerning Pulp Mills on the River Uruguay (Argentina* v. *Uruguay)*, Judgment of 20 April 2010, ICJ Reports 2010 (hereafter *Case concerning Pulp Mills*), para. 167. See also the Joint Dissenting Opinion of Judges Al-Khasawneh and Simma, para. 6.

[66] *Ibid.*, Separate Opinion of Judge Greenwood, para. 28.

[67] *Ibid.*, para. 27, citing Watts, 'Enhancing the effectiveness of procedures of international dispute settlement' in Frowein and Wolfrum (eds.), *Max Planck Yearbook of United Nations Law*, vol. 5, 2001, pp. 29–30. See also Jolowicz, *On Civil Procedure*, 235.

[68] *Ibid.*, para. 27.

It would be more helpful to the Court for such individuals to appear as experts. This would also alleviate unfairness vis-à-vis the other party, although in this case unfairness was less of an issue as both parties had their experts appear as counsel.[69] It was important that the provisions of the Rules of the Court applying to expert testimony not be circumvented through the further use of this practice.[70]

Even with cross-examination there will still be an unclear boundary between experts appearing as advocates and experts who participate in proceedings as expert witnesses. In the *Case concerning Land Reclamation by Singapore in and around the Straits of Johor (Malaysia* v. *Singapore)*[71] the content of the expert reports submitted by Malaysia[72] was presented orally by Professor Sharifah Mastura, a geomorphologist from the Department of Geography at Malaysia's University of Kebangsaan, whose unit had authored one of the reports. After her presentation Professor Sharifah was cross-examined by Singapore. In its Award, the Tribunal stated that she was 'examined as an expert', although Malaysia referred to this as 'questioning' rather than examination.[73] In the record of proceedings for the *Land Reclamation* case, Professor Sharifah's name was included in the list of technical advisers forming part of the Malaysian delegation. Her curriculum vitae had not been submitted to the Tribunal, and she spoke as a representative ('I shall summarise our concerns . . .').

To what extent might a court or tribunal be prepared to rely on the input of an expert acting as an advocate? In the *Case concerning Pulp Mills*, Judge Bennouna asked the parties themselves what they understood in referring to an 'independent expert' to whom they had had recourse, and in particular whether it was possible 'for an expert commissioned by one or other of the Parties to be considered as an independent expert'.[74] Argentina and Uruguay took different positions in response to this question. Argentina considered that its scientific advocates, Professors Wheater and Colombo, were independent, and was prepared also to include one of Uruguay's scientific delegation members in this

[69] *Ibid.*, para. 28. [70] *Ibid.*, para. 27.

[71] *Case concerning Land Reclamation by Singapore in and around the Straits of Johor (Malaysia* v. *Singapore) (Provisional Measures)*, Order of 8 October 2003 (hereafter *Land Reclamation (Provisional Measures)*), decision available at www.itlos.org.

[72] Excluding that of Professor Falconer, Professor of Water Management at Cardiff University. See p. 99.

[73] Verbatim Record, Saturday, 27 September 2003, 9.30 am, 16, line 44.

[74] Verbatim Record, Tuesday, 22 September 2009, translation, 56.

category. In Argentina's view, 'independence is not a matter of compensation alone, it is also a question of frame of mind'.[75] Professors Colombo and Wheater were 'respected senior academics' who had their international reputations to protect.[76] The reports that they had prepared on the Botnia Mill should be given weight according to their own characteristics: depth of analysis, exhaustiveness, accuracy of data, clarity and coherence of conclusions.[77] Argentina advocated the practice of oral advocacy by such scientists, without cross-examination and without prejudice to the question of their independence, including those who had written reports incorporated in the party's pleadings, as a practical way to deal with cases like the *Case concerning Pulp Mills* and the *Gabčíkovo-Nagymaros* case. The International Court of Justice was a large court, and the time for examination and cross-examination was limited: it was important to be aware of 'the realities and practicalities of international litigation'.[78] On the other hand, a permanent full-time employee of the state like Ms Torres on the Uruguayan delegation could not be regarded as independent.[79] Nor, according to Argentina, could Uruguayan delegation member Mr McCubbin be regarded as independent, as he was an author of the Hatfield Report prepared for the International Financial Corporation (IFC) of the World Bank, from whom funding had been sought for the mills' construction.[80]

Uruguay took the view that retained experts, by definition, could not be independent. Their evidence was admissible, but could not be given the same weight as evidence from unaffiliated experts.[81] Further, advocates were 'clearly partisan'.[82] As they were not subject to cross-examination like an expert witness, particular note should be taken of their partisanship. Uruguay therefore regarded as independent only evidence from the work of the agencies that had been retained by the IFC.[83] The findings of these agencies should be given considerable weight, because they were disinterested, applied exacting standards,

[75] Verbatim Record, Monday 28 September 2009, translation, 12.

[76] Verbatim Record, Tuesday 29 September 2009, 23.

[77] Verbatim Record, Monday, 28 September 2009, 12. [78] *Ibid.*, 26.

[79] Verbatim Record, Tuesday, 29 September 2009, 23, citing Salmon, J. (ed.), *Dictionnaire de Droit International Public*, 2001.

[80] Verbatim Record, Tuesday, 29 September 2009, 24.

[81] Verbatim Record, Thursday, 24 September 2009, 33–4; Verbatim Record, Friday, 2 October 2009, 33–4.

[82] Verbatim Record, Thursday, 24 September 2009, 36, quoting Watts, 'Burden of proof', 299.

[83] Verbatim Record, Thursday, 24 September 2009, 33 ff.

and were part of a project review with multiple layers.[84] Uruguay said it was also troubled by the phenomenon of the introduction of new evidence during the oral hearings by the expert advocates on the Argentinian delegation, evidence that had not been included in the written proceedings.[85] The Court recorded the parties' views on the relative independence of the various studies and reports placed before it, and of experts appearing as counsel. However, the Court did not find it necessary to enter into a general discussion on their merits, reliability and authority.[86]

As an alternative to having their scientists appear as advocates, the parties may have their legally trained advocates present scientific arguments supporting their claims. This will require a serious commitment on the part of the lawyer, particularly where the scientific history of a dispute is long and complex.[87] To take an example, in the *Land Reclamation* case, Singapore chose to have one of its legal advocates, Mr Lowe, present a technical critique of Malaysia's expert evidence.[88] Mr Lowe set out to highlight to the Tribunal how, in Singapore's view, Malaysia's expert evidence had failed as a whole to indicate the urgency necessary to sustain a request for provisional measures.[89] Mr Lowe discussed various limitations on the scope of the reports submitted by Malaysia,[90] querying assumptions in the Department's report in relation to factors such as erosion, peak velocities and wave height.[91] In relation to Malaysia's reliance on interviews with 800 Malaysian fishermen, most of whom perceived Singapore's land reclamations to have adversely affected their catches, Mr Lowe observed that the terms of the question that had actually been put to the fishermen had not been revealed to the Tribunal. He also noted contrary reference to trends in catch figures.[92] So far as navigation was concerned, Mr Lowe noted that alterations to water velocity would generally be greatest in the centre of a channel, but that ships did not attempt to travel in the centre of the route because of the presence of the Guillemard Rocks and the Merlin

[84] *Ibid.*, 37–8.

[85] Verbatim Record, Friday, 2 October 2009, 31. See the rejection of Argentina's official request to introduce late evidence in the verbatim record of Monday, 28 September 2009, translation, 2.

[86] *Case concerning Pulp Mills*, paras. 166, 168.

[87] See e.g. the presentations made by Mr Samuel Wordsworth in the *Gabčíkovo-Nagymaros* case, in the Verbatim Record of Monday 24 March, from 41 and 61, and of the morning of Tuesday 25 March, from 10.

[88] See below. [89] Verbatim Record, Friday, 26 September 2003, at 3.00 pm, 16.

[90] *Ibid.*, 17–25. [91] *Ibid.*, 19, 23. [92] *Ibid.*, 20.

Rocks.[93] He compared the 1.5 cm of erosion that was expected to occur in the seabed in the time before the constitution of the Annex VII Tribunal to hear the merits of the dispute with the 25 cm margin of error permitted in seabed mapping under the standards promulgated by the International Hydrographic Organization.[94] In response, Mr Crawford, as counsel for Malaysia, noted there were many points that could be made. For example, the interviews with local fisherman had focused on twenty or so fishing villages precisely in the affected area, whereas the catch figures cited related to Johor as a whole.[95] However, he suggested that the Tribunal did not need to descend into such detail and observed that it would be rare for scientific assessments to be entirely univocal. The basic point at the provisional measures stage was that all four of the reports submitted by Malaysia showed serious grounds for concern.[96]

Evidence generated by administrative procedures

In some cases, evidence submitted by the parties may have been produced in the course of various administrative procedures. This information will not necessarily address all scientific questions thoroughly in the way that will best help an international court or tribunal. For example, in the *Case concerning Pulp Mills* both at the provisional measures stage and at the merits stage the International Court of Justice received documentation produced in the course of the World Bank's consideration of whether to fund the pulp mills' construction. The Spanish and Finnish companies investing in the two Uruguayan pulp mills had applied for finance from the IFC and guarantees from the Bank's Multilateral Investment Guarantee Agency. In addition the Court received documentation from the Dirección Nacional de Medio Ambiente (DINAMA), the Uruguayan government agency responsible for the environmental oversight of such projects.

The IFC had commissioned a number of independent reports on the pulp mills, that were referred to in the proceedings before the International Court of Justice. These included a Cumulative Impact Statement (CIS), which had been produced for the IFC by two independent experts. Following a review by the IFC's independent compliance advisory ombudsman the IFC had then sought an independent review of

[93] *Ibid.*, 22. [94] *Ibid.*, 24.
[95] Saturday, 27 September 2003, at 9.30 am, 19, lines 15–21. [96] *Ibid.*, 19.

the CIS by the Hatfield firm of consultants. At the time when Argentina's request for provisional measures was being considered, a new set of independent technical experts had been appointed to evaluate all of the environmental studies that had been completed to date. Funding remained contingent on their report,[97] which was expected within some three months.[98] By the time of the proceedings on the merits, a final cumulative impact statement had been prepared for the IFC by a firm called EcoMetrix, on the basis of which the project was approved by the IFC. Within a year, in 2007, the Uruguayan authorities had authorised operations to begin. Before the commencement of operations, the IFC had two further reports prepared by 'independent external consultants', EcoMetrix and AMEC, an international engineering firm.[99] The IFC concluded that the Botnia Mill was ready to operate. After the first six months of operation, EcoMetrix prepared another report for the IFC in mid 2008,[100] and another at the end of 2008 reviewing the first year of operations.[101] The Uruguayan authorities also prepared a report on performance up until mid 2009.[102] Uruguay sought to rely on the positive statements in these reports.

Conflicting use will be made of such extensive reports. Uruguay referred to remarks in the Hatfield report that 'comments expressing concern that the mills will cause catastrophic environmental damage are unsupported, unreasonable and ignore the experience in many other modern bleached kraft pulpmills'.[103] Yet Argentina highlighted the IFC ombudsman's confirmation of the projects' transboundary impact, including on water and water quality,[104] as well as the findings of the ombudsman[105] and the Hatfield report[106] that many issues remained to be addressed and that insufficient information had been provided to permit completion of a full environmental impact assessment.[107] According to Uruguay, even at the time of Argentina's request for provisional measures many of the criticisms put forward in the Hatfield report had already been addressed in the course of Uruguay's

[97] Verbatim Record, Thursday 8 June 2006, 3.00 pm, 47.
[98] Verbatim Record, Friday 9 June 2006, at 10.00 am, 33.
[99] Verbatim Record, Monday 21 September 2009, 24.
[100] *Ibid.*, 24. [101] *Ibid.*, 25. [102] *Ibid.*, 25.
[103] Verbatim Record, Thursday 8 June 2006, 3.00 pm, 18.
[104] Verbatim Record, Friday 9 June 2006, 10.00 am, 11. [105] *Ibid.*, 11.
[106] Verbatim Record, Thursday 8 June, 10.00 am, 44; Friday 9 June, 10.00 am, 11, 33; Friday 9 June, 10.00 am, translation, 38.
[107] *Case concerning Pulp Mills (Provisional Measures)*, para. 51.

own environmental oversight processes. However Argentina sought to emphasise the deficiencies in the EIAs submitted to the Uruguayan authorities,[108] noting that DINAMA itself had pointed out lack of information, contradictions and unsatisfactory answers in Botnia's EIA for the CMB plant.[109] In its decision on Argentina's request for provisional measures the Court took note of Argentina's observation that DINAMA had classified the plants as projects presenting a risk of major negative environmental impact, and had characterised the technical processes to be used at the plants as inherently polluting,[110] although this did not lead to an order of provisional measures in favour of Argentina.

At the provisional measures stage Uruguay also produced evidence generated by Argentina characterising the plants as innocuous. Such a statement had also been made by Argentina's Chief Technical Adviser at the Executive Commission for the River Uruguay, Dr Armando Darío Garín, to the effect that:

> It must be pointed out, with complete and absolute emphasis that none of the different technical reports evidence that the activity in question causes an irreversible and unavoidable damage to the environment, at least of a sufficient level that would warrant the suspension of the plant or opposition to its construction, at least with any scientific basis ...[111]

Such 'own goals' are seen also in other disputes. Where politics within a defending party revolve around a federal structure this may be particularly likely. In *Metalclad Corporation* v. *United Mexican States*[112] a number of technical studies took place before and during the events leading up to the eruption of a full dispute between Metalclad and Mexico over the refusal of the Municipality of Guadalcázar (the Municipality) to grant a municipal construction permit for a hazardous waste landfill plant that had been authorised at federal level consistent with Mexican law. The Autonomous University of the State of San Luis Potosi, where Guadalcázar is located, issued a study confirming earlier findings that the landfill site was geographically suitable.[113] The same conclusion

[108] Verbatim Record, Friday 9 June, 10.00 am, 12.

[109] *Ibid.*, 31; Verbatim Record, Thursday 8 June 2006, 10.00 am, 65–6.

[110] *Case concerning Pulp Mills (Provisional Measures)*, para. 8.

[111] Verbatim Record, Thursday, 8 June 2006, 3.00 pm, 54–5; Verbatim Record, Friday 9 June 2006, 4.30 pm, 33; and for Argentina's response Verbatim Record, Friday 9 June 2006, 10.00 am, translation, 19.

[112] *Metalclad Corporation* v. *United Mexican States*, Award of 20 August 2000, 5 ICSID Reports 209.

[113] *Ibid.*, para. 44.

was reached in a site audit carried out by the Mexican Federal Attorney's Office for the Protection of the Environment, an agency of the Federal Secretariat of the Mexican Environment, Natural Resources and Fishing.[114] Nevertheless, the Municipality had retained the view that the site was geologically unsuitable and that there were grounds for concern about potential adverse environmental effects.[115] Accordingly, the dispute proceeded to arbitration.[116]

The party-appointed independent expert

Scientific evidence may also come before an international court or tribunal through its presentation by an expert selected and appointed by one of the parties but requested to act in an 'independent capacity'. Generally in international cases any relations between witnesses and the parties in whose favour they testify may be taken into account in the weighing of the evidence.[117] Scepticism as to whether an appointee can present a truly independent view might be expected, as in national law. The French distrust of oral evidence is reflected in the maxim '*qui mieux abreuve, mieux preuve*'[118] and the problem of bias has always been understood in the common law.[119] Regardless of remuneration or reward, research has shown that even inadvertent bias is likely for expert

114 *Ibid.*, para. 44. 115 *Ibid.*, para. 106.

116 The use of expert scientific evidence from national documentation is common in human rights cases. For example see *Hatton and others* v. *The United Kingdom*, Judgment of 8 July 2003, 37 EHRR 28, in which the European Court of Human Rights found a violation of Articles 8 (the right to respect for family and private life) and 13 (the right to a remedy for violation of rights) of the European Convention on Human Rights in relation to sleep disturbance and prevention caused by night flights at Heathrow Airport; *López Ostra* v. *Spain*, 9 December 1994, 20 EHRR 277, a case where the Court also found a violation of Article 8, in relation to the pollution emanating from a waste treatment plant servicing local tanneries; and the case of *Guerra and others* v. *Italy*, 19 February 1998, 26 EHRR 357, where a violation of the same provision was established in relation to a fertiliser factory. See also *Oneryildiz* v. *Turkey*, 30 November 2004, 41 EHRR 20. However, a government will not always release relevant material, as seen in *Fadeyeva* v. *Russia*, 9 June 2005, 45 EHRR 10, a case concerning the operation of a steel plant where a violation of the right to respect for private and family life was also found.

117 Amerasinghe, *Evidence*, pp. 201–2 and 226, referring to the *Walfish Bay* case (1911) Award, 11 UNRIAA 263 at 302 and 303.

118 Beardsley, 'Proof of fact', 478 citing Loysel, Antoine in Dupin Laboulaye, *Instituts Coutumiers* (1846) Sec 770, and translating the maxim as 'a witness who is well wined and dined will testify well'.

119 In 1901 Judge Learned Hand wrote that, already: 'Enough has been said elsewhere as to the natural bias of one called in such matters to represent a single side and liberally paid to defend it.' Hand, 'Historical and practical considerations', 53.

witnesses operating in an adversarial context.[120] An expert's outlook on the types of issues arising in the parties' dispute is likely to be consonant with the appointing party's own approach and the expert may have become familiar with that party's case in the course of his or her appointment.

Additionally or alternatively it might be asked whether an 'independent' party-appointed expert should be expected to act any differently to any other party-appointed expert. Several factors ought to be taken into account. Experts appear only very rarely before international courts and tribunals and they are likely to be individuals of high professional calibre. Their standing within their own scientific communities will be high, and they are unlikely to harbour intentions to execute their duties as technical experts in a way that could prejudice this standing. While generally it can be expected that all party-appointed experts may be remunerated by the parties at a level consistent with their qualifications and experience, this ought not necessarily be considered to undermine their sense of duty to the court and their own commitment to providing impartial advice.

However, an independent party-appointed expert may perhaps be tasked differently from other party-appointed experts, to good effect. One particular task that may be requested of a party-appointed independent witness is that he or she put forward a review of the advice that a party has relied upon in its dealings with the other party. This role was performed by Professor Sir John Beddington in the *Southern Bluefin Tuna cases (New Zealand* v. *Japan; Australia* v. *Japan)*.[121] Reviewing the opinion of Australia's scientists Dr Polacheck and Ms Preece, Professor Beddington conveyed lucidly the view that carried the day: 'Clearly, any increase in captures over those taken in 1997 can only further decrease the probability that the desired recovery can be achieved.'[122] A distinctive feature of Professor Beddington's appearance was that the International Tribunal for the Law of the Sea entertained his examination on the voir dire. Questions on the voir dire were restricted to points relating to the independence of the witness rather than his scientific

[120] Lind and Tyler, *The Social Psychology*, p. 115.

[121] *Southern Bluefin Tuna cases (New Zealand* v. *Japan; Australia* v. *Japan)*, Order of 27 August 1999, 38 ILM 1624 (hereafter *Southern Bluefin Tuna (Provisional Measures)*).

[122] Opinion of Professor Sir John Beddington, presented in evidence by Australia and New Zealand, para. 64. Comments on the Issues raised by T. Polacheck and A. Preece, 'A scientific overview of the status of the southern bluefin tuna stock' and by Talbot Murray's 'Comment' on that overview.

credentials.[123] This contrasted with the *South West Africa* cases, where examination on the voir dire was limited to the expertise of the witness although not permitted to extend to the witness's views on the subject matter at hand.[124]

In the *Land Reclamation* case Mr Roger Falconer, Professor of Water Management at Cardiff University, appeared as an independent expert before the Tribunal. Professor Falconer had authored one of the four reports submitted to the International Tribunal for the Law of the Sea by Malaysia with its request for provisional measures. Malaysia had then asked him to appear before the Tribunal as an independent consultant.[125] Malaysia's examination of Professor Falconer illustrates how this process can be used to generate the space for an expert to explain the salient points from his or her study. In the course of the examination, Professor Falconer explained that an increase in the velocity of water flows by some 70 per cent (according to Singapore's studies, which indicated an increase from 0.7 to 1.2 metres per second) would result in a threefold increase in the transportation of mud and a fifteenfold increase in the transportation of sand or silt south of Pulau Tekong. In this respect, Professor Falconer considered that the Malaysian government's own study seriously understated the potential impact of the reclamation works because that study assumed only the transportation of mud and not of silt or sediment.[126] The professor also identified how the flow around the headland was disrupted and, with the narrowing of the water channel, this created eddies (as predicted in computer simulations by both Malaysia and Singapore) which trapped and redeposited sediment and mud along the beaches.[127] He recommended carrying out simulations to look at how the shape of the reclamation might be modified to deal with the impact on the coastline.[128] In addition, Professor Falconer considered it essential that longer-term studies be carried out.[129] Clearly, Professor Falconer's scientific input was valuable

[123] Verbatim Record, 18 August 1999, 38, line 27; *Southern Bluefin Tuna (Provisional Measures)*, para. 25.

[124] *South West Africa cases (Ethiopia* v. *South Africa; Liberia* v. *South Africa)*, ICJ Pleadings 1966, vol. X, 340, 341. For discussion, see Jessup, 'Foreword' in Sandifer, *Evidence*, p. x; Sandifer, *Evidence*, pp. 340–1; Schwarzenberger, *International Law*, pp. 648–9; Highet, 'Evidence and proof of facts', 360–1. On the use of voir dire proceedings to establish the status of experts in the international criminal tribunals, see Tochilovsky, *Jurisprudence of the International Criminal Courts*, pp. 466–8.

[125] Verbatim Record, Thursday, 25 September 2003, 11.00 am, 32, 33.

[126] *Ibid.*, 33. [127] *Ibid.*, 33. [128] *Ibid.*, 34. [129] *Ibid.*, 34–5.

in moving the dispute forward towards the investigative processes that led promptly to its resolution.

Party-appointed independent experts have also been used in the WTO. For example, in *European Communities – Measures Affecting Asbestos and Asbestos-Containing Products*, Canada sought to convey that it wished two experts on its delegation to be viewed as impartial by informing the meeting that in this case they were 'serving as honorary members of the delegation and have declined to accept any compensation from Her Majesty in order that both their independence and the appearance thereof may be guarded'.[130] The requirement that party-appointed witnesses generally act independently of the parties is seen increasingly commonly in national jurisdictions, and also in international commercial arbitration.[131]

Cross-examination

Cross-examination increasingly features in the proceedings of international courts and tribunals and is an important method for testing out the evidence adduced from a party's expert witness.[132] This may not be a comfortable experience for an expert witness. Weaknesses in experts' testimony are likely to be made to appear even where the experts are extremely good scientists, particularly in a case in which scientific uncertainty is genuinely present. For example, in the *Land Reclamation* case, Mr Lowe's cross-examination, for Singapore, of Malaysian expert witness Professor Falconer sought to place a question mark over his testimony as a whole. First, Mr Lowe clarified that the scope of the witness's expertise, and of his report, were limited.[133] Mr Lowe had Professor Falconer confirm that he had been remunerated by Malaysia for the written report he had produced.[134] Mr Lowe then followed a line of questions that showed the witness's work to be confined to an

[130] *European Communities – Measures Affecting Asbestos and Asbestos-Containing Products*, Complaint by Canada (WT/DS135), Report of the Panel (hereafter *EC – Asbestos* PR) DSR 2001: VIII, 3305, Annex VI, Transcript of Joint Meeting with Experts JM 7. Canada made use of the experts on the Canadian delegation in questioning the correctness of particular points of record asserted by the Panel's experts. JM 107, 189.

[131] IBA Rules, Article 5(2)(c).

[132] Riddell and Plant, *Evidence*, p. 194. For discussion of practice in the ICJ as it developed in the *Corfu Channel* and *South West Africa* cases, Rosenne, *The Law and Practice*, pp. 1311–12, 1317–19.

[133] *Land Reclamation (Provisional Measures)* Thursday, 25 September, am, 35.

[134] *Ibid.*, 36 and see above.

evaluation of the modelling carried out by the Malaysian Department of Irrigation and Drainage and not to involve the evaluation or taking of primary data, nor the reading of the data compiled by the Department.[135] The witness was then asked to confirm that most of the predictions in the Department's report were based on mathematical modelling.[136] Mr Lowe also elicited the information that the witness had not attempted to visit the reclamation sites in Singapore, although he had looked at them from the Malaysian side on the day before he met with Malaysian officials.[137] However, when Mr Lowe pressed the witness for comment on whether the changes to the marine environment that he had described would be gradual or dramatic, Professor Falconer insisted that sediment transport rates could change quite significantly and suddenly in response to only slight alterations in velocity.[138]

Parties may regard the opportunity to cross-examine as a valuable component of their armoury, and as important for bringing out the truth of a situation. Strategically, they may even prefer to see their own experts cross-examined by the opposing party, if they believe the experts will stand up to this well and impress the court or tribunal. This approach was effective for the US in the *Methanex* case. The *Methanex* Tribunal rejected a suit by a major methanol producer under Chapter 11 of the North American Free Trade Agreement in relation to a Californian Executive Order banning the gasoline additive methyl tertiary-butyl ether, for which methanol is an important ingredient. The Tribunal was persuaded that the scientific study relied on by the state of California, which had been carried out by the University of California, constituted serious and objective science. This undoubtedly predisposed the Tribunal well toward the US defence.

From the point of view of an international court or tribunal, however, it may be more helpful to introduce a procedure that also contains a strong investigative element, rather than relying solely on the process of examination and the complementary, usually deconstructive, process of cross-examination. An investigative procedure led by the court

[135] *Ibid.*, 36–7; See also Friday, 26 September 2003, 3.00 pm, 19, lines 33–44.

[136] *Ibid.*, 37. Professor Falconer made the point that the Department had set out to have the report produced within a six month timeframe, when typically two to three years' field measurements would be needed to ascertain the impact of reclamations. In re-examination for Malaysia, Mr Crawford obtained confirmation from Professor Falconer that mathematical modelling was the usual way to address questions of environmental impact in this context. *Ibid.*, 38.

[137] *Ibid.*, 37. [138] *Ibid.*, 37–8.

or tribunal, or a process where experts are brought together for discussion before the court or tribunal, may better enable the court or tribunal to build up a solid and coherent understanding of the science. Examples of procedures being developed in the WTO and in investment treaty arbitration are discussed below. These processes contrast with the traditional adversarial model, which dismantles experts' evidence, leaving the court or tribunal to assess the remnants.[139]

Consultation of international organisations

In pursuit of a better understanding of a case, international courts and tribunals may seek advice from international organisations specialising in relevant fields. Provision is made in the Statute of the International Court of Justice for the Court to request the provision of information by public international organisations,[140] and to receive from them information provided at their own initiative that is relevant to cases before the Court.[141] Indeed, the Court has 'attached considerable probative value to reports compiled and communicated by UN agencies'.[142] Taking an example, the Court considered a report prepared at the request of the World Health Organization's Director-General in its Advisory Opinion on the *Legality of the Use by a State of Nuclear Weapons in Armed Conflict*.[143]

A proactive approach was taken early on by the GATT Panel dealing with *Thailand - Cigarettes*, where the Panel consulted representatives of the World Health Organization (WHO). This was done at the request of Thailand and in accordance with an understanding between the parties, on technical aspects of the case including the health effects of cigarette use.[144] The practice of consulting specialised agencies on technical

139 As one writer has described it, cross-examination 'privileges skepticism over consensus'. Jasanoff, 'What judges should know', 353.

140 Statute of the International Court of Justice, Article 34(2). See also International Court of Justice Rules of Court (1978), adopted on 14 April 1978 and entered into force on 1 July 1978, Article 69(4). Amerasinghe, *Evidence*, 159.

141 International Court of Justice Rules of Court (1978), adopted on 14 April 1978 and entered into force on 1 July 1978, Article 69(2).

142 Riddell and Plant, *Evidence*, p. 237, see also pp. 398–400.

143 *Effects of Nuclear War on Health and Health Services*, 2nd edn (Geneva: WHO, 1987), cited in *Legality of the Use by a State of Nuclear Weapons in Armed Conflict* (Advisory Opinion), 8 July 1996, ICJ Reports 1996 66, 78.

144 GATT Panel Report, *Thailand – Restrictions on Importation of and Internal Taxes on Cigarettes*, DS10/R, adopted 7 November 1990, BISD 37S/20.

questions has effectively been continued by WTO panels.[145] In *EC – Hormones*,[146] for example, one of the experts included in the consultation process was from the Codex Alimentarius Commission, the international agency responsible for setting standards in food safety. The Codex Secretariat was sent written questions as part of the Panel's written consultations with experts.[147] In *European Communities – Measures Affecting the Approval and Marketing of Biotech Products*, the Panel consulted with the parties as to which international organisations should be contacted by the Panel.[148] The Panel decided to consult the secretariats of the Convention on Biological Diversity, the Codex Alimentarius Commission, the Food and Agriculture Organization of the United Nations, the International Plant Protection Convention, the World Organisation for Animal Health, the United Nations Environment Programme, and the WHO.[149] The agencies were asked for their input in the form of standard references to assist the Panel in ascertaining meanings of particular terms, such as 'pest', the interpretation of which goes to the scope of the SPS Agreement.[150] This process was opposed unsuccessfully by the complainant,[151] but the parties were provided with the opportunity to comment on the international organisations' input.[152]

The WTO panel charged with the *Continued Suspension of Obligations* cases in the growth-promotion hormones dispute consulted the Codex Alimentarius Commission, and the Joint Expert Committee on Food Additives of the Food and Agriculture Organization and the WHO, as well as the International Agency for Research on Cancer.[153] The parties were invited to comment on the replies of these organisations together with the replies of the panel-appointed scientific experts, and then to comment on the comments made by the other parties. Representatives

[145] Grando reports on the consultation of the International Monetary Fund in *India – Quantitative Restrictions on Imports of Agricultural, Textile and Industrial Products*, Complaint by the United States (WT/DS90), Report of the Appellate Body, DSR 1999: IV, 1763. Grando, *Evidence*, p. 130.

[146] *European Communities – Measures Concerning Meat and Meat Products (Hormones)*, Complaint by Canada (WT/DS48), Complaint by the United States (WT/DS26). Two identically constituted WTO dispute settlement Panels (the Panel) circulated parallel reports in this case: Report of the Panel (Canada) DSR 1998: II, 235 (hereafter *EC – Hormones*, Complaint by Canada, PR), Report of the Panel (United States) DSR 1998: III, 699 (hereafter *EC – Hormones*, Complaint by the US, PR). See also the Report of the Appellate Body DSR 1998: I, 135 (hereafter *EC – Hormones* ABR).

[147] *EC – Hormones*, Complaint by Canada, PR, para. 6.7; Complaint by the US, PR, para. 6.8.

[148] *EC – Biotech* PR, para. 7.31. [149] *Ibid.*, para. 7.31.

[150] *Ibid.*, paras. 7.19, 7.31. [151] *Ibid.*, para. 7.19. [152] *Ibid.*, para. 7.31.

[153] *Canada – Continued Suspension* PR, Annex E.

from the three international organisations participated in the oral stage of the Panel's consultation with the experts it had approached to assist it. Their contributions during the meeting focused on explaining the institutional functioning of their respective agencies, as well as clarifying their agencies' written responses. One of the representatives of the international organisations, Dr Cogliano, head of the Carcinogen Identification and Evaluation Group at the International Agency for Research on Cancer, served at the same time as one of the six independent experts appointed by the Panel.[154]

The parties may also invoke the views of UN specialised agencies and other intergovernmental organisations as well as of national authorities in other jurisdictions.[155] For example, in its WTO case against the EC ban on chrysotile asbestos, *European Communities – Measures Affecting Asbestos and Asbestos-Containing Products*, Canada referred to views of the Directorate-General XXIV of the EC, the United States Occupational Safety and Health Administration, the United States Environmental Protection Agency and the WHO's International Agency for Research on Cancer.[156] Reference was also made in the *Case concerning Pulp Mills* to the WHO as an authoritative source of technical information. Argentina observed that the WHO had classified dioxins and furans as 'known human carcinogens' linked with problems in neurological development of newborns and to a variety of immunological diseases. In the *Nuclear Tests cases (New Zealand* v. *France) (Australia* v. *France)* New Zealand cited in support the 1962 conclusions of the United Nations Scientific Committee on the Effects of Atomic Radiation (UNSCAER).[157] UNSCAER was set up by the General Assembly in 1955 to collect and study radiological information including on fallout from nuclear weapons tests.[158] According to UNSCAER, it was clearly established that exposure to radiation could give rise to cancer, leukaemia and detectable or undetectable inherited abnormalities.

[154] *Continued Suspension* JM.

[155] See *Application of the Convention on the Prevention and Punishment of the Crime of Genocide*, paras. 227ff.

[156] *EC – Asbestos* PR, paras. 3.178, 3.327.

[157] *Nuclear Tests case (Australia* v. *France) Request for the Indication of Interim Measures of Protection*, Order of 22 June 1973, ICJ Reports 1973 99; *Nuclear Tests case (New Zealand* v. *France) Request for the Indication of Interim Measures of Protection*, Order of 22 June 1973, ICJ Reports 1973 135; *Nuclear Tests case (Australia* v. *France)*, 20 December 1974, ICJ Reports 1974 253; *Nuclear Tests case (New Zealand* v. *France)*, 20 December 1974, ICJ Reports 1974 457.

[158] Request for the Indication of Interim Measures of Protection submitted by the government of New Zealand, para. 8.

Genetic damage had occurred at the lowest levels experimentally tested to date, and the assumption of UNSCAER and the International Commission on Radiological Protection (ICRP) was that any exposure to radiation could have irreparable and harmful physical effects.[159] The ICRP had, however, set dose limits for radiation, on the basis that the related risks should be no greater than other risks regularly accepted in everyday life.[160] Australia also relied on the work of UNSCAER.[161]

In the *Case concerning Pulp Mills*, Uruguay considered that the independent consultants' reports prepared for the financing decisions of the IFC should be regarded as evidence from an international organisation.[162] Yet these reports had been prepared by consultants rather than the IFC itself. Argentina also argued that certain individual consultants were not altogether independent.[163] Argentina observed that the IFC had a limited sphere of competence, specifically concentrated on the execution of operations in the promotion of private investment.[164] Uruguay responded that the mandate of the IFC related only to projects that were socially and environmentally sustainable, and the reports in question were intended to ensure that funded projects were consistent with this mandate.[165] Uruguay referred to dicta of the Court in the *Application of the Convention on the Prevention and Punishment of the Crime of Genocide* (*Bosnia and Herzegovina* v. *Serbia and Montenegro*) to the effect that the United Nations Secretary-General's 1999 report 'The Fall of Srebrenica'[166] possessed considerable authority because of the 'care taken in preparing the report, its comprehensive sources and the independence of those responsible for its preparation'.[167] A distinction should perhaps be drawn between the views

[159] Application Instituting Proceedings of New Zealand, para. 14; Request for Provisional Measures of New Zealand, paras. 39–40.

[160] Request for the Indication of Interim Measures of Protection submitted by the government of New Zealand, para. 37.

[161] Request for the Indication of Interim Measures of Protection submitted by the government of Australia, paras. 7, 13.

[162] See above the discussion on which sources of evidence in this case were to be regarded as 'independent'.

[163] See Argentina's arguments in the Verbatim Record, Monday, 28 September 2009, translation, 28–9. See also at 57–9.

[164] *Ibid.*, 27. [165] Verbatim Record, Thursday 1 October 2009, 35.

[166] Report of the United Nations Secretary-General 'The Fall of Srebrenica', UN Doc. A/54/549.

[167] Verbatim Record, Friday 2 October 2009, 40–1, citing *Application of the Convention on the Prevention and Punishment of the Crime of Genocide*, 135–7. See also Verbatim Record, Thursday 24 September 2009, 38.

expressed by the IFC itself, which had concluded that the Botnia Mill would 'not cause harm to the environment',[168] and the reports prepared by consultants to the IFC.

Site visits

International courts and tribunals may have an inherent power to make a site visit or *descente sur les lieux* in order to acquaint themselves with the physical aspects of a dispute 'on the ground'.[169] Specific provision for site visits may also be made in courts' and tribunals' governing documents.[170] Arbitral tribunals have conducted site visits on a number of occasions,[171] including a site visit by a tribunal consisting of judges of the International Court of Justice in the *Beagle Channel Arbitration (Argentina* v. *Chile)*[172] and a site visit in the *Dispute concerning the Course of the Frontier between BP62 and Mount Fitzroy (Argentina/Chile) ('Laguna del Desierto')*.[173] In both instances the visit took place before the opening of the oral proceedings. A tribunal may even take with it an expert or experts on such a visit.[174] A formal site visit, by the International Court of Justice at least, would be expected to involve all the members of the Court, rather than a delegate or subcommittee.[175] Such a visit will not necessarily involve the formal taking of evidence as envisaged under Article 66 of the Court's Statute.[176] However, it will provide the opportunity for the court or tribunal to receive technical explanations that complement the evidence it receives via the parties' pleadings and the evidence they submit formally to the Court.

[168] Verbatim Record, Thursday 24 September 2009, 40.

[169] Brown, *A Common Law*, p. 111. Rosenne, 'Visit to the site', 461; Bedjaoui, 'La "Descente"', 2. Jenks notes the absence of specific provision for site visits in the Statute and Rules of the ICJ, but canvasses the various precedents for such visits. Jenks, *The Prospects*. On site visits by the international criminal tribunals, see Tochilovsky, *Jurisprudence of the International Criminal Courts*, pp. 373–4.

[170] See e.g. the ICSID Arbitration Rules, 32(4)(b) and 37, which provide for visits and enquiries at places connected with a dispute. Schreuer, *The ICSID Convention*, pp. 670–1.

[171] Rosenne, 'Visit to the site', 470–72; Hudson, 'Visits'.

[172] *Beagle Channel Arbitration (Argentina* v. *Chile)* 18 February 1977 52 ILR 93.

[173] *Dispute concerning the Course of the Frontier between BP62 and Mount Fitzroy (Argentina/Chile) ('Laguna del Desierto')* 21 October 1994, 113 ILR 1, paras. 10, 11.

[174] *Decision of the Arbitral Tribunal established to settle the dispute concerning the course of the boundary between Austria and Hungary near the lake called 'Meerauge'*, Decision of 13 September 1902, 28 UNRIAA (2007) 379.

[175] Bedjaoui, 'La "Descente"', 8–9.

[176] Statute of the International Court of Justice, Article 66. Watts, 'Burden of proof', 301; Riddell and Plant, *Evidence*, p. 67.

In the *Gabčíkovo-Nagymaros* case, following an invitation by Slovakia, and Hungary's expression of co-operation, arrangements were made for a site visit in a Protocol of Agreement concluded between the parties and supplemented by Agreed Minutes.[177] Conscious that the harmful effects of the dam project on the groundwater and acquifers would not be apparent from a visual inspection nor so soon after the river's diversion, Hungary sought to condition the Court to this in advance.[178] The Court was in the area for four days between the first and second rounds of oral proceedings, visiting locations on the Danube and taking note of 'technical explanations given by the representatives who had been designated for the purpose by the parties'.[179] This site visit gave the Court the opportunity to deepen its understanding of the system of locks being constructed on the Danube. The International Court of Justice had not previously conducted a site visit, although the Permanent Court of International Justice carried out a three-day visit in the *Case concerning Diversion of Water from the Meuse (Netherlands* v. *Belgium)*, hearing technical explanations on site and seeing practical demonstrations of the locks and installations.[180] No site visit was made in the *Case concerning Pulp Mills*.[181] In the *Corfu Channel* case it was the Court's experts who made a site inspection, between the two rounds of oral pleadings in the case, which included inspecting the vessel alleged to have laid the mines in the Corfu Channel and conducting night-time observation tests with a blacked-out vessel from Albanian lookout points.[182]

[177] *Case concerning the Gabčíkovo-Nagymaros Project (Hungary/Slovakia)*, Order of 5 February 1997, ICJ Reports 1997 3, 5.

[178] *Gabčíkovo-Nagymaros* case, Verbatim Record, Friday 7 March, 70–1 and translation, 52–3.

[179] *Case concerning the Gabčíkovo-Nagymaros Project (Hungary/Slovakia)*, Judgment of 25 September 1997 ICJ Reports 1997 7 (hereafter *Gabčíkovo-Nagymaros* case), para. 10.

[180] *Diversion of Water from the Meuse (Netherlands* v. *Belgium)*, Judgment of 28 June 1927, PCIJ Series A/B, No. 70, 9. On the documentation of the visit, see Bedjaoui, 'La "Descente"', 19.

[181] This was regretted by Judge Cançado Trindade in his Separate Opinion, para. 151.

[182] See below, pp. 110–13. Consider also the wide-ranging enquiries conducted in the *Behring Fur-Seals* case. *Behring Fur-Seal Arbitration (Great Britain/United States of America)*, 1893 1 Moore International Arbitrations 945. For a more recent example, although a maritime boundary arbitration, consider the visit to the site in the *Guyana* v. *Suriname* arbitration under Annex VII of the United Nations Convention on the Law of the Sea. This visit was made by the Tribunal's hydrographer, Dr Gray, accompanied by party representatives and a Tribunal registry official. Award of the Arbitral Tribunal Constituted Pursuant to Article 287, and in Accordance with Annex VII, of the United Nations Convention on the Law of the Sea, 17 September 2007; Tribunal Hydrographer's Site Visit Report, 30 July 2007, both available at www.pca-cpa.org.

During the site visit in the *Gabčíkovo-Nagymaros* case, on-site technical presentations were made by representatives of the respective parties, and the Court asked questions, although pleading was precluded. In practice this 'led, at times, to an interchange of views with an immediacy of response that can rarely have been seen before the Court'.[183] In the second round of oral pleadings, following the visit, the parties responded further to the Court's questions,[184] as well as referring at various points to what the Court had seen. One of Hungary's advocates, scientist Dr Carbiener, made a presentation on the lessons learnt from the visit.[185] Given the mass of scientific evidence in this case, the opportunity for the Court to ground its appreciation of the issues by visiting the site has been described as '*incomparablement utile*'.[186] Yet it must also be taken into account that in this case much of the real environmental damage was invisible, and will take time to manifest itself.

The court-appointed expert

In addition to hearing party-appointed experts a court or tribunal itself may also appoint experts to provide input into its work. Appointment of experts by international tribunals is an accepted practice, owing its status perhaps partly to civil law traditions in the appointment of experts as judicial auxiliaries.[187] Tribunals' statutes and rules of procedure frequently set out their powers to appoint independent experts.[188] Article 50 of the Statute of the International Court of Justice, which replicates Article 50 of the Statute of the Permanent Court of International Justice, provides an example,[189] providing that 'The Court may, at any time, entrust any individual, body, bureau, commission or other organization that it may select, with the task of carrying out an enquiry or giving an expert opinion.' The provision is thought to have been inspired by Article 90 of the 1907 Hague

[183] Tomka and Wordsworth, 'The first site visit', p. 139. See also Thouvenin, 'La Descente'.
[184] *Gabčíkovo-Nagymaros* case, Verbatim Record, Thursday 10 April 1997, 11.
[185] *Gabčíkovo-Nagymaros* case, Verbatim Record, Friday 11 April, 57–61.
[186] Bedjaoui, 'La "Descente"', at 21.
[187] Allison and Holtzmann, 'The Tribunal's use of experts', 281; Jolowicz, *On Civil Procedure*, pp. 230–1, 234.
[188] Brown, *A Common Law*, pp. 114–15. White, *The Use of Experts*, p. 75. Indeed, both authors consider tribunals may have inherent powers to appoint experts. *Ibid.*, pp. 28–9, 73–9; Brown, *A Common Law*, p. 115; Tams, 'Article 50', 1110.
[189] See also Rules of Court of the International Court of Justice, Articles 51 and 67. For commentary, Rosenne, *The Law and Practice*, pp. 1116–17, 1325–32.

Convention for the Pacific Settlement of International Disputes.[190] The UNCITRAL Rules[191] and the Iran–US Claims Tribunal Rules[192] also provide for the reference of technical issues to independent experts appointed by a tribunal, and the Iran–US Claims Tribunal has made use of independent experts in a number of cases.[193] The procedure followed by the expert is reminiscent of French procedures in certain respects, including the provision in Article 27(2) of the Tribunal Rules for experts to invite party representatives to attend any site inspection that might be made by the expert. Provisions regarding expert evidence are often quite precise in the case of those specialised tribunals dealing with subjects that are likely to raise technical or scientific issues. Article 289 of the LOSC provides that:

> In any dispute involving scientific or technical matters, a court or tribunal exercising jurisdiction under this section may, at the request of a party or proprio motu, select in consultation with the parties no fewer than two scientific or technical experts chosen preferably from the relevant list prepared in accordance with Annex VIII, article 2, to sit with the court or tribunal but without the right to vote.[194]

Provision for the appointment of experts is additionally found in the rules of international administrative tribunals,[195] and experts have been appointed in a number of cases.[196] The North American Free Trade Agreement envisages the consultation of experts by panels at the request of a disputing party or on their own initiative provided the parties agree.[197] Panels may also, unless the parties disapprove, request a 'written report of a scientific review board on any factual issue concerning environmental,

190 White, *The Use of Experts*, p. 36.

191 UNCITRAL Arbitration Rules 1976, Article 27. On practice under the UNCITRAL Rules, and also the International Chamber of Commerce Arbitration Rules, see Eijsvoogel, *Evidence*, p. 22; Sanders, 'Commentary'.

192 Iran–United States Claims Tribunal Final Rules of Procedure, 3 May 1983, 1 Iran–US CTR 57 (hereafter Iran–United States Claims Tribunal Rules of Procedure), Article 27.

193 Amerasinghe, *Evidence*, pp. 156 and 396.

194 Articles 15, 77, 79, 82, and 83 of the Rules of Procedure of ITLOS provide in further detail for the Tribunal's consultation of experts. Rules of the International Tribunal for the Law of the Sea, www.itlos.org. The power of arbitral tribunals constituted under Annex VII of the Convention to consult experts is also specifically recognised in Article 6 of Annex VII. See also Permanent Court of Arbitration Optional Rules for Arbitrating Disputes Relating to Natural Resources and/or the Environment, www.pca-cpa.org, Article 27.

195 Amerasinghe, *Evidence*, p. 306.

196 *Ibid.*, 307 ff.

197 North American Free Trade Agreement, San Antonio, 17 December 1992, 32 ILM 289, 605, in force 1 January 1994, Chapter Twenty, Article 2014.

health, safety or other scientific matters raised by a disputing Party in a proceeding'.[198] The European Courts' Statutes and Rules of Procedure set out the Courts' power to commission expert advice, though this is less common in the European Courts than elsewhere.[199] However, in the European Court of Justice it is expected as a matter of course that the Court will take an active role.[200] The power to appoint experts may also be regarded as an inherent power of international courts and tribunals.[201]

The power to appoint experts at its own initiative was used only once by the Permanent Court of International Justice, in the *Case concerning the Factory at Chorzów*,[202] and has been used only in one case in the International Court of Justice, in the *Corfu Channel* case.[203] A Commission of Experts was tasked with making an independent study of the facts in dispute between the parties in this case and was asked to prepare a report dealing with the likelihood of Albanian knowledge of the minelaying in the Corfu Channel.[204] Following the delivery of the report, Albania complained of gaps in the report and further information was obtained from the Yugoslav government, with the experts also carrying out a site visit to Sibenik and Saranda.[205] When

198 *Ibid.*, Article 2015 (1). Model Rules of Procedure for Chapter Twenty of the North American Free Trade Agreement, www.nafta-sec-alena.org, Rules 38 to 48.

199 Plender, 'Procedure in the European Court', 154; Lasok, *Law and Institutions*, p. 297.

200 MacLennan, 'Evidence', 268; Lasok, *The European Court*, pp. 422, 423. Where significant evidence lies within the possession of one party, that party may, however, be allocated a burden with respect to its production. Brealey, 'The burden of proof', 260. It is accepted that there may be a proof-taking stage between the written and oral proceedings, with a judge-rapporteur designated by the President to conduct these proceedings. Lasok, *Law and Institutions*, pp. 293–4. Greater use of experts appointed by the Luxembourg courts has been advocated for scientific cases. MacLennan, 'Evidence', 283–8.

201 Amerasinghe, *Evidence*, p. 306. White, *The Use of Experts*, pp. 73–6.

202 *Case concerning the Factory at Chorzów (Germany* v. *Poland) (Claim for Indemnity – Merits)* (1928) PCIJ Series A, No. 13, para. 8 and Order of 13 September 1928, Permanent Court of International Justice Series A, No. 17. Sandifer, *Evidence*, p. 333. A Commission of Experts was appointed to estimate indemnity due to Germany in respect of Polish possession of the factory at Chorzów. However the Commission was dissolved when the case was settled.

203 Riddell and Plant, *Evidence*, pp. 62–6; *Corfu Channel case (United Kingdom* v. *Albania)*, Order of 17 December 1948, ICJ Reports 1947–1948 124. For the use also of expert evidence in assessing compensation in this case, see the Order of 19 November, 1949 ICJ Reports 1949 237.

204 *Corfu Channel case (United Kingdom* v. *Albania)*, ICJ Reports 1949 2 (hereafter *Corfu Channel* case), 142, Annex 2, Experts' Report of 8 January 1949.

205 *Corfu Channel* case, 151, Decision of the Court, dated 17 January 1949, regarding an Enquiry on the Spot.

the Commission's second report was presented,[206] an additional short hearing was held and the experts were asked to respond to questions from members of the Court.[207] The Court accorded 'great weight' to the experts' opinion, considering their examination at the locality to have been carried out in such a way as to guarantee that their information was correct and impartial.[208]

Subsequent requests for the Court to appoint experts have been declined.[209] In the past, many of the cases coming before the Court may not have required the consultation of independent experts. However, at this point in history, it would seem that 'the tide has turned in favor of increased numbers of disputes in which the determination of the facts [is] important'.[210] In order to deal effectively with such cases, particularly those where scientific uncertainties are involved, hesitance will need to be overcome. The appointment of an independent expert may be particularly helpful for an international court or tribunal where the evidence presented by the parties' own experts conflicts.[211] It will have to be accepted, as it is in the WTO, that a certain delay will be engendered. Many individual judges have recorded their encouragement for the Court's potential appointment of its own experts.[212]

The question whether the Court should appoint independent experts divided the Court in the *Case concerning Pulp Mills*. The majority of the Court did not find this necessary, and was prepared to weigh and evaluate the data before it without assistance in order to determine whether Uruguay had breached its obligations under the Statute of the River Uruguay.[213] Judge Kenneth Keith explained in his Separate

[206] *Corfu Channel* case, 152, Experts' Report dated 8 February 1949, on the Investigations and Tests at Siberisk and Saranda.

[207] *Corfu Channel* case, 163, Questions put by three Members of the Court on 10 February 1949. The experts replied subsequently. *Corfu Channel* case, 165, Experts' Replies, dated 12 February 1949, to Questions put by Three Members of the Court; White, *The Use of Experts*, p. 112. For a description of the procedures that were followed, Rosenne, *The Law and Practice*, pp. 1326–36.

[208] *Corfu Channel* case, 22.

[209] Rosenne, *The Law and Practice*, pp. 1329–30, discussing the requests put to the Court in Application for Revision and Interpretation of the Judgment of 24 February 1982 in the *Case concerning the Continental Shelf (Tunisia/Libyan Arab Jamahiriya) (Tunisia* v. *Libyan Arab Jamahiriya)*, Judgment of 10 December 1985, ICJ Reports 1985 192, 228; *Case concerning the Land, Island and Maritime Frontier Dispute (El Salvador/Honduras: Nicaragua intervening)*, Judgment of 11 September 1992, ICJ Reports 1992 350, 351, 361, 400.

[210] Riddell and Plant, *Evidence*, p. 310.

[211] *Ibid.*, p. 339, see also at 419 where Riddell and Plant recommend a greater use of the powers of the ICJ to obtain the testimony of court-appointed experts.

[212] *Ibid.*, p. 334.

[213] *Case concerning Pulp Mills*, para. 236.

Opinion that the Court saw the task in this case as 'assessing, by reference to the raw data, the impact of the operation of the plant on the water quality'.[214] He commended the parties for providing additional scientific and technical data during the hearings, supplementing the data provided previously and in the course of their prior provisional measures requests.[215] This data was important as the Botnia plant had only begun operations approximately three months before Argentina had had to file its Reply.[216] Particularly helpful was an Argentinian scientific and technical report summarising the research done by the National Universities of La Plata and Buenos Aires during the first eighteen months of the plant's operation.[217] On the basis of the data before it, the Court made a series of factual findings to the effect that Argentina had not established a case that the mill's operation had affected water quality. The Court considered whether effluent discharges were within the regulatory limits,[218] and the impact of the discharges on water quality and biodiversity,[219] including with respect to the effects of dissolved oxygen,[220] phosphorus,[221] phenolic substances,[222] nonylphenols,[223] and dioxins and furans.[224] However a number of the judges were dissatisfied with the Court's decision not to take further steps to investigate the scientific issues before it. Judge Al-Khasawneh, Judge Simma, Judge Yusuf, Judge Cançado Trindade and Judge ad hoc Vinuesa considered that the Court should have taken a markedly more proactive role and appointed independent experts to assist it.[225] The Joint Dissenting Opinion of Judges Al-Khasawneh and Simma manifested these concerns in the strongest terms. They considered that the Court had 'omitted to resort to the possibilities provided by its Statute and thus simply has not done what would have been necessary in order to arrive at a basis for the application of the law to the facts as scientifically certain as is possible in a judicial proceeding'.[226]

There are occasions where the views of experts have great weight with a tribunal, as explicitly acknowledged by the International Court

[214] *Ibid.*, Separate Opinion of Judge Keith, para. 8. See also Separate Opinion of Judge Greenwood, para. 24.

[215] *Ibid.*, para. 3. [216] *Ibid.* [217] *Ibid.*, para. 4. See also above, p. 85.

[218] *Case concerning Pulp Mills*, paras. 227–8. [219] *Ibid.*, paras. 229–62.

[220] *Ibid.*, paras. 238–9. [221] *Ibid.*, paras. 240–50. [222] *Ibid.*, paras. 251–4.

[223] *Ibid.*, paras. 255–7. [224] *Ibid.*, paras. 258–9.

[225] *Ibid.*, Joint Dissenting Opinion of Judges Al-Khasawneh and Judge Simma, Declaration of Judge Yusuf, Separate Opinion of Judge Cançado Trindade, Dissenting Opinion of Judge ad hoc Vinuesa.

[226] *Ibid.*, para. 2.

of Justice in respect of the experts' report in the *Corfu Channel* case.[227] Further, experts are sometimes proactive in their relationship with tribunals, and this is not inconsistent with experts' basic function. In the United Nations Compensation Commission Category 'C' Claims procedures, for example, the panel of psychological and other experts appointed to assist the Commission in matters concerning compensation for mental pain and anguish criticised the ceilings which had been set for compensation by the Governing Council of the Commission.[228]

Both party-appointed and tribunal-appointed experts have been used simultaneously in international cases, as in the *Corfu Channel* case.[229] In WTO cases involving scientific experts, such as *European Communities – Measures Concerning Meat and Meat Products (Hormones)*,[230] both tribunal-appointed and party-appointed experts have participated in joint meetings with experts, in their different capacities. In *EC – Hormones* the active contribution to discussion of the nine scientific experts on the EC delegation added a distinctive dimension. The EC experts spoke with authority and in some instances made discursive explanatory interjections, whereas the experts on the Canadian and US delegations hardly participated in recorded discussion at all. Delegation experts were not examined by the representatives of the parties. However, the Panel heard the views of its own experts on the opinions of the EC experts.[231] In the *Continued Suspension of Obligations* cases the Panel invited the participation of the parties' experts in its joint meeting with experts. The EC brought in seven experts, four of whom made interventions of some substance,

[227] *Corfu Channel* case, 22. The Court rejected Albanian complaints that the experts had exceeded their mandate in interpreting their own findings of fact, and it is clear from the judgment that the Court made its own findings. *Corfu Channel (United Kingdom of Great Britain and Northern Ireland* v. *Albania)*, ICJ Pleadings, vol. 5, 115; White, *The Use of Experts*, p. 180.

[228] *UNCC Expert Report Category 'C' Claims (First Instalment)*, 2 September 1994, 109 ILR 205, Annex VI, Expert Report on Mental Pain and Anguish, 436. Reference might be made also the case of *Loayza Tamayo* v. *Peru*, in which the IACHR relied on the diagnosis of a court-appointed expert that the victim suffered from post-traumatic stress syndrome as a result of her systematic torture and rape. *Loayza Tamayo* v. *Peru* (Reparations) (1998) 42 Inter-Am. Ct. H.R. (Ser. C), paras. 74–6.

[229] Alford, 'Fact finding by the World Court', 361.

[230] *EC – Hormones*, Complaint by Canada, PR; Complaint by the US, PR.

[231] Annex, Transcript of the Joint Meeting with Experts, attached to the panel reports in both the complaint by Canada and the complaint by the US (hereafter *EC – Hormones* JM), paras. 315–16, 319, 718, 719. See also, for example, *Japan – Measures Affecting Agricultural Products*, Complaint by the United States (WT/DS76), Report of the Panel DSR 1999: I, 315 (hereafter *Japan – Agricultural Products* PR), paras. 10.87, 10.257; and *EC – Asbestos* JM, 359.

occasionally to the consternation of Canada.[232] Both party-appointed and tribunal-appointed expert witnesses are used in cases under the Convention on the Settlement of Investment Disputes between States and Nationals of other States (the ICSID Convention).[233]

The WTO system for expert evidence

A significant development in the taking of scientific evidence by international courts and tribunals is the system that has developed in the WTO. The WTO system for taking expert evidence was devised as a response to the needs of the dispute resolution process in cases involving complex scientific questions.[234] The system was not specifically envisaged in the WTO Dispute Settlement Understanding (DSU),[235] but rather was developed by panels to meet their needs, taking into account the relevant provisions of the DSU. For panels, the divisions of the secretariat who assist them, and the parties in the early cases it was a matter of 'learning by doing'. The system that hasevolved is presently a 'de facto standard procedure' in the WTO.[236] In cases where expert advice will be needed, a panel will adopt the necessary working procedures. Yet each case is dealt with independently and the procedures commonly used could be altered by a panel at any time.

The consultation of tribunal-appointed scientific experts by WTO panels may take place even where the parties have not so requested,[237] or the parties do not agree that this is necessary.[238] Between three and six experts have been appointed in each case. A consultation process with two stages has been developed. In the written phase of the consultation a list of written questions is submitted to the experts, and each

[232] *Canada - Continued Suspension* JM, e.g. paras. 252–7, 1056–7.

[233] Convention for the Settlement of Investment Disputes between States and Nationals of other States, Washington, 18 March 1965, in force 14 October 1966, 575 UNTS 159, Schreuer, *The ICSID Convention*, p. 665.

[234] Grando notes that experts have been used exceedingly rarely in other types of case, for example translation experts were appointed by the panel in *Japan - Measures Affecting Consumer Photographic Film and Paper* Complaint by the United States (WT/DS44), Report of the Panel, DSR 1998: IV, 1179. Grando, *Evidence*, p. 342.

[235] Understanding on Rules and Procedures Governing the Settlement of Disputes, WTO, *The Legal Texts: The results of the Uruguay round of multilateral trade negotiations*, p. 354.

[236] Conversation with WTO practitioner, Geneva, 2007.

[237] *United States - Import Prohibition of Certain Shrimp and Shrimp Products*, Complaint by India (WT/DS58), Complaint by Malaysia (WT/DS58), Complaint by Pakistan (WT/DS58), Complaint by Thailand (WT/DS58), Report of the Panel DSR 1998: VII, 2821 (hereafter *US - Shrimp* PR), paras. 7.52, 7.55. 5.1.

[238] *EC - Biotech* PR, para. 7.16.

expert is asked to respond in writing to those questions corresponding to his or her area of expertise. The parties are asked for suggestions for written questions to be put to the experts. In *European Communities – Approval and Marketing of Biotech Products* the EC identified a number of scientific and technical questions that the Panel might put to the experts, including on the state of scientific understanding on the adverse consequences of genetically modified organisms.[239]

Should they wish to do so, parties to WTO proceedings are free to submit written comments on the replies received from the experts. In *EC – Biotech*, for example, lengthy comments were received from all four parties.[240] Where necessary, additional written questions may be sent to the experts, with the parties given the chance to comment again.[241] The parties will also be given an opportunity to comment on one another's comments, and all of the parties' comments will be provided to all of the experts.[242] A summary or compilation of the experts' written answers may be prepared by staff from the WTO secretariat and reviewed by the experts to ensure it is correct.[243] The experts' written answers have been incorporated in panels' reports in compiled form. The Panel may send sections of its report dealing with the factual aspects of a case to the experts for confirmation that they reflect accurately the scientific evidence and the experts' opinions.[244]

The second phase consists of an oral consultation or 'joint meeting'. Joint meetings with experts are generally held between the two substantive meetings between a panel and the parties, i.e. the two rounds of hearings, frequently immediately preceding the second substantive meeting.[245] The joint meetings take place over a one- to two-day period,

239 *Ibid.*, Annex C, Replies by the Parties to Questions posed by the Panel on 3 June 2004, paras. 52–7.

240 *EC – Biotech* PR, Annex I, Comments by the Parties on the Replies by the Scientific Experts to the Questions posed by the Panel.

241 See e.g. *EC – Biotech* PR, para. 7.29.

242 See e.g. *ibid.*, para. 7.29.

243 *Continued Suspension* JM, para. 49.

244 This additional step was taken in *Japan – Agricultural Products*. The experts' confirmations raised only a couple of points, and were provided to the parties at the same time as the Panel's interim report. *Japan – Agricultural Products* PR, paras. 6.116–6.119. The Panel also sent to the experts for their comments a draft of those parts of the draft Panel report which concerned the possibility of testing for differences in sorption instead of conducting the variety by variety tests being used by Japan, before the Panel issued its interim report. *Ibid.*, para. 8.74.

245 As one Panel recorded, 'the meeting with experts advising the Panel took place the day before the second substantive meeting so parties could incorporate in their rebuttal statements, comments and conclusions drawn from the scientific evidence'. *Australia – Measures Affecting Importation of Salmon*, Complaint by Canada (WT/DS18), Report of the Panel DSR 1998: VIII, 3407 (hereafter *Australia – Salmon*), para. 8.2.

and are attended by the panel, its experts, the parties and their experts. A copy of the transcript of the joint meeting is checked by the experts for accuracy and incorporated in the panel's report, as well as a copy of the experts' responses to the panel's questions and the parties' comments on the written consultation and on one another's comments.

The time available at a joint meeting is in practice apportioned depending on the needs presenting themselves. Time constraints make imperative a close focus on garnering information on key points from the experts, and learning from them as much as possible about the scientific subject matter of the dispute. Experience suggests that a good deal of ground can be covered if the meeting is chaired skilfully and flexibly. In *US – Shrimp*, the first case where a joint meeting was held, the chair interceded from time to time to steer the discussion in directions the Panel might find helpful,[246] and to help ensure the best use was made of the short time available.[247] The pattern that has developed in joint meetings is as follows. First, there are introductory statements by the experts. They may be given an opportunity to outline the main differences between their own views and those of their colleagues, and put forward their primary arguments. They are usually invited also to react to the parties' comments on their written responses to the Panel's questions. Then discussion will begin on the substantive issues. Dealing with distinct topics one by one has proved a helpful way to proceed.[248] As the Chair explained in *Australia – Measures Affecting Importation of Salmon*, 'so that we do not subsequently crisscross backwards and forwards between the subjects – if we get into a subject let us deal with it and dispose of it'.[249]

An extensive but moderated discussion of the scientific issues has been encouraged. In *Australia – Salmon*, for example, the Chair emphasised that it was really up to the experts how they responded to parties' questions. In his experience past proceedings had been very satisfactorily conducted. He noted:

> this is not an interrogation or court of law, they should feel relaxed about it and obviously offer their expertise as they see fit.[250]

[246] *US – Shrimp* PR, Annex IV, Transcript of the Joint Meeting with Experts (hereafter *US – Shrimp* JM), paras. 25, 34, 54, 119, 167.

[247] *Ibid.*, paras. 164, 175–9, 181.

[248] *Continued Suspension* JM, para. 44.

[249] *Australia – Salmon* PR, Annex 2, Transcript of the Joint Meeting with Experts (hereafter *Australia – Salmon* JM), para. 7.

[250] *Ibid.*, 7.

In *EC – Hormones*, the Chair made it clear that the consultation process was not intended to elicit consensus[251] or to put a deal together.[252] The purpose of the joint meeting was described as an opportunity for the experts to expand upon their written answers to the Panel's written questions and answer further questions, and for views to be challenged.[253]

The floor is given to the parties in turn. The parties may follow up any points made by the experts during the written stage of consultations, and any points they make in the course of the joint meetings. The experts generally answer the parties' questions at some length. Written questions or comments may be submitted to the experts for oral answer during the meeting by parties or the panel.[254]

Members of the panel are most often silent during joint meetings, leaving it to the Chair to ensure all necessary points are covered.[255] At the end of joint meetings, panels will take the opportunity to ask for clarification from the experts on any points that may remain unclear. The panel-appointed experts are invited to make closing statements to emphasise the points they consider most important. Transcripts of the meetings are prepared, circulated and included in panels' reports. Providing experts with the opportunity to read and comment upon transcripts of their evidence before they are finalised provides a safeguard in respect of their accuracy and completeness.[256] In some reports bibliographical information is included.[257]

No true cross-examination is involved in WTO 'joint meetings', although there is something of the cross-examination style in some of the parties' questions. For example, in *US – Shrimp* the US was the party showing most readiness to put questions to the experts orally. US participation in the joint meeting with experts included rhetorical

[251] *EC – Hormones*, Complaint by Canada, PR, para. 8.9; Complaint by the US, PR, para. 8.9.

[252] *EC – Hormones* JM, paras. 45, 241, 808; *EC – Hormones*, Complaint by Canada, PR, para. 8.9; Complaint by the US, PR, para. 8.9. To save time, the experts were advised that they did not need to take the floor where they agreed with a point made by another expert.

[253] *EC – Hormones* JM, para. 1.

[254] See e.g. *Australia – Salmon* JM, paras. 140, 220, 222.

[255] See e.g. *Australia – Salmon* JM, paras. 276, 289; *Canada – Continued Suspension* JM, paras. 626, 647, 656, 659, 663, 805, 807, 869.

[256] This practice has also been adopted elsewhere. In the *Corfu Channel* case transcripts were made available immediately for the parties' witnesses to correct in accordance with the Rules of the Court.

[257] For example, in *US – Shrimp* the scientific evidence included in the annexure of the Panel report includes a list of literature cited by the experts and two background papers by one of them.

questioning, a focus on the detail of comments made by particular experts, reductionism, and the use of imagery.[258] The US was also the more active participant in the joint meeting in *Japan – Measures Affecting the Importation of Apples*.[259] In *EC – Hormones*, US questioning was likewise directed to establishing clearly a number of propositions on which the US case was built.[260] In *EC – Biotech* Canada pursued a line of questions intended to show that there was discrimination in respect of genetically modified crops compared with modified crops produced through conventional breeding.[261] Pleading is not generally permitted during the joint meetings, but may resume at the subsequent substantive meeting after the experts are discharged.[262] Certainly, although the experts are appointed and consulted by panels, in practice the major part of joint meetings is given over to the questioning of the independent experts by the parties.

Conducting a written consultation in advance of holding a meeting or hearing with experts appears to lay the groundwork well for such an oral session. The bulk of the technical and scientific information pertinent to a case can be recorded in the course of the written consultation. This means that at the hearing adjudicators and litigants can focus on making sure that key points are understood and the way the experts' advice fits into the overall context of the case is clear.

Although the primary purpose of the joint meeting with experts is for a panel to listen to the input of the panel-appointed experts, disputing parties' own scientific experts also have a role in the meeting. The disputants' legal representatives may find it helpful to have their scientific advisers at hand in the room with them for whispered consultation on points arising in the course of the meeting. As determined within each delegation, party-appointed experts may also make occasional interventions addressing some of the more sophisticated scientific issues arising.[263]

258 *US – Shrimp* JM, paras. 96–101.

259 *Japan – Measures Affecting the Importation of Apples*, Complaint by the United States (WT/DS245), Report of the Panel DSR 2003: IX, 4481, Annex 3, Transcript of the Joint Meeting with Experts.

260 *EC – Hormones* JM, paras. 241, 242, 245, 246.

261 *EC – Biotech* PR, Annex J, Transcript of the Joint Meeting with Experts, paras. 121–65, 381–95, 474, 500–77, 623, 710, 716, 723.

262 See e.g. *EC – Hormones* JM, para. 344; *Australia – Salmon* JM, para. 8, but also at 77; *Japan – Agricultural Products* JM, paras. 10.87, 10.100.

263 See above, pp. 113–14.

The evolution of a system for expert consultation with a strong oral phase and an unscripted dynamic is particularly noteworthy in a forum where the parties have traditionally relied predominantly on their written submissions as the way to communicate their arguments and evidence to a panel. The chief benefit of oral consultation with experts is the scope it provides for explanation of the concepts, methods and principles that underlie scientific arguments. In nearly all cases this is invaluable for improving the overall level of understanding of technical issues for all participants in a case, on both sides of the bench. Views on the science can be tested against one another. Different topics can be addressed in their entirety, eliminating to some extent the need to move back and forth between issues that is likely to characterise any procedure where experts take the stand in isolation and in succession. At the second substantive hearing following the joint meeting with experts, the parties may comment on the joint meeting, drawing from the experts' remarks those points most pertinent to their cases.[264]

WTO panels' procedures for taking expert advice are still evolving. For example, in the *EC – Biotech* case, procedures were put in place for protecting strictly confidential information because of commercial sensitivities in the EC.[265] Some regard the periods of time dedicated to meetings with experts as adequate, while others consider that a one- or two-day meeting over-compresses proceedings.[266] There are also disadvantages to the informal way joint meetings have been conducted. In *EC – Hormones* an expert commented at one stage that 'we are responding somewhat on the fly'.[267] Questions to experts sometimes elicited answers that covered only half an issue, and it could be difficult to tell when an expert was speaking from extensive knowledge of a matter and when he or she was speaking from a less profound knowledge base. There has been a suggestion that experts need to avoid 'back of the envelope' calculations, as a mere guess by an expert may carry

[264] See e.g. the Second Oral Statement of the European Communities on the Meeting with Experts and Additional Scientific Evidence in *EC – Biotech* PR, paras. 4.1094–4.1120.

[265] *EC – Biotech* PR, para. 7.43, footnote 233.

[266] For example, in contrast, the hearing of the parties' witnesses in the *Corfu Channel* case ran for a three-week period, from 22 November to 14 December 1948.

[267] *EC – Hormones* JM, para. 227. For example, the discussion introduced by the EC on the sensitivity of adolescent sectors of the population to growth-promotion hormones led to a divergent series of what seemed to be quite rough calculations of adolescents' likely hormonal residue excesses, based on the generalisation that the diet of American children consisted of two 'Whopper' hamburgers a day. *Ibid.*, paras. 234–98, see also 269.

disproportionate weight with a panel.[268] The view expressed by one expert in *EC – Hormones* that use of growth-promotion hormones in cattle could cause cancer for up to one individual in every million consumers provides an example.[269]

An additional particularity of the WTO dispute resolution system is the interim review stage of panels' proceedings, required under Article 15 of the DSU. Prior to the interim review stage, the factual and descriptive sections of panels' reports are circulated for written comment. Following this, panels' interim reports are submitted to the parties *in toto*, and the parties may submit written requests for review of precise aspects of these reports, and indeed there is provision for requiring a meeting to be held between the panel and the parties to discuss such issues if necessary.[270] The parties' opportunity to comment on and correct questions of fact at the interim review stage is important, as errors of fact cannot be addressed on appeal.[271] However, in scientific disputes there may be time pressures. In the *Continued Suspension of Obligations* cases the EC said it was not possible in the time available to indicate all the Panel's alleged errors and omissions on the scientific issues underpinning the dispute.[272]

The availability of technology and pressure to make the inner workings of the WTO more transparent have also led to innovation. In the *Continued Suspension of Obligations* cases it was decided for the first time, at the parties' request, that the panel's meetings with the parties would be held as open sessions, which the public would be free to observe on closed-circuit television.[273] There was a concern that the dynamics of a joint meeting with experts might alter when it was accorded such transparency. In the past, the confidential nature of panel meetings has meant that panels have sought advice from experts in a closed

[268] Pauwelyn, 'Expert advice', 248.

[269] *Ibid.*, 248. See the recurrence of this idea in the *Continued Suspension of Obligations* cases, JM, paras. 726–8.

[270] Dispute Settlement Understanding, Article 15.

[271] Article 17.6 of the DSU provides that '[a]n appeal shall be limited to issues of law covered in the panel report and legal interpretations developed by the panel'. Thus the Appellate Body has no power to make findings of fact, although factual issues could be addressed indirectly if the Appellate Body found that a panel had failed to make an objective assessment of the facts as required under Article 11 of the DSU.

[272] *Canada – Continued Suspension* PR, para. 6.12; *US – Continued Suspension* PR, para. 6.13. The Panel regretted the EC's approach. *Canada – Continued Suspension* PR, para. 6.15; *US – Continued Suspension* PR, para. 6.16.

[273] *Canada – Continued Suspension* PR, Annex A-2 Working Procedures for the Panel, para. 2; *US – Continued Suspension* PR, Annex A-2 Working Procedures for the Panel, para. 2.

setting, where a collegial atmosphere prevails. The consultation process has been amicable and productive. There was also a concern that the manner in which the disputants' advocates addressed the experts might be influenced by a pressure to play to certain of the advocates' domestic constituencies. These anxieties have proved largely unfounded. Nor has attendance at the television broadcasts been high, although third parties to the disputes have attended with relative consistency. This procedure has been followed subsequently, in *Australia - Measures Affecting the Importation of Apples from New Zealand*.[274]

WTO panels have relied on experts' advice in determining the issues before them. For example, the *EC - Hormones* Panel relied on the advice of its experts in determining the comparability of risks from growth-promotion hormones with risks from hormones occurring endogenously in foods and risks from hormones administered for therapeutic and zootechnical purposes. To take a further example, the WTO panel that dealt with the *Continued Suspension of Obligations* cases was clearly reliant on its appointed experts' advice.[275] If the Panel had not been overruled by the Appellate Body, the points in relation to which the Panel relied on expert evidence would have been dispositive of the overall case. Although subsequently overruled, the Panel found that the EC had failed to base its sanitary and phytosanitary measures on a risk assessment in accordance with Article 5.1 of the WTO Agreement on Sanitary and Phytosanitary Measures (SPS Agreement),[276] and that the EC could not rely on the provision in Article 5.7 allowing temporary measures without a risk assessment. Therefore the Panel determined that the EC had failed to establish the respondents' breach of Article 22.8 of the Dispute Settlement Understanding (DSU) and thus of Article 23.1 of the DSU.[277] In reaching the conclusion that the EC had failed to

[274] *Australia - Measures Affecting the Importation of Apples from New Zealand*, Complaint by New Zealand, DS 367.

[275] *Canada - Continued Suspension of Obligations in the EC - Hormones Dispute*, Complaint by the EC (WT/DS321) Report of the Panel, Report of the Appellate Body, adopted 14 November 2008; *US - Continued Suspension of Obligations in the EC - Hormones Dispute*, Complaint by the EC (WT/DS320), Report of the Panel, Report of the Appellate Body, adopted 14 November 2008 (hereafter respectively *Canada - Continued Suspension* PR, *US - Continued Suspension* PR, and, referring to the identical paragraphs of the two Appellate Body reports, *Continued Suspension* ABR).

[276] Agreement on the Application of Sanitary and Phytosanitary Measures, WTO, *The Legal Texts: The results of the Uruguay round of multilateral trade negotiations*, p. 59.

[277] Article 22.8 of the DSU states that a suspension of concessions or other obligations shall be temporary and shall only be applied until such time as a measure found to be inconsistent with a covered agreement has been removed. Article 23.1 requires a

comply with Article 5.1 in relation to oestradiol-17ß the Panel summarised and relied on the views of the experts on whether the EC's internal opinions had identified the potential for adverse effects on human health and the extent to which the opinions evaluated the potential occurrence of these effects.[278] At the same time, the Panel made it clear that it had itself 'examined and evaluated the evidence', which included the information it had received both from the experts and from the parties' submissions.[279] Yet the Panel did rely on the experts' input. When it came to the applicability of Article 5.7 the Panel drew heavily on the experts' advice.[280] At the same time, this was done explicitly within a framework designed to limit the Panel's analysis to issues and explanations advanced by the parties, in order to avoid 'making a case' for either party in light of the remarks of the Appellate Body in *Japan – Measures Concerning Agricultural Products*,[281] discussed further below. Yet, again, the Panel did rely on the experts' input.

Interestingly, the Appellate Body reversed the Panel's findings in relation to Articles 5.1 and 5.7, because in its view the Panel had applied the wrong legal tests when it made use of expert testimony.[282] The Appellate Body found that the purpose of a panel's consultation with experts in relation to Article 5.1 was not to test 'whether the panel-appointed experts would have done a risk assessment in the same way as a disputant', and reached the same conclusions.[283] The purpose was to help the panel verify 'that a risk assessment was supported by coherent reasoning and respectable scientific evidence, and in this sense was objectively justifiable'.[284] The Panel had overstepped the mark by

member seeking redress of a violation of obligations under the covered agreements to have recourse to the rules and procedures of the DSU. The EC's reasoning was that, as the EC had brought itself into compliance with the SPS Agreement, the respondents' suspension of their obligations to the EC had to be lifted in accordance with Article 22.8. In continuing with the suspension of obligations in these circumstances, the respondents were seeking redress of a violation otherwise than in accordance with the DSU and so were in breach of Article 23.1.

278 *Canada – Continued Suspension* PR, paras. 7.492–7.509, and see paras. 7.525–7.538; *US – Continued Suspension* PR, paras. 7.520–7.537 and see paras. 7.557–7.570.

279 *Canada – Continued Suspension* PR, paras. 7.432, 7.540; *US – Continued Suspension* PR, paras. 7.443, 7.572.

280 *Canada – Continued Suspension* PR, paras. 7.640–7.823; *US – Continued Suspension* PR, paras. 7.663–7.837.

281 *Canada – Continued Suspension* PR, paras. 7.635–7.638; *US – Continued Suspension* PR, paras. 7.658–7.661.

282 *Continued Suspension* ABR, paras. 278, 315–16, 581, 617, 619, in relation to Article 5.1, and, in relation to Article 5.7, *ibid.*, 734.

283 *Ibid.*, para. 592.

284 *Ibid.*, para. 590.

undertaking a role exceeding what was required in order to assess compliance with Article 5.1, and in doing so had misused the advice of the panel-appointed experts. When it came to Article 5.7, the Appellate Body considered that the Panel had again erred, adopting an incorrect legal test for determining the insufficiency of scientific evidence, and therefore incorrectly appreciating the significance of the evidence before it.[285] The test applied by the Panel was whether there was a 'critical mass' of new evidence and/or information that called into question the fundamental precepts of previous knowledge and evidence so as to render previously sufficient evidence insufficient. The Appellate Body considered this threshold too high.[286] It should be emphasised that the Appellate Body was not criticising the Panel for relying on expert evidence, but for making errors of law in relation to the interpretation of Articles 5.1 and 5.7.

Expert witness-conferencing in international arbitration

The procedure seen in the WTO has much in common with developments in international arbitration in recent years towards a greater use of expert witness-conferencing, also seen in many national jurisdictions. Expert witness-conferencing is used by some tribunals in international investment disputes, as well as in international commercial arbitration. It involves hearing more than one expert witness simultaneously, and encouraging the experts to comment on one another's views.[287] Such conferencing is to be distinguished from the practice of directing the parties' experts to meet with one another before a hearing with a view to reaching agreement on the factual aspects of a case.[288] Witness-conferencing is also distinct from more procedurally oriented pre-hearing preparatory conferences convened by arbitral tribunals.[289] At an expert conference the experts for each party present their views in one another's presence, and respond to questions from the tribunal in relation to issues where there is contradictory evidence and on points requiring clarification. The parties do not examine or cross-examine the experts, although they may ask supplementary questions.

Disputing parties' growing support for witness-conferencing procedures is allied closely with a renewed commitment to the fundamental goal of establishing the facts as a sound basis for an arbitral

[285] *Ibid.*, para. 731. [286] *Ibid.*, para. 712.
[287] See for example the IBA Rules, Article 8(3)(f).
[288] See above, p. 79. [289] See Amerasinghe, *Evidence*, p. 115.

decision, rather than seeking merely to attack through cross-examination the testimony for the opposing party.[290] As recently as 2006, the practice of witness-conferencing was considered still to be in 'relative infancy' within international arbitration[291] yet in 2009 it was described as the normal method for examining experts and greater use of the same procedure for taking evidence from non-expert witnesses of fact was being encouraged.[292] Certainly, tribunals will want to consult with parties beforehand where the use of witness-conferencing is contemplated, to make sure the parties are willing, which can be done at the stage of a preparatory conference.[293]

There are various forms that may be taken by witness-conferencing. The preference may be for a relatively 'free-flowing' panel discussion between the experts, chaired by the tribunal, where counsel have the liberty to ask questions and intervene.[294] Alternatively, a more formal approach is for the experts each to give evidence, followed by a period of cross-examination incorporating rebuttal from opposing experts, followed by any questions from the tribunal.[295] Thorough preparation by the tribunal will be important in order to draw the most from the interchange, and to guide the process appropriately as necessary.[296] The utility of the conference depends on the tribunal having had the time to absorb the scientific evidence available to it before the expert conference is held, and to develop a sense of the questions that it would like to see addressed.

Indeed, the oral procedure may be preceded by a written phase, as in the WTO. Various arbitration rules envisage the prior submission of expert reports. The tribunal may then prepare an agenda setting out the issues to be traversed at the hearing.[297] A witness conference involving the court or tribunal may also be supplemented by a meeting between the party-appointed experts before the hearing, as referred to above, where they will prepare lists of the matters on which they agree and the matters on which they do not agree, giving reasons where they do not agree.[298]

The result of all this preparation should be a focused and productive session where the experts' sense of independence is enhanced and the discussion is like a 'roundtable discussion between colleagues'.[299] Such

[290] Peter, 'Witness conferencing', 159. [291] Hunter, 'Expert conferencing', 823.
[292] Hwang, 'Witness conferencing and party autonomy', 25.
[293] Raeschke-Kessler, 'Witness conferencing', 422.
[294] Hwang, 'Witness conferencing', 3; Peter, 'Witness conferencing', 168–9.
[295] Hwang, 'Witness conferencing', 3. [296] *Ibid.*, 4; Hunter, 'Expert conferencing,' 822.
[297] Hunter, 'Expert conferencing,' 822. [298] See above, pp. 79, 123.
[299] Jones, 'Party appointed expert witnesses', 148.

panel procedures have also been called 'hot-tubbing', in reference to the aim of a relaxed sense of collegiality during the hearing.[300] The effect of the new procedure has been powerful. Hearings are greatly reduced in length, as relevant points are brought out more easily and differences between experts' views reduced down to a few vital points.[301]

An explicit intention behind the development of witness-conferencing has been to transcend the divide between civil law and common law procedure.[302] At the same time, there has been a certain influence from reforms in civil procedure in England promoting active judicial case management including pre-trial meetings between experts and from the development of 'hot-tubbing' in Australian jurisdictions.[303] Witness-conferencing has been found to reduce the need for the appointment by a tribunal of its own expert witnesses.[304] Advocates for increased recourse to this option within common law civil procedure have acknowledged their inspiration by French procedures,[305] although the French *expertise* procedure involves a highly self-contained role for the expert. The French procedure devolves an authoritative investigative role to the expert, which may include making site visits and taking further information from the parties.[306]

The prominent distinction between procedures for taking expert evidence in the WTO, and witness-conferencing as seen in mixed and private international arbitration, is that the WTO process has been developed for obtaining evidence from experts appointed by WTO panels themselves, whereas witness-conferencing is used mainly with party-appointed experts.

Expert adjudicators and assessors

Alternatives to reliance on expert evidence include the appointment of technical experts as tribunal members.[307] The appeal of this option lies

300 *Ibid.*, 147. 301 Peter, 'Witness conferencing', 159 and 165.

302 Raeschke-Kessler, 'Witness conferencing', 417.

303 Hodgkinson and James, *Expert Evidence*, 700. See also the discussions of Right Hon. Lord Woolf MR, *Access to Justice*, Ch. 13, paras. 42–51.

304 Peter, 'Witness conferencing', 166.

305 Brown, 'Oral evidence', 77–85. On the influence within international adjudication of developments in civil procedure at the national level, see above, Chapter 1, pp. 21–9.

306 Brown, 'Oral evidence', 77–8.

307 The combination of juridical and technical knowledge has a long history in certain legal traditions, as seen in the multidisciplinary education of the rabbi during the Talmudic period of the fourth century: Taylor, 'A comparative study', 184.

particularly in its potential to bridge the differences in the conceptual and linguistic vocabularies employed by members of these two communities. Inclusion of a scientifically qualified and experienced professional on a tribunal may also help a tribunal to identify the scientific issues it must address. On the other hand, concerns have been expressed that, unlike that of an expert witness, the input of an expert who is also a tribunal member will not be put before the parties for comment.[308] Further, his or her influence within the court or tribunal may be stronger than that of an expert witness.[309]

Selection of a full tribunal solely on the basis of technical expertise is rare except in disputes confined to clearly defined sector-specific issues.[310] Even the appointment of technical experts to sit as tribunal members alongside other members with legal qualifications and experience itself is not common. In a case soon to be dealt with by an arbitral tribunal constituted under the Permanent Court of Arbitration's Optional Rules for Arbitration of Disputes Relating to Natural Resources and/or the Environment,[311] the appointment of a three-person tribunal is expected, comprising two scientists with a lawyer presiding. Distinctive features of these optional rules include provision for a panel of arbitrators with 'expertise in the subject-matters of the dispute at hand'.[312] Where the Optional Rules are used, the Secretary-General will make available lists of persons with appropriate expertise, in order to assist the parties.[313] Within the WTO there is also the possibility of including a technically qualified professional on panels dealing with scientific cases.[314] This

308 Freyer, 'Assessing expert evidence,' 436.

309 Pauwelyn, 'The use of experts', 345.

310 White refers to examples from the fields of fisheries and oil concessions. White, *The Use of Experts*, p. 181.

311 Permanent Court of Arbitration Optional Rules for Arbitration of Disputes Relating to Natural Resources and/or the Environment.

312 Article 8(3). The Arbitral Tribunal is also expressly given the power under the Optional Rules to request the parties to submit a non-technical document that summarises and explains the background to 'any scientific, technical or other specialized information which the Arbitral Tribunal considers to be necessary to understand fully the matters in dispute'. Article 24(4).

313 Article 8(3). The Secretary-General will also provide a list of persons who are considered to have the requisite expertise in the relevant scientific and technical matters in order to assist with the process of appointing experts to report to the Tribunal. Article 27(5).

314 For example, in *Canada – Patent Protection* a medically qualified panel member was appointed. *Canada – Patent Protection of Pharmaceutical Products*, Complaint by the European Communities (WT/DS114), Report of the Panel DSR 2000: V, 2289. Conversation with WTO practitioner. See also Pauwelyn, 'Expert advice', 247; Iynedjian, 'The case'.

panel member would assist the others in developing their understanding of the advice received from the experts appointed by the panel. Indeed, there is scope for a specialist panel to be appointed at the discretion of the parties under Article 25 of the DSU.

Reference may also be made to the provision made for specialist arbitral tribunals under Annex VIII of the LOSC. Special Arbitral Tribunals constituted under Annex VIII of the LOSC consist of experts, and are intended to be constituted from lists of such experts in the fields of fisheries, protection and preservation of the marine environment, marine scientific research, and navigation, including pollution from vessels and by dumping. Nominations for members of the lists are received from states, and the lists of experts are drawn up by the United Nations Food and Agriculture Organization (fisheries), the United Nations Environment Programme (environment), the Intergovernmental Oceanic Commission (marine scientific research) and the International Maritime Organization (navigation), or appropriate subsidiary bodies. The notion of drawing up and maintaining lists of experts in the subject matter of the LOSC, reminiscent of French arrangements for taking expertise,[315] could be applied also in other fora such as the WTO, although the frequency with which lists would have to be updated and the wide range of scientific fields from which the experts would need to be drawn would probably make this an unfeasible process.

A further option for obtaining technical expertise in international adjudication is the co-option onto a tribunal of technical assessors.[316] The appointment of assessors approximates more closely the practice of consulting tribunal-appointed experts than that of appointing technically qualified members of tribunals, as referred to above, as an assessor usually lacks voting rights.[317] In this regard, the position of assessors is

[315] de Hautecloque, 'French judicial expertise', 79.

[316] Rosenne, *The Law and Practice*, pp. 1114–16; Amerasinghe, *Evidence*, p. 158; White, *The Use of Experts*, 46–7. See also Permanent Court of International Justice, Rules of Court Adopted on March 1936, www.icj-cij.org, Articles 7 and 8.

[317] Under Article 30(2) of the Statute of the International Court of Justice the Court is permitted to provide in its rules of procedure for assessors to sit with it, but without the right to vote. Provision for the appointment of assessors by secret ballot is made in Article 9 of the Court's Rules of Procedure, and they are to make a solemn declaration before beginning their duties. In English civil procedure, too, the role of the single joint expert and that of an assessor are very similar, especially in a case where it is the primary function of the assessor to prepare a report to assist the court. Although an assessor is not subject to cross-examination, importance is attached to ensuring that

quite distinct from that of ad hoc judges. Although they may not vote, assessors will take part in the deliberations of the Court.[318] In this respect, the role of assessors differs from that of court-appointed experts. There is potentially considerable flexibility in the procedures which may be used to consult assessors.[319] Assessors may be appointed by a tribunal or by one of the parties, and may work with the tribunal and/or with tribunal-appointed experts. Appointment of assessors is not common in practice, however.[320] Neither the Permanent Court of International Justice nor the International Court of Justice have ever made an appointment.[321] In the view of at least one commentator, it might have been helpful for the Court to do so in the *Gabčíkovo-Nagymaros* case.[322]

Perhaps more likely is the gradual accretion of expertise in the handling of certain types of environmental dispute by particular courts or tribunals, or individual adjudicators. However, views on the need for a specialist international environmental court are mixed.[323] The Chamber for Environmental Matters of the International Court of Justice, established in 1993, remained unused during its thirteen-year life and has not been reconstituted since the Court decided not to elect a Bench for the Chamber in 2006. Commentators remark that the flexibility of the existing mechanisms available in many international adjudicatory fora may provide what is needed 'provided this system is used intelligently and appropriately'.[324] Within the LOSC there is a choice of tribunal, with an arbitral procedure there is always a choice of arbitrators, and in every forum there is scope for the consultation of experts.

the parties have the opportunity to comment on the assessor's advice. Following the Woolf reforms in civil procedure, assessors may be used more widely than in the past, their use previously having been limited mainly to nautical matters in Admiralty proceedings, as well as patents cases and questions of costs. Zuckerman, *Civil Procedure*, pp. 742–3. Although see the continued resistance to the use of experts encountered by Lord Woolf, *ibid.*, Ch. 13, para. 59.

318 Rules of Court of the International Court of Justice, Article 21(2).

319 Highet, 'Evidence and proof of facts', 372 considers that provisions for the appointment of assessors could be relied upon in the appointment by international tribunals of special masters for findings of fact, as used historically to report on questions of evidence in the Chancery courts in England, and increasingly in the US in present-day cases involving scientific or financial complexities.

320 See *Chorzów Factory* case, Order of 15 December 1928, PCIJ Series A, Nos. 14–24.

321 Rosenne, *The Law and Practice*, p. 1115.

322 Okowa, 'Case concerning the *Gabčíkovo-Nagymaros* Project', 695.

323 For discussion, Okowa, 'Environmental dispute settlement', 168. Birnie *et al. International Law*, pp. 255–7; Stephens, *International Courts*, pp. 56–61.

324 Birnie *et al.*, *International Law*, p. 257.

Procedures like those seen in the *Trail Smelter* arbitration demonstrate what can be achieved when a practical approach is taken.[325]

Determination by a neutral expert

An alternative form of dispute resolution is to have a case determined by a neutral expert. In case of an expert determination, the expert is entrusted with making a decision on the basis of his or her expertise in order to resolve the parties' dispute. The aim is to produce an inexpensive and prompt outcome.[326] An expert determination took place in the Baglihar Hydroelectric Plant dispute between India and Pakistan, decided in favour of India on 12 February 2007.[327] The Baglihar dispute arose when India began in 2002 to build the Baglihar Hydroelectric Plant in Jammu and Kashmir approximately 100 km upstream from the border with Pakistan on the Chenab River. Under the Indus Waters Treaty of 1960, in accordance with a plan originally proposed by the World Bank, the three eastern rivers of the Indus Basin (the Sutlej, the Beas and the Ravi) are allocated to India and the three western rivers (the Indus, the Jhelum and the Chenab) are allocated to Pakistan.[328] However, the Treaty permits India to use the western rivers for certain specified uses, including generation of hydroelectric power through new run-of-the-river plants subject to the provisions of Annexure D to the Treaty. The question whether the plant had been designed in such a way as to conform with the requirements of Annexure D depended on the determination of certain technical points over which the parties differed. The matter could not be resolved in the Permanent Indus Commission established under the Treaty and accordingly the parties' 'difference' was referred by Pakistan to the World Bank. The process through which the dispute was then determined was co-ordinated through the International Centre for the Settlement of Investment Disputes.

The Treaty provided that any such differences were to be determined by a neutral expert,[329] and accordingly a highly qualified engineer of

[325] *Ibid.*, p. 256. On the *Trail Smelter* arbitration see above, Ch. 2, p. 32.

[326] Freyer, 'Assessing expert evidence,' at 437.

[327] Executive Summary of the Expert Determination in the Baglihar Hydroelectric Plant Dispute between India and Pakistan, available on the World Bank website, www.worldbank.org/indus.

[328] Indus Waters Treaty 1960 (hereafter Indus Waters Treaty), available on the World Bank website, www.worldbank.org/indus.

[329] *Ibid.*, Annexure F, part 2, para. 4.

the Laboratory of Hydraulic Constructions at the Federal Institute of Technology of Lausanne was appointed. He was charged with making a final and binding determination of the case, in accordance with the Treaty. An international law expert was subsequently selected at his request to assist him, Professor Laurence Boisson de Chazournes of the University of Geneva, as well as a senior engineer.

The parties had, respectively, carried out a range of studies on the plant. The parties' delegations also included experts and engineers. In the course of the dispute's determination, the parties visited the neutral expert's home laboratory, where the neutral expert took advice from colleagues, and he also visited a hydraulic laboratory in India in order to inspect a model of the plant's operation. Further, a site visit was made to the plant itself. The entire process was concluded in accordance with a structured timetable over a period of approximately eighteen months. The neutral expert posed written questions to the parties in the course of proceedings, and issued to them a draft final report for comment, to help ensure it was free from error. The Executive Summary of the Expert Determination indicates that the report contained a thorough and carefully laid out assessment of the points of difference between the parties.

For the parties to a case such as this, the specific provisions and objectives of the Treaty are expected to be determinative of the situation. The difficulty may be that a technical expert's primary focus rests on the provision of expert guidance on the appropriate and best design for such a plant, based on his or her professional expertise in light of the state of the art in the field. For example, the neutral expert recommended that the height of the dam be reduced by a metre and a half below the specification in the Indian design and, with reference to the volume of water that the dam would be able to hold,[330] also considered that the maximum pondage, or portion of water stocked for operational purposes, should be greater by several magnitudes than that envisaged by Pakistan. The neutral expert based this calculation on the need to meet consumer demand in India, using as his base data a graph of power demand in the Baglihar region for December 2004. In contrast the Treaty's specified definition controlling the maximum power permitted to be produced at the plant was based on a minimum mean discharge at the site as calculated from data collected for as long a period as possible, with a minimum of five years for small plants.[331] From

[330] Indus Waters Treaty, see Annexure D, part 3, para. (a).
[331] *Ibid.*, see Annexure D, part 1, 2(i) and part 3 para. (c).

Pakistan's point of view, India's capacity to interfere with the waters of the Chenab was a significant issue. There was precedent for the cutting off of Pakistan's water supplies in the region, in the form of a temporary failure by India to supply canals fed by the eastern rivers following the partition of Pakistan from India in 1947. Of parallel concern for Pakistan was the possibility that a sudden release of water from Baglihar could cause serious flood damage downstream on the plains in Pakistan. Pakistan's objective was to ensure that India adjusted the design of the plant to be strictly consistent with Annexure D, the relevant provisions of which would help ensure that the design of such a plant would afford India only minimal opportunity to exercise control over the flow of the western rivers.

As a model for the process of expert determination, the Baglihar case accordingly calls attention to the difficulties of achieving an outcome that satisfactorily moulds legal interpretation with the application of technical expertise. The Treaty, under which the parties' difference had been notified, called for the exercise of judgement in both spheres. This may not be a task that it is reasonable to ask of an expert where his or her professional formation lies in a distinct technical field, even where the expert is provided with the services of an individual international legal adviser. In practice it may be necessary to allow more fully for a treatment that engages both legal and technical aspects of a disagreement. This may involve treating many such disagreements as primarily legal disputes, despite their high level of technical content. Indeed, the Indus Waters Treaty provides for the establishment of a Court of Arbitration where a neutral expert determines that a difference falls outside his or her mandate.

Conclusion

The diversity of procedures through which international courts and tribunals may make use of expertise is striking. Until recent years practice has been relatively confined to the traditional adversarial process, where each party appoints its own experts, expert reports are submitted in evidence and the experts may be called to testify during the hearing. The challenges posed by disputes involving scientific uncertainty and potential future harm have gradually led to greater use of the many different mechanisms available for receiving expert input. The steps taken in the various international courts and tribunals vary, but the unmistakable trend is towards the use of procedures that bring greater judicial involvement in the scientific aspects of these cases.

Expert evidence is likely to be given a higher profile in international judgments and awards in future. In the past its profile has sometimes been low. The scientific evidence presented by the parties in the *Gabčíkovo-Nagymaros* case was referred to briefly in the judgment of the International Court of Justice.[332] In dealing with the Hungarian plea of ecological necessity, the Court noted the impressive amount of scientific material placed on record by the parties and stated that it had given most careful attention to this material, but concluded that there was no need to determine which of the parties' scientific points of view was better founded.[333] It has been asked whether 'it would not have been better for the Court to have sought impartial technical information and thus rendered a judgment more specific on these scientific matters'.[334] Yet the site visit in the *Gabčíkovo-Nagymaros* case was a notable step for the International Court of Justice, indicating the Court's preparedness to take a proactive approach in engaging with scientific and technical issues.

The WTO has evolved its own extremely practical system for panels to take independent expert advice in the many disputes involving scientific uncertainty now arising in multilateral trade. In international arbitration, the rise of the expert witness conference provides similar benefits. A significant change in the practice of litigants was also introduced in the Court in the *Gabčíkovo-Nagymaros* case, when advocates presented the science as party representatives and full members of their delegation, although this approach was strongly criticised in 2010 in the *Case concerning Pulp Mills*.[335] In the International Tribunal

[332] Reference even to the views of the Hungarian Academy of Sciences was made initially only in the form of an excerpt from a communication between the Hungarian Deputy Prime Minister and his Czechoslovak counterpart explaining the Hungarian change of position in relation to the completion of the project. *Gabčíkovo-Nagymaros* case, para. 35. The Committee had considered environmental, ecological, and seismological issues, as well as issues related to water quality, and adopted the view that there was inadequate knowledge of the consequences of environmental risks associated with the project. The Committee found the risks associated with implementation of the project according to the original plan to be unacceptable. Further thorough and time-consuming studies were recommended by the Committee (although the Hungarian government noted that it could not be stated for certain that adverse impacts would ensue).

[333] *Ibid.*, para. 54. Yet the Court clearly did adopt an informal position on the science, albeit a tacit one. James Crawford, Remarks, European Society of International Law and American Society of International Law Joint Research Forum 'Changing futures? Science and international law', Helsinki, Finland, 2–3 October 2009.

[334] Rosenne, 'Fact-finding', 242.

[335] See above, pp. 88–93.

for the Law of the Sea disputants have relied successfully on party-appointed 'independent' experts of high standing, as seen in the *Southern Bluefin Tuna* and *Land Reclamation* cases.

WTO Panels frequently make express reference to the views of the experts they consult. For instance, in the highly scientific case *Japan – Measures Affecting the Importation of Apples*, the Panel relied freely and directly on the experts' advice both during the original proceedings and subsequently at the compliance stage. However, even in the WTO, the full impact of expert evidence is not always apparent on the face of a final report. For example in *United States – Import Prohibition of Certain Shrimp and Shrimp Products*, the Appellate Body's final disposal of the case was undoubtedly informed by the experts' advice that sea turtles faced different problems in different locations, but in reaching this decision the Appellate Body did not directly rely on the panel's consultation of scientific experts.[336]

From a court or tribunal's point of view, it can be advantageous to hear experts in person, as this provides the opportunity to assess experts' reasoning more closely than in the case of written evidence.[337] It may also enable a court or tribunal to clarify the exact status of an expert's qualifications and experience, and the boundaries of his or her discipline. In addition, it is helpful for a court to be able to ask questions of several experts together. There is also a distinct potential benefit to be gained from creating the opportunity for a tribunal to hear experts respond to one another's contentions and explanations. At the same time, insights may be gained from allowing the parties and their experts to question points made by court-appointed experts. This means of taking expert evidence helps eliminate the possibility of biased evidence and gives a tribunal more direct access to an expert or experts. The tribunal may request reports and schedule special meetings with experts as it considers necessary, and may expect full responses from experts on all points on which it seeks further information. The parties may also be invited to comment on the experts' written reports, in draft or final form.[338] In many ways the combined written and oral model for expert consultation seen in the WTO is an appealing one. Judges of the

336 This is consistent with the task of the Appellate Body as a body charged with hearing appeals on matters of law. The Appellate Body found that US requirements for turtle excluder devices were discriminatory.

337 Alford, 'Fact finding by the World Court', 73.

338 Amerasinghe, *Evidence*, p. 397 refers to the *Richard D. Harza and others* case (1986) 11 Iran–US CTR at 76, and others.

ICJ have regarded the WTO practice as contributing most to the development of a 'best practice' in 'consulting outside sources'.[339]

A more widespread trend toward greater orality and immediacy in the consultation of experts would carry forward at an international level the ongoing historical move away from the mediaeval European *ius commune*, which was characterised by an emphasis on formal proof and written procedures.[340] Greater space for judges to develop dialogues with experts, including independent experts appointed by courts and tribunals themselves, would provide the opportunity for them to discover more about the essence of the issues under dispute and to help deal with issues requiring particular clarification.[341] Complete passivity on the part of decision-makers is certainly not desirable.[342]

However, the use of these new procedures brings with it a range of difficulties. As indicated at the start of this chapter, the root of the problem lies in the closeness of fact and law in many scientific disputes. The legal rules governing the parties' relationships commonly give rise to mixed questions of fact and law. Expert input will be central to the interpretation and application of these provisions. This raises a disharmony within the rationalist tradition, experienced at a practical level as a discomfort in relation to the potentially overly influential role played by experts. Tribunals, practitioners and scholars have always held to the view that the roles of the expert and the tribunal are distinct. Chapter 4 investigates the ways in which this may no longer be so. Experts may effectively participate in the tribunal's interpretation of legal rules. Experts' evidence may in practice help discharge the burden of proof. Experts may also have valuable insights to offer into the need for

339 *Case concerning Pulp Mills*, Joint Dissenting Opinion of Judges Al-Khasawneh and Simma, para. 16.

340 See Cappelletti and Garth, 'Introduction', 5–13.

341 Okowa has suggested specifically that environmental disputes involving scientific uncertainty may be 'more suited to an inquisitorial than an adversarial process'. Okowa, 'Environmental dispute settlement', 169. In the *Case concerning Pulp Mills* Judges Al-Khasawneh and Simma underlined that the advantages of 'recourse to outside expertise' included 'interaction with experts in their capacity as experts and not as counsel'. *Case concerning Pulp Mills*, Joint Dissenting Opinion of Judges Al-Khasawneh and Simma, para. 13. See also para. 16.

342 *Ibid.*, 96. Indeed, as Fuller observed in respect of the judge's engagement in a case, 'the critical value [is] not passivity, but detachment'. Bone, 'Lon Fuller's theory', 1310. Although often welcomed as an indication of neutrality in an adversarial context, passivity may remove decision-makers' capacity to clarify significant points at crucial moments in the development of their understanding. Damaška, *Evidence Law Adrift*, p. 96.

precaution in a case. Would the remedy for the tendency towards integration of the roles of adjudicators and experts be to restructure international adjudication into two stages: a fact-finding stage and a legal stage? On closer examination this does not seem workable. Instead, it seems that the current situation has to be accepted, with best efforts made to maintain transparency and courts' and tribunals' assumption of responsibility for their own decision-making.

4 The role of adjudicators and the role of experts

A close engagement with the science, and with the testimony of scientific experts, is becoming an inevitable feature of the international adjudication of disputes involving potential harm to human health or the environment. Even the most traditional of the international courts, the International Court of Justice, has been giving careful consideration to this issue.[1] Greater use of the diverse procedures addressed in the previous chapter, particularly the consultation of experts appointed by a court or tribunal, will require a revisitation of the fundamental tenets of international adjudication. Perhaps the most central of these tenets is that the tribunal to which a dispute is submitted alone has the authority to take a binding decision on the issues raised by a case, and that a tribunal's findings must be based on its own convictions.[2]

[1] In the *Case concerning Pulp Mills* in 2010, Judges Al-Khasawneh and Simma lamented that the Court had missed 'what can aptly be called a golden opportunity to demonstrate to the international community its ability, and preparedness, to approach scientifically complex disputes in a state-of-the-art manner'. However, the majority of the Court did not agree that it was necessary in the circumstances of the case for the Court to take a more forward approach. See above, Ch. 3, pp. 111–12. *Case concerning Pulp Mills on the River Uruguay (Argentina* v. *Uruguay)*, Judgment of 20 April 2010, ICJ Reports 2010 (hereafter *Case concerning Pulp Mills*), Joint Dissenting Opinion of Judges Al-Khasawneh and Simma, para. 28.

[2] This rule is well explained by the Franco-Italian Conciliation Commission in its decision in the *I.V.E.M. Claim* 7, March 1955 22 ILR 875. Mani, *International Adjudication*, p. 237; White, *The Use of Experts*, pp. 142–3. The Iran–US Claims Tribunal has also observed: 'No matter how well qualified an expert may be ... it is fundamental that an arbitral tribunal cannot delegate to him the duty of deciding the case.' *Starrett Housing Corporation, Starrett Systems Inc. and Starrett Housing International Inc.* v. *Government of the Islamic Republic of Iran, Bank Omran, Bank Mellat and Bank Markazi* Interlocutory Award 19 December 1983; Final Award 14 August 1987 16 Iran–US CTR 112, 565.

The need for tribunals to be alert to the possibility of inadvertent delegation to experts was emphasised by White in 1965.[3] White underlined that the role of the independent expert was limited to assisting a tribunal in the establishment or elucidation of matters of fact. In principle, it is the tribunal and not the expert who is tasked with identifying the relevance and significance of the factual aspects of a case.[4] Thus Sandifer has emphasised 'the importance of limiting the use of experts to questions susceptible to resolution by reference to reasonably well established scientific and technical standards'.[5] Indeed, in the merits phase of the *South West Africa* cases a question on cross-examination was disallowed by the President of the International Court of Justice precisely because it was one of the very questions that the Court was going to have to determine.[6]

The envisaged division of labour between adjudicators and experts is closely connected with the traditionally fundamental distinction between law and fact. The law is normative, facts are physical.[7] The distinction is an important aspect of the rationalist tradition[8] and contributes to a sense of fairness about the adjudicatory process.[9] Ajudication is regarded as the relatively straightforward application of the law to the facts.[10]

Mixed questions of fact and law

Examining the practice of international courts and tribunals, the starting point must therefore be to ask whether the task of experts

[3] White, *The Use of Experts*, pp. 11–12, and Ch. 9.

[4] *Ibid.*, p. 164 citing Lauterpacht, *The Development of International Law*. Documents governing the use of experts by international tribunals reflect the distinction between the role of tribunals and the role of experts. For example, as a general rule these documents do not give experts voting rights, as specified in Article 289 of the United Nations Convention on the Law of the Sea. United Nations Convention on the Law of the Sea, Montego Bay, 10 December 1982, in force 16 November 1994, 21 ILM 1261 (hereafter LOSC). Experts may, however, participate in the judicial deliberations of the International Tribunal for the Law of the Sea. Rules of the International Tribunal for the Law of the Sea, www.itlos.org, Article 42. Article 10 of the Resolution on the Internal Judicial Practice of the Tribunal provides for experts to receive the necessary papers, and to be consulted by the Drafting Committee as appropriate. Resolution on the Internal Judicial Practice of the Tribunal adopted on 31 October 1997, www.itlos.org.

[5] Sandifer, *Evidence*, p. 467.

[6] *South West Africa cases (Ethiopia* v. *South Africa; Liberia* v. *South Africa)*, ICJ Pleadings, vol. X, 636.

[7] Ress, 'Fact-finding', 177–203.

[8] On the rationalist tradition, see Ch. 1, above, pp. 5–6.

[9] Alvarez, 'Burdens of proof', 411. [10] Bentham, *Rationale*, see Ch. 1, above, p. 1.

can simply be to supply the facts needed by the court or tribunal in order to apply the law? The reality is not so clear-cut. Indeed, as foreshadowed in the previous chapter, disputes involving scientific uncertainties are often governed by legal provisions involving mixed questions of fact and law. These mixed questions of fact and law include tests governing how states should act in situations of incomplete scientific knowledge, for example by requiring them to act only in ways that are reasonable, necessary or proportionate, or to co-operate appropriately with one another.[11]

To take an example of the problem of mixed fact and law, reference may be made to disputes relating to environmental protection under the United Nations Convention on the Law of the Sea (LOSC).[12] Had the *Southern Bluefin Tuna cases (New Zealand* v. *Japan; Australia* v. *Japan)* proceeded to the merits, the International Tribunal for the Law of the Sea would have had to ascertain whether Japan had fulfilled its obligations to co-operate in relation to measures necessary for the conservation of the living resources of the high seas under Articles 64 and 116–19 of the LOSC.[13] Determining the necessity of environmental measures and the appropriate extent of co-operation in the circumstances will involve judgments combining an appreciation of the science with a sense of the legal principles at issue under such provisions. Likewise in the *Dispute concerning the MOX Plant, International Movements of Radioactive Materials and the Protection of the Marine Environment of the Irish Sea (Ireland* v. *United Kingdom)* Ireland alleged inter alia that the United Kingdom's authorisation and operation of the Mox Plant would breach the obligations of co-operation to protect the marine environment found in Articles 123 and 197 of the LOSC.[14] Here, too, an assessment of the co-operation that was needed in order to protect the marine environment would have had to be made. However, again the case did not reach the merits stage.

[11] On the first three of these examples, see Bilder, 'Some limitations of adjudication'.

[12] United Nations Convention on the Law of the Sea, Montego Bay, 10 December 1982, in force 16 November 1994, 21 ILM 1261.

[13] *Southern Bluefin Tuna cases (New Zealand* v. *Japan; Australia* v. *Japan) (Provisional Measures)*, Order of 27 August 1999, 38 ILM 1624; *Southern Bluefin Tuna cases (Australia and New Zealand* v. *Japan) Jurisdiction and Admissibility*, 4 August 2000, 39 ILM 1359, 12.

[14] *Dispute concerning the MOX Plant, International Movements of Radioactive Materials and the Protection of the Marine Environment of the Irish Sea (Ireland* v. *United Kingdom) Request for Provisional Measures*, Order of 3 December 2001, 41 ILM 405; *Mox Plant case (Ireland* v. *United Kingdom) (Suspension of Proceedings on Jurisdiction and Merits and Request for Further Provisional Measures)*, Order of 24 June 2003, 42 ILM 1187.

Compliance with similar obligations may also become the subject of disputes under bilateral agreements. In the *Case concerning Pulp Mills* Argentina asserted that Uruguay had violated obligations under the 1975 Statute of the River Uruguay inter alia to take all necessary measures for the rational and optimal utilisation of the river and to preserve the aquatic environment through appropriate measures.[15] Determining the necessity of environmental measures and the appropriate extent of co-operation in the circumstances could have involved judgment combining a close appreciation of the science with the legal principles at issue, had the Court not readily found that the scientific evidence put forward by Argentina was insufficient to establish a case against Uruguay, except in regard to violation of procedural rights. Judges Al-Khasawneh and Simma observed in their Joint Dissenting Opinion that 'The conclusions of scientific experts might be indispensable in distilling the essence of what legal concepts such as "significance" of damage, "sufficiency", "reasonable threshold" or "necessity" come to mean in a given case.'[16]

There are many other potentially close connections between scientific fact and law in the various legal rules that may govern different disputes in the WTO. In WTO law, the exception in Article XX(b) of the General Agreement on Tariffs and Trade (GATT) is couched in terms of the necessity of measures to protect human, animal or plant life and health. A similar necessity test has been adopted also under Article 2.2 of the WTO Agreement on Sanitary and Phytosanitary Measures (the SPS Agreement), as well as under Article 2.2 of the WTO Agreement on Technical Barriers to Trade.[17] It is primarily in WTO cases that science and law have come closest to convergence. For example, in *Australia – Salmon* the Panel consulted the panel-appointed experts on comparisons between risks,[18] in order to deal with the legal question of whether

[15] *Case concerning Pulp Mills*, Application Instituting Proceedings filed in the Registry of the Court on 4 May 2006.

[16] *Ibid.*, Joint Dissenting Opinion of Judges Al-Khasawneh and Simma, para. 17.

[17] Compliance with Article 2.2 has been at issue in *Australia – Measures Affecting Importation of Salmon*, Complaint by Canada (WT/DS18), Report of the Appellate Body DSR 1998: VIII, 3327, Report of the Panel DSR 1998: VIII, 3407 (hereafter *Australia – Salmon* PR); and *Japan – Measures Affecting Agricultural Products*, Complaint by the United States (WT/DS76), Report of the Appellate Body DSR 1999: I, 277 (hereafter *Japan – Agricultural Products* ABR); Report of the Panel DSR 1999: I, 315; and in *Australia – Measures Affecting the Importation of Apples from New Zealand*, Complaint by New Zealand, DS 367.

[18] *Australia – Salmon* PR, Part VI, Written Consultation with Experts, Compiled Responses, questions 5, 6, 9, 10 and 11.

Australia's practices were discriminatory. The Panel relied on the experts' advice in reaching a finding of discrimination between imports of salmon and imports of herring for bait and live ornamental finfish.[19] The Panel also required expert input in interpreting what might be meant by the term 'risk assessment' in the SPS Agreement. The Panel wanted to know from the experts whether in their view risk assessment had to be conducted on a disease by disease basis,[20] whether an 'option by option' assessment was a minimum requirement of a risk assessment,[21] and whether they considered risk assessments inherently had to be quantitative or could instead take a qualitative form.

Further examples abound. In *Japan – Measures Affecting Agricultural Products* the Panel asked the experts whether they considered there was an objective or rational relationship between the varietal testing requirement imposed by Japan and any of the evidence the parties had submitted. This went to the legal question whether Japan's measures were based on a risk assessment.[22] In *European Communities – Measures Affecting Asbestos and Asbestos-Containing Products* the experts were involved in the Panel's task of assessing whether or not the EC measures could be considered 'necessary' to protect human life or health under Article XX(b) of the GATT. This included assessing whether there were any reasonably available alternatives to the EC asbestos ban. The Panel asked the experts to make comparisons between risks in respect of the French policy of using substitute products in place of asbestos. One expert considered for example that chrysotile was very potent, and as none of the substitute fibres demonstrated carcinogenicity in humans he believed that in terms of public health it would be beneficial to use some of these substitutes.[23]

[19] *Australia – Salmon* PR, paras. 8.135, 8.138.

[20] The Panel ultimately found that a risk assessment did have to identify risk on a disease-specific basis. *Australia – Salmon* PR, para. 8.74.

[21] The Panel held an option by option assessment was a minimum requirement of a risk assessment. *Australia – Salmon* PR, para. 8.88. The Panel referred to relevant opinions expressed by the Panel-appointed experts in making its finding, as well as the OIE Guidelines on Risk Assessment. *Ibid.*, 8.86–8.87.

[22] *Japan – Measures Affecting Agricultural Products*, Complaint by the United States (WT/DS76), Report of the Panel DSR 1999: I (hereafter *Japan – Agricultural Products* PR), paras. 8.32, 8.35.

[23] *European Communities – Measures Affecting Asbestos and Asbestos-Containing Products*, Complaint by Canada (WT/DS135), Report of the Panel DSR 2001: VIII, 3305 (hereafter *EC – Asbestos* PR) Annex VI, Transcript of Joint Meeting with Experts JM, para. 381. Two of the other experts agreed. *Ibid.*, paras. 383, 385.

Variations in the degree of closeness between fact and law in a complex WTO SPS dispute may be demonstrated with reference to *European Communities – Approval and Marketing of Biotech Products*. In *EC – Biotech*, the Panels' written consultation with its experts focused around three issues, which were flagged to the parties in advance.[24] Fact and law potentially ran together in relation to all three of the issues. The panel portrayed the role of the independent experts that it consulted as the provision of 'the necessary scientific input to assist the Panel in understanding the issues raised by the Parties and to resolve the trade dispute before it'.[25]

The first of the three issues on which the Panel consulted the experts involved background information to assist in determining whether there were unjustified delays in EC regulatory processes. This went to whether or not the EC had breached the requirement to avoid 'undue delay' in Article 8 and Annex C(1)(a) of the SPS Agreement. The experts were asked to address various aspects of the way that the approvals process had been operating, specifically: scientific and technical grounds for comments and objections by Member States; scientific and technical grounds for requests for additional information from applicants; and justifications on scientific and technical grounds for time taken to evaluate additional information.[26] The Panel's final report referred at various points to the advice provided by experts,[27] but on this issue the input from the scientific experts was generally highly scientific in nature, directed toward answering relatively narrow questions posed by the Panel. Fact and law were not as close as they could have been.

The second issue related to EC Member States' individual safeguard measures. The Panel wanted to know from the experts how the scientific and other documentation relied upon by individual states compared with the existing international standards. These standards were found in IPSM 11, Codex Alimentarius and the Cartagena Protocol on Biosafety. The Panel also wanted to know whether this information was 'sufficient to support' the safeguard measures. In relation to the second issue the Panel set out for the experts the definition of 'risk assessment' from the SPS Agreement, as well as the text of Article 5.2 and 5.3 of the

[24] *EC – Biotech* PR, para. 7.18. The parties were invited to suggest specific questions for the experts on each issue, which they did. *Ibid.*, para. 7.20.

[25] *EC – Biotech* PR, para. 7.30.

[26] *EC – Biotech* PR, Annex H, Replies by the Scientific Experts, p. 57.

[27] See e.g. *EC – Biotech* PR, paras. 7.873–7.874. 7.894, 7.922–7.923, 7.927–7.928, 7.930.

SPS Agreement.[28] The Panel asked the experts about the extent to which individual Member States' evidence and documentation evaluated the risks of the biotech products.[29] The Panel was also interested in whether Member States' documentation was 'sufficient to support' the safeguard measures because this was necessary to fulfil the requirements of Article 5.1 that sanitary and phytosanitary measures be 'based on' a risk assessment. In *EC – Hormones* the Appellate Body had interpreted Article 5.1 as requiring that the results of the risk assessment must 'sufficiently warrant – that is to say, reasonably support – the SPS Measure at stake'.[30] The expert advice on these matters thus went closely to the legal questions before the Panel in relation to compliance with the Article 5.1 requirement to base SPS measures on a risk assessment.[31]

Expert advice provided in relation to the second issue also went to the matter of whether the EC should be able to rely on Article 5.7 of the SPS Agreement in relation to individual Member States' safeguard measures: the experts were asked whether the evidence from the individual Member States supported the adoption of a temporary prohibition on biotech products[32] and whether the scientific evidence available to individual Member States was insufficient to permit a risk assessment.[33] Fact and law also ran closely together here.

The third issue in the written consultation related to the question of discrimination. The experts were asked to assist the Panel in determining whether there were significant differences in the risks from the biotech products at issue in the case and (a) biotech products approved in the EC before October 1998, (b) comparable novel non-biotech products (such as plant products from selective breeding, cross-breeding and mutagenesis) and (c) foods produced with biotechnology processing aids such as genetically modified yeasts, bacteria and enzymes.[34] The intention was for the Panel to assess whether there was any basis for finding the EC to be out of compliance with Article 5.5 of the SPS Agreement, which prohibits arbitrary or unjustifiable

[28] *EC – Biotech* PR, Annex H, Replies by the Scientific Experts, p. 170.

[29] *Ibid.*, questions 60, 64, 67, 70, 73, 76, etc.

[30] *European Communities – Measures Concerning Meat and Meat Products (Hormones)*, Complaint by Canada (WT/DS48), Complaint by the United States (WT/DS26), Report of the Appellate Body DSR 1998: I, 135 (hereafter *EC – Hormones* ABR), para. 193.

[31] For the text of Article 5.1 see Ch. 1, note 61.

[32] *EC – Biotech* PR, Replies by the Scientific Experts, questions 61, 65, 68, 71, 74, 77, etc.

[33] *Ibid.*, questions 59, 63, 66, 69, 72, 75, 78, etc.

[34] *Ibid.*, 226.

distinctions in the levels of protection that Member States consider to be appropriate in different situations where these distinctions result in discrimination or a disguised restriction on international trade.

These examples from *EC – Biotech* demonstrate that in a scientific case the insights necessary to make sound legal decisions may come from the experts consulted by the tribunal, even though it is the international adjudicatory body that has exclusive authority to carry out tasks such as the interpretation of legal terms and the legal categorisation of factual issues. However, in the event it was in relation to the scope of the SPS Agreement, and the question of compliance with the procedural obligation under Annex C(1)(a) to process import applications without undue delay, that express reliance was placed on the experts' evidence.[35] For example, the Panel defined 'pest' with reference to expert advice on many points. Genetically modified plants could be 'pests' in various respects, including where their introduction led to plants growing where they were undesired, crossbreeds with undesirable traits[36] and organisms with pesticide resistance,[37] as well as through their effects on non-target organisms.[38] Reliance on the experts' advice on issues going to the scope of the SPS Agreement is notable because of the significance of the Panel's findings not only for future litigation but also within the broader WTO context.[39]

It is clear that there will be instances in the future where international courts and tribunals have to engage closely and overtly in mixed questions of fact and law, and they will doubtless have to do so on occasion with definitive consequences. For example, in the *Continued Suspension of Obligations* cases, it seemed likely that a WTO panel constituted under Article 21.5 of the DSU would have had to assess whether EC compliance with its obligations in relation to five of the six hormones in question was insufficient for a risk assessment and a temporary ban on this substance was therefore justified.[40]

[35] For discussion of Panel's decision to make such issues the central focus of the case, rather than assessing compliance with the core SPS disciplines, see Foster, 'Prior approval systems'.

[36] See the lengthy footnote referring to expert advice on this point. *EC – Biotech* PR, para. 7.256 and note 408.

[37] Again, there was a moderately long footnote here referring to expert evidence. *EC – Biotech* PR, para. 7.260 and note 412.

[38] *EC – Biotech* PR, para. 7.269.

[39] The Panel's broad interpretation of the applicability of the SPS Agreement has even been described as 'SPS imperialism'. Scott, *The WTO Agreement*, p. 17.

[40] For discussion on the *Continued Suspension of Obligations* cases, see below, Ch. 8.

The closeness between fact and law may often be less overt in investment law, but scientific determinations will also be of considerable potential significance in investment disputes.[41] In both investment and trade disputes, the legal issues before the court or tribunal may depend on an assessment of the motive behind a state's adoption of measures affecting trade or investment. Frequently, such assessments will need to be based on inference, and to a degree science may come to be used as an 'objective proxy' for an assessment of motive.[42] So long as the science relied upon by a state appears to cross a threshold of acceptability, it becomes difficult to draw inferences about adverse motives on the part of the state. For example, motive is relevant when assessing whether a measure taken by a host state is 'for a public purpose' as part of determining whether the measure is an exercise of the host state's 'police powers' and therefore does not constitute expropriation.[43] To take another example, in the case of *Methanex Corp.* v. *United States of America* the Tribunal found that it had no jurisdiction to determine the merits of the dispute, on the basis that Methanex had failed to establish that the US measures in question were intended to harm foreign methanol producers or to benefit domestic ethanol producers. Accordingly, the US measures did not 'relate to' Methanex or its investments and jurisdiction was lacking under Article 1101(1) of the North American Free Trade Agreement (NAFTA).[44] To the extent that motive is at issue, reference to scientific considerations is not the only evidence that will be relevant in investment cases, as there may well be other evidence that indicates a state's motivations.[45] However, tribunals have pronounced obliquely on the correctness of the science.[46]

[41] Wagner, 'International investment', 530–34; Orellana, 'The role of science'.

[42] Lévesque, Céline 'Science in the hands of international investment tribunals: A case for "scientific due process"'.

[43] See e.g. *Técnicas Medioambientales Tecmed S.A.* v. *The United Mexican States*, Award of 29 May 2003, 43 ILM 133 (hereafter the *Tecmed* case).

[44] *Methanex Corp.* v. *United States of America*, 3 August 2005, Part IV, Chapter E, para. 22, decision available at http://ita.law.uvic.ca.

[45] See e.g. the examination in the *Methanex* case of the 'scientific *and administrative* record'. *Methanex*, Part IV, Chapter E, para. 20, emphasis added. Note also that in the *Tecmed* case the Tribunal turned to evidence that the Mexican decision not to renew authorisation for the operation of the investor's landfill was driven mainly by sociopolitical factors.

[46] For example, the *Methanex* Tribunal found that 'the question is whether the scientific conclusions which were presented to the Governor were so faulty that the Tribunal may reasonably infer that the science merely provided a convenient excuse for the hidden regulation of methanol producers'. *Ibid.*, Part IV, Chapter E, para. 19. The Tribunal

Science may also be relevant in determining whether there may be any genuine reason to treat a foreign investor differently from locals. Here it is not just that the absence of a convincing scientific rationale for differing treatment may be a factor indicating discriminatory intent; the science may also provide an objective justification for differing treatment. Similarly, science may be relevant in determining whether an investor has been accorded fair and equitable treatment, although the degree of relevance may depend on the standard that is applied to gauge fair and equitable treatment. Arbitrators may need to assess the objective value of the science relied upon by host states, although they should still not necessarily find themselves obliged to determine whether the science is correct in all respects.

The root of the difficulty in the consultation of experts lies in the distinction between the particular and the general. A court's or tribunal's determination of what is sufficient, insufficient, discriminatory, necessary, reasonable, proportionate or 'for a public purpose' may draw on more than the factual advice provided by experts relative to the particular case. It may also draw on the experts' assessments of what is, in *general*, sufficient, insufficient, discriminatory, necessary, reasonable, proportionate or 'for a public purpose'.[47] Yet it is the members of international courts and tribunals, rather than the scientific experts, who should be responsible for the broader long-term implications of the way in which a legal term is understood and applied in a given case. It is the court or tribunal that is vested with the authority to carry out this quintessentially legal function, and the court or tribunal is expected to do so in accordance with the legal rules governing interpretation. Thus, in the *Case concerning Pulp Mills*, Judges Al-Khasawneh and Simma conceded that experts 'would be drawn into question of legal interpretation through their involvement in the application of legal terms',[48] while continuing to envisage a division in function:

said that it was 'not persuaded that the [University of California] Report was scientifically incorrect'. *Ibid.*, Part III, Chapter A, para. 101.

[47] As explained by Walker: 'This preference for rule-based reasoning over generalisation-based reasoning creates a tendency for the legal fact-finding process to transform generalisations into rules. This natural tendency can easily operate through the mechanism previously discussed: Individual scientists testify before fact-finding panels about their scientific reasoning, fact-finding panels adopt some of that reasoning as their own, some of that reasoning becomes 'soft rules' as the Appellate Body defers to it and later panels follow it, and some generalisations are explicitly converted into default rules of law.' Walker, 'Transforming science into law', 185.

[48] *Case concerning Pulp Mills*, Joint Dissenting Opinion of Judges Al-Khasawneh and Simma, para. 16.

> In short, in a scientific case such as the present dispute, the insights to make sound legal decisions necessarily emanate from experts consulted by the Court, even though it certainly remains for the Court to discharge the exclusively judicial functions, such as the interpretation of legal terms, the legal categorisation of factual issues, and the assessment of the burden of proof.[49]

Similarly, Judge Yusuf gave a number of reasons why he did not consider that resorting to an expert opinion would undermine the function of the Court by taking away the role of the judge. In his view the expert's task was to elucidate the facts, the Court's task was to weigh them, and expert assistance would not be required 'wholesale' but only in relation to certain selected facts.[50]

The concern that expert evidence should be particular rather than general, or 'specific rather than conclusory', has been recognised in national law.[51] In most instances the members of a court or tribunal have had decades of training equipping them for their task. In contrast, technical experts are highly specialised in their own fields, but without legal expertise. As stated in strong terms by one commentator:

> Supplying sufficient intelligence to decision makers is one function; applying policy to the facts of a dispute is another. There are no indications that the technical specialist is a specialist in the application of policy, that his training gives him a perception of inclusive interests, that he grasps the techniques of authoritative decisions or is in any sense expert in its strategies.[52]

Associated with this issue is the tendency for courts and tribunals to rely on the credentials and credibility of individual scientists contributing evidence to a case.[53] The scientific aspects of a dispute need to be determined based on the science itself, rather than with reference to the attributes of the individuals conveying the science.[54]

The need to maintain a distinction between the role of the court and the role of the expert is familiar in both common and civil law systems. Yet in both systems it is accepted that there needs to be a modus operandi allowing courts to seek assistance even on matters intrinsically connected with legal issues where necessary. In the common law, a central principle has been that expert testimony will be admissible only on matters that it is not within the competence of the court, or a jury, to

[49] *Ibid.*, para. 12. See also para. 3.
[50] Declaration of Judge Yusuf; para. 10. See also paras. 11–12.
[51] Mueller and Kirkpatrick, *Evidence*, p. 636. [52] Reisman, *Nullity and Revision*, p. 453.
[53] Rosenne, 'Fact-finding', 244–5. [54] *Ibid.*, 244–5.

judge.[55] For a period, this was reflected in the 'ultimate issue' rule, precluding witnesses from addressing an ultimate issue before a court. Despite the abolition of the 'ultimate issue' rule in many common law jurisdictions, there is still a 'tradition against the testimony expressing legal conclusions'.[56] Further, it is understood that the interpretation of words with a specific legal meaning is the task of the court. However, in limited circumstances it is accepted that it may be beneficial to hear an expert view on the meaning of a term, such as a technical term in a statute or legal document.[57] In the French context the underlying concern has perhaps been greater because court-appointed experts' reports are frequently used and will most often be decisive.[58] Although these reports are not partisan, neither are they subjected to the rigours of the common law adversarial process. Yet it is accepted, too, that French experts may be asked 'questions which require the application of legal concepts to the facts which they find'.[59] While the French judge is expected to retain full responsibility for the decision in a case, he or she is permitted to seek the advice of an expert even on matters involving the legal qualification of facts, provided that this requested advice is limited to matters that he or she cannot resolve without help.[60]

Once it is accepted in the international legal context that there will inevitably be some involvement on the part of experts in issues of legal interpretation, it is possible to identify a number of appropriate safeguards that may go some way towards addressing the problem. It is important that everything practicable is done to try and ensure the continued fairness of international adjudicatory decision-making and, to the extent possible, certainty in the law. First, a tribunal should always make it clear it has gone through a process of forming its own views on those matters requiring it to do so – and this is particularly necessary where a tribunal decides to adopt the same views as an expert.[61] This is a responsibility that must be shouldered despite the complexity of a dispute. The tribunal can be taken to be aware of the

[55] Hodgkinson and James, *Expert Evidence*, pp. 3, 12–25, 279–80; Zuckerman, *Civil Procedure*, 714–15.

[56] Mueller and Kirkpatrick, *Evidence*, p. 638.

[57] Hodgkinson and James, *Expert Evidence*, 289–90.

[58] See above, Ch. 1, p. 28. Beardsley, 'Proof of fact', 481; and see Ngwasiri, 'Some problems of expertise', 168–83, 170, 182.

[59] Bell *et al.*, *Principles of French Law*, p. 100. [60] Jolowicz, *On Civil Procedure*, pp. 225, 233.

[61] Consider White's example of the *North Atlantic Coast Fisheries case* where a committee of experts was tasked with determining both factual questions about the fishery and also the appropriateness, necessity, reasonableness and fairness of the disputed

need for legal interpretations to be of general application and to carry a responsibility for helping ensure that will be the case even where expert input is significant for determining legal issues in a particular instance. Secondly, maximum transparency must be accorded to the reasoning behind the decisions in these cases. Thirdly, certain safeguards for the parties can be built into the consultation process. The parties should be given the opportunity to comment on the written questions that a panel intends to put to the experts, and identify questions that they consider would be likely to elicit from the experts their views on legal questions. The parties must be given the opportunity to comment on experts' written responses to the panel's written questions. Indeed, practice in the WTO demonstrates a high level of awareness of these requirements. Indeed, the expert consultation in the International Court of Justice envisaged by Judges Al-Khasawneh and Simma in the *Case concerning Pulp Mills* would have taken place 'in full public view and with the participation of the parties'.[62] These remedies are only partial, however, and cannot altogether resolve the underlying issue.

Experts and the burden of proof

Provision of decisive factual advice by independent scientific experts may raise concerns that the experts are discharging the burden of proof on behalf of litigating parties.[63] The notion that a court can only find facts on the basis of the evidence from the parties will be familiar to common lawyers.[64] Arguably the approach taken within French law is

legislation. These questions clearly involved analysis and value judgement. The tribunal in this case was careful to retain a discretion in its handling of the report of the committee of experts. In any event the establishment of a Permanent Mixed Fisheries Commission superseded reliance upon the committee of experts. White, *The Use of Experts*, p. 167. *Award of the Tribunal of Arbitration in the Question Relating to the North Atlantic Coast Fisheries (Great Britain/United States of America)*, 7 October 1910 XI UNRIAA 167.

62 *Case concerning Pulp Mills*, Joint Dissenting Opinion of Judges Al-Khasawneh and Simma, para. 17. See also para. 23 and the discussion at para. 14 decrying the Court's use of invisible or 'phantom' experts behind the scenes. As in the WTO, the judges envisaged the parties' consultation also in regard to the selection of experts. *Ibid.*, para. 13. Suggesting that the Court's private use of experts be restricted at least to issues of minor significance, Tams, 'Article 50', 1118.

63 Martha, 'Presumptions', 98. Consider the comments of Arbitrator Mosk, dissenting in the case of *Behring International Inc.* v. *Iranian Air Force*, who considered the appointment of an expert in engineering to inventory Air Force property as a way 'to assist one of the parties to obtain evidence'. *Behring International, Inc.* v. *The Islamic Republic Iranian Air Force, and others*, 19 December 1983, 4 Iran–US CTR 89, 92.

64 Zuckerman, *Civil Procedure*, p. 752.

more grounded. As a practical matter, the French have long discarded what was earlier regarded as a fundamental premise of French civil procedure: that it is not the judge's task to seek out evidence that may support or weaken the parties' claims.[65] *Mesures d'instruction* are not to be employed merely to make up for shortfalls in the parties' own evidence. The principle underlying their use is to acquire crucial evidence on which the outcome of a case depends.[66]

This issue arose square-on in *Japan - Agricultural Products*,[67] where a WTO Panel used the information provided by the experts appointed by the Panel in a way that was relatively out of the ordinary. The Panel reasoned, based on the scientific evidence received from the independent experts, that comparing sorption tests for different varieties of fruit was a less trade-restrictive measure which Japan could have employed in place of its current requirements for full phytosanitary testing on all varieties of US fruit,[68] and therefore Japan was in breach of the SPS Agreement. That is, the Panel devised from the scientific evidence an alternative phytosanitary measure that the Panel considered a disputant might have been expected to adopt. The Appellate Body would not accept this.[69] Although the Appellate Body noted that panels had a 'significant investigative authority', panels could not use this authority to find in favour of a complainant which had not established a prima facie case based on the specific claims it had put forward.[70] The sorption testing option was, subsequently, agreed upon by the parties, bringing their dispute to a close.[71]

The Appellate Body's approach in *Japan - Agricultural Products* was criticised.[72] It is difficult fully to sustain the argument that where a tribunal relies on independent expert advice that means the advice is being used inappropriately towards discharging a burden or burdens of proof.[73] Tribunals receive potentially relevant information

[65] Beardsley, 'Proof of fact', 460–1, citing Aubry and Rau, *Cours de droit civil pratique Français*, 5th edn (1922), XII, p. 74.

[66] Bell *et al.*, *Principles of French Law*, p. 97. See also Jolowicz, *On Civil Procedure*, pp. 234–5, 238–9.

[67] *Japan - Agricultural Products* PR. [68] *Ibid.*, para. 8.74.

[69] *Japan - Agricultural Products* ABR. [70] *Ibid.*, paras. 129–30.

[71] Pauwelyn, 'The use of experts', 354; Pauwelyn, 'Expert advice', 249.

[72] Pauwelyn, 'Expert advice', 249–51. Grando, *Evidence*, pp. 345–8, taking the view that it is open to a panel to consider all the evidence before it in order to make an objective assessment of the case.

[73] Indeed, Schwarzenberger talks of the Court itself assuming a 'burden' of proof in advisory proceedings. Schwarzenberger, *International Law*, p. 651.

and opinions from many sources. Parties' duties to collaborate in the production of evidence before international tribunals,[74] and a tribunal's own role in seeking out all available evidence,[75] are indeed regarded by some writers as part of burden of proof rules.[76] In the end, the quasi-investigative aspect of the inquiry increasingly seen in cases involving scientific uncertainty marks it out from a strictly adversarial encounter in which information assisting in the discharge of the burden of proof can only come from the parties to the dispute. It is surely artificial to maintain the view that the evidence that goes to discharge the burden of proof is strictly limited to that submitted by each party?[77] After all, no one complains about the issue when a litigating party relies on points made by experts appointed by the opposing party, yet it could readily be said that the first party has not discharged its burden of proof on its own. From time to time, information provided by the panel-appointed experts will naturally be of genuine significance to a party's case, whether because of the light it casts on that party's evidence or more directly. Indeed, the parties may base some of their arguments on experts' advice. For example, in *United States – Import Prohibition of Certain Shrimp and Shrimp Products* the US and Thailand drew strongly on the experts' individual and collective opinions to support their own views as presented in their comments on the written consultation with the experts.[78] This will of course be a selective practice. The parties in the *US – Shrimp* case also attacked the experts' evidence, including that of particular experts, as

[74] Sandifer, *Evidence*, pp. 115–17; Lachs, 'Evidence', 267. See e.g. Article 3.10 of the WTO Dispute Settlement Understanding.

[75] Damaška, *Evidence Law Adrift*, p. 82. For background drawn from comparative law, see also Jolowicz's survey of courts' roles in adducing evidence in different jurisdictions. Jolowicz, 'The active role'.

[76] Kazazi builds a concept of burden of proof with three limbs: *actori incumbit probatio*, the collaboration of the parties, and the fact-finding role of the tribunal. Kazazi, *Burden of Proof*. Witenberg focuses on a duty of collaboration, and a special duty of the international judge to search out the truth, as principles running parallel to the rule on burden of proof. Witenberg, '*Onus probandi*'. Cf. White, *The Use of Experts*, p. 9.

[77] Amerasinghe, *Evidence*, pp. 148 and 161.

[78] *United States – Import Prohibition of Certain Shrimp and Shrimp Products*, Complaint by India (WT/DS58), Complaint by Malaysia (WT/DS58), Complaint by Pakistan (WT/DS58), Complaint by Thailand (WT/DS58), Report of the Panel DSR 1998: VII, 2821 (hereafter *US – Shrimp* PR), in respect of the US, paras. 5.402, 5.420, 5.422; in respect of Thailand, paras. 5.366, 5.369, 5.388–5.392, 5.378–5.385. See also in respect of India paras. 5.294, 5.302, 5.303 and in respect of Malaysia para. 5.337.

incorrect, as constituting generalisations or invalid extrapolations, and as unpersuasive, idealistic or speculative.[79]

There is a suggestion in the jurisprudence that there is some identifiable point at which a prima facie case can be considered to be established, and that once a claimant can be seen to have reached this point in its pleadings a panel is free to take into account the evidence of panel-appointed experts as information that endorses the party's case. For example, in *EC – Asbestos* the Panel observed it was necessary that the party making the claim 'spontaneously makes' its own prima facie case:

> Information provided by the experts consulted by the Panel pursuant to Article 13 of the Understanding 'to help it to understand and evaluate the evidence submitted and the arguments made by the parties', even where it has been requested by the Panel, can under no circumstances be used by a panel to rule in favour of a party which has not established a prima facie case based on specific legal claims or pleas asserted by it.[80]

Yet a panel will obviously reach its conclusions on the factual aspects of a case in the light of all it hears during the proceedings, both from the parties and from the experts.[81] Indeed, this has been acknowledged by panels.[82] It is not going to be possible to determine from a panel's expression of its findings the relative weight that members of the panel may have attributed to the parties' arguments, the parties' evidence and the advice of independent experts. In practice, the evidence and information before a panel will be evaluated as a package. The Panel's own reasoning in *EC – Asbestos* demonstrates its reliance

[79] *Ibid.*, for comments by India, paras. 5.296, 5.300; by Malaysia, paras. 5.340, 5.337; by Thailand, paras. 5.376, 5.377, 5.386–5.387; and by the US, paras. 5.422–5.432. Also see e.g. *Australia – Salmon* PR, comments by Canada, paras. 4.39, 4.157, 4.72, 4.82, 4.109, 4.110, 4.137, 4.140, 4.97, 4.128, 4.202, 4.209 (ii), 4.209 (iii), 4.199; and by Australia, paras. 4.79, 4.145, 4.146, 4.146, 4.148, 4.150, 4.189, 4.205, 4.223, 4.224, and *Australia – Salmon* JM 84. See *Japan – Agricultural Products* PR, paras. 4.67, 4.135, 4.114, 4.130, 4.134, 4.166, 4.167, 4.87. Also *EC – Asbestos* PR, paras. 3.323, 3.324, 3.325, 3.334, 3.335, 3.325, 3.341, 3.342, 3.350, 3.354, 3.355, 4.87, 5.440, 5.439, 5.582.

[80] *EC – Asbestos* PR, para. 8.81, citing *Japan – Agricultural Products*.

[81] See Grando, *Evidence*, pp. 113–14, citing findings of the Appellate Body to the effect that it is open to panels to consider all the evidence in determining whether a prima facie case has been made. See also at pp. 310–11, 357.

[82] See e.g. *Japan – Agricultural Products* PR, paras. 7.9, 7.10, and for explicit use of the experts' input, see paras. 8.33–8.41.

on the experts.[83] A more limited use of experts' input will not be workable.[84]

An analogy can also be drawn between benefits derived by a party from the presentation to a tribunal of independent expert advice and benefits derived by a party through evidence presented by an intervening party. Alternatively, an analogy might be drawn with tribunals' long-standing practice of taking judicial notice of facts such as historical events and well-publicised political situations. Additionally, it may be observed that there is scope for the International Court of Justice to be guided by expert input in giving advisory opinions under Chapter IV of its Statute.[85] Further, it is instructive to consider working procedures within the United Nations Compensation Commission (UNCC). Following Iraq's invasion and occupation of Kuwait in 1991, the United Nations Compensation Commission performed a fact-finding function with certain quasi-judicial aspects, although admittedly this was not a truly adjudicatory forum. In the UNCC it was understood that under Article 35(1) of the Rules, 'Each claimant is responsible for submitting documents and other evidence which demonstrate satisfactorily that a particular claim or group of claims is eligible for compensation, pursuant to Security Council resolution 687(1991).'[86] Nevertheless, it was clear that much of the decision-making would be undertaken on the basis of 'professional judgment reports' prepared by expert consultants.[87] The Panel also requested information from international organisations.[88] Additionally, discussions were held by the Secretariat, sometimes with expert involvement, with representatives of the claimants in order to obtain additional information requested by the Panel.[89]

Why has the question of the relationship between the taking of independent expert advice and the application of burden of proof

[83] On the Panel's reliance on the experts' advice see the remarks above, p. 140, and see *EC – Asbestos* PR, paras. 8.186, 8.188, 8.189, 8.191, 8.192, 8.193. On the health risk associated with chrysotile, see also para. 8.194, and on the question of substitute fibres, paras. 8.220, 8.222. On controlled use there were a range of factual findings drawing on the input of experts, at paras. 8.200, 8.201, 8.202, 8.209, 8.211, 8.213, 8.215.

[84] Pauwelyn, 'The use of experts', 352.

[85] Indeed, Schwarzenberger talks of the Court itself assuming a 'burden' of proof in advisory proceedings. Schwarzenberger, *International Law*, p. 651.

[86] See e.g. United Nations Compensation Commission Governing Council, Report and Recommendations made by the Panel of Commissioners concerning the First Instalment of 'F4' Claims, discussed further below. UN Doc S/AC/26/2001/16, 22 June 2001, para. 50.

[87] *Ibid.*, para. 43. [88] *Ibid.*, para. 43. [89] *Ibid.*, para. 45.

rules courted so much attention in the context of WTO dispute resolution? As a political matter, WTO dispute resolution continues to depend on the membership's sense of control over the dispute settlement process. At the same time, the process derives a legitimacy by 'outsourcing' to qualified scientists those issues requiring specialist knowledge.[90] However, this does not override the instinct of the membership to ensure that the dispute resolution process does not 'take on a life of its own'. It is desirable to return here to the basic aims of the dispute settlement process, and to the governing text, the Dispute Settlement Understanding. A panel is obliged to make a full assessment of the facts of a case in accordance with Article 11 of the DSU, which requires that 'a panel make an objective assessment of the matter before it'. The quality and status of dispute settlement outcomes will be improved through adjudicators' access to information from neutral expert sources. There should be little harm in acknowledging more openly the quasi-investigative aspect of the system that has evolved in the WTO.

Precaution in the views of experts

Related with the question of the weight to be given to expert evidence is the point that precaution is likely to inform the testimony of all scientists heard by the court, whether as advocates or witnesses, in varying degrees. As a technical matter, of course experts may indicate that certain objective qualifications apply to the evidence on the table, or express doubts or reservations in relation to scientific hypotheses, and these comments will naturally form part of the body of information that a tribunal will need to take into account. In addition, individual experts will have their own perspectives on the risks addressed by the litigation in which they are involved. Experts in fields connected with the prevention and management of harm will be likely to have pre-established commitments to principles for dealing with risks. Such perspectives may lead experts to adopt a precautionary approach in relation to the issues before the tribunal. This is true even of witnesses appointed by a party engaging in a risk-bearing activity, as these experts may have to defend their opinion before their peers and the court or tribunal. The degree of precaution reflected in the experts' input will vary, depending on their backgrounds, experience and allegiances. Experts

[90] On the legitimacy of expertise, Bodansky, 'The legitimacy', 619 ff.

may demonstrate awareness that their advice may have implications for the development of international law on the regulation of risks. In some instances this could lead to a desire to exert a positive influence over such development in the direction of a more precautionary interpretation and application of international law.

An international court or tribunal will generally seek to understand individual scientists' beliefs and commitments in relation to the types of risk at issue in the case. This is usually done without any direct investigation of the experts' views on the subject of precaution.[91] The parties' advocates may seek to highlight and investigate the note of precaution implicit in an expert's testimony. At the risk of complicating proceedings, perhaps it might additionally be helpful for tribunal members to ask experts directly about their views on the appropriateness or otherwise of precautionary approaches in particular circumstances? Arguably it is better for a tribunal, and for the parties, to have a full picture of experts' reasoning. Transparency, and the indication of assumptions on which reports are based, is regarded as a duty of the expert within the common law system.[92] Once an expert's views on the appropriateness of precaution have been openly discussed, how should the expert's testimony be regarded? It could be argued that highly qualified and experienced scientific experts are well placed to give an authoritative opinion on the appropriateness of precautionary action in circumstances of scientific uncertainty, because they are able to evaluate the uncertainties in the applicable science as a whole and with relative ease.

Direct reference by experts to precautionary approaches and to the precautionary principle should not come as a surprise. Recognition of the place precaution must take in responsible environmental policy cannot necessarily be disaggregated from the scientific methodologies they favour.[93] For example, the experts consulted in *EC – Asbestos* and *US – Shrimp* demonstrated a personal and professional commitment to aspects of the precautionary principle in situations of scientific

[91] Peel remarks that: 'it may be difficult for decision-makers to isolate the extent to which 'expert' evaluations of threats are themselves influenced by value judgments and subjective opinions', Peel, *The Precautionary Principle*, p. 157.

[92] Zuckerman, *Civil Procedure*, p. 718. See also Peel, *The Precautionary Principle*, pp. 156–7.

[93] MacDonald, 'Appreciating the precautionary principle', 262. Cf. in the EC Communication on the Precautionary Principle there is an attempt to separate out the precautionary principle proper from the employment of prudence or caution in scientific assessment and in risk analysis.

uncertainty, and we find specific articulations by the experts of precautionary values. Dr Henderson considered that when a government had to make a decision in a context of scientific uncertainty as to causes and effects, and the potential environmental consequences of action or inaction were generally considered to be serious or irreversible, then the precautionary principle was an important factor. In his view, the precautionary principle complemented science-based approaches for risk management. Indeed, in the context of mineral exploitation, invocation of the precautionary principle was premised on a recognition that scientific understanding of the potential magnitude and consequence of consequent effects on human health and the environment might be incomplete.[94] Given the extent, complexity, contradictions and uncertainties of the scientific literature on asbestos, Dr Henderson did not think that differences of view would be resolved in the foreseeable future,[95] yet there did exist 'a substantial body of independent scientific and medical opinion' that chrysotile was carcinogenic, that there was no delineated threshold level for carcinogenicity and that all aspects of chrysotile use could not be controlled, while existing scientific evidence indicated that safer substitute materials were available.[96] He noted that in national policy for occupational health and safety a prudent approach was often adopted, based on the 'first do no harm' principle[97] and conservative estimates of worst-case scenarios. The same was appropriate in national health policy.[98] Dr de Klerk essentially agreed.

In *US – Shrimp* the precautionary approach featured strongly in the views of Dr Frazier and Dr Eckert. Dr Frazier noted that defensible conclusions could not be drawn on the basis of the lack of information, but that absence of information was no proof of the absence of a phenomenon.[99] Where conservation decisions had to be made with 'imperfect knowledge', he espoused an approach of 'conservative' decision-making, referring to the precautionary approach in the Code

[94] *EC – Asbestos* PR, para. 5.624. [95] *Ibid.*, para. 5.654. [96] *Ibid.*, para. 5.655.

[97] *EC – Asbestos* JM 145. The principle *primo non nocere* is referred to a number of times in expert testimony at the meeting. For example, *ibid.*, 140, 145, 182; *EC – Asbestos* PR, para. 5.623.

[98] *EC – Asbestos* PR, para. 5.435.

[99] *US – Shrimp* PR, para. 5.273; JM, para. 35 *US – Shrimp* PR, Annex IV, Transcript of the Joint Meeting with Experts (hereafter *US – Shrimp* JM). This point has been echoed by experts in later cases, for example in *EC – Biotech* the Panel noted the advice of Dr Andow that panels should not infer an absence of effect from an absence of information. *EC – Biotech* PR, para. 7.269 note 422.

of Conduct for Responsible Fisheries of the United Nations Food and Agriculture Organization (FAO).[100] Dr Eckert observed in a similar vein that the fact there was no evidence for something did not mean it did not exist. He considered that any problem with sea-turtle populations should be immediately addressed, rather than waiting ten or twenty years for further research to be carried out.[101]

In *EC – Biotech*, the panel-appointed experts also conveyed their awareness of the limits of scientific knowledge. For example, in his concluding remarks during the oral phase of expert consultation, Dr Andow remarked wryly in relation to the particular issue of insecticide resistance, 'For each new insecticide product that came out, the entomologists thought that insects couldn't evolve resistance to "this one" (the new insecticide). By the 1980s, the entomologists gave up on that argument, because every time they said it, they were proved wrong.'[102] Throughout the case there was a particular emphasis on the scientific uncertainties associated with genetically modified crops. During the 1990s it had become accepted that research at a small scale was 'insufficient to provide knowledge of the spread, persistence and ecological effects of biotech crops at scales of field and landscape'.[103] Upscaling assumptions were scientifically unreasonable and therefore scientific studies with broad parameters were required.[104] Dr Squire also commented that 'current knowledge seems insufficient to model and predict the extent of a potential problem'.[105] In the *Continued Suspension of Obligations* cases, Dr De Brabander expressed the view that the science increasingly supported a ban on growth-promotion hormones, and that 'the economical [*sic*] profits resulting from using hormones do not balance the potential danger in all of its aspects'.[106]

An impetus towards placing considerable weight on precautionary insights from experts may become particularly strong where all the experts appointed by a panel share the view that a precautionary approach would be the most appropriate stance to adopt in a given situation. For example, in *Japan – Measures Affecting the Importation of*

[100] *US – Shrimp* PR, paras. 5.12, 5.83, 5.85; JM, para. 134.
[101] *US – Shrimp* JM, paras. 33, 122.
[102] *EC – Biotech* PR, Annex J, Transcript of the Panel's Joint Meeting with Scientific Experts of 17 and 18 February 2005 (hereafter *EC – Biotech* JM), Dr Andow, para. 1193.
[103] *EC – Biotech* PR, Annex H, Replies by the Scientific Experts, p. 16, para. 39, Dr Squire.
[104] *Ibid.*, 15, paras. 37–8, Dr Squire. [105] *Ibid.*, 14, para. 28, Dr Squire.
[106] *EC – Biotech* PR, Annex D, Replies by the Scientific Experts to Questions posed by the Panel, para. 394. See also at paras. 368–70 and 400–1.

Apples the panel-appointed experts all agreed, at the conclusion of the original proceedings, that for Japan to continue to maintain certain of the requirements it was implementing in respect of US apples would be an appropriate response to the biosecurity risk posed by fireblight.[107] Nor did the Panel find otherwise. However, at the compliance stage it seemed that there had been a reduction in the degree of precaution that the Panel was prepared to tolerate. At the parties' request, the Panel considered more closely the various distinct requirements imposed by Japan on US apples. Only one requirement was judged to be consistent with the SPS Agreement: Japan's requirement that apples exported by the US be certified as free from fireblight.

The relatively informal nature of discussion at WTO joint meetings with experts is important in making transparent and enabling panels to gauge the precautionary content of scientists' views. At the same time, where an independent expert considers precaution integral to his or her assessment of a situation, this may carry weight in a panel's own decisions about a case.[108] On the other hand, there will be occasions on which the experts demur at responding to questions they consider are governed by value judgements.[109]

In all of this it should not be discounted that the evidence of party-appointed experts may also contribute to a tribunal's appreciation of the seriousness or urgency of a risk. In the *Southern Bluefin Tuna* case the Australian scientists annexed to their report extracts from the Reports

[107] *Japan – Measures Affecting the Importation of Apples*, Complaint by the United States (WT/DS245), Report of the Panel DSR 2003: IX, 4481 (hereafter *Japan – Apples* PR), Annex 3, Transcript of the Joint Meeting with Experts, paras. 388–419. See also *Japan – Apples* PR, paras. 8.173–8.175 and *Japan – Apples* Report of the Appellate Body DSR 2003: IX, 4391, paras. 239–41.

[108] Jolowicz, describing the French system of consulting experts, highlights the weight that attaches to a single, non-partisan, expert report even though the judge is not bound by it. Jolowicz, *On Civil Procedure*, p. 231.

[109] See e.g. *European Communities – Measures Concerning Meat and Meat Products (Hormones)*, Complaint by Canada (WT/DS48), Complaint by the United States (WT/DS26). Two identically constituted WTO dispute settlement Panels (the Panel) circulated parallel reports in this case: Report of the Panel (Canada) DSR 1998: II, 235 (hereafter *EC – Hormones*, Complaint by Canada, PR), Report of the Panel (United States) DSR 1998: III, 699 (hereafter *EC – Hormones*, Complaint by the US, PR). See also the Report of the Appellate Body DSR 1998: I, 135 (hereafter *EC – Hormones* ABR). See the Complaint by Canada, PR paras. 6.143, 6.233, Complaint by the US, paras. 6.144, 6.234; and the Annex, Transcript of the Joint Meeting with Experts, attached to the panel reports in both the Complaint by Canada and the Complaint by the US (hereafter *EC – Hormones* JM), paras. 402–3. See also *Australia – Salmon* JM, para. 295; *EC – Asbestos* PR, paras. 5.332, 5.334.

of the Scientific Committee of the Commission for the Conservation of Southern Bluefin Tuna from 1991 to 1998 strongly recommending against increases in the catch of tuna given the uncertainties in the science.[110] Professor Beddington, asked by Australia and New Zealand to provide an independent report on the views of Australian and New Zealand scientists, as referred to above, saw the precautionary principle as central to dealing with scientific uncertainty in fisheries management. He referred to elements of the FAO's guidelines for precautionary measures in over-utilised fisheries. According to Professor Beddington, the SBT stock had undeniably been overfished. Spawning stock and recruitment figures were at historically low levels and assessment of the stock's prognosis for recovery was problematic given the lack of information about the behaviour of the stock at such low levels. Therefore, he considered that a precautionary approach to the management of the tuna stock was essential. In his view, any increase over 1997 catch levels would run counter to a precautionary management approach.[111]

Two-stage adjudicatory procedures

One way to deal with the issues that have been raised in this chapter in relation to the role of experts within adjudicatory processes would potentially be to separate out their role structurally. Specialist fact-finding is, effectively, often seen in the French system of expertise, and also historically in the common law.[112]

Could specialist fact-finding form part of a two-stage adjudication process in international courts and tribunals? The fact-finding phase

[110] See above, Ch. 2, p. 42.

[111] Opinion of Professor Sir John Beddington, presented in evidence by Australia and New Zealand, paras. 11, 12, 28, 42, 64, 66. Comments on the Issues raised by T. Polacheck and A. Preece, 'A scientific overview of the status of the southern bluefin tuna stock' and by Talbot Murray's 'Comment' on that Overview. In contrast, the independent report provided by the members of a 1998 review panel, annexed to the pleadings of Japan before ITLOS, took the view that it would be possible to compensate for any detectable negative effects of the experimental fishing programme by decreasing Japan's quota in future years if necessary. Panel Statement on Experimental Fishing Program by Maguire, Sullivan, Mohn and Tanaka, presented in evidence by Japan, 4.

[112] Special juries were used in England during the fourteenth century, frequently composed of tradesmen or craftsmen from relevant fields. Hand, 'Historical and practical considerations', pp. 41–2. As late as 1838 the jury *de ventre inspiciendo*, composed of married women, was empanelled to assess whether a prisoner was with child. Rosenthal, 'The development of the use of expert testimony', 407.

need not necessarily come first. Such a process might fit one of two models. Under one model, the first stage would be to ask a scientific panel or commission for findings on scientific questions, and the second stage would be to have a legal tribunal decide on the legal questions.[113] Indeed, a 'distinct procedure for establishing the facts' has been recommended as a general matter within the procedure of the International Court of Justice, in order to improve the efficacy of international litigation.[114] Under an alternative model, the judicial stage might come first, followed by the scientific stage.[115] This second model could perhaps be regarded as applying primarily in boundary disputes in which technical experts perform the clearly defined role of demarcating boundaries after an award has been made. Yet it might also be applicable in other disputes. However, on closer investigation it becomes clear that the primary difficulty with proposals for two-stage adjudication in cases involving scientific uncertainty and potential future harm is that, as discussed earlier, factual and legal issues are often not easily separable in practice, compared with instances where the mechanism of inquiry operates.

Provisions for the operation of Commissions of Inquiry were incorporated in Articles 9–14 of the 1899 Hague Convention for the Pacific Settlement of Disputes, and with greater elaboration in Articles 9–35 of the 1907 Hague Convention for the Peaceful Settlement of Disputes. As recently as 1997 the Permanent Court of Arbitration adopted Optional Rules of Procedure for Fact-Finding Commissions of Inquiry.[116] The independent mechanism of inquiry has proved helpful for resolving international disputes of high fact intensity, such as disputes over border incidents or acts of sabotage.[117] The power of inquiry as a method of dispute settlement may often be to cast a definitive light

[113] This model has similarities with the model applied in 1976 by a US taskforce when it proposed the establishment of a Science Court to resolve scientific disputes impeding administrative decision-making. Task Force of the Presidential Advisory Group on Anticipated Advances in Science and Technology, 'The Science Court Experiment: An Interim Report' (1976) 193 *Science* 653–6. The proposal was not implemented. Among the concerns expressed by critics were difficulties associated with separating out facts and values in relation to the kinds of case where the Science Court would be used. Wesley, 'Scientific evidence', 687 f; Wirth, 'The role of science', 844; Thibaut and Walker, 'A theory of procedure'.

[114] Rosenne, *The Law and Practice*, p. 1340. [115] White, *The Use of Experts*, p. 87.

[116] Permanent Court of Arbitration Optional Rules of Procedure for Fact-Finding Commissions of Inquiry, www.pca-cpa.org.

[117] Bar-Yaacov, *The Handling of International Disputes by Means of Inquiry*.

on the facts such that the claims of one of the parties are clearly substantiated.[118] There are also specialised provisions for processes in the nature of inquiry under particular agreements. Under the United Nations Agreement relating to the Conservation and Management of Straddling Fish Stocks and Highly Migratory Fish Stocks, states may establish ad hoc expert panels to help in the speedy resolution of disputes.[119] Under Article 5 of Annex VIII of the LOSC a Special Tribunal may be tasked with carrying out an inquiry in order to establish the facts giving rise to a dispute.[120] Under the 1977 Convention on the Non-Navigational Uses of International Watercourses the parties are obliged to have recourse to an impartial fact-finding mechanism unless they have agreed to another form of dispute settlement.[121]

Inquiry is seen additionally in the context of post-conflict claims settlements. In carrying out their work, the UNCC's panels assessed each claim by reference to generally accepted scientific criteria and methodologies,[122] assisted by expert consultants from many fields including chemistry, toxicology, biology, medicine, epidemiology, economics, geology, atmospheric sciences, oil spill assessment and response, rangeland management and accounting. The governments of Kuwait, Iran, Jordan and Saudi Arabia received compensation for loss of natural resources, crops, livestock, water resources and damage to public health, as well as for measures of remediation. It is interesting to note that the first instalments of environmental claims dealt with in the UNCC related to the monitoring and assessment of environmental damage. This included investigating whether environmental damage had occurred, quantifying the resulting loss and assessing methodologies to mitigate the damage.[123] In terms of their relationship to questions of liability, it was admittedly unusual to consider such claims

[118] *Ibid.*, pp. 324–7.

[119] *United Nations Agreement for the Implementation of the Provisions of the United Nations Convention on the Law of the Sea of 10 December 1982 Relating to the Conservation and Management of Straddling Fish Stocks and Highly Migratory Fish Stocks* 1995, New York, 4 August 1995, in force 11 December 2001, Article 29. Orrego Vicuña, *The Changing International Law*, pp. 272–3.

[120] See above, pp. 109, 127.

[121] See Article 33(3) of the Convention on the Non-Navigational Uses of International Watercourses, New York, 21 May 1997, 36 ILM (1997) 700.

[122] United Nations Compensation Commission Governing Council, Report and Recommendations made by the Panel of Commissioners concerning the First Instalment of 'F4' Claims, paras. 35, 43.

[123] *Ibid.*, para. 28.

before deciding claims for damage themselves. It was necessary to do so as monitoring and assessment activities might be critical in enabling quantification of claims for damage.[124] It was expected that some monitoring and assessment activities might need to be conducted for several years.[125] This accommodation of the need for further research over the medium term calls to mind the approach taken in the *Trail Smelter* arbitration.[126]

Although these processes of inquiry have proved helpful in the situations where they have been employed, inquiry in its purest form cannot as a general rule be expected to offer a final resolution to the type of dispute discussed in this book. In these cases, where mixed questions of fact and law will usually require resolution, inquiry into the facts can only ever constitute one aspect of a broader process. Reference might be made to the work of the Commission on the Limits of the Continental Shelf, established under Article 76(8) of the LOSC to make recommendations relating to the determination of the outer limits of states' continental shelves.[127] The Commission has twenty-one elected members, who are highly experienced experts in geology, geophysics and hydrography. Although the starting point for the Commission's work is the Convention's legal definition of the continental shelf, legal expertise on the Commission is limited. Tellingly, experience has suggested that it is important for submitting states to work closely in relation to the legal issues with the members of the subcommissions responsible for each state's submission.

Further illustrating the point, an Inquiry Commission reported in 2006 for the first time under Article 3 and Appendix IV of the Espoo Convention on Environmental Impact Assessment in a Transboundary Context. The Inquiry related to concerns raised by Romania concerning the Ukraine's development of an economically poor region through a construction project to enhance navigation: the Danube–Black Sea Deep-water Navigation Canal in the Ukrainian section of the Danube Delta, or 'Bystroe Canal Project'.[128] The Inquiry Commission conducted

[124] *Ibid.*, paras. 29, 30, 38, 39. [125] *Ibid.*, para. 40. [126] See above, Ch. 2, p. 32.

[127] Analysing 'the complex legal-scientific-technical interface of Article 76', Kwast suggests that the work of the Commission is best seen as only one aspect of what must be understood more broadly as the co-operative endeavour of implementing Article 76. Kwast, 'Cooperating on the law of UNCLOS Article 76'.

[128] Convention on Environmental Impact Assessment in a Transboundary Context, Espoo, 25 February 1991, in force 27 June 1997, 30 ILM (1971). For the Inquiry Commission's Report on the Likely Significant Adverse Transboundary Impacts of the

a site visit, which it also strongly recommended for future inquiries, and took advice from four experts, in the fields of hydro-morphology, geochemistry, fisheries and birdlife. The Commission concluded that the Ukraine's project was, in the terms of the Convention, 'likely to have a significant adverse transboundary impact', and recommended that Romania and the Ukraine organise a bilateral research programme. The Ukraine continued its activities and, in the light of the Commission's work, was found by the Convention's Implementation Committee to be out of compliance with its obligations under the Convention. This finding was adopted in May 2008 by the Meeting of the Parties to the Convention,[129] and the matter will be addressed again by the Meeting of the Parties in June 2011. Although the Inquiry Commission was tasked with investigating the legal question of whether the Ukraine's activity was 'likely to have a significant adverse transboundary impact', the Commission determined that in the light of the complexities associated with evaluating the impacts of human activities on the natural world an element of technical or scientific judgement would always be present in making such a determination.[130] A 'comprehensive consideration of the characteristics of the activity and its possible impact' would be made, but this had to be combined with 'knowledge and experience(s) from other, more or less similar areas or phenomena'.[131] Accordingly, the Commission had sought the best professional advice from experts of international renown.[132] In many respects what might have been regarded as an inquiry involving an application of the law to the facts came down to a purely factual enquiry.

In disputes coming before international courts and tribunals, factual investigation and legal reasoning will need to proceed in tandem. This is illustrated with reference to Singapore's assertions in the provisional measures proceedings in the *Case concerning Land Reclamation* that Malaysia had not built into its submissions the necessary bridges between the expert evidence that it laid before the International

Danube–Black Sea Navigation Route at the Border of Romania and the Ukraine, see www.unece.org (hereafter 'Report'). There have also been other international fact-finding missions in relation to this project. See in particular the Joint Mission of the Expert Team of the European Convention and International Conventions on the 'Bystroe project' in the Ukrainian part of the Danube Delta (6–8 October 2004) Mission Report of the Expert Team 17 November 2004, available at http://ec.europa.eu.

[129] Report of the Meeting of the Parties to the Convention on Environmental Impact Assessment in a Transboundary Context on its Fourth Meeting, held in Bucharest from 19 to 21 May 2008, UN DOC. ECE/MP.E1A/10.

[130] Report, 14. [131] *Ibid.*, 14. [132] *Ibid.*, 14.

Tribunal for the Law of the Sea and its legal claims that a state of urgency prevailed. At the heart of Singapore's assertions, whether they were valid or not, lay an important point. Singapore's descriptions of the Malaysian case underline the need in such cases to weave a tangible legal analysis out of the various threads that dangle from the often complex factual material submitted to the Court: 'it is not enough to present this Tribunal with a sort of do-it-yourself set of materials from which it might rustle up some sort of case'.[133] In this case the Tribunal did find the circumstances sufficiently urgent to require prompt and effective co-operation in the implementation of commitments made by the parties at the Tribunal's final sitting, which led successfully to joint studies on the issues under dispute. Where an international court or tribunal is dealing with the merits of a case, and not simply a requirement for provisional measures, the situation may be even more challenging.

The *Arbitration Regarding the Iron Rhine* also raises questions about the severability of fact and law such that a court or tribunal may always readily reserve to itself the task of addressing the legal issues, while leaving the scientific questions to experts. In the *Arbitration Regarding the Iron Rhine ('Ijzeren Rijn') Railway (Belgium and the Netherlands)*[134] the Tribunal recommended that the parties establish a committee of independent experts within four months of the date of the award to determine the costs of reactivating the Iron Rhine Railway, the costs of alternative autonomous development by the Netherlands and the quantifiable benefits accruing to the Netherlands by reason of the reactivation.[135] The Tribunal considered it appropriate to leave these issues to experts: 'Nor is it the task of this Tribunal to investigate questions of considerable scientific complexity as to which measures will be sufficient to achieve compliance with the required levels of environmental protection.'[136] The Tribunal envisaged that the work by the experts

[133] Friday 26 September, 2003, 3.00 pm, 15, lines 3–5. 'Singapore submits that Malaysia cannot simply lob four volumes of graphs and tables at the Tribunal and assert that somewhere in them there is some pretty powerful scientific evidence to back up their case.' Page 20, lines 42–4.

[134] *Arbitration Regarding the Iron Rhine ('IJZEREN RIJN') Railway (Belgium/Netherlands)*, Award of 24 May 2005, www.pca-cpa.org.

[135] *Ibid.*, para. 235.

[136] *Ibid.*, para. 235. In the *Case concerning Pulp Mills* Judges Al-Khasawneh and Simma considered the *Iron Rhine* Tribunal's 'hybrid approach' to appointing experts as a helpful example of how experts might be deployed. *Case concerning Pulp Mills*, Joint Dissenting Opinion of Judges Al-Khasawneh and Simma, para. 15.

would complete the resolution of the parties' dispute by giving concrete shape to the rulings made by the Tribunal.

What is distinctive about the Tribunal's rulings in *Iron Rhine* is the central aspect of the Tribunal's decision, that the costs of reactivation, including associated environmental measures, should be allocated in a way reflecting the 'balance' between the parties inherent in the 1839 Treaty between Belgium and the Netherlands Relative to the Separation of their Respective Territories (the Treaty of Separation). This was the instrument under which Belgium derived its right of transit across the Netherlands and the Iron Rhine Railway had been constructed. Essentially, the Tribunal held that the Netherlands was to cover the costs of the economic benefits and other benefits it would derive from reactivation of the railway and the remainder was to be covered by Belgium. A particularly expensive feature of the reactivation was likely to be the requirement for a tunnel to be built in the Meinweg area, which had been designated as a national park by the responsible Netherlands minister, and as a 'silent area' by the Province of Limburg. Here the Tribunal again applied the notion of the balance in the Treaty of Separation, this time so as to require the parties to share equally in the costs of constructing the railway in this sector. Thus it was as a result of relying on the notion of balance that the Tribunal did not have to engage closely with the science in order to assess whether a tunnel was indeed necessary to achieve 'compliance with the required levels of environmental protection'. The method employed in this case served as a unique means to separate out matters of factual enquiry from questions of law. However, the Tribunal did not clearly convey with reference to the rules on treaty interpretation how the principle of balance had been derived from Article XII of the Treaty of Separation. If similar approaches are to be used by other international courts and tribunals it will be important to articulate links back into the applicable international legal provisions, so that the method by which fact and law are separated is clearer.

From discussions earlier in this chapter, it is apparent that without the opportunity to come to terms closely with the scientific questions in a case a court or tribunal is likely to find it difficult to make findings on points such as whether a party has acted as 'necessary' or 'reasonably' in the circumstances. Yet such points cannot be determined by an expert fact-finding group. They are matters that a tribunal alone will have the authority to decide. Accordingly, an opportunity for international courts and tribunals to examine the scientific evidence themselves and to discuss these issues with scientists would seem to be of the essence in the adjudication of international disputes involving scientific uncertainty. Conferring independent jurisdiction on experts to decide factual questions would not provide the assistance that is really needed by international courts and tribunals in many cases. There is also the possibility that an extra layer of jurisdiction could lead to confusion and delay. In *Compagnie d'Electricité de Varsovie* the Polish government proposed that 'differences with regard to the interpretation of the Convention should be referred to a legal arbitrator (*arbitre juriste*) whereas those relating to the application of Articles 5 and 11 should be solved by an expert arbitrator (*arbitre expert*)'.[137] The arbitrator, while allowing for his power to consult experts, did not, however, find any intention to create such a dualism of jurisdiction, 'a dualism which cannot fail to produce interruptions and delays'.[138] On balance, the idea of using two-stage adjudication for scientific disputes does not seem worth pursuing further at this point.

The Expert Review Group in the World Trade Organization

A number of variations on two-stage adjudication may additionally be mentioned. One variation that could be useful is the employment of an expert to help draw up the terms of reference for an expert group.[139] A further variation is found in the practice of international administrative tribunals, in that these tribunals may have access to the prior factual findings of international organisations' internal dispute-resolution bodies such as joint appeals boards in the United Nations or appeals committees such as in the World Bank.[140] Potentially more significant is the provision in Article 13.2 of the WTO DSU which enables panels to

[137] *France* v. *Poland (In the Matter of the Dispute between the Compagnie d'Electricité de Varsovie and the Municipality of Warsaw)*, 30 November 1929, 5 ILR 387, 388.

[138] *Ibid.*, 390. In a number of disputes over oil concessions the parties have, however, clearly intended to create dual arbitral jurisdiction. White, *Use of Experts*, p. 175.

[139] Amerasinghe reports that this was contemplated but not pursued by Chamber One of the Iran–US Claims Tribunal in the *Starrett* case. Amerasinghe, *Evidence*, pp. 157–8. *Starrett Housing Corporation, Starrett Systems, Inc., Starrett Housing International, Inc.* v. *The Government of the Islamic Republic of Iran, Bank Markazi Iran, Bank Omran, Bank Mellat*, Order of 20 September 1982, 4 Iran–US CTR 122, Part V.

[140] Amerasinghe, *Evidence*, p. 281.

seek an advisory report from an 'expert review group'.[141] Panels have not pursued this option, and have continued to consult experts individually,[142] despite the urging of the EC instead to appoint and consult individual experts.[143] Panels have relied on Article 13.1 and 13.2 of the DSU, which provides for them to seek information and technical advice. In *European Communities – Measures Concerning Meat and Meat Products (Hormones)* the Panel decided that the right in Article 13.1 and 13.2, and in Article 11.2 of the SPS Agreement, was not limited by the references to establishment of an expert review group in those provisions, despite EC protestations.[144] The Appellate Body commented that there was no legal obstacle to the Panel drawing up ad hoc rules for these particular proceedings in consultation with the parties, as Appendix 4 of the DSU, which sets out rules and procedures applicable to expert

[141] Article 13.2 states that: 'Panels may seek information from any relevant source and may consult experts to obtain their opinion on certain aspects of the matter. With respect to a factual issue concerning a scientific or other technical matter raised by a party to a dispute, a panel may request an advisory report in writing from an expert review group. Rules for the establishment of such a group and its procedures are set forth in Appendix 4.'

Article 13.2 is very similar to provisions for seeking input from expert review groups in the 1979 Tokyo Round TBT Agreement on Technical Barriers to Trade. For further background, Christoforou, 'WTO Panels', 243–65. Appendix 4 to the DSU now sets out rules and procedures that apply to expert review groups established in accordance with Article 13.2. Appendix 4 of the WTO DSU provides explicitly that the final report of an 'expert review group' shall be advisory only. The assumption has been made that Appendix 4 of the DSU applies to the possible use of expert review groups in disputes arising under the SPS Agreement, even though Article 11.2 of the SPS Agreement refers to an 'advisory' 'technical expert group' rather than an 'expert review group'. There are also specific provisions on consultation of expert groups by panels under Article 11.2 of the SPS Agreement, and Article 14.2 of the TBT Agreement. Annex 2 to the TBT Agreement sets out provisions that apply to 'technical expert groups' appointed by panels to assist with disputes falling under the TBT Agreement. See Pauwelyn, 'The use of experts', Note 14. Panels may also have recourse under Article 4.5 of the WTO Agreement on Subsidies and Countervailing Measures to the Permanent Group of Experts established under Article 24 of that Agreement. Likewise, Article 18.2 and Annex II of the WTO Customs Valuation Agreement establish a Technical Committee on Customs Valuation, from which panels may request a report under Article 19.4. The Rules of Conduct for the DSU, adopted by the DSB on 11 December 1996 (WT/DSB/RC/1), apply to all experts participating in the dispute settlement mechanism pursuant to Article 13 of the DSU or the specific provisions under the three other WTO agreements.

[142] The provisions of Appendix 4 have been applied by analogy. Pauwelyn, 'The use of experts', 340.

[143] *Canada – Continued Suspension* PR, paras. 6.20, 7.63–7.73; *US – Continued Suspension* PR, paras. 6.21, 7.65–7.75.

[144] *EC – Hormones*, Complaint by Canada, PR, para. 8.7; Complaint by the US, PR, para. 8.7. See also *EC – Asbestos* PR, paras. 5.1, 5.4, 5.12, 5.17, 5.18, 8.10.

review groups, did not apply.[145] The possible use of expert review groups has not had a high profile within the WTO membership in general, and there is no impetus to amend Article 13.2 of the DSU.

What would be the advantages and disadvantages of using an expert review group? Advantages include a potential boost in the assistance provided to panels. For example, as part of its role the group could be asked to undertake the task of refining and synthesising, or systematising, the relevant scientific information in the field. The group might be asked to identify the existing range of views among the contemporary scientific community on the issues arising in the dispute at hand.[146] Using a system of appointing individual experts requires panels to appreciate where the common ground may lie between a range of scientific views, and this will sometimes be a challenging task.[147] Especially in complex cases, this is a demanding role to expect of any adjudicatory body, even a domestic court with years of experience in dealing with scientific evidence. A particular concern is that errors by panels in the ascertainment of fact cannot easily be challenged, unless there is egregious error.[148] On balance, it would not be surprising if WTO panels were to give further consideration to the possibility of using expert review groups.

However, the case for using an expert group is not entirely persuasive. At its best, a group procedure might produce a comprehensive response to a particular question based on an integrated application of the individual experts' scientific knowledge. However, much of this is achievable by making imaginative and patient use of the existing processes of consultation with individual experts. Further, as a practical matter it has to be accepted at the outset that the views of an expert review group would not be monolithic. Room would certainly have to be left for the expression of minority views, and panels would have to take these views into account in their decision-making. There is also a broader problem. Whether experts from a range of different disciplines would be prepared to put their names to a group report incorporating the perspectives of their colleagues from fields with which they were individually unfamiliar would remain to be seen. Additionally, although the established procedure for the consultation of experts as individuals is

[145] *EC – Hormones* ABR, 148. [146] Conversation with WTO practitioner.

[147] Pauwelyn, 'The use of experts', 329–30, 355; Christoforou, 'WTO Panels in the face of scientific uncertainty'.

[148] *EC – Hormones* ABR, para. 133. See Article 17.6 of the DSU, above, Ch. 3, p. 120.

time-consuming, largely because of the difficulties associated with the selection of experts, the appointment of a group could be more time-consuming, because these difficulties might become even more pronounced.[149] Where an expert group with distinct responsibilities was being appointed, efforts would have to be redoubled to avoid any perceived or actual bias or conflict of interest. The decision-making process would also become lengthier.[150]

The important question would also remain of how best to deal with closely mixed questions of fact and law if an expert group was used. Discussion on this issue earlier in this chapter has suggested that it is helpful for adjudicators to have experts' input on such questions, but that the experts' input should be transparent and courts and tribunals should continue to take responsibility for the decisions adopted. Consideration should be given to how to carry these insights through into an expert review-group system. For example, questions relating directly to matters such as the necessity of a measure, or the sufficiency of scientific evidence, could be included among those asked of the expert review group. The scientists could also be asked, for example, whether a risk assessment relied upon by a member is scientifically sound and complete. This advice might go to a legal question such as whether a risk assessment merits designation as such. In preparing its written report, an expert review group could be asked to disaggregate its views, setting out why the members consider a measure 'necessary' or the science 'sufficient'. That is to say, both particular and more general reasons could be given for the group's advice. Being provided with all of this material would put a panel in a stronger position to make the best use of the scientific evidence. However, an expert group could be given no discrete mandate or jurisdiction to determine such issues, which are clearly for the panel. Panels would need to retain the opportunity to meet with the experts for discussion of the scientific points that would help the panel to develop its understanding of crucial issues.

The bottom line then, is that the scientific and legal stages of dealing with a dispute cannot readily be altogether separated out. The overall effect of using an expert review group in WTO dispute settlement might well be largely presentational: the consultation with experts would appear more distinct from the other stages involved in a panel's consideration of a case. As a result, adjudicatory decision-making within the WTO might gain a political buffer against error in the appreciation of

[149] Conversation with WTO practitioner. [150] Pauwelyn, 'Expert advice', 237.

the science. Potentially the use of an expert group might even create more scope for the exercise of a power of revision by the dispute settlement body if this appeared necessary in the light of new scientific evidence.[151] However, the use of an expert group would in practice not truly create two-stage adjudication. In any event, using an expert review group might not help increase transparency within the WTO. The accountability of the scientific participants would be diluted by the requirement to produce a joint report, even where allowance was made for the expression of minority views. The dynamics between the individual scientists would not be open to observation. Further, it is possible that disproportionate weight might be given to such a report merely because it was a group product. The political response might be to ask why, instead, the WTO dispute settlement system did not rely on the expert work of international organisations such as the World Organisation for Animal Health (OIE – previously the Office International des Épizooties).

The expert dispute settlement mechanisms in the OIE and under the International Plant Protection Convention (IPPC)[152] could indeed form a prelude to WTO dispute settlement. However, in neither case are experts tasked with resolving legal issues. Under Article XIII of the IPPC the Director General of the FAO will appoint a committee of experts on the request of a party or parties to report in relation to any dispute over the Convention's interpretation and application or:

> if a contracting party considers that any action by another contracting party is in conflict with the obligations of the latter under [the provisions of the Convention dealing with phytosanitary certification and import requirements] especially regarding the basis of prohibiting or restricting the imports of plants, plant products or other regulated articles coming from its territories.

A number of the IPPC obligations regarding import requirements are similar to the obligations under the SPS Agreement, for example the obligation in Article VII(2)(a) of the IPPC not to take phytosanitary measures unless necessary and technically justified. The Committee will include representatives designated by each party and will take into account evidence from the parties. The Convention expressly envisages that a copy of the report may be requested by the WTO, 'the

[151] On the question of revision, see below, Ch. 7.

[152] International Plant Protection Convention, Rome, 6 December 1951, in force 3 April 1952 (as amended by the FAO Conference at its Twentieth Session (November 1979) and at its Twenty-ninth Session (November 1997) UNTS 1952, 68.

competent body of the international organization responsible for resolving trade disputes'.[153] However the Committee's report will deal only with the technical aspects of the dispute and is not binding.

In the OIE an expert mediation procedure will operate by consent of the parties.[154] The expert mediators are to be recommended by the Director General of the OIE, usually from OIE Reference Laboratories or Consulting Centres. They will endeavour to find a technically sound consensus or compromise solution that will allow trade to be established or re-established between the parties. This process is confidential. Thus neither the IPPC nor the OIE procedure involves a legal ruling on whether a party is acting consistently with its WTO obligations. That is left to be dealt with through the WTO dispute-settlement mechanisms. However, IPPC recommendations might form part of the evidence put before a WTO dispute-settlement panel.

In conclusion, where fact and law are close an international court or tribunal has little choice but to come to terms with the science. The challenges this poses may be considerable, but the task cannot be delegated. Given this imperative, the point that predominates is the value of the dialogue that presently takes place between panels or tribunals and individually appointed experts especially in addressing mixed questions of fact and law. Establishing an altogether distinct scientific fact-finding stage within international adjudication, or a 'tribunal within a tribunal'[155] would not appear easily to meet the needs of such cases. Clearly, it would be of immense help to an international court or tribunal if it were possible to be provided with an independent scientific overview of a case at the outset of proceedings. The ideal scientific overview would identify the scientific issues relevant to the legal problems before the court or tribunal, and explain the state of the science on important scientifically disputed or uncertain points. However, producing such a summary would require both legal and scientific expertise, and the summary would have to be adjusted in the course of proceedings to reflect the new insights gained through the adversarial process. Certainly, a working summary might be a useful internal document for a court or tribunal to make use of as it comes to grips with the relevance of the science in the case before it.

153 *Ibid.*, Article 13(3).

154 The procedure is described in *International Trade: Rights and obligations of OIE members*, available on the OIE website, www.oie.int/.

155 Pauwelyn, 'Expert advice', 237.

The help of a scientific assessor or assessors would most likely be needed to create and develop such a document.

Selection of experts by international courts and tribunals

As the inevitable expert involvement in the interpretative and decision-making processes of international courts and tribunals increases, the pressure will go on to ensure experts are appropriately selected. Experience in the WTO has shown that there may be considerable difficulty with the selection of its own independent experts by an international court or tribunal. In the WTO, considerable effort is expended in attempting to select appropriately qualified experts who are acceptable to the parties. WTO panels have adopted a practice of requesting lists from specialised international agencies identifying possible candidates for appointment as experts. Inter-agency consultation, along with all other administrative aspects of WTO dispute resolution, is facilitated by the WTO secretariat. The involvement of the specialised agencies assists the WTO in a practical sense, and at the same time the involvement of the agencies as neutral third parties in the nominations process enhances perceptions of the chosen experts as independent.

In particular, panels have approached those agencies listed in Annex A, paragraph 3, of the SPS Agreement. In *EC – Hormones*, for example, in addition to appointing one expert selected by each party, the Panel appointed two experts from lists sought from the Secretariat of the Codex Alimentarius Commission and the International Agency for Research on Cancer.[156] In *Australia – Salmon*, the Panel consulted with the OIE,[157] while in the *Japan – Agricultural Products* case names of experts were requested from the Secretariat of the IPPC.[158] In *EC – Biotech*, the Panel sought names of experts from the secretariats of the Convention on Biological Diversity, the Codex Alimentarius Commission, the FAO, the IPPC, the OIE and World Health Organization. This produced a list of thirty names, and names were also requested from the parties, producing another seventy names.[159] The Secretariat contacted the individuals named by the international organisations, and this produced

[156] *EC – Hormones*, Complaint by Canada, PR, para. 6.5; Complaint by the US, PR, para. 6.6.
[157] *Australia – Salmon* PR, para. 6.2. [158] *Japan – Agricultural Products* PR, para. 6.2.
[159] *EC – Biotech* PR, paras. 7.21, 7.22.

nineteen curricula vitae, with twenty-nine curricula vitae coming from the experts named by the parties.[160]

Generally the parties will then be given an opportunity to comment on the proposed experts on the basis of their curricula vitae. The parties may be asked to rank the nominees in order of preference and state any 'major' or 'compelling objections' to individual experts.[161] Where positive agreement cannot be secured, the aim will be to compile a list of individuals in relation to whom no party has raised a compelling objection. In *EC – Biotech*, for example, the parties submitted many compelling objections.[162] Parties will be asked for their reasons for any such objections.[163] Where it becomes clear that the selection process has not produced experts in all the necessary fields of expertise, an additional selection round may be held. This took place in the *EC – Biotech* case, on the basis of a list of experts named by the parties.[164] Altogether, the group of experts consulted in *EC – Biotech* included scientists specialising in entomology, food technology, ecology and biology, crop research, food standards and crop genetics.[165] In *EC – Hormones* the EC emphasised that all the requisite areas of expertise should be covered when experts were selected, and accordingly the Panel appointed an additional expert with expertise in the carcinogenic effects of hormones.[166]

The panel will also be aware of the need for some diversity of views among the experts to be selected. If the science in a particular field is not settled, it is important that a panel avoid appointing a set of experts whose advice is unlikely to reflect the actual divergence of views within the scientific community.[167] Given that the number of recognised worldwide experts in a particular scientific subdiscipline may be limited, this can be awkward in practice. For example, there could be as few as five experts who might potentially be approached for advice on a particular topic. These experts, who may have had no reason previously to be aware of the activity of the WTO or its dispute resolution procedures, will have to be approached to see if they would be willing and available to assist the panel.[168] They must be asked to confirm their suitability for appointment in terms of the areas of expertise in which

[160] *Ibid.*, paras. 7.21 and 7.22.
[161] See e.g. *Australia – Salmon* PR, para. 6.3; *Japan – Agricultural Products* PR, para. 6.2; *EC – Asbestos* PR, paras. 5.8, 5.20.
[162] *EC – Biotech* PR, paras. 7.21, 7.23, 7.27. [163] Pauwelyn, 'The use of experts', 344.
[164] *EC – Biotech* PR, para. 7.27. [165] *Ibid.*, paras. 7.25, 7.27.
[166] *EC – Hormones*, Complaint by Canada, PR, para. 6.6; Complaint by the US, PR, para. 6.7.
[167] Conversation with WTO practitioner. [168] Conversation with WTO practitioner.

the panel requires assistance. Perhaps it then becomes apparent that two of these five experts actually work for the government in one of the disputing members' own countries, or for private parties whose interests stand to be affected by the outcome of the dispute in question. Perhaps the parties then object to the remaining names on the list. In such circumstances the selection of experts rapidly becomes very awkward. Accordingly, it is understood that a panel may override parties' reluctance in relation to the appointment of particular individuals, in order for dispute resolution to proceed. Panels will be aware that the unfortunate result of too readily accepting all the objections raised by the parties could be a catastrophic loss of access to the best available international expertise.[169] Problems with gaining the parties' agreement to experts proposed following such procedures led to a reversal of approach in the *EC - Biotech* case. Not since the *EC - Hormones* case had the parties been invited to nominate experts themselves. In *EC - Hormones* the Panel selected two experts from the lists of nominees put forward by the EC and the US.[170] In *EC - Biotech* the Panel again invited nominations from the parties, and then used their lists in its selection process.[171] However, objections remained a problem.

The extent to which the parties can expect automatically to be involved in the selection of experts in international courts and tribunals more generally is limited. In principle, it is for the international court to select its own experts, though the parties may be consulted. The extent to which this is so will depend on the practice of the particular tribunal and on the circumstances of the case. For example, under the rules of the Iran–US Claims Tribunal, experts could be selected in a number of ways: by agreement between the parties, on the recommendation of professional associations or at the recommendation of the Chair of the Tribunal.[172] In some instances joint nomination may prove an efficient way of eliminating arguments about the competence of the experts while also ensuring that they are seen as completely objective and impartial. In the *Case concerning Delimitation of the Maritime Boundary in the Gulf of Maine area (Canada/United States of America)*, a boundary dispute,

[169] Pauwelyn, 'Expert advice', 246.

[170] Pauwelyn, 'The use of experts', 342. Canada initiated its parallel complaint against the EC later than the US, and so missed the opportunity to nominate experts itself. It was agreed that the same experts would be consulted and Canada was invited to comment on the experts who had been identified for the US case.

[171] Conversation with WTO practitioner.

[172] Amerasinghe, *Evidence*, p. 396; van Hof, *Commentary on the UNCITRAL Rules*, pp. 194–7.

the parties required in their Special Agreement the appointment of a jointly nominated expert by the International Court of Justice. This appointment was made under Article 50 of the Court's Statute.[173] The expert, Mr Peter Bryan Beazley, a retired commander in the British Navy, submitted a technical report and was also available for consultation by the Court. Mr Beazley took part directly in the Court's deliberations and his input enabled the Court to delimit the boundary between the parties, as requested by the parties.[174] His report does not appear to have been provided to the parties, although it is annexed to the judgment.[175] Joint nomination may be less politically feasible in the type of case addressed in this book, where scientific uncertainty is high and there are risks of harm to individuals or the environment.[176]

When appointing experts, international courts and tribunals will need to be conscious of potential conflicts of interest on the part of the experts. In the *Continued Suspension of Obligations* cases, the Appellate Body found that the Panel had infringed the EC's due-process rights in consulting two experts. These two experts had previously been members of the Joint FAO/WHO Expert Committee on Food Additives (JECFA), the international standard-setting body that had evaluated the growth-promotion hormones, and they had participated in these evaluations.[177] The experts' institutional affiliation 'compromised their appointment and thereby the adjudicative independence and impartiality of the Panel'.[178] The US and Canada took exception to this finding.[179] The US was concerned that the Appellate Body's standard for independence and impartiality could disqualify experts who, like the individuals

[173] *Case concerning Delimitation of the Maritime Boundary in the Gulf of Maine area (Canada/United States of America)*, Order of 30 March 1984, ICJ Reports 1984, 165.

[174] For these reasons, his role has been likened to that of an assessor rather than an expert. Riddell and Plant, *Evidence*, p. 335, citing Rosenne, *Procedure*, p. 32; Rosenne, *The Law and Practice*, pp. 1326, 1328. *Case concerning Delimitation of the Maritime Boundary in the Gulf of Maine area (Canada/United States of America)*, Judgment of 12 October 1984, ICJ Reports 1984 (hereafter *Gulf of Maine* case).

[175] *Gulf of Maine* case, 174. Rosenne, *The Law and Practice*, p. 1326.

[176] Allison and Holtzmann, 'The Tribunal's use of experts'.

[177] *Continued Suspension* ABR, paras. 437–84.

[178] *Ibid.*, para. 736(b). For the Panel's defence of the appointments in the light of EC concerns, see *Canada – Continued Suspension* PR, para. 6.21; *US – Continued Suspension* PR, para. 6.22.

[179] Communication from the United States on concerns regarding the Appellate Body's Report, WT/DS320/16, 12 November 2008, paras. 23–9. For Canada's concerns, see Minutes of Meeting held in the Centre William Rappard on 14 November 2008, Dispute Settlement Body, 4 February 2009, WT/DSB/M/258.

in question, 'had an intimate understanding and well-developed ability to communicate matters of extreme technical, scientific, and conceptual complexity, by virtue of their familiarity with the risk assessment at issue',[180] and that panels could be entrusted with taking into account experts' prior involvement in related processes.[181] This finding can be contrasted with the Appellate Body's rejection of EC complaints at the appeal stage in the *EC – Hormones* case that one of the experts selected by the Panel had links to the pharmaceutical industry and was a national of a party or third party.[182]

The limits of scientific expertise

Issues may also arise in relation to the boundaries of the knowledge and expertise of experts, or indeed of international organisations consulted by an international court or tribunal. During the consultation of experts, tribunals may need to rely on the experts for indications of the limits of their respective scientific disciplines. For example, in *EC – Asbestos*, both in their written comments and at the joint meeting the experts indicated from time to time that matters fell outside their area of expertise. In other instances it has been the parties who have raised objections in this regard. For example, in assessing the necessity of Thailand's restrictions on the import of US cigarettes in *Thailand – Cigarettes*, the GATT Panel charged with deciding the case relied in part on the advice of the WHO representatives that bans on advertising could curb demand for cigarettes,[183] but the Panel did not adopt the view expressed by the WHO representatives that experience elsewhere had shown that if multinational tobacco companies entered closed markets then an increase in smoking resulted.[184] The Panel did not give reasons for this, but US objections that WHO opinion on this point was not within its area of recognised expertise, or within the scope of the parties' understanding on the purpose of consultation with WHO, may have carried some weight.[185]

Scientific experts' special expertise will not necessarily extend to social questions connected with parties' disputes. Yet their views have been sought on such questions. For example, in *EC – Hormones* at various

[180] *Ibid.*, para. 25. [181] *Ibid.*, para. 24. [182] *EC – Hormones* ABR, para. 148.

[183] GATT Panel Report, *Thailand – Restrictions on Importation of and Internal Taxes on Cigarettes*, DS10/R, adopted 7 November 1990, BISD 37S/20, 78.

[184] *Ibid.*, 55. [185] *Ibid.*, 58.

points in the joint meeting with experts the Chair also put questions to the experts on topics that might not be strictly regarded as scientific, although could be considered subjects of technical expertise with which a Panel might require some assistance. Several of these questions could equally have been put to regulators or administrators, and even to the representatives of the parties, although the scientists provided a perspective on the points that may have been of some assistance. For example, in *EC – Hormones* the Panel was seeking to understand the extent to which abuse and overuse of growth-promotion hormones was widespread. In response to one question on this point, one expert replied 'it is not a scientific question ... do you think people drive faster than allowed in any country or in another one [*sic*]?'[186] However, two of the other experts spoke on the issue, drawing on surveys that had been carried out and referring to the detectability of residues as a deterrent. The Panel also sought the experts' views during the written stage of consultation on how the EC ban was implemented in practice, internally and at its borders.

In *EC – Asbestos* the experts were also asked about the effectiveness of training to assist controlled-use policies. One expert listed human error, wilful non-compliance, poor judgement, accidents and the impossibility of training the population that would be exposed to asbestos as factors making it impossible to be sure of a certain minimum exposure level even under controlled-use policies.[187] However he suggested that whether controlled-use or prohibition policies would achieve the elimination of chrysotile from the workplace and the human environment in general was essentially 'a societal question and a public health policy issue'.[188] Expert input on the question whether controlled use was a feasible policy was essentially based on general knowledge and experience rather than scientific knowledge.[189]

In WTO cases it is probable that panels will seek expert assistance in dealing with the social and legal comparison of risks and appropriate measures to respond to them. In *EC – Hormones* a topic that was of considerable significance in the legal framework in the case, but to

[186] *EC – Hormones* JM, para. 170. See also the Chair's remark in the *Continued Suspension of Obligations* cases that the experts might not be in a position to respond to questions about the extent to which good veterinary practice was used. *Continued Suspension* JM, para. 834; see also para. 839. When one of the experts did respond, Canada took issue with this and the expert clarified that it went beyond his role as an expert to comment on the matter. See paras. 875–7, 882–6.

[187] *EC – Asbestos* PR, para. 5.360. [188] *Ibid.*, para. 5.435. [189] *Ibid.*, paras. 5.336, 5.343–5.

which science could only partially contribute, was the question referred to earlier of whether bans on growth-promotion hormones were arbitrarily discriminatory. The Chair repeated questions to the experts to try and establish whether carbadox, which worked only indirectly as a growth promoter through its effect on intestinal bacteria, could be 'compared with' hormonal growth-promotion agents, or whether there was a 'critical distinction' between them.[190] The Chair explained that because the agreement required 'legally consistent policies' the Panel needed to know from the scientific point of view whether these agents could be compared.[191] The experts appeared reluctant to respond, perhaps considering this a comparison which rather required an assessment on the basis of non-scientific considerations. One expert, sensing the Panel's need for assistance, ventured a reply. He said that the hour was late and he was 'going to go out on a limb'.[192] He said that even though a number of the experts had consistently said they felt uncomfortable with drawing comparisons, carbadox was a genotoxic carcinogen, while there was much debate over whether growth-promotion hormones were genotoxic carcinogens. Within the toxicological community, they would attach greater concern to a compound which was a genotoxic carcinogen than to one with a different kind of effect.

International courts and tribunals should retain an awareness of the distinctions that may be drawn between scientific and social questions. Turning to the experts for advice, as well as to the parties, may help a court or tribunal to inform itself on certain issues that are more social than scientific in character. However, it will be important to listen to the caveats placed on experts' responses and to allow the parties full opportunity to comment on experts' contributions to non-scientific questions. Often, there will be a connection with the legal issues before the court or tribunal.

[190] *EC – Hormones* JM, paras. 767, 770.

[191] *EC – Hormones* JM, para. 772. Although the Chair reined in a question by the EC dealing with the relative safety of growth-promotion hormones and carbadox. *Ibid.*, para. 347.

[192] Comments of Dr Ritter, *EC – Hormones* JM, paras. 773, 776. The Chair also asked the experts whether, if evidence of the possible genotoxicity of hormones was a reason to ban their use in growth promotion, it was also a reason to ban their other uses. Comment was offered by Dr Arnold and Dr André on the justification for use of hormones in their therapeutic applications. *Ibid.*, paras. 861, 863. Pauwelyn observes that 'Upon some insisting by the panel, an expert may nonetheless be tempted to make a guess.' Pauwelyn, 'The use of experts', 349–50.

The quality of scientific evidence

Clearly, scientific evidence relied upon by an international court or tribunal needs to be of high quality if the authority and finality of its judgments are not to be undermined. Courts' and tribunals' freedom to assess evidence and accord it such weight as they consider appropriate allows them to disregard any evidence which does not appear sufficiently reliable. Decisions about the weight to attribute to evidence are usually made as they arise. International courts and tribunals apply no general rules, for example rules requiring that weight will only be placed on scientific evidence that has been subject to peer review and publication.[193] This may be important in the context of potential harm. For example, in *EC – Asbestos* the EC argued that governments should not be prevented from taking action quickly when they were presented with the substantive results of significant reports, as it could take quite some time for formal scientific publication.[194]

There is also the question of the extent to which reliance should be placed on personal communications with scientists. For example, in *Australia – Salmon* one of the panel-appointed experts, Dr Rodgers, observed the degree of reliance by both parties on 'personal communications with respected fish pathologists' and suggested these 'should be accepted at face value', as there was not time to corroborate all the information they contained. He noted the unpublished status of the data, and that it 'could contain an element of subjective opinion and assumption'. However, there was a problem with the published scientific literature in that it could quickly become out of date. Further, Canada had access to data from 'research projects, veterinary reports and monitoring and surveillance programmes', not always publicly available in the scientific community.[195]

One example of scientific evidence of unsuitable quality to form the basis of a judicial decision is found in the *Japan – Apples* case. Numerous studies indicated that mature, symptomless apples did not harbour endophytic populations of fireblight.[196] Japan cited a study by van der Zwet that was said to have recorded findings of the fireblight bacterium in mature fruit. Although the van der Zwet study had recorded

[193] See above, Ch. 1, pp. 12–14.

[194] *EC – Asbestos* PR, para. 3.29. In *US – Shrimp*, research still too recent to have been published was put forward on its own merits as expert opinion. *US – Shrimp* JM, para. 115.

[195] *Australia – Salmon* PR, para. 6.87.

[196] *Japan – Apples* PR, para. 8.123.

fireblight in harvested fruit the authors had not specified the maturity of this fruit or whether the fruit was symptomless. The US had sought clarification from the main authors of the van der Zwet study but this had only cast further doubt on the proposition that the fireblight bacterium might be found in commercially mature fruit. The Panel reached the view that the van der Zwet findings were unclear and disputed.[197]

As well as the science cited by the parties, the advice of international standard-setting bodies may also come under scrutiny. In *Australia – Salmon* Australia argued that OIE advice that evisceration be regarded as a standard measure against transmission of fish diseases did not reflect the significance to Australia of diseases that were endemic in major aquaculture fishing nations but exotic to Australia.[198] Australia argued that the OIE Code was not to be regarded as adequate in the particular circumstances of the case in terms of international guidelines, because it was 'under substantial revision, not representative of global conditions, not grounded on a scientific basis and the result of non-transparent decision-making'.[199] The panel was interested to assess how the OIE operated. At the meeting with experts another of the panel-appointed experts, Dr Winton, explained how the Fish Diseases Commission (FDC), which was the relevant specialist commission of the OIE, worked. It was not necessarily the repository of all available data and opinion. The FDC gathered information through its large collegial networks,[200] but did not try to consider 'every possible disease risk between any possible trading partners'.[201] Periodically they invited input from experts in particular areas where the FDC had weaknesses. Their procedure was informal, and based on the consensus of the five members.[202] The emphasis tended to fall on uncontrollable diseases with a proven etiology with a limited geographic distribution and robust diagnostic methods.[203] The Panel recalled that the SPS Agreement explicitly directed it to the OIE's standards, guidelines and recommendations.[204] The validity of the OIE Code for the Panel's purposes was not altered due to its being subject to revision or because of the way it was adopted.[205]

[197] *Ibid.*, para. 8.127. [198] *Australia – Salmon* JM, para. 326.
[199] *Australia – Salmon* PR, para. 7.10. [200] *Australia – Salmon* JM, para. 40.
[201] *Ibid.*, para. 43.
[202] *Ibid.*, para. 44. It was 'a very dynamic process' and, he said, 'we will probably never get it completely right'. *Ibid.*, para. 43 (see also *Australia – Salmon* PR para. 6.135, Written Consultation with Experts, Dr Winton's response to Question 21).
[203] *Australia – Salmon* PR, para. 6.137. [204] SPS Agreement, Article 5.1, Annex A, para. 3(b).
[205] *Australia – Salmon* PR, para. 7.10.

Such generic issues in relation to professional standards in scientific evidence that are likely to arise repeatedly: whether research cited is the most recent, whether it is reliable, whether publication is required as an indicator of reliability, and whether reports of personal communications with scientists carry weight. Tribunals presently assess the probative value of proffered evidence on a case-by-case basis, and indeed, given the complexity and variety of disputes which may arise, this may be the most appropriate response. The adoption of specific rules on the weight of different forms of evidence might be more of a hindrance than a help, particularly if these rules were to go beyond mere guidelines.

The responsibility of the court or tribunal

International courts and tribunals should not fight shy of taking overall responsibility for the determination and decisions made in a case. As in the common law, 'A Court trying a dispute ... must itself decide the issues between the parties, no matter how difficult the issues, or how much their determination may require specialist knowledge.'[206] In contrast, under Roman law a judge might refuse to pronounce judgment if neither party to a dispute could provide a convincing case.[207] The doctrine of *non liquet* could result in deferral of a decision in the absence of sufficient information about the facts of the case.[208] There is no authority for the recognition of such a doctrine in international law. International courts have a duty to reach a decision on disputes properly brought before them. The best way to avoid the real danger of reaching a decision based on facts that a court or tribunal does not properly comprehend is to make use of the best available means for the consultation of appropriate experts.

Comfort may be drawn from the realisation that there will seldom be a suggestion that international courts and tribunals should make narrow or specific findings involving taking a precise position on scientific issues. While the science must be thoroughly interrogated, a court's findings on mixed questions of science and law will be predicated only on such views on the science as must be formed in order to make these findings. For example, in the *Gabčíkovo-Nagymaros* case, Hungary emphasised that the ICJ 'does not have to pronounce definitively on

[206] Zuckerman, *Civil Procedure*, p. 731, footnote omitted. [207] Sandifer, *Evidence*, p. 126.
[208] White, *The Use of Experts*, p. 87.

contested scientific issues, but it does have to decide whether there were serious scientific concerns on issues affecting vital resources'.[209] In the *Case concerning Pulp Mills*, counsel for Argentina urged the Court not to focus solely on the issue of whether or not the plant was causing harm, although it was necessary for the Court to consider these risks.[210] Judges Al-Khasawneh and Simma observed that 'the task of a court of justice is not to give a scientific assessment of what has happened, but to evaluate the claims of the parties before it and whether such claims are sufficiently well-founded so as to constitute evidence of a breach of a legal obligation'.[211] The same point was made by Judge Keith who stressed that the 'responsibility of making decisions on the matters of scientific dispute arises only if the matters require decision in the course of the Court determining whether or not Argentina had made out its claim. A number of issues debated before the Court, such as the river flow and the best ways of measuring it, did not have to be decided in the course of making that determination'.[212]

Conclusion

States are likely on the whole to support approaches to international adjudication under which every practicable and reasonable measure is taken to produce outcomes that will be accepted by litigants and by the international community.[213] Fairness between litigants and fairness to the wider community may often be well served where international courts and tribunals appoint and consult closely with independent advisers when necessary.[214]

The tensions canvassed in this chapter will be at their most tangible in relation to the testimony of independent experts appointed by international courts and tribunals. Problems may also potentially arise where international courts and tribunals seek advice from international organisations specialising in relevant fields. The issues are less likely to arise as intensely in relation to party-appointed expert witnesses, as a

209 Verbatim Record, Monday 3 March 1997, 94–5. See also the Verbatim Record of Thursday 10 April, 15–16.

210 Verbatim Record, Monday 14 September 2009, translation, 13–19.

211 *Case concerning Pulp Mills*, Joint Dissenting Opinion of Judges Al-Khasawneh and Simma, para. 4.

212 *Ibid.*, Separate Opinion of Judge Keith, para. 11.

213 Lawrence and Slaughter, 'Toward a theory of effective supranational adjudication'

214 Stein, *Foundations of Evidence Law*, p. 237.

court or tribunal is less likely to rely as directly and overtly on evidence understood by all participants as partisan in some degree. Even where evidence from party-appointed experts is persuasive, their evidence is naturally a step removed from the court or tribunal by virtue of having been introduced by a party and subjected to the adversarial process. Further, the evidence will be framed by that party's understanding of the case. It may or may not be directed to relevant mixed questions of fact and law as perceived by the court or tribunal. For all this, the problem will not be altogether absent in relation to the evidence of party-appointed experts. Difficulties are most likely in relation to testimony from a party-appointed expert who expressly appears in an independent capacity, especially if he or she is questioned by the court or tribunal.

Although there will be different patterns in relation to evidence sourced from experts in different capacities, overall it is clear that some involvement of experts in legal issues will be unavoidable. There are remedies, but these remedies are only partial. Further, caution and an adherence to the precautionary principle will form part of the world-view and even the disciplinary outlook of individual experts. As with the influence of expert testimony on other matters connected with the normative content of a case, the best way to deal with this is also to ensure maximum transparency and always to allow the parties the opportunity to comment on material that may be adverse to their cases. The injection of precautionary considerations by well-informed scientists should be welcomed rather than rejected. If the best and most experienced scientific minds are concerned about states' responses to an environmental or health risk, it is better for international courts and tribunals to know this.

PART III

Burden of proof

5 Getting to the heart of the rules on burden of proof[1]

The exercise of the international adjudicatory function in disputes involving scientific uncertainty may meet its greatest test in relation to the allocation of the burden of proof. The traditional rule on the burden of proof has the potential to provide a high degree of predictability in international adjudication, yet there may arise cases where fairness calls strongly for an international court to reassess or adjust the allocation of the burden of proof. This may especially be so in the light of the precautionary principle. This chapter investigates the origins and the logic of the rule on burden of proof, establishing its parameters and the desirable directions for its future development. Chapter 6 then explores the potential for a modification in the articulation or application of the existing rules on burden of proof, in order to permit the reversal of the burden of proof to give effect to the precautionary principle.

The rule on the allocation of the burden of proof that is applied in international courts and tribunals is that the party making an assertion must prove that assertion: *actori incumbit probatio*.[2] The rule derives from the rule applying in civil trials in Roman law: *ei incumbit probatio qui dicit non qui negat*. According to the maxim *reus in exceptione fit actor*, a party relying on an exception in the substantive law will attract the burden of proving the applicability of the exception or defence. Thus, as Rosenne has written:

[1] An article developing aspects of this chapter and Ch. 8 is to be published in the *Australian Yearbook of International Law*. See C. E. Foster, 'Burden of Proof'.

[2] Rosenne, *The Law and Practice*, p. 1040; Kazazi, *Burden of Proof*, p. 54; Brown, *A Common Law*, p. 92; Sandifer, *Evidence*, pp. 123 ff; Amerasinghe, *Evidence*, pp. 61–2; Pauwelyn, 'Evidence', 235, 237; Martha, 'Presumptions', 98, Lasok, *The European Court*, pp. 420–38.

Generally, in application of the principle *actori incumbit probatio* the Court will formally require the party putting forward a *claim or a particular contention* to establish the elements of fact and of law on which the decision in its favour might be given.[3]

Adjudication of disputes under public international law has, in general, more frequently involved addressing the legal questions dividing the parties, rather than points of fact.[4] This has contributed to the view that the burden of proof should not be overemphasised. Although seldom referring directly to the issue, the Permanent Court of International Justice did expressly apply the rule that a party asserting a fact bore the burden of proving it,[5] but the Court's decisions generally rested on uncontested facts.[6] The International Court of Justice has likewise usually hinged its decisions on legal questions and based them on undisputed facts, making little reference to the burden of proof.[7] Courts and tribunals are aware that litigants' satisfaction is likely to be greater where outcomes are based on material points.[8] The rules on allocation of the burden of proof are usually

[3] Rosenne, *The Law and Practice*, p. 1040.

[4] Hudson, *The Permanent Court*, p. 500; Kazazi, *Burden of Proof*, p. 83; Thirlway, 'Procedural law', 302.

[5] *The Mavrommatis Jerusalem Concessions*, Judgment of 26 March 1925 [1925] PCIJ Series A, No. 5; *Legal Status of Eastern Greenland*, Judgment of 5 April 1933 [1933] PCIJ Series A/B, No. 53, 49. Riddell and Plant, *Evidence*, p. 89.

[6] 'As regards matters of evidence, a review of the jurisprudence of the PCIJ reveals that the Court's general approach was to establish and rely on the facts which were not in dispute between the parties.' Kazazi, *Burden of Proof*, p. 75. See also Sandifer, *Evidence*, p. 132.

[7] Rosenne, *The Law and Practice*, p. 1039; Sandifer, *Evidence*, p. 134; Kazazi, *Burden of Proof*, p. 83; Hudson, *The Permanent Court*, 500; Thirlway, 'Procedure'; Riddell and Plant, *Evidence*, p. 74. For example, the International Court of Justice assessed closely a large body of evidence in the *Case concerning Armed Activities on the Territory of the Congo*, yet, without reference to the allocation of the burden of proof, made findings on questions such as the defences asserted by Uganda of consent and self-defence. *Case concerning Armed Activities on the Territory of the Congo (Democratic Republic of the Congo* v. *Uganda)*, Judgment of 19 December 2005, ICJ Reports 2005 (hereafter *Case concerning Armed Activities on the Territory of the Congo)*. See also the *Case concerning the Application of the Convention on the Prevention and Punishment of the Crime of Genocide (Bosnia and Herzegovina* v. *Serbia and Montenegro)*, Judgment of 26 February 2007, ICJ Reports 2007 (hereafter *Case concerning the Application of the Convention on the Prevention and Punishment of the Crime of Genocide)*. In this case the Court rested many of its factual findings on prior conclusions of the International Criminal Tribunal for the former Yugoslavia. For discussion, Sivakumaran, 'Application of the Convention', 706–8.

[8] Bilder, 'The fact/law distinction', 97; Sandifer, *Evidence*, pp. 24–8, 132.

applied retrospectively by a tribunal, if at all, once most or all of the evidence is in.[9]

In practice, arguably the duties on litigants to co-operate with international courts and tribunals in all matters relating to proof[10] are considerably more significant than the rule on the allocation of the burden of proof.[11] These duties follow from a general duty to act in good faith in international dispute settlement.[12] The fulfilment of the international judicial function depends on states' provision of adequate information to international courts and tribunals,[13] and on their co-operation at all stages of the proceedings, especially during hearings.[14] Yet the rules on the burden and standard of proof remain a permanent feature of international adjudication. International courts have a duty to reach a decision on disputes properly brought before them. The concept of the burden of proof is intended to help ensure that a decision is reached in every case.[15] Litigators take into account the rules on burden of proof in determining their strategies as they prepare their cases, and the rules are connected closely with disputants' responsibilities to the court.[16]

The rules on the burden of proof come further into their own in cases where evidence is unclear or incomplete.[17] This is frequently the case in the disputes that are under study in this book. Here, the application of these rules may determine the outcome of international litigation. For example, in the *Case concerning the Gabčíkovo-Nagymaros Project (Hungary/Slovakia)*,[18] Hungary bore the burden of proof in relation to its assertion of ecological necessity. Hungary asserted that ecological necessity precluded its responsibility for the breach of its 1977 Treaty with Slovakia that took place when Hungary suspended work on building a system of locks and dams on the River Danube. The necessity of stopping work on the Gabčíkovo-Nagymaros project was the subject of ongoing scientific research and a full factual case could not be provided in Hungary's defence. The Court found that it had not

[9] Schwarzenberger, *International Law*, p. 644. [10] Witenberg, '*Onus probandi*', 331–3.
[11] Kolb, 'General principles', 828. [12] *Ibid.*, 828. [13] *Ibid.*, 828–9.
[14] Rosenne, *The Law and Practice*, p. 1340.
[15] Schwarzenberger, *International Law*, p. 643, Note 18. Amerasinghe, *Evidence*, p. 34, citing Dalloz (1969) 2 *Répertoire de Droit International* 627, Article 2.
[16] Waincymer, *WTO Litigation*, p. 536. [17] Pauwelyn, 'Evidence', 258.
[18] *Case concerning the Gabčíkovo-Nagymaros Project (Hungary/Slovakia)*, Judgment of 25 September 1997, ICJ Reports 1997 7 (hereafter *Gabčíkovo-Nagymaros* case).

been established that there was a state of ecological necessity. Accordingly, Hungary's defence failed.[19]

To take another example, as discussed in the introductory chapter, the World Trade Organization (WTO) Panel that dealt with the trans-Atlantic dispute about the use of growth-promotion hormones in cattle in *European Communities – Measures Concerning Meat and Meat Products (Hormones)*[20] allocated to the EC the burden of proving that trade-restrictive measures adopted to counter health risks from hormone-treated beef complied with all the applicable provisions of the WTO Agreement on Sanitary and Phytosanitary Measures (SPS Agreement).[21] The EC was not able to discharge this burden, and the Panel found the EC's measure to be inconsistent with Articles 3.1, 5.1 and 5.5 of the Agreement. The Appellate Body subsequently overruled the Panel regarding the allocation of the burden, although agreeing that the EC had acted inconsistently with Article 5.1. Through this decision, and subsequent cases decided under the SPS Agreement, determinations on the allocation of the burden of proof have gained particular prominence in scientific disputes in the WTO. Indeed, in the growth-promotion hormones dispute:

> It [was] widely thought that fear of bearing the full burden of proof in a scientifically complex and politically sensitive dispute – like all those involving public health – [was] the main factor impeding the initiation of substantive compliance proceedings by any party

leading to a long, drawn-out, political battle.[22]

[19] See above, Ch. 2, pp. 37–41.

[20] *European Communities – Measures Concerning Meat and Meat Products (Hormones)*, Complaint by Canada (WT/DS48), Complaint by the United States (WT/DS26). Two identically constituted WTO dispute settlement Panels (the Panel) circulated parallel reports in this case: Report of the Panel (Canada) DSR 1998: II, 235 (hereafter *EC – Hormones*, Complaint by Canada, PR), Report of the Panel (United States) DSR 1998: III, 699 (hereafter *EC – Hormones*, Complaint by the US, PR).

[21] Agreement on the Application of Sanitary and Phytosanitary Measures, WTO, *The Legal Texts: The results of the Uruguay round of multilateral trade negotiations*, p. 59.

[22] EU takes first step to clarify beef hormones science, *Bridges Review*, December 2008–January 2009, vol. 12, No. 6, 14. The Appellate Body remarked in the *Continued Suspension of Obligations cases* dealing with Article 22.8 of the WTO Dispute Settlement Understanding that 'Much of the reluctance of the parties to secure a definitive determination in respect of Article 22.8 is the apprehension that, upon initiation, a party will attract the full burden of proof.' *Canada – Continued Suspension of Obligations in the EC – Hormones Dispute*, Complaint by the EC (WT/DS321), *US – Continued Suspension of Obligations in the EC – Hormones Dispute*, Complaint by the EC (WT/DS320), Report of the Appellate Body, adopted 14 November 2008 (hereafter, referring to the identical paragraphs of the two Appellate Body reports, *Continued Suspension* ABR), para. 359. For further discussion, see below, Ch. 8.

Principles underlying the rules on the burden of proof

Ripert observed in 1933 that the rule on burden of proof in international law rested on a logic that had never been discussed.[23] In national law, the rule on burden of proof has been seen as helping maintain fairness in adjudication by providing a rough equality between the parties in the form of a tie-breaker rule requiring each party to prove his or her own allegations.[24] Although the underlying aim of the adjudicatory process is a proper application of the law to the facts,[25] the rules on burden of proof have been developed in the knowledge that there are always risks of an erroneous outcome. In cases where the rules come into operation, they will allocate such risks between the parties. Aiming for more than a rough equality between the parties has not been possible. To require a court to allocate the burden based on a sophisticated estimate of what each party is risking in a case would be to impose a legislative role upon an adjudicatory body. The same is true in international law, where this would be of particular concern. The underlying aim of fairness, rather than equality per se, is therefore a stronger contender as a principle that has guided the development of international rules relating to the burden of proof.[26] Fairness is especially important in international law. Submission to jurisdiction is voluntary, and the implementation of adjudicatory decisions and ongoing use of adjudicatory mechanisms is highly contingent on states' perceptions of their fairness.

Sitting alongside the rationale of fairness is an additional underpinning of the rules on burden of proof in international law, in the form of the presumption of compliance. The presumption of compliance is applicable in all cases involving allegations of non-compliance with international legal obligations. The presumption of compliance is not unique to international law. It is found in most domestic legal systems,[27] consistent with an expectation that the actors in the system will continue to go about their day-to-day activities in a law-abiding manner. The presumption respects the dignity of each member of a

[23] 'Le principe que le fardeau de la preuve incombe au demandeur est admis sans hésitation devant les jurisdictions internationales. Il repose sur les idées de justice et de logique qui n'ont jamais été discutées.' Ripert, 'Les Règles', 646.

[24] Cf. Stein, *Foundations*, p. 222. [25] Bentham, *Rationale*. See above, Ch. 1 p. 5.

[26] Indeed, commentary on equality as a principle of international procedure has omitted reference to the rule on burden of proof in discussing the procedural rules that give effect to equality. Kolb, 'General principles', 800–2, see also at 818–20; Rosenne, *The Law and Practice*, pp. 1048–52.

[27] Kazazi, *Burden of Proof*, pp. 57–66.

community in assuming they are committed to the good of the community and have acted consistently with its norms.[28] The presumption is supported by the idea that what is normal is to be presumed and any other state of affairs is subject to proof. Thus, 'It may also be said that what is customary, normal or more probable is presumed and that anything to the contrary must be shown to exist by the party alleging it.'[29] This is consistent with theories of proof in French law. From the French perspective, it is taken as a starting point that 'les individus soient libres les uns à l'égard des autres' and therefore a claimant must prove 'le lien juridique qui assujettit celui qu'il désigne comme son débiteur'.[30] The presumption of compliance by states with their legal obligations has been an important contributing factor in consistency of practice in the rules on burden of proof internationally. The presumption corresponds reasonably well to the reality of states' international legal behaviour in general and helps protect states from vexatious claims that they are in breach of their obligations. A claimant who so asserts must expect to bear the burden of proving the applicability and breach of the rules invoked.[31]

The presumption of compliance sits well with the norm *pacta sunt servanda*, although not deriving its force directly from this norm. Although the two are allied, especially through the respect they accord to the dignity of states, the presumption of compliance does not equate directly with the notion that states act in good faith. In the *Continued Suspension of Obligations* cases in the WTO, the Panel viewed the presumption of compliance as a presumption of good faith compliance, referring to the obligation reflected in Article 26 of the Vienna Convention on the Law of Treaties that parties perform their international treaty

[28] Nance, 'Civility and the burden of proof', 653. See also Stein, *Foundations*, p. 222.

[29] Amerasinghe, *Evidence*, pp. 215–16.

[30] Ghestin *et al.*, *Traité de Droit Civil*, p. 619. An explanation of the French approach has also been offered which suggests that the effect of taking a court action is to destroy the appearance of the lack of an obligation towards the claimant, and therefore the claimant must prove that the reality differs from the apparent situation. Larroumet, *Droit Civil*, p. 341. See also Malaurie and Morvan, *Droit Civil*, p. 127.

[31] As observed by Judge ad hoc Ečer in his Dissenting Opinion in the *Corfu Channel case (United Kingdom* v. *Albania)*: 'There is a *presumptio juris* that a State behaves in conformity with international law. Therefore, a State which alleges a violation of international law by another State must prove that this presumption is not applicable . . .'. *The Corfu Channel case (United Kingdom* v. *Albania)*; Judgment of 9 April 1949, ICJ Reports 1949 2, Dissenting Opinion of Judge Ečer, 119. See also Amerasinghe, 'Presumptions', 398. Amerasinghe, *Evidence*, p. 215.

obligations in good faith.[32] The Appellate Body did not accept the Panel's approach.[33] The Appellate Body reasoned that even if the EC is presumed to have acted in good faith it would not necessarily follow that the EC had achieved compliance with its obligations.[34]

Are there other theoretical and practical approaches to the question of the burden of proof that merit consideration? For example, within the dispute settlement processes of the World Trade Organization should there be a law-and-economics-based determination of where the burden of proof should lie? One law-and-economics perspective is that the assessment of the relative costs of proof, the costs of error and the estimated likelihood that complaints will be well-founded is part of the legislative function and negotiators will have already taken these factors into account in the drafting of legal provisions. On this approach the burden of proof will usually lie with a complainant unless otherwise specified.[35] This perspective offers another possible rationalisation for accepting that the burden of proof usually lies with the complainant, and may complement the rationalisations of the rule on the burden of proof outlined above.

An alternative proposed law-and-economics approach would involve panels and the Appellate Body assessing legal provisions individually and deciding whether there is reason to allocate the burden of proof to the defending party rather than the complaining party in relation to each provision through reference to the relative costs of proof, the costs of error and the estimated likelihood that complaints will be well-founded.[36] In the absence of direction from the WTO membership, this approach would require panels and the Appellate Body to make substantive determinations of how the burden should be allocated in relation to the various and multitudinous provisions of WTO law. The task is not only onerous, but also overtly legislative in nature. The

[32] *Canada – Continued Suspension of Obligations in the EC – Hormones Dispute*, Complaint by the EC (WT/DS321) Report of the Panel, 31 March 2008, paras. 7.312–7.323. See also *US – Continued Suspension of Obligations in the EC – Hormones Dispute*, Complaint by the EC (WT/DS320) Report of the Panel, 31 March 2008. References below are from the report in the Canadian case (hereafter *Canada – Continued Suspension* PR). The presumption of compliance and the expectation that states will act in good faith were conflated both by the EC in its pleadings in these proceedings (see e.g. the Closing Statement of the EC, 15 September 2005, 2–3) and by the Panel itself. *Canada – Continued Suspension* PR, paras. 7.312–7.357; *US – Continued Suspension* PR, paras. 7.312–7.359.

[33] *Continued Suspension* ABR, paras. 278, 315–16, 581.

[34] *Continued Suspension* ABR, para. 315. [35] Grando, *Evidence*, pp. 203, 358.

[36] *Ibid.*, pp. 203–4, 224.

resulting loss of certainty or predictability has been admitted.[37] The constitutional problems that would be associated with such an approach in national law take on new dimensions in international law, a voluntary and horizontal legal system where it is important to constrain the judicial function. The multilateral trade regime of the WTO may be considered to possess differentiating features marking it out from the general international legal system, in the form of a compulsory system of dispute resolution by adjudication and close to universal participation in a package of trade agreements covering a large part of the field of international economic regulation. Yet the underlying political and legal structures remain those of public international law, primarily a reactive system in which adherence to obligations is founded on the voluntary consent of notionally sovereign equals. States require certainty in their international legal relations, and this is better attained through an approach to the burden of proof conceiving of the adjudicatory role as neutral, and devoid of the complexity involved in developing a provision-by-provision approach. Further, it would be unhelpful if practice in relation to burden of proof in the WTO were to diverge from practice in other international courts and tribunals at a time when a more or less 'common law of evidence' is emerging across these bodies, helping bring WTO law into the broad fold of public international law.

In summary, considerations of fairness between states and of respect for the dignity of the states both remain important factors lying behind the rules on burden of proof in international law. In disputes involving state responsibility the presumption of compliance is of particular significance as an underpinning of the rules because of the certainty it engenders for actual and potential litigants. It is desirable for international courts and tribunals to accord priority to such certainty and to keep in check the exercise of judicial discretion in the application of the rules on burden of proof. However, there remains scope for flexibility in the application of the rules in cases where this is necessary. A departure from the usual practice may be required when the standard approach would create an 'improper inequality' in a way that affects the fairness of the proceedings.[38] An international court or tribunal must

[37] *Ibid.*, p. 215.

[38] Kolb, 'General Principles', 802. For example, in order to avoid serious inequality between the parties, the ICJ declined to hear oral argument from UNESCO in *Judgments of the Administrative Tribunal of the ILO* and subsequent cases, because the individual civil servants affected were not entitled to appear before the Court. *Judgments of the*

ensure that neither party obtains, 'some unfair advantage over the other, where that is due to the particular circumstances of the case'.[39] Scope for the exercise of judicial discretion in order to try and ensure fairness is discussed further below.

Legal sources of the rule on the allocation of the burden of proof

There is no reason to doubt the validity of the usual sources of international law in relation to procedural law.[40] However, an unusual feature of the rules on burden of proof is that they appear to derive simultaneously from several sources. The rules may also derive from the inherent or implied powers of international courts and tribunals.

Provisions on the allocation of the burden are found in the constituent documents and rules of procedure of only a few international courts and tribunals. The statutes of the Permanent Court of International Justice, the International Court of Justice and the International Tribunal for the Law of the Sea are silent on the subject, and, indeed, they say little on questions of procedure more generally. Article 30 of the Statute of the International Court of Justice provides specifically that the Court shall frame rules for carrying out its functions, including procedural rules.[41] The same provision is found in Article 16 of the Statute of the International Tribunal for the Law of the Sea.[42] However, no provisions dealing explicitly with the burden or standard of proof have been included in the rules of procedure adopted by either body.[43] The WTO

Administrative Tribunal of the ILO upon Complaints Made Against UNESCO, Advisory Opinion of 23 October 1956, ICJ Reports 1956 77, 85–6.

[39] Rosenne, *The Law and Practice*, p. 1049.

[40] Thirlway, 'Procedural law', 389; Brown, *A Common Law*, p. 37. Rosenne writes: 'Since there is no essential difference between substantive and adjectival law in the broad sense, it follows that they have similar, if not identical, origins, whether customary or conventional.' Rosenne, *The Law and Practice*, p. 1027.

[41] Statute of the International Court of Justice, San Francisco, 26 June 1945, 3 Bevans 1153, in force 24 October 1945.

[42] Statute of the International Tribunal for the Law of the Sea, United Nations Convention on the Law of the Sea, Montego Bay, 10 December 1982, in force 16 November 1994, 21 ILM 1261, Annex VI.

[43] Under Article 48 of the Statute of the International Court of Justice, replicated in Article 27 of the Statute of the International Tribunal for the Law of the Sea, the Court is also to make orders for the conduct of individual cases including in relation to the form and timeframes for the submission of argument and in relation to all matters connected with the taking of evidence. See also Articles 49–52 of the Statute of the International

Dispute Settlement Understanding (DSU) does not go much further. Article 12(1) provides that panels are to follow the working procedures found in Appendix 3 of the DSU, while the Appellate Body was to draw up working procedures for appellate review under Article 17(a).[44] Neither set of working procedures addresses the burden of proof.

The *actori incumbit probatio* rule was discussed in the Report on Arbitral Procedure of 1950 by Georges Scelle, the Special Rapporteur of the International Law Commission,[45] but not included in the Commission's 1958 Model Rules on Arbitral Procedure.[46] Although the 1899 and 1907 Hague Conventions on the Pacific Settlement of Disputes are silent on burden of proof, Article 24(1) of the Optional Arbitration Rules of the Permanent Court of Arbitration incorporates the rule, stating that:[47]

> Each party shall have the burden of proving the facts relied on to support its claim or defence.

The rule was included in Article 24 of the Iran–US Claims Tribunal's Rules of Procedure,[48] mirroring Article 24 of the UNCITRAL arbitration rules,[49] and is considered to represent 'generally accepted principles of international arbitration practice and contribute to the effective resolution of cases before the Tribunal'.[50] A number of Iran–US Claims Tribunal decisions have been based around the allocation of the burden of proof, and questions of burden of proof also have a high profile in the

Court of Justice, concerning requests for the production of evidence from the parties and the taking of expert testimony.

44 Working Procedures for Appellate Review, 7 October 2004, www.wto.org.

45 Model Rules on Arbitral Procedure (1950) II *Yearbook of the International Law Commission* 114 at 134.

46 (1958) II *Yearbook of the International Law Commission* 82.

47 Permanent Court of Arbitration Optional Rules for Arbitrating Disputes between Two States; see likewise Article 24(1) of the Permanent Court of Arbitration Optional Rules for Arbitrating Disputes between Two Parties of which Only One is a State; Permanent Court of Arbitration Optional Rules for Arbitration involving International Organizations and States; Permanent Court of Arbitration Optional Rules for Arbitration between International Organizations and Private Parties; Permanent Court of Arbitration Optional Rules for Arbitration of Disputes relating to Natural Resources and/or the Environment. These rules of procedure are available at www.pca-cpa.org.

48 Article 24 states that 'each party shall have the burden of proving the facts relied on to support his *claim or defence*'. Emphasis added, Final Tribunal Rules of Procedure, 3 May 1983, 1 Iran–US CTR 57, Article 24.

49 United Nations Commission on International Trade Law (UNCITRAL) Arbitration Rules 1976, www.uncitral.org.

50 Kazazi, *Burden of Proof*, p. 104; *Islamic Republic of Iran* v. *United States of America*, Case A-20, 10 July 1986, 11 Iran–US CTR 271 at 274.

views of dissenting arbitrators.[51] It may be noted also that Rules 33 and 34 of the Model Rules of Procedure for Chapter 20 of the North American Free Trade Agreement (NAFTA) explicitly state that a claimant must prove that a respondent's actions are inconsistent with NAFTA, and that a party asserting that a measure is covered by an exception must so prove.[52]

In his 1975 work *Evidence before International Tribunals*, Sandifer described international rules about evidence and proof as 'tantamount to a customary law of evidence'.[53] Explicit support for the rules as currently formulated may be found in the arguments of states' representatives before international tribunals (although the value of pleadings as evidence of *opinio juris* must be subject to considerable qualification). States' implementation of the decisions of international tribunals,[54] and their continued participation in international litigation, could be regarded as acquiescence to the rules on burden of proof usually applied by courts and tribunals. Objections raised in relation to the rules about proof tend to focus on the application of the rules rather than on their content. It is therefore possible to view the rules on burden of proof as founded in customary international law. However, it is clear that the support for this is more limited and of a different character to the support usually required to support the existence of a rule of customary international law. The threshold for customary international law is high. In principle a general and consistent practice is required on the part of states, in which they engage because of their belief in a rule they are obliged to follow.[55]

International courts and tribunals do aim for consistency in their procedural decisions,[56] and remark has been made that 'the practice of an international tribunal may in general, if sufficiently consistent, generate a procedural rule which that particular tribunal, at least, may not lightly depart from, and which possibly also has some degree of

[51] Kazazi, *Burden of Proof*, pp. 108, 112–13. For example, *Islamic Republic of Iran* v. *United States of America*, Case A/1 (Issues I, III, and IV), 30 July 1982, I Iran–US CTR 189; *Flexi-Van Leasing, Inc.* v. *The Islamic Republic of Iran*, Order of 15 December 1982, 12 Iran–US CTR 335.

[52] Model Rules of Procedure for Chapter 20 of the North American Free Trade Agreement, www.nafta-sec-alena.org.

[53] Sandifer, *Evidence*, p. 458. On the burden of proof rules as customary international law see also Witenberg, '*Onus probandi*', 327. Cf. Thirlway, 'Procedure', 1128; and the hesitation observed by Amerasinghe, *Evidence*, p. 26.

[54] Brown, *A Common Law*, p. 53 at note 106.

[55] Brownlie, *Principles of Public International Law*, pp. 8–10.

[56] *Ibid.*, p. 21. See also Riddell and Plant, *Evidence*, p. 31.

general validity as a component of the general corpus of procedural law of international tribunals'.[57] References to the 'customary practice' of international courts and tribunals,[58] 'international judicial practice'[59] and 'customary rules developed in international judicial practice'[60] convey a certain status. Still, international courts' borrowing from one another of practices and methods that have proved themselves successful and efficient cannot, strictly, be regarded as more than a practically motivated activity lacking the power directly to generate new procedural norms.[61] Clearly, the customary practice of international tribunals cannot be directly equated with state practice in terms of its power to create binding new rules of customary international law.[62] Such activity may nevertheless be a most important plank in the practical development of procedural rules. International law is understood to develop inter alia via soft law generated through usage and expectation.

On the other hand, the rules on burden of proof may arguably find their source in general principles of law.[63] Rules on evidence in international courts are often put forward among the relatively scarce examples of general principles of law as referred to in Article 38(1)(c) of the Statute of the International Court of Justice.[64] There are differing views on what is meant by the reference to general principles of law in Article 38(1)(c). One view is that general principles of law as referred to in Article 38(1)(c) may be extracted from principles or rules common among municipal legal systems. Frequently, general principles argued to be derived in this way are held to include rules of procedure and evidence. Few writers explicitly suggest that the rules about burden of proof are under contemplation, but a particular strength of the rule on the burden of proof is its commonality across domestic legal systems.[65] On another view, the drafters of Article 38(1)(c) shared an intention that their

[57] Thirlway, 'Dilemma or chimera', p. 623. [58] Brown, *A Common Law*, p. 54.

[59] *Ibid*., p. 53. [60] *Ibid*., p. 229.

[61] Thirlway, 'Procedure of international courts and tribunals', 1128.

[62] Thirlway, 'Dilemma or chimera?', 623–4.

[63] Amerasinghe prefers to let this explanation suffice, as it reflects the approach taken by international courts themselves. Amerasinghe, *Evidence*, p. 26. See also Brown, *A Common Law*, pp. 93, 118; Kolb, 'General principles', 793; Cheng, *General Principles of Law*, p. 335, describing the rule on burden of proof and related rules as created by certain 'general principles of law based on common sense and developed through human experience'.

[64] Article 38(1)(c) of the Statute of the International Court of Justice sets out the law to be applied by the Court in deciding the disputes submitted to it, and is commonly regarded as articulating the recognised sources of international law.

[65] Shaw, *International Law*, pp. 98–105; Brownlie, *Principles of Public International Law*, pp. 16–18.

reference to general principles of law was intended to relate to objective principles of justice, to be understood at the level of general propositions.[66] Such latent principles of law should guide international judges, enabling them gradually to determine the content of international law more closely.[67] The view has been taken that general principles of law in this sense include the rule on the allocation of the burden of proof (*actori incumbit probatio*),[68] as well as a number of other principles of judicial procedure, including the rule that no one may be a judge in their own cause (*nemo debet esse judex in propria sua causa*), the due process rule (*audi alteram partem*), the principle that the court knows the law (*jura novit curia*) and the principle of res judicata.[69] In practice the two views regarding general principles of law overlap. Often domestic principles reflect universal notions of justice or effectiveness. The rule on the burden of proof may qualify as a general principle of law on both views.

Additionally, a procedural and evidentiary rule-making capacity may be regarded as an inherent power of a tribunal, whether domestic or international, deriving from the need to ensure that tribunals are fully equipped to carry out the judicial function.[70] The view has consistently been taken that the judicial function involves the settlement of disputes and the sound administration of justice.[71] The International Court of Justice has observed that such powers inhere automatically in international judicial organs, and that their purpose is to protect the basic functions of international judicial bodies.[72] This approach has won support, and probably represents the best way to understand the inherent powers of international courts and tribunals.[73] The alternative view is that these powers are not inherent, but rather are to be implied from the constituent documents of international courts and tribunals in much the same way as international organisations' powers can be implied from

[66] Cheng, *General Principles of Law*, pp. 18, 24. [67] *Ibid.*, pp. 18–19. [68] *Ibid.*, p. 327.

[69] Brown, *A Common Law*, Ch. 2, p. 16; Cheng, *General Principles of Law*, pp. 257–301.

[70] Brown, *A Common Law*; Simpson and Fox, *International Arbitration*, pp. 147, 152; Kazazi, *Burden of Proof*, p. 177. On international courts' and tribunals' inherent powers, see further below, Ch. 6, pp. 249–53.

[71] Brown, *A Common Law*, pp. 72–8; Gaeta, 'Inherent powers of international courts and tribunals', 354–5.

[72] *Nuclear Tests case (Australia* v. *France) (Jurisdiction)*, 20 December 1974, ICJ Reports 1974 253, 259–60; *Nuclear Tests case (New Zealand* v. *France) (Jurisdiction)*, 20 December 1974, ICJ Reports 1974 457, 463.

[73] Brown, *A Common Law*, 71; See also Gaeta, 'Inherent powers of international courts and tribunals', 364–8.

their constituent documents.[74] On this view, international judicial organs are impliedly attributed the powers necessary to carry out their role on the same basis as other international institutions established by states.[75] However, examples of where international courts have adopted the language of implied powers are very rare.[76]

A further potential source of rules on evidence and proof in international courts and tribunals may be identified in the form of the specific provisions in the constitutive documents of a number of tribunals envisaging that tribunals will develop their own rules of procedure. Such provisions could be regarded as delegating to international courts and tribunals the authority to make and develop rules on proof, and to respond to procedural issues arising in cases on an ad hoc basis. Generally, tribunals consult with disputants over particular procedures that may be required to deal with a case, and may issue interim orders on procedural points if this is considered necessary.

The rules governing the burden of proof in international law are therefore highly distinctive among international legal rules, because of the multiplicity of their sources. This may endow the rules with particular flexibility, as they could be developed or amended in many different ways. In practice, there has been relative consistency in the articulation of the rules.

Judicial articulation of the rule on burden of proof

International adjudication functions on the basis that a court is expected to know the law in accordance with the maxim *jura novit curia*,[77]

[74] Brown, *A Common Law*, p. 69; Gaeta, 'Inherent powers of international courts and tribunals', 360, 362.

[75] *Reparation for Injuries suffered in the service of the United Nations, Advisory Opinion*, 11 April 1949, ICJ Reports 174, 182–4.

[76] Brown, *A Common Law*, p. 69. Gaeta refers to the phrasing used by Trial Chamber II of the International Criminal Tribunal for the former Yugoslavia in *Prosecutor* v. *Blaskic*, but the Appeals Chamber preferred the language of 'inherent powers', considering that 'the International Tribunal must possess the power to make all those judicial determinations that are necessary for the exercise of its primary jurisdiction'. *Prosecutor* v. *Blaškić*, 18 July 1997, 110 ILR 608, 704. In *Mexico – Taxes on Soft Drinks*, the WTO Appellate Body indicated the same preference, disregarding the appellant's use of the term 'implied powers' in stating 'We agree with Mexico that WTO panels have certain powers that are inherent in their adjudicative function'. *Mexico – Tax Measures on Soft Drinks and Other Beverages*, Complaint by the United States (WT/DS308), Report of the Panel DSR 2006 I, 43 (hereafter *Mexico – Soft Drinks* PR).

[77] *Fisheries Jurisdiction case (United Kingdom of Great Britain and Northern Ireland* v. *Iceland)*, Judgment of 25 July 1974, ICJ Reports 1974 1, 9; cf. *Case concerning the Land, Island and*

and there is no need to prove the law. A clear distinction is to be drawn between fact and law, in that facts require proving while the law does not.[78]

As articulated in the decisions of international courts and tribunals, a party will bear the burden of proving all the facts it asserts. This was rearticulated in 2010 in the *Case concerning Pulp Mills on the River Uruguay (Argentina* v. *Uruguay)*, where the Court said:

> To begin with, the Court considers that, in accordance with the well-established principle of *onus probandi incumbit actori*, it is the duty of the party which asserts certain facts to establish the existence of such facts. This principle which has been consistently upheld by the Court . . . applies to the assertions of fact both by the Applicant and the Respondent.[79]

There has been a consistent line of authority to this effect. The International Court of Justice observed in its judgment on jurisdiction and admissibility at the provisional measures stage in 1984 in the case of *Military and Paramilitary Activities in and against Nicaragua (Nicaragua* v. *United States of America)* that:

> any judgment on the merits in the present case will be limited to upholding *such submissions* of the Parties as have been *supported by sufficient proof of relevant facts*, and are regarded by the Court as sound in law . . . Ultimately, however, *it is the litigant seeking to establish a fact who bears the burden of proving it.*[80]

Maritime Frontier Dispute (El Salvador/Honduras), Judgment of 11 September 1992, ICJ Reports 1992 350, 376; Pauwelyn, 'Evidence, proof and persuasion', 585; Kazazi, *Burden of Proof*, p. 43.

78 Although in practice advocates regularly lay out their view on the content of the law, and tribunals are assumed to find this helpful. Kazazi, *Burden of Proof*, p. 49, n. 1.

79 *Case concerning Pulp Mills on the River Uruguay (Argentina* v. *Uruguay), Request for the Indication of Provisional Measures*, Order of 15 July 2006, ICJ Reports 2006 (hereafter *Case concerning Pulp Mills*), para. 162. See also Separate Opinion of Judge Greenwood, para. 24.

80 Emphasis added. *Case concerning Military and Paramilitary Activities in and against Nicaragua (Nicaragua* v. *United States of America) (Jurisdiction and Admissibility)*, Judgment of 26 November 1984, ICJ Reports 1984 169, para. 101. See also *Avena and other Mexican Nationals*, where the Court referred in 2004 to the 'well-settled principle' in international law that a litigant seeking to establish the existence of a fact bears the burden of proving it, *Avena and other Mexican Nationals (Mexico* v. *United States of America)*, ICJ Reports 2004, para. 55 (hereafter *Avena and other Mexican Nationals*); *Case concerning the Land and Maritime Boundary between Cameroon and Nigeria (Cameroon* v. *Nigeria) (Preliminary Objections)* Judgment of 11 June 1998, 1998 ICJ Reports 275, 319; *Case concerning the Land and Maritime Boundary between Cameroon and Nigeria (Cameroon* v. *Nigeria, Equatorial Guinea Intervening)*, Judgment of 10 October 2002, ICJ Reports 2003 303, 453; and *Case concerning the Frontier Dispute (Burkina Faso and Mali)*, para. 65.

In 2007 in the *Case concerning the Application of the Convention on the Prevention and Punishment of the Crime of Genocide (Bosnia and Herzogovina* v. *Serbia and Montenegro)* the Court said:

On the burden or onus of proof, it is well established in general that the applicant *must establish its case* and that a party *asserting a fact must establish it* . . .[81]

In WTO jurisprudence the leading case on the allocation of the burden of proof is *United States – Measure Affecting Imports of Woven Wool Shirts and Blouses from India (US – Wool Shirts).*[82] In that case, the Appellate Body stated:

various international tribunals, including the International Court of Justice, have generally and consistently accepted and applied the rule that the party *who asserts a fact*, whether the claimant or the respondent, is responsible for providing proof thereof. Also, it is a generally-accepted canon of evidence in civil law, common law and, in fact, most jurisdictions, that the burden of proof rests upon the party, whether complaining or defending, *who asserts the affirmative of a particular claim or defence.*[83]

Similarly in investment arbitration the burden is allocated to the party making a claim, but also lies with the party asserting a fact.[84]

From these references it can be seen that the requirement for a party to prove all the facts it asserts is generally taken as convenient shorthand for the requirement that a party should prove all the facts going to

[81] *Case concerning the Application of the Convention on the Prevention and Punishment of the Crime of Genocide*, para. 204.

[82] *United States – Measure Affecting Imports of Woven Wool Shirts and Blouses from India*, Complaint by India (WT/DS33), Report of the Appellate Body DSR 1997: I (hereafter *US – Wool Shirts* ABR), 323, Report of the Panel DSR 1997: I, 343.

[83] *Ibid.*, p. 14, emphasis added. For reiterations that continue to incorporate this formula, see *Turkey – Restrictions on Imports of Textile and Clothing Products*, Complaint by India (WT/DS34), Report of the Panel DSR 1999: VI, 2363, para. 9.57, citing *Argentina – Measures Affecting Imports of Footwear, Textiles, Apparel and Other Items*, Complaint by the United States (WT/DS56), Report of the Panel DSR 1998: III, 1033, paras. 6.34–6.40.

[84] Schreuer, *The ICSID Convention*, p. 669. See also, in the International Tribunal for the Law of the Sea, Vice-President Wolfrum's approach in his Separate Opinion in the *M/V 'Saiga' (No. 2)* case. Vice-President Wolfrum was prepared to determine that St Vincent and the Grenadines bore the burden of proof due to its position as claimant, but referred to the principle *actori incumbit probatio* as putting the burden of proof on a party asserting a fact. *M/V 'Saiga' (No. 2) (St Vincent and the Grenadines* v. *Guinea) (Admissibility and Merits)*, 1 July 1999, 38 ILM 1323 (hereafter *M/V 'Saiga' (No. 2)*), paras. 7 and 8.

make up its legal case. The assumption is that the facts a party asserts will be those required for its case. An emphasis on each party's burden of proving the facts necessary to support its contentions is most natural in boundary disputes, where rival claims are presented.[85] In disputes involving state responsibility the presumption of compliance comes into play and would indicate a greater emphasis on the need for a party to establish its legal claims, rather than merely the facts supporting these claims.[86] Further, there is the possibility that a responding party may assert a defence, which will attract the burden of proof in respect of all the facts necessary to support that defence.

An emphasis on claims and defences rather than on facts is frequently seen in national law. In Roman law a party making a legal claim bore the burden of proving the facts needed to substantiate the claim.[87] A party asserting a defence bore the burden of establishing the facts necessary to support the defence.[88] The claim and the defence were tried separately, one after the other.[89] In relation to the trial of the claim, the

[85] Thus, to take an example, in the *Temple of Preah Vihear* case, Cambodia and Thailand each based their claims on a series of facts and contentions, and it was for each party to establish the facts underlying its claims. *Case concerning the Temple of Preah Vihear (Cambodia* v. *Thailand)*, Judgment of 15 June 1962, ICJ Reports 1962 615–16. See also *Case concerning the Frontier Dispute (Burkina Faso and Mali)*, Judgment of 22 December 1986, ICJ Reports 554, 587–8, para. 65. In 2008 in *Pedra Branca* the International Court of Justice stated that '[i]t is a general principle of law, confirmed by the jurisprudence of this Court, that a party which advances a point of fact in support of its claim must establish that fact'. *Sovereignty over Pedra Branca / Pulau Batu Puteh, Middle Rocks and South Ledge (Malaysia/Singapore)*, Judgment of 23 May 2008, para. 45. Similarly in 2009 in the *Black Sea* case, the Court reiterated that 'the party asserting a fact as a basis of its claim must establish it'. *Maritime Delimitation in the Black Sea (Romania* v. *Ukraine)*, Judgment of 3 February 2009, para. 68.

[86] On the presumption of compliance, see above, on the principles underlying the burden of proof, see pp. 189–90. Grando interprets the dicta of the International Court of Justice – on the need for each party to prove the facts it asserts – as referring only to auxiliary propositions and not to 'the burden of proof *stricto sensu*'. Grando, *Evidence*, p. 199.

[87] Berger, *Encylopedic Dictionary of Roman Law*, p. 652, citing the Digest of Justinian. The Roman law origins of the rule on burden of proof have been noted by a number of writers. Lachs, 'Evidence', 267; Witenberg, '*Onus probandi*', 232; Mani, *International Adjudication*, p. 202.

[88] Berger, *Encylopedic Dictionary of Roman Law*, p. 652, citing the Digest of Justinian.

[89] 'The Praetor sent to the judex a *formula* containing a brief indication of the plaintiff's claim, of the affirmative defence, if any, of the affirmative replication, if any, and so on – with instructions to hear the parties and their witnesses, and then decide the case. No denials were mentioned in the formula, but each affirmative case was understood to be denied. Then followed a trial of each of these cases separately.' Thayer, 'The burden of proof', 56.

claimant was the *actor* and bore the burden of proof. In relation to the trial of the defence, the defendant was the *actor* and bore the burden of proof.[90] The term *actor* derives from the verb *agere*, literally *to act*, but referring in the legal context to the act of pleading or making a case.[91]

Both common law and civil law conceptions of the allocation of the burden of proof effectively centre on the parties' assertions as to the existence of an obligation or a defence. In French law, under Article 9 of the New Code of Civil Procedure:

> Each party is under a duty to prove in accordance with the law those facts which are necessary for the success of his *claim*.[92]

The French Supreme Court has added that 'the uncertainty or doubt subsisting after the production of evidence should necessarily be retained to the detriment of the one who had the burden of proof'.[93] German law envisages that 'Each party must prove those facts *which gave rise to the rights or defences* on which it relies.'[94] The law of the Netherlands

[90] Thayer, 'The burden of proof', 56. 'In general, he who seeks to move a court to take action in his favour, whether as an original plaintiff whose facts are merely denied, or as a defendant, who, in setting up an affirmative defence, has the rôle of *actor* (*reus excipiendo fit actor*), must satisfy the court of the truth and accuracy of the grounds of his claim, both in point of fact and law.' Thayer, 'The burden of proof', 57.

[91] Amerasinghe, *Evidence*, p. 62, note 2.

[92] Emphasis added. Dalloz (1970) Répertoire de Procédure Civile, p. 5, quoted by Kazazi, *Burden of Proof*, p. 60, with historical background. For an alternative translation, see New Code of Civil Procedure at http://lexinter.net/ENGLISH/code_of_civil_procedure.htm. In the French: 'Il incombe à chaque partie de prouver conformément à la loi les faits nécessaires au succés de sa prétention.' Nouveau Code de Procédure Civile, Delvolvé, Jean-Louis, *Arbitration in France* (The Hague; New York: Kluwer, 2003), 100, quoted by Kazazi, *Burden of Proof*, p. 60. See also Larroumet, *Droit Civil*, pp. 340–1.

[93] 'L'incertitude ou le doute subsistant à la suite de la production d'une preuve doivent nécessairement être retenus au détriment de celui qui avait la charge de cette preuve.' Cass. Fr., 31 January 1962, Bull. Cass., 1962, C.I.V.IV, No. 105 as cited by Hanotiau, 'Satisfying the burden', 343. See also Taruffo, 'Rethinking', 673, describing this point as the basic mechanism of the burden of proof in civil law systems. In Belgium, the rule on the allocation of the burden is expressed both in terms of the proof of asserted facts and in terms of proof of the facts supporting a party's claim or defence. Article 870 of the Code Judiciaire states that in civil cases: 'Chacune des parties a la charge de prouver les faits qu'elle allègue.' Article 1315 of the Civil Code provides that: 'Celui qui réclame l'exécution d'une obligation doit la prouver. Réciproquement, celui qui se pretend libéré doit justifier le payement ou le fait qui a produit l'extinction de son obligation.' Kazazi, *Burden of Proof*, p. 61. Hanotiau cites also Belgian decision Cass., 10 December 1976, Pas., 1977, I, at 410.

[94] Emphasis added. Kazazi, *Burden of Proof*, p. 64, citing Cohn, E.J., 'Law of civil procedure' in E.J. Cohn (ed.), *Manual of German Law* (Dobbs Ferry, NY: Oceana, 1968–1971), II, pp. 162–260, 219.

provides that where the legal rules applying to a case '*attach a certain legal consequence* to the existence of certain facts, he who claims to be entitled to this consequence must prove the facts'.[95] In Italian law the burden of proof has been described as 'the burden of persuading the court of the truth of the allegations *underlying a claim or defense*'.[96] Iranian civil law is based on Islamic law, but is also inspired in some parts by the codes of the civil law countries.[97] In Iranian law, Article 1257 of the Civil Code provides that:

> Whosoever *claims a right* must prove it and *if the defendant, in defence, claims a matter which requires proof* it is incumbent upon him to prove that matter.[98]

The UNIDROIT Principles of Transnational Civil Procedure provide that 'each party has the burden to prove all the material facts *that are the basis of that party's case*'.[99] To the extent that there is an emphasis on proof of facts per se in civil law jurisdictions, this may be partly because the relationship between fact and law differs from this relationship in the common law. Establishing the facts establishes the existence of an obligation towards a claimant.[100] For example, in the French law of delict human deeds causing harm to another are constitutive of obligations of compensation.[101] However, even in the civil law it can clearly be said that proof of facts will only be significant when it supports a legal claim or defence.

Although they have often placed emphasis on the need for parties to prove all the facts they assert, commentators have also described the burden of proof as a way of allocating the duty to bring forward

95 Emphasis added. Kazazi, *Burden of Proof*, p. 64, citing Stein, P. A. 'Civil procedure' in D. C. Fokkema, J. M. J. Chorus, E. H. Hondius and E. Ch. Lisser (eds.), *Introduction to Dutch Law for Foreign Lawyers* (Deventer: Kluwer, 1978), pp. 231–62, 246.

96 Emphasis added. Sandifer, *Evidence*, pp. 126–7, quoting M. Cappelletti and J. M. Perillo (eds.), *Civil Procedure in Italy* (The Hague: Nijhoff, 1965). See also Prieto-Castro y Ferrandiz, *Derecho Procesal Civil*, p. 149.

97 Kazazi, *Burden of Proof*, p. 62, referring to France, Switzerland and Belgium.

98 Emphasis added. Translated from Persian. Kazazi, *Burden of Proof*, p. 62.

99 Emphasis added. American Law Institute UNIDROIT, *Principles of Transnational Civil Procedure* (Cambridge University Press, 2006), Principle 21.1. See the accompanying proposed Rule 28.1.

100 Prieto-Castro y Ferrandiz, *Derecho Procesal*, p. 151, referring to facts constitutive of juridical relationships.

101 Bell *et al.*, *Principles of French Law*, p. 355. Equally, a respondent who believes him or herself to be free from an obligation must prove the fact that extinguishes the obligation. Ghestin *et al.*, *Droit Civil*, p. 620. For discussion, Malaurie and Morvan, *Droit Civil*, p. 125.

evidence that will substantiate the contentions that the parties develop in their pleadings[102] and stated that the burden of proof applies to the facts that underlie a claim.[103] They note also that the burden of proof will be allocated to the 'real' claimant actually putting forward a legal claim: the burden is not allocated to the party who is merely the claimant in a procedural sense, for example by virtue of having initiated dispute resolution.[104]

As a practical matter, it must be acknowledged that the remaining aspect of the rule on burden of proof, according to which a party must prove all the facts that it asserts, may come into play independently in some cases. An example of the invocation of the second aspect of the rule on burden of proof is seen in the *Japan – Measures Affecting the Importation of Apples* case in the WTO in 2003. In this case the US claimed that Japan's quarantine requirements for US apples were inconsistent with Article 2.2 of the WTO Agreement on Sanitary and Phytosanitary Measures because they were maintained without sufficient scientific evidence. As complainant, the US bore the burden of proof to establish this. The US accordingly laid out a case that there was not sufficient scientific evidence to support the phytosanitary requirements on apples from the US, based on the fact that these apples were expected all to be mature and symptom-free and therefore could not be infected by fireblight. However, the Panel allocated the burden of proof to Japan to prove particular facts asserted by Japan, for example that there was sufficient evidence that fireblight bacteria carried by an infected US apple could be transferred to a host plant in Japan by means of rainsplash.[105] This assertion formed part of a counter-argument put forward by Japan based on the possibility of the US accidentally exporting apples that were not mature and symptomless and that could pose phytosanitary risks.[106] The Appellate Body's analysis

[102] Sandifer, *Evidence*, pp. 123, 127 and see 135. Alford, 'Fact finding', 83. Kazazi, *Burden of Proof*, p. 30; Witenberg, '*Onus probandi*', 2. Cheng, *General Principles of Law*, p. 334, refers to the Latin: *actore non probante reus absolvitur.*

[103] Amerasinghe, *Evidence*, p. 50. See also Kolb, 'General principles', 819.

[104] An example often cited is the *Rights of Nationals of the USA in Morocco* case. In this case France took the position of the plaintiff in order to bring the matter before the ICJ, yet the Court's approach was to examine and reject in turn each of the rights asserted by the US. *United States Nationals in Morocco (France* v. *United States)*, Judgment of 27 August 1952, 1952 ICJ Reports 176. Amerasinghe, *Evidence*, p. 65.

[105] *Japan – Measures Affecting the Importation of Apples*, Complaint by the United States (WT/DS245), Report of the Panel DSR 2003: IX, 4481 (hereafter *Japan – Apples* PR), para. 8.168.

[106] *Japan – Measures Affecting the Importation of Apples*, Complaint by the United States (WT/DS245), Report of the Appellate Body DSR 2003: IX, 4391, para. 228.

of the burden's allocation in this case emphasised 'the principle that the party that asserts a fact is responsible for providing proof thereof'.[107]

Common lawyers might seek to explain the situation in *Japan – Apples* by saying that sufficient evidence had been submitted in relation to the US claim notionally to 'shift' the 'evidential' or 'tactical' burden onto the respondent, who could, by providing enough persuasive evidence supporting its own argument, potentially throw that burden back onto the complainant.[108] On a common law analysis of the example from the *Japan – Apples* case the US carried the legal burden of proof, but it would have been in Japan's interest to establish the fact in question regarding transfer by rainsplash in case the Panel considered Japan's line of argument to be a persuasive counterweight to the US case. The common law concept of the 'evidential' burden of proof is not generally recognised in international tribunals.[109] The sense in which reference to the burden of proof is usually made in international law is the sense shared by the common law and the civil law, coinciding with the common law conception of the 'legal' or fixed burden of proof.[110] Indeed, the concept of an evidential burden was rejected by the International Court of Justice in *Avena and other Mexican Nationals (Mexico* v. *United States of America)*.[111]

Nor has the idea of a shifting burden of proof been taken up as a general practice by international courts and tribunals, although the idea has been in vogue in dispute settlement within the WTO. Indeed, in *US – Wool Shirts* the Appellate Body conceptualised the

[107] *Ibid.*, para. 157.

[108] The common law distinguishes between the 'true' 'legal' burden of proof (also known as the 'persuasive burden') and the 'evidential' burden. The allocation of the legal burden may determine whether a party will lose the case or the point at issue, whereas the evidential burden is only a requirement to produce evidence to counter the evidence already produced by the other party. The evidential burden has been described as shifting from one party to another during proceedings, while the legal burden remains fixed. Tapper, *Cross and Tapper on Evidence*, pp. 130–8.

[109] Alford, 'Fact finding', 83 in relation to the practice of the ICJ. Waincymer, *WTO Litigation*, pp. 536–7.

[110] Kazazi, *Burden of Proof*, p. 31.

[111] *Avena and other Mexican Nationals*, paras. 56–7, as interpreted in the Declaration of Judge Ranjeva, para. 2. Amerasinghe, *Evidence*, pp. 37 and 43, although see pp. 87–8. There are of course requirements in international courts that applicants submit with their statements of claim the facts they assert and 'the nature of the evidence they intend to rely on'. See e.g. Article 38(2) Rules of Court of the International Court of Justice. These requirements are not to be equated with the discharge of the common law 'evidential burden'. They are designed to inform a tribunal, to ensure respondents know the case they are answering, and to set a framework for judgment *infra petita*. Brealey, 'The burden of proof', 251.

judicial weighing of evidence in these terms.[112] However, the notion of a shifting burden of proof was found unsatisfactory, perhaps because WTO practice lacked a concomitant distinction between the evidential burden and the legal burden. Explicit reference to the shifting of the burden of proof therefore has not been a consistent feature of WTO dispute resolution.[113] The aspect of the rule on burden of proof that is oriented around the proof of facts may thus help fill the gap left by the absence of a concept of evidential or tactical burden in international law.

There have been some areas of uncertainty in the articulation of the rules on burden of proof. For example, there has been uncertainty accompanying the idea that the burden of proof should be allocated to the litigant who asserts the positive aspect of a given factual proposition. This proposition derives some of its persuasive power from the view put forward by Bentham that 'he should have the burden on whom it would sit lightest'.[114] In Roman law an actor who had to prove a negative proposition could be freed from his duty through the rule *negativa non sunt probanda* or *negantis nulla probatio*.[115] However, it is understood that this rule does not apply today, domestically or internationally.[116] Clearly, in certain circumstances an international

[112] As cited above, 'If that party adduces evidence sufficient to raise a presumption that what is claimed is true, the burden then shifts to the other party, who will fail unless it adduces sufficient evidence to rebut the presumption.' *US – Wool Shirts* ABR, 14.

[113] See *Korea – Dairy*, where the Panel stated that as a matter of law the burden of proof rested with the complainant, and did not shift during the proceedings, but remained with the claimant throughout. The Panel would then weigh together all the evidence it had received and decide if it thought the complainant's claims well founded. *Korea – Definitive Safeguard Measure on Imports of Certain Dairy Products*, Complaint by the European Communities (WT/DS98), Report of the Panel DSR 2000: I, 49, para. 7.24. Nevertheless, as discussed below a WTO panel will commonly state that it has reached the view that a party has established a prima facie case and that this case has remained unrebutted by the other party. In contrast, the idea that the burden of proof shifts upon the establishment of a prima facie case is still found in international investment arbitration. Schreuer, *ICSID*, p. 669. Investment arbitration differs from the practice of other international courts and tribunals in this respect, and may have been influenced more significantly by national practice. Investment tribunals have referred to the remarks of the Appellate Body in *US – Wool Shirts*. *International Thunderbird Gaming Corporation* v. *The United Mexican States*, Award of 26 January 2006, para. 95, Arbitral Tribunal constituted under Chapter Eleven of the North American Free Trade Agreement (UNCITRAL); *Marvin Feldman* v. *Mexico*, Award of 16 December 2002, para. 177.

[114] Thayer, 'The burden of proof', 59, citing *The Works of Jeremy Bentham* (Edinburgh; London: William Tait; Simpkin, Marshall, & Co., 1843), VI, pp. 136, 139.

[115] Kolb, 'General principles', 824.

[116] *Ibid.*, 824. Grando, 'Allocating the burden', 641. For further discussion, including with reference to WTO practice, Grando, *Evidence*, pp. 193–6.

litigant will be put in the position of being required to prove a negative. For example, in *Southern Bluefin Tuna cases (New Zealand* v. *Japan; Australia* v. *Japan)*, Australia and New Zealand were claiming that Japan had not co-operated with them in relation to measures necessary for the conservation of the living resources of the high seas under Articles 64 and 116–19 of the LOSC.[117] Had the case reached the merits stage this would have required proof of a negative proposition. Experience with the application of the SPS Agreement has also provided many examples of the need for a claimant to establish factual propositions taking a negative form. Within the articulation of the rule on burden of proof, contemporary practice regarding negative propositions in disputes involving state responsibility has thus been consistent with an appreciation of the certainty engendered by the presumption of compliance and a consistent articulation of the rules on burden of proof. Where necessary, a court or tribunal may allow a claim on the basis of an unrebutted prima facie case in order to accommodate considerations of fairness arising from the assertion of negative propositions, as discussed further below.[118]

On occasion it is also sometimes suggested that the burden of proof should be allocated to the litigant with the best access to relevant information.[119] For example, counsel drew on this notion in the *Case concerning Pulp Mills*, pointing out that the parties were not on an equal footing. While Argentina had to rely on experts' reports and processes of deduction, Uruguay had much greater access to evidence concerning the Botnia Mill because of its right to exercise governmental functions in its own territory.[120] The idea of allocating the burden to the litigant with the best access to information is also consonant with the proposal that 'he should have the burden on whom it would sit lightest', but has been described as potentially 'theoretically disputable'.[121] In practice a litigant may well carry the burden of proof

[117] *Southern Bluefin Tuna cases (New Zealand* v. *Japan; Australia* v. *Japan)*, Order of 27 August 1999, 38 ILM 1624; *Southern Bluefin Tuna case (Australia and New Zealand* v. *Japan)*, Award on Jurisdiction and Admissibility, 4 August 2000, 119 ILR 509.

[118] See below, pp. 229–30.

[119] *Lighthouses Arbitration between France and Greece*, Claim No. 6, 24 July 1956, 23 ILR 677, 678 (hereafter *Lighthouses Arbitration*, Claim No. 6). Canvassing further authorities and discussing associated issues, see Grando, *Evidence*, p. 196.

[120] Verbatim Record, Monday 28 September 2009, translation, 10–11.

[121] van Hof, *Commentary on the UNCITRAL Rules*, pp. 162–3. For further criticism see Grando, *Evidence*, p. 147, discussing WTO practice. Grando's overall approach to burdens of proof is based on an assumption that the parties have equal access to the evidence

even though it is likely that the other party has better access to the relevant information. An illustration from the jurisprudence of the International Court of Justice is seen in the *Case concerning Avena and other Mexican Nationals (Mexico* v. *United States of America).* In this case the Court found that the US had not discharged the burden of showing that Mexican nationals were also US nationals, even though necessary information, such as their dates of birth and their parents' marital status at that time, was thought to be held by Mexico.[122] An asymmetry in the parties' ability to produce evidence to support their claims and defences may be inherent in the circumstances of certain cases, but this does not alter the application of the rules on burden of proof.[123] Nor has the WTO Appellate Body been prepared to accept that disputants' relative ease of access to pertinent information determines the allocation of the burden of proof.[124] Thus, contemporary practice in the articulation of the rules on burden of proof in relation to litigants' relative ease of access to information in disputes involving state responsibility has also been consistent with an appreciation of the certainty engendered by the presumption of compliance, and a consistent articulation of the rules on burden of proof. Where this places a party in an awkward position, it may be of some help to recall litigants' duty to co-operate with international courts and tribunals in bringing forward evidence that will help them to decide the case.[125] In case of non-co-operation, adverse inferences may be drawn.[126] Again, some relief may be possible through a discretionary application of the prima facie case rule.[127]

needed to prove their cases, and her primary recommendation for addressing asymmetries is to institute a mechanism ensuring better access to the evidence rather than to consider adjusting the allocation of the burden of proof. *Ibid.*, pp. 318, 361.

122 The US had not demonstrated adequate efforts to obtain the information from the Mexican authorities. *Avena and other Mexican Nationals*, paras. 41 and 55–7. Rosenne, *The Law and Practice*, p. 1042.

123 Separate Opinion, Judge Owada, *Case concerning Oil Platforms (Islamic Republic of Iran* v. *United States of America)*, Judgment of 6 November 2003, ICJ Reports 2003 (hereafter *Case concerning Oil Platforms*), paras. 42–6.

124 *European Communities – Trade Description of Sardines*, Complaint by Peru (WT/DS231/R), Report of the Panel DSR 2002: VIII, 3451 (hereafter *EC – Sardines* PR), para. 281. See below.

125 Riddell and Plant, *Evidence*, p. 49. Amerasinghe, *Evidence*, pp. 96 ff.

126 Cheng, *General Principles of Law*, pp. 324–30; Amerasinghe, *Evidence*, pp. 43, 132–7 and 141–2, and see also p. 206. Note also the jurisprudence of the UN Human Rights Committee and the Inter-American Court for Human Rights in drawing adverse inferences against a state.

127 See below, pp. 229–30. In contrast, see Grando, *Evidence*, pp. 330–1, 361–2. Where mechanisms for equalising access to evidence fail, Grando envisages either a reversal of the burden of proof or the application of new legal presumptions to enable findings to be made on the basis of facts that can be proven from the available evidence.

Overall, then, although it is not explicitly acknowledged, the judicial articulation of the rules on burden of proof today in disputes involving state responsibility is often relatively consistent with a prioritisation of certainty in the system. This is apparent in three ways. The first is seen in the practical but unarticulated subservience of the second aspect of the burden of proof to its first aspect: the first aspect being the requirement for a party to prove all facts necessary to support *a claim or defence*. This first aspect of the rule on burden of proof is underpinned by the presumption of compliance and is designed not to vary according to judicial discretion. The second way in which the judicial articulation of the rules on burden of proof is consistent with the prioritisation of certainty in international law lies in the common acceptance in many cases today that parties may sometimes have to prove negative assertions. The third way lies in the non-acceptance of the variation of the rules on burden of proof that would allocate the burden according to which party has access to relevant information. In these three ways, certainty in relation to the rules on burden of proof is sustained. The practical need to alleviate the burden may, in rare cases, be met through the use of a prima facie case approach in the application of the rules on proof, as discussed further below.

Judicial application of the rules on burden of proof

There remains considerable scope for the exercise of discretion in the application of the rules on burden of proof. This is notably the case in connection with determining whether a rule is a general rule or an exception, and also with the choice of a standard of proof, including where a court or tribunal allows a party to prevail on the basis of a prima facie case established to an unspecified standard of proof.

Distinctions between general rules and exceptions

International courts and tribunals have the task of ascertaining whether a rule is a general rule, or whether it is a defence or exception. The principle that the burden of proof will be allocated to a party seeking to rely on an exception is recognised in states' approach to the conduct of proceedings in international tribunals,[128] and has been

[128] See e.g. the arbitral award in *Libyan Arab Foreign Investment Company (LAFICO) and the Republic of Burundi*, 4 March 1991, 96 ILR 279 at 309–20, where Burundi attempts to

followed clearly and consistently since early in international judicial practice.[129] It is reflected in the writings of commentators,[130] and occasionally in tribunals' rules of procedure. The term 'exception' bears a close connection with the Roman law concept of the *exceptio*, which described an affirmative defence in the formulary system.[131] The *exceptio* was an assertion that was put forward in opposition to the plaintiff's claims, but was more than a mere denial of the claim.[132] An *exceptio* was also included as a negative condition in the *interdict*, and permitted the defendant to disregard the praetor's order if the condition applied. Certain exceptions were an integral part of an *interdict*, while others were inserted by the praetor at the request of the defendant.[133]

Exceptions may also be referred to as defences. When the defence of necessity was raised by Hungary in the *Gabčíkovo-Nagymaros* case, the International Court of Justice indicated that it viewed the defence as an exception, remarking that an assertion of necessity 'could only be accepted on an exceptional basis'.[134] The Court noted that the International Law Commission had explained that not only did it view the justification of necessity 'as really constituting an exception' but also 'one even more rarely admissible than is the case with the other

justify the expulsion of Libyan nationals from Burundi; and the earlier *Naulilaa* case, in which Germany sought to justify aggression in Angola, relying on a thesis based on the right to conduct reprisals. *Responsabilité de L'Allemagne à Raison des Dommages causés dans les Colonies Portuguaises du Sud de L'Afrique*, Sentence sur le principe de la responsabilité, 31 July 1928, II RIAA 1012 at 1025–8. On the same point, see also *Responsabilité de L'Allemagne à Raison des Actes commis Postérieurement au 31 Juillet 1914 et avant que le Portugal ne participât à la Guerre*, 30 June 1930, II RIAA 1035 (hereafter *Cysne* case), 1056.

129 *Asylum case (Colombia/Peru)*, Judgment of 20 November 1950, ICJ Reports 266, 282; *Cysne* case, 1056.

130 Amerasinghe, *Evidence*; Brown, *A Common Law*; Pauwelyn, 'Evidence', 232, 235; Martha, 'Presumptions', 87 f, reviewing GATT panels' practice in relation to the general exceptions under Article XX of GATT, commercial and economic defences, exceptions to the prohibition on qualitative restrictions, safeguard provisions, and security exceptions. Cf. Grando, *Evidence*, pp. 187–8. Grando questions the distinction between general rules and exceptions.

131 Hunter, *Introduction to Roman Law*, p. 183. Fergusson, 'A day in court in Justinian's Rome', 763.

132 Rosenne, *The Law and Practice*, p. 806.

133 Berger, *Encylopedic Dictionary of Roman Law*, 458.

134 *Gabčíkovo-Nagymaros* case, para. 51. Similarly, in the *M/V 'Saiga' (No. 2)* case ITLOS considered that the burden of proof lay with Guinea to prove the applicability of the defence of necessity. Guinea failed to show grave and imminent peril to its essential interests justifying the application by Guinea of its customs laws in its exclusive economic zone. *M/V 'Saiga' (No. 2)*, paras. 132–5.

circumstances precluding wrongfulness'.[135] Hungary had not established to the satisfaction of the Court that the construction of the project would have led to the consequences alleged.[136] As discussed earlier, Hungary might have been able to sustain a defence of ecological necessity if there had been more scientific evidence supporting the Hungarian argument of 'imminent peril'.[137]

There are a number of other circumstances in which the wrongfulness of a breach of international law is precluded as a matter of secondary international law. The six potential defences identified in the International Law Commission's Articles on State Responsibility are: the consent of the affected state, self-defence, *force majeure*, distress, necessity and the adoption of countermeasures in response to an internationally wrongful act by another state.[138] A party arguing that responsibility for its conduct is precluded on such grounds will bear the burden of proof in relation to that defence.[139] In relation to waivers of rights adopted prior to or at the time of the commission of what would otherwise be a breach of an obligation owed to the party or parties who have adopted the waiver, the defence of consent, referred to above, will apply.[140] This is a helpful explanation for the WTO Appellate Body's characterisation of the Enabling Clause in *European Communities – Conditions for the Granting of Tariff Preferences to Developing Countries* as an exception, discussed further below.

[135] *Gabčíkovo-Nagymaros* case, para. 50, citing the International Law Commission's Draft Articles on the Responsibility of States for Internationally Wrongful Acts (1998) II(2) *Yearbook of the International Law Commission* 26, also published in Crawford, *The International Law Commission's Articles*.

[136] *Gabčíkovo-Nagymaros* case, Separate Opinion of Judge Koroma.

[137] Foster, 'Necessity and precaution'.

[138] Draft Articles on the Responsibility of States for Internationally Wrongful Acts, Articles 20–5, (2001) II *Yearbook of the International Law Commission* 26, also published in Crawford, *The International Law Commission's Articles*.

[139] In relation to the defence of necessity see the *Cysne* case, 1056, although the burden of proof in this matter was indicated in the Declaration of London, which the parties had each declared would govern their conduct of hostilities, 1052. In relation to the defence of *force majeure*, see the *Russian Indemnity* case, *Affaire de L'Indemnité Russe*, 11 November 1912, XI UNRIAA 421, 443. The allocation of the burden is not referred to in every case where the application of the defences is considered. See e.g. the award of the France–New Zealand Arbitral Tribunal in the case of the *Rainbow Warrior (New Zealand* v. *France)*, 30 April 1990, 82 ILR 499.

[140] Draft Articles on the Responsibility of States for Internationally Wrongful Acts, commentary to Article 20, paras. 2 and 3, (2001) II(2) *Yearbook of the International Law Commission* 26, also published in Crawford, *The International Law Commission's Articles*.

Examples of exceptions in the primary law are found in the various bodies of international law. In the *United States – Wool Shirts* case the WTO Appellate Body observed that Articles XX and XI:2(c)(I) of the General Agreement on Tariffs and Trade (GATT) could be categorised as exceptions or 'affirmative defences'.[141] The point was confirmed in *United States – Standards for Reformulated and Conventional Gasoline*[142] and the same practice has been followed in subsequent cases.[143] Exceptions are also found elsewhere in WTO law.[144] Likewise, the Iran–US Claims Tribunal has required parties to prove the applicability of the exceptions on which they rely.[145] The European Court of Justice, too, has held that 'the burden of proving circumstances justifying a derogation from the principle of the free movement of goods rests on the Member State whose legislation is responsible for the obstruction'.[146] Defences may simultaneously be available both in primary and in secondary law. In the *CMS Gas Transmission Co.* v. *Argentina* annulment decision it was held that the principles of *lex specialis* required that the relevant provision in the applicable treaty should be applied first, and only then should a tribunal consider the applicability of the necessity exception in the secondary law on state responsibility.[147]

[141] *US – Wool Shirts* ABR, 16. An 'affirmative defence' may be contrasted with a defence that consists merely of the denial of a plaintiff's claim. Thayer, 'Burden of proof'.

[142] *United States – Standards for Reformulated and Conventional Gasoline*, Complaint by Brazil (WT/DS4), Complaint by Venezuela (WT/DS2), Report of the Panel DSR 1996: I, 29, paras. 6.20, 6.31, 6.35; *United States – Standards for Reformulated and Conventional Gasoline*, Report of the Appellate Body DSR 1996: I, 3, 22–3.

[143] *United States – Import Prohibition of Certain Shrimp and Shrimp Products*, Complaint by India (WT/DS58), Complaint by Malaysia (WT/DS58), Complaint by Pakistan (WT/DS58), Complaint by Thailand (WT/DS58), Report of the Panel DSR 1998: VII, 2821 (hereafter *US – Shrimp* PR), para. 7.30. *Korea – Measures Affecting Imports of Fresh, Chilled and Frozen Beef*, Complaint by Australia (WT/DS169), Complaint by the United States (WT/DS161), Report of the Panel DSR 2001: I, 59, para. 8.177. *United States – Measures Affecting the Cross-Border Supply of Gambling and Betting Services*, Complaint by Antigua (WT/DS285), Report of the Panel DSR 2005: XII, 5797, paras. 6.12 and 6.449–6.451. *Mexico – Soft Drinks* PR, para. 8.166. *Brazil – Measures Affecting Import of Retreaded Tyres*, Complaint by the European Communities (WT/DS332), Report of the Panel DSR 2007: V, 1649, para. 7.669.

[144] Grando, *Evidence*, p. 155. See e.g. *Canada – Patent Protection of Pharmaceutical Products*, Complaint by the European Communities (WT/DS114), Report of the Panel DSR 2000: V, 2289, para. 7.16.

[145] In particular, see *R. N. Pomeroy and others*, 8 June 1983, 2 Iran–US CTR 372 at 382.

[146] See e.g. Case 304/84, *Ministère Public* v. *Claude Muller and others* [1986] ECR I-1511, para. 16.

[147] *CMS Gas Transmission Co.* v. *Argentina*, Decision on Annulment, ICSID Case No. ARB/01/8, paras. 130–6, decision available at http://ita.law.uvic.ca.

Courts and tribunals must act with great care in determining whether a rule is a general rule, or whether it is a defence or exception.[148] In relation to a general rule, a defending state's compliance with international law is presumed. Where a state has to rely on an exception, the state's compliance is no longer presumed. The determination of whether a provision is a general rule or an exception may thus involve a tacit but potentially significant normative judgment.[149] Those who rely on provisions deemed to be general rules are privileged over those who rely on exceptions. In this respect there is an implicit hierarchy between general rules and exceptions. The reasoning underlying the distinction may be that day-to-day implementation of general rules is more common than reliance on exceptions. There is consistency here with the notion that what is more normal or probable is to be presumed.[150] This perspective on the character of exceptions also resonates with the principle according to which exceptions are to be narrowly construed.

On the other hand, it is important not to undermine the significance of the policies often encapsulated in exceptions. The Appellate Body has been at pains to emphasise that the importance of the policies represented in exceptions should not be underappreciated. In *EC – Tariff Preferences*, the Appellate Body emphasised that the characterisation of the enabling clause as an exception did not diminish its status in any way.[151] The reports of the Appellate Body to date in cases involving environmental exceptions within the multilateral trade framework also demonstrate a determination to avoid this pitfall. From a policy perspective, there should not be a punitive dimension in allocating the burden to a party relying on an exception. Deviation from the general rule may be necessary to protect important interests.

The interests of certainty and stability in international law demand that decisions to create exceptions in the law need to be regarded as having been taken at the time that such provisions are created, their character from then on generally being immutable. Determining whether

[148] Thayer, 'The burden of proof', 46 and 58–9. 'Once the norm is assumed, the burden of proof will weigh heavily against the supposed deviation'. Gordon, 'The World Court', 807.

[149] Grando recognises this, and takes a position that is wary of adjudicators second-guessing the relative importance attached by drafters to the provisions they crafted. Grando, *Evidence*, pp. 169, 177, 184–5.

[150] See above.

[151] *European Communities – Conditions for the Granting of Tariff Preferences to Developing Countries*, Complaint by India (WT/DS246), Report of the Appellate Body DSR 2004: III, 951 (hereafter *EC – Tariff-Preferences* ABR), para. 98.

a provision embodies a general rule or an exception is part of the interpretation of the provision. Established customary and conventional rules on the interpretation of treaties are applicable, and their reasoned application should help reinforce objectivity in the determinations that are made. However, a particular challenge may arise for adjudicators where the categorisation of the legal provisions applying to a given dispute involves taking a position on the reconciliation of competing policy goals within a high-intensity regime.

(a) *The struggle within WTO dispute settlement*

An intriguing example of the struggle that may ensue is the development within WTO jurisprudence of various categories of rule in addition to the notions of general rule and exception. A number of forms of provision have been identified that permit deviations from a rule but have not been denoted exceptions. These categories of provision have been described as 'exemptions' and 'autonomous rights', and do not attract the burden of proof. Only in relation to exceptions does a respondent bear the burden of proof; in relation to exemptions and autonomous rights the burden of proof will lie with the complainant, as usual.

Whether these analytical categories are justifiable has been questioned.[152] Is designation as an 'autonomous right' merely a way of adding judicial emphasis to the importance of a general rule? Certainly, the content of the 'autonomous right' identified by the Appellate Body in the form of Article 3.3 of the SPS Agreement in *EC – Hormones* is of particular social significance.[153] Article 3.3 says that members may introduce or maintain measures resulting in a higher level of protection than would be achieved by measures based on the relevant standards, guidelines or recommendations if there is a scientific justification or as a result of the level of protection considered by the member to be appropriate in accordance with Article 5.1–5.8.[154]

[152] Broude, 'Genetically modified rules'.

[153] *EC – Hormones* ABR, para. 104. The provision in Article 3.3 has also been described as containing a 'conditional' right because a respondent has a right to act in the way discussed in the provision provided the respondent's action falls within the provision's terms or conditions. The provision in Article 27(4) of the WTO Agreement on Subsidies and Countervailing Measures has been described in the same way, and Article 6 of the Textiles Agreement would seem to share the same features. *US – Wool Shirts* ABR, 16. Remarks by Pauwelyn, Joost in 'Internet roundtable: The Appellate Body's GSP decision' (2004) 3(2) *World Trade Review* 239, 257.

[154] Such measures are also not to be inconsistent with any other provisions of the Agreement.

The effect of the Appellate Body's categorisation of the rule in Article 3.3 was significant, as noted earlier. The *EC – Hormones* Panel had characterised Article 3.3 of the SPS Agreement as an exception to the obligation contained in Article 3.1.[155] Article 3.1 of the SPS Agreement provides that members are to base their SPS measures on international standards except as otherwise provided in the Agreement. The Panel referred to Article 3.2, which embodies a presumption of consistency with the SPS Agreement for measures that 'conform to' international standards. The Panel reasoned that this presupposed that the burden of proof fell on a member imposing measures under Article 3.3 that were not 'based on' international standards.[156] According to the reasoning of the Panel, once the complaining party provided a prima facie case that the measures were not consistent with Article 3.1, the burden fell on the party that had instituted the measures to prove consistency with Article 3.3.[157] The Panel thus concluded that, as it had already been found that the EC's measures were not based on the international standards that existed, the burden of proof in this case rested on the EC to prove its compliance with Article 3.3.[158] Because compliance with Article 3.3 depends on compliance with all the provisions of the Agreement, and particularly Article 5, the implication of this finding was to place on the EC the burden of proving compliance and consistency with each of the elements of the applicable provisions of Article 5.[159] Thus in assessing the EC's compliance with Article 5.1 in respect of five of the six hormones at issue, the Panel proceeded to require the EC to submit evidence that its measures were based on a risk assessment.[160]

The Appellate Body disagreed with the Panel's reasoning. According to the Appellate Body, the relationship between Article 3.1 and 3.3 was qualitatively different to that between Articles I or III and Article XX of the GATT 1994.[161] The Panel had erred in law.[162] The right of a member to establish its own level of sanitary protection was an autonomous

[155] *EC – Hormones*, Complaint by Canada, PR, paras. 8.88, 8.89; Complaint by the US, PR, paras. 8.85, 8.86.
[156] *Ibid.*, Complaint by Canada, PR, para. 8.57; Complaint by the US, PR, para. 8.54.
[157] *Ibid.*, Complaint by Canada, PR, para. 8.90; Complaint by the US, PR, para. 8.87.
[158] *Ibid.*, Complaint by Canada, PR, para. 8.91; Complaint by the US, PR, para. 8.88.
[159] *Ibid.*, Complaint by Canada, PR, paras. 8.103, 8.168; Complaint by the US, PR, paras. 8.100, 8.165.
[160] *Ibid.*, Complaint by Canada, PR, para. 8.104; Complaint by the US, PR, para. 8.101.
[161] *Ibid.*, Complaint by Canada, PR, para. 8.104; Complaint by the US, PR, para. 8.101.
[162] *EC – Hormones* ABR, para. 108.

right independent from the provisions of Article 3.1.[163] Article 3.1 simply excluded from its ambit situations covered by Article 3.3. Under Article 3.3 of the SPS Agreement a member had an important right to set for itself a level of SPS protection different from that implicit in international standards, and this was not merely an exception to the obligation in Article 3.1.[164]

A similar dynamic is seen in jurisprudence under the Agreement on Technical Barriers to Trade (TBT Agreement).[165] In *European Communities – Trade Description of Sardines*, a WTO Panel found that an EC regulation preventing Peruvian exporters from describing their product as 'sardines' was inconsistent with Article 2.4 of the TBT Agreement. Article 2.4 provides that WTO members are to base their technical regulations on international standards, except where such standards would be an ineffective or inappropriate means to fulfil the legitimate objectives.[166] The Panel viewed Article 2.4 as containing an exception or affirmative defence,[167] but the Appellate Body did not share the view that there was a general rule–exception relationship between the first and second parts of Article 2.4.[168] The Appellate Body rested its determination of the point on the strong conceptual similarities with the issues that had arisen in *EC – Hormones* concerning the relationship between Article 3.1 and Article 3.3 of the SPS Agreement.[169] Again, the content of the second part of Article 2.4 is of especial significance, socially and in environmental terms.

Both Article 3.3 of the SPS Agreement and Article 2.4 of the TBT Agreement run counter to the trade-related objectives of the WTO regime, narrowly understood. The value of the designation 'autonomous right' may lie in the recognition especially accorded to these

[163] *Ibid.*, para. 172. [164] *Ibid.*, para. 172.

[165] Agreement on Technical Barriers to Trade 1995, WTO, *The Legal Texts: The results of the Uruguay round of multilateral trade negotiations*, p. 121.

[166] Article 2.4 states: 'Where technical regulations are required and relevant international standards exist or their completion is imminent, Members shall use them, or the relevant parts of them, as a basis for their technical regulations except when such international standards or relevant parts would be an ineffective or inappropriate means for the fulfilment of the legitimate objectives pursued, for instance because of fundamental climatic or geographical factors or fundamental technological problems'.

[167] *EC – Sardines* PR, para. 7.50.

[168] *European Communities – Trade Description of Sardines*, Complaint by Peru (WT/DS231/R), Report of the Appellate Body DSR 2002: VIII, 3359 (hereafter *EC – Sardines* ABR), para. 275.

[169] *Ibid.*, para. 274.

provisions, ring-fencing them from designation as exceptions. The Appellate Body is refusing to accept that the proper interpretation of these provisions would place them lower in the hierarchy of applicable rules, stripping the presumption of compliance from parties who rely on them, with potentially concrete consequences in cases where the evidence may be finely balanced.

The concept of an 'exemption' has also been referred to in disputes under the Agreement on Sanitary and Phytosanitary Measures, specifically in relation to Article 5.7 of the Agreement. Article 5.7 of the SPS Agreement is a provision allowing a WTO member to adopt SPS measures without a risk assessment, as a temporary response to a risk and under strict conditions.[170] Article 5.7 was first categorised as an 'exemption' by the Appellate Body in *Japan – Agricultural Products*, albeit a 'qualified exemption'.[171] In the *Japan – Apples* case there was a temporary deviation in the categorisation of Article 5.7, and the burden of proof was allocated to the respondent, Japan, in relation to Article 5.7.[172] On the facts of *Japan – Apples* the burden's allocation under Article 5.7 probably made little difference. As there was a 'large quantity' of 'high quality' scientific evidence in which 'the experts have expressed strong and increasing confidence',[173] even if the burden had been correctly allocated to the US it was clear that Article 5.7 was inapplicable. However, the question was revisited and corrected in *European Communities – Measures Affecting the Approval and Marketing of Biotech Products*, where it was made clear that Article 5.7 does not attract the burden of proof and is not an exception, either to Article 2.2 or Article 5.1 of the SPS Agreement. The Panel in this case referred to Article 5.7 as a 'qualified right' rather than an exemption.[174] The notion of a 'qualified right' is reminiscent of the term 'autonomous right' used to describe Article 3.3 of the SPS Agreement.

[170] For the terms of Article 5.7, see above, p. 65, n. 212.

[171] *Japan – Measures Affecting Agricultural Products*, Complaint by the United States (WT/DS76), Report of the Appellate Body DSR 1999: I, 277, para. 80.

[172] *Japan – Apples* PR, paras. 7.26, 8.212, 8.222. The question of the burden of proof under Article 5.7 was not raised by Japan on appeal.

[173] *Ibid.*, para. 8.219.

[174] *European Communities – Measures Affecting the Approval and Marketing of Biotech Products*, Complaint by United States, Canada, Argentina (WT/DS291, WT/DS292, WT/DS293), Report of the Panel DSR 2006: III, 847 (hereafter *EC – Biotech* PR), paras. 7.2969–7.2983. Note the EC argument to this effect at para. 7.2952. See, though, para. 7.3254 where the term exception is used, perhaps inadvertently.

The WTO Appellate Body applied a legal test for determining whether a provision embodies an exception in *EC – Tariff Preferences*.[175] On this test, an exception will usually apply simultaneously with a general rule, although the exception will govern the situation.[176] In *EC – Tariff Preferences* it was found that the enabling clause of GATT applied simultaneously with Article I(1), although the enabling clause took precedence over Article I(1).[177] It was found that the enabling clause was an exception.

The *EC – Tariff Preferences* case concerned a complaint by India against the EU's Drug Arrangements, which were designed to combat drug production and trafficking. The Drug Arrangements were one of the programmes forming part of the EC's 2001 Generalised System of Preferences (GSP) for developing countries. Under the Drug Arrangements, only twelve selected developing countries, not including India, were eligible for tariff-free access to EU markets, provided they complied with conditions laid down by the EU for combating drug production and drug trafficking. India argued that the EC Drug Arrangements breached the most favoured nation rule in Article I of the GATT, which required all WTO members to be treated equally. India also argued that the Drug Arrangements were not protected by the 1979 enabling clause, a waiver of the rights adopted by the contracting parties to the GATT that permitted preferences to be granted to developing countries under GATT in exceptional circumstances.[178] India won the case. The enabling clause was found to apply only to GSP schemes that were non-discriminatory.[179] As the EU's tariff preferences were discriminatory they were not protected by the exception found in the enabling clause.[180] The EC could not rely on the exception embodied in the enabling clause. Characterisation of the enabling clause as an exception was one of the important outcomes in this case.

[175] See also the prior decision in *Brazil – Export Financing Programme for Aircraft*, Complaint by Canada (WT/DS46), Report of the Appellate Body, DSR 1999: III, 1161 at para. 139. The Appellate Body agreed with the Panel that allowance for the non-application of the WTO prohibition on export subsidies as a transitional measure did not amount to an exception. See Report of the Panel, DSR 1999: III, 1221, paras. 7.50–7.56.

[176] Citing *EC – Hormones*, ABR, 104; *EC – Sardines* ABR, para. 275. See also *Brazil – Export Financing Programme for Aircraft*, Complaint by Canada (WT/DS46), Report of the Appellate Body DSR 1999: III, 1161, paras. 139–41.

[177] *EC – Tariff-Preferences* ABR, para. 90.

[178] See Article XXV(5) of GATT 1947 and now Article IX(3) of the WTO Agreement.

[179] *EC – Tariff-Preferences* ABR, paras. 145 and 190.

[180] *EC – Tariff Preferences* ABR, paras. 180–4 and 188.

On the Appellate Body's approach a provision that applies instead of another provision, rather than simultaneously, will not be an exception. Applying the Appellate Body's test, Articles 3.3 and 5.7 of the SPS Agreement and Article 2.4 of the TBT Agreement would not amount to exceptions. Accordingly, they would not attract the burden of proof. Yet at the same time, the Appellate Body indicated in *EC – Tariff Preferences* that the distinction in this respect between exceptions and other permissive provisions might not always be able to be drawn, and might not always be evident. The distinction between provisions that create exceptions and provisions that may exclude the application of other provisions has been criticised for its artificiality.[181]

The Appellate Body also suggested in *EC – Tariff Preferences* that an adjudicatory body may be expected to apply a general rule before proceeding to apply an exception.[182] Indeed, there was some consternation when the *EC – Biotech* Panel decided to examine the EC's compliance with Article 5.1 of the SPS Agreement before applying Article 5.7, because this could be taken to infer that Article 5.7 was an exception when it has been recognised as constituting only an exemption.[183]

However, other international courts and tribunals do not always follow the order of analysis proposed by the Appellate Body in *EC – Tariff Preferences*. A court or tribunal may decide to omit making a finding on whether there is a breach of a general rule and proceed directly to considering the applicability of an exception. In the *Case concerning Oil Platforms (Islamic Republic of Iran* v. *United States of America)*[184] by addressing the exception first, the International Court of Justice was enabled to make findings on the question of US compliance with the law on the use of force, an issue of the highest importance to the international community.[185] This case concerned two United States attacks on Iranian oil production complexes in 1987 and 1988 during the 1984–8 tanker war. Iran complained that these attacks were in breach of the parties' 1955 bilateral Treaty of Amity (the Treaty). The Court considered first whether the US might be exculpated under the rubric of self-defence by virtue of a savings clause in Article XX(1)(d) of the Treaty allowing

181 Grando, *Evidence*, pp. 181–4. 182 *Ibid.*, para. 102.

183 Broude, 'Genetically modified rules'. 184 *Case concerning Oil Platforms*, p. 160.

185 *Ibid.*, para. 38. Cf. the views of Judge Higgins, Judge Buergenthal and Judge Owada, who considered that the finding on Article X(I) did not merit the place it was given in the Court's *dispositif*. Separate Opinion of Judge Higgins, paras. 22–3 and 49; Separate Opinion of Judge Buergenthal, para. 30; Separate Opinion of Judge Owada, para. 12.

the parties to protect essential security interests.[186] The burden of proof was allocated to the US to prove that its actions were consistent with the law on self-defence, a recognised exception to the international legal prohibition on the use of force by one state against another.[187] The Court found that the US had failed to prove that its actions could be justified as a matter of self-defence and were therefore not justified under Article XX(1)(d) of the Treaty.[188] The Court then considered whether the US attacks had, as alleged, breached the obligations to allow freedom of commerce and navigation found in Article X(1) of the Treaty, but as there had been no interference with commerce in oil between the territories of the parties the Court found there to be no violation.[189]

One further feature of the *EC – Tariff Preferences* case deserves mention. Although exceptions are usually raised by respondents as defences, in this case in light of the special characteristics of the enabling clause, combined with the circumstances of the case,[190] the Appellate Body considered that a complaining party would not be fulfilling its legal responsibilities as claimant if it omitted reference to the clause and its relevant subparagraphs from its claims and did not address the subject of the clause's application in its written submissions.[191] The Appellate Body emphasised that the enabling clause was critical for developing countries, and accordingly played a vital role in promoting trade. In the event, India had appropriately incorporated such references and material.[192] As alluded to above, these responsibilities are distinct from the burden of proof.

[186] Article XX(1)(d) provided that:

> the present Treaty shall not preclude the application of measures: ...
> (d) necessary to fulfil the obligations of a High Contracting Party for the maintenance or restoration of international peace and security, or necessary to protect its essential security interests.

[187] *Case concerning Oil Platforms*, para. 57.

[188] *Ibid.*, paras. 79 and 125(1).

[189] *Ibid.*, paras. 99 and 125(1). Arguably, this finding rendered the finding on self-defence immaterial to the legal dispute before the Court. In the instance of the *Oil Platforms* case there is also room for discomfort on other grounds in relation to the Court's decision to address initially the US claim of self-defence, rather than starting with the question of whether the US had committed a breach of its obligations to Iran under the bilateral treaty. Jurisdiction on the subject of the use of force had been rejected at the preliminary objections stage. The Court had taken jurisdiction under the Treaty of Amity only in relation to the subject of freedom of commerce and navigation. *Case concerning Oil Platforms (Preliminary Objections)*, Judgment of 12 December 1966, ICJ Reports 1996 803.

[190] *Ibid.*, para. 106. [191] *Ibid.*, paras. 106, 118.

[192] *Ibid.*, para. 119. For further discussion see Harrison, James 'Legal and Political Oversight of WTO Waivers' (2008) 11(2) *Journal of International Economic Law* 411–25.

Why, it might be asked, is the identification of such 'exemptions' and 'autonomous rights' a particular feature of the WTO and SPS and TBT Agreements? The high 'regime-intensity' of the SPS and TBT Agreements may be the most significant factor in producing provisions that will be treated by the WTO judiciary in this way. Both agreements contain a dense set of rules tightly marshalled around a central policy: they are designed as bulwarks against economic protectionism. Yet other goals are also important within the deregulated international economic system, and should not be allowed to remain below the radar. WTO adjudicators have demonstrated an increasing awareness of this aspect of WTO law. If the rules in Articles 3.3 and 5.7 of the SPS Agreement and Article 2.4 of the TBT Agreement were redrafted as exceptions, that would lessen their utility as important counterweights that can be employed by adjudicators, and indeed policy-makers, administrators and negotiators, to help balance out the policy content of the agreements in favour of other interests.

The true analytical need for maintaining distinct sub-categories of general rules such as 'exemptions' and 'autonomous rights' may be minimal. However, the WTO experience highlights the discretion lying in the hands of international courts and tribunals when it comes to the application of the rules on burden of proof. The principled and reasoned exercise of this discretion will be important for the stability of international adjudication. For example, in the *EC – Hormones* case referred to above, the WTO Appellate Body looked beyond the regime's immediate demands to combat economic protectionism that had so strongly influenced the Panel at first instance. The Appellate Body took into account the importance, both socially and in terms of the balance necessary for the regime's survival, of recognising that WTO Members had not forgone the right to establish their own desired level of protection against sanitary and phytosanitary risks, even if this were a higher level of protection than that afforded by international standards, without attracting the burden of proof in relation to the conformity of their sanitary and phytosanitary measures with WTO law.

(b) Segmentation of legal claims

There are certain fields of international law where a practice has developed of segmenting out distinct elements of a legal claim for the purposes of allocating the burden of proof. In the law relating to diplomatic protection, a respondent asserting that a claim is precluded by the availability of local remedies must prove the availability of such remedies. However, if a claimant then asserts that such remedies are ineffective, the claimant must prove their ineffectiveness.[193] In international human rights law, where the power differential between the parties will normally be particularly wide, the segmentation is different: in a case where it is not clear that there is access to effective local remedies, a respondent state may be required to demonstrate both the availability and the effectiveness of the local remedies.

Segmentation has also been contemplated in relation to the environmental defences in WTO law. In WTO jurisprudence the test of whether a measure is 'necessary' in terms of the relevant exceptions in Article XX of GATT and Article XXIV of the General Agreement on Trade in Services (GATS) incorporates a test of whether there are any reasonably available alternative measures.[194] For example, in *European Communities – Measures Affecting Asbestos and Asbestos-Containing Products*, Canada argued that the EC could not rely on Article XX(b) of the GATT because there was a reasonably available alternative to the banning of chrysotile asbestos by the EC: to adopt safer 'controlled use' policies for the use of chrysotile. The Panel did not consider that Canada's argument was sufficiently well supported by the evidence to rebut the EC's prima facie case that its ban on chrysotile was necessary to the protection of human life and health in accordance with Article XX(b) of GATT.[195] In *United States – Measures Affecting the Cross-Border Supply of Gambling and Betting Services*, the Appellate Body observed that it was not incumbent upon a responding party who asserted that a measure fell within the scope of XIV(a) of GATS to address all potential alternative measures with which its own

[193] Brownlie, *Principles of Public International Law*, pp. 492–501; Watts and Jennings, *Oppenheim's International Law*, p. 526. Amerasinghe, *Evidence*, pp. 78 ff. In Article 15(a) of the International Law Commission's 2006 draft Articles on Diplomatic Protection this was cast as an exception to the local remedies rule.

[194] GATT Panel Report, *United States Section 337 of the Tariff Act of 1930*, L/6439, adopted 7 November 1989, BISD 36S/345, para. 5.26; *Korea – Measures Affecting Imports of Fresh, Chilled and Frozen Beef*, Complaint by Australia (WT/DS169), Complaint by the United States (WT/DS161), Report of the Appellate Body DSR 2001: I, 5, 165; *European Communities – Measures Affecting Asbestos and Asbestos-Containing Products*, Complaint by Canada (WT/DS135), Report of the Panel DSR 2001: VIII, 3305, Report of the Appellate Body DSR 2001: VII, 3243, 171.

[195] *European Communities – Measures Affecting Asbestos and Asbestos-Containing Products*, Complaint by Canada (WT/DS135), Report of the Panel DSR 2001: VIII, 3305, para. 8.222; *EC – Asbestos* ABR, para. 175.

measure was to be compared.[196] If a complainant raised a possible alternative measure then the responding party would have to address the alternative that had been identified.[197]

This has led at least one writer to ask whether complainants should specifically be allocated the burden of proving the positive assertion that alternative measures are reasonably available.[198] However, even though this might make it easier for respondents to rely successfully on the Article XX exceptions, it is simplest to continue with an approach under which the burden of proof revolves around the parties' claims.[199] The relevant assertion of law here would be that paragraph (a) of Article XX was applicable. International courts and tribunals should be wary of exercising discretion in a way that introduces greater segmentation into the rules on burden of proof. This is an activity involving normative judgments that should not lightly be taken on by an adjudicative body.

Standards of proof

International jurisprudence 'has always avoided a rigid rule regarding the amount of proof necessary to support the judgment'[200] and standards of proof are not a strong focus of attention in international tribunals.[201] However, a certain level of probative evidence has always been required. That point is clear even in the decision-making of the Iran–US Claims Tribunal, where evidence has frequently been difficult to locate.[202] Generally, the standard of proof applied requires a case to be

[196] *United States – Measures Affecting the Cross-Border Supply of Gambling and Betting Services*, Complaint by Antigua (WT/DS285), Report of the Appellate Body DSR 2005: XII, 5663, paras. 309, 320, 326.

[197] See also *Brazil – Measures Affecting Import of Retreaded Tyres*, Complaint by the European Communities (WT/DS332), Report of the Appellate Body, DSR 2007: IV, 1527, para. 156.

[198] Bartels, 'Commentary', 222.

[199] Grando characterises the Appellate Body's approach as imposing on the claimant a burden of pleading a sub-element of a claim but discourages this practice. Grando, *Evidence*, pp. 212–15.

[200] *Velásquez-Rodríguez* case, Judgment of 29 July 1988, IACHR, Ser. C, No. 4; 28 ILM 291, 315–16. The Court referred to the decisions of the International Court of Justice in the *Corfu Channel* case, see n. 31 above and *Case concerning Military and Paramilitary Activities in and against Nicaragua*, see n. 277 below.

[201] Schwarzenberger, *International Law*, pp. 192, 643. Pasqualucci, *The Practice and Procedure*, p. 213. Amerasinghe, *Evidence*, p. 232.

[202] *Jalal Moin* v. *Islamic Republic of Iran*, 25 May 1994, 30 Iran–US CTR 71, 75. Amerasinghe, *Evidence*, p. 367.

established as a minimum on the preponderance of the evidence.[203] Yet standards of proof alter from case to case, depending on the nature of the issues.[204] Where the charges levelled against a state are considered to be particularly serious there has been some inclination to maintain a higher standard of proof. To take an example, a high standard of proof is found in the *Partial Awards of the Eritrea–Ethiopia Claims Commission on the Treatment of Prisoners of War*. In light of submissions made by the parties, the Commission considered that:

> Particularly in light of the gravity of some of the claims advanced, the Commission will require clear and convincing evidence in support of its findings.[205]

Similarly in the *Genocide* case the International Court of Justice took the view that the Court 'had to be fully convinced' that allegations of genocide and other acts had been clearly established.[206] These comments were reminiscent of the Court's comments in the *Corfu Channel* case. In the *Corfu Channel* case the UK argued that it could satisfy the burden of proof by showing with reasonable certainty the complicity of Albania in minelaying in the Channel. The Court said, however, that 'a charge of such exceptional gravity against a State would require a high degree of certainty that has not been reached here'.[207] An interesting feature of the formulation in the *Genocide* case is that it is cast in terms of the subjective state of mind of the Court: the Court 'had to be fully

[203] Amerasinghe, *Evidence*, p. 245.

[204] Watts, 'Burden of proof', 289; Kazazi, *Burden of Proof*, p. 323. See also Amerasinghe, *Evidence*, Ch. 12.

[205] *Partial Awards on Prisoners of War between the State of Eritrea and the Federal Democratic Republic of Ethiopia: Eritrea's Claim* 17, 42 ILM 1083 (2003), paras. 43 *et seq.*; *Ethiopia's Claim* 4, 42 ILM 1056 (2003), paras. 34 ff.

[206] *Case concerning the Application of the Convention on the Prevention and Punishment of the Crime of Genocide*, 209.

[207] *Corfu Channel* case, 17. See also the Separate Opinion of Judge Shahabuddeen in *Qatar* v. *Bahrain* (Jurisdiction and Admissibility), Judgment of 15 February 1995, ICJ Reports 5, 63. A similar approach is taken in human rights cases. In the *Velásquez-Rodríguez* case, relating to the forced disappearance of Manuel Velásquez-Rodríguez, the Inter-American Court of Human Rights considered it was appropriate to apply a high standard of proof in order to reflect the seriousness of the charge against Honduras. See e.g. the *Velásquez-Rodríguez* case, para. 135. See also *Godínez Cruz*, 20 January 1989, IACHR Ser. C, No. 5, para. 135. The European Court of Human Rights has also required proof beyond reasonable doubt in relation to serious allegations. See *Ireland* v. *United Kingdom*, 18 January 1978 ECHR Ser. A, No. 25; 58 ILR 264 (hereafter *Ireland* v. *United Kingdom*); case of *Cyprus* v. *Turkey*, 10 May 2001, paras. 112–15.

convinced'. This is reminiscent of the civil law approach to standard of proof, where the standard being applied goes unpronounced.[208]

The variability in standards of proof and the need to ensure a greater element of predictability for litigants have become a focus of concern in relation to international adjudication. There has been a call for the adoption of a formal standard of proof in the International Court of Justice. Judge Higgins, then President of the Court, commented in the *Oil Platforms* case that:

> The principal judicial organ of the United Nations should .... make clear what standards of proof it requires to establish what sorts of facts.[209]

It has been argued that the adoption of a formal standard or standards of proof in international adjudicatory decision-making would be a positive step, accentuating the significance of the judicial weighing of evidence, and leading to increased transparency in the articulation by international courts and tribunals of how persuasive they find particular evidence.[210] Scope for the arbitrary application of the rules on proof would be diminished. Such expectations of transparency in the appreciation of evidence are shared by common and civil law systems alike.[211] The question is how to encourage their consistent application in international courts.

In the International Tribunal for the Law of the Sea, Vice-President Wolfrum has remarked on the need for a more consistent approach to the standard of proof.[212] In the Iran–US Claims Tribunal a standardisation in the rules of evidence has been encouraged.[213] Adoption of a consistent standard of proof in the European Court of Justice has likewise been advocated, the formula suggested being that of a 'reasonable degree of certainty'.[214] Arguments have also been made for a pre-determined standard of proof to be established in the WTO to provide

[208] Likewise see the variable adoption of subjective and objective standards in *Case concerning Armed Activities on the Territory of the Congo*, at paras. 207 and 237, and the *Oil Platforms* case at e.g. paras. 71 and 76. On the civil law approach in relation to standards of proof, see below, pp. 227–9; Grando, *Evidence*, pp. 88–9.

[209] *Oil Platforms* case, para. 33. See also the Separate Opinions of Judge Buergenthal and Judge Owada, and see Green, 'Fluctuating evidentiary standards'.

[210] Prager, 'Procedural developments at the International Court of Justice'.

[211] Taruffo, 'Rethinking the standards of proof', 668.

[212] Separate Opinion of Vice-President Wolfrum, *M/V Saiga (No. 2)*, para. 2.

[213] Brower, 'Evidence'.

[214] Lasok, *The European Court*, p. 431; Plender, 'Procedure', citing Advocate General Gand in Case 8/65, *Acciaierie e Ferriere Publiese* v. *High Authority* [1966] ECR 1, 12.

more consistency and predictability.[215] In *United States - Import Prohibition of Certain Shrimp and Shrimp Products*[216] the Panel observed that the parties' submissions had raised questions about 'how much' had to be proved. However, the Panel considered that:

> We [therefore] have to assess the evidence before us in the light of the particular circumstances of this case. This implies that we may consider any type of evidence, and also that we may reach our conclusions regarding a particular claim on the basis of the level of evidence that we consider sufficient.[217]

In the *EC - Biotech* case, the Panel used a wide variety of expressions to convey the level of proof that had been achieved in relation to factual propositions underlying the claim that the EC had been maintaining a de facto moratorium on approval of biotech products. For example, the Panel 'had seen no evidence' and was therefore 'not persuaded',[218] the 'record does not disprove the claim',[219] the proposition was 'plausible'[220] and, frequently, the circumstances were 'consistent' with a moratorium.[221] Certainly the standard applied here seems to have been a low one. Perhaps this is to be explained on the basis that establishing a de facto moratorium is not easy, and necessarily may be based on inference. When it came to making findings against the EC under Article 5.1 of the SPS Agreement, the Panel said that the facts did not naturally lead to the conclusion that a prohibition on imports was warranted, and 'strongly suggest[ed]'[222] that the EC had not fulfilled the requirements of Article 5.1 in relation to individual Member States' safeguard measures. Even this does not seem a high standard of proof. In the investment context, reference has been made, for example, to 'the balance of probabilities'[223] with remarks

[215] Pauwelyn, 'The use of experts', 360; Cameron and Orava, 'GATT/WTO Panels', 235. See also Grando, *Evidence*, pp. 92, 132, 147, 356–7.

[216] *United States - Import Prohibition of Certain Shrimp and Shrimp Products*, Complaint by India (WT/DS58), Complaint by Malaysia (WT/DS58), Complaint by Pakistan (WT/DS58), Complaint by Thailand (WT/DS58), Report of the Panel DSR 1998: VII, 2821 (hereafter *US - Shrimp* PR).

[217] *US - Shrimp* PR, para. 7.14. [218] *EC - Biotech* PR, paras. 7.1020, 7.1022.

[219] *Ibid.*, para. 7.1034. [220] *Ibid.*, para. 7.1039.

[221] Although see *ibid.*, para. 7.1028, where the circumstances were found to 'support the contention' of the complaining parties.

[222] *Ibid.*, para. 7.3064.

[223] See the finding of the *Methanex* Tribunal on the question of jurisdiction, *Methanex*, Part IV, Chapter E, para. 18. *Methanex Corp.* v. *United States of America*, 3 August 2005, decision available at http://ita.law.uvic.ca.

also such as 'that proposition is simply not tenable on the evidential record'.[224]

Analyses suggest that if the standards of proof presently applied by international courts and tribunals are extrapolated from their decisions these standards fall into several identifiable clusters, including proof beyond reasonable doubt, proof on the balance of probabilities and conclusive proof.[225] This clustering may represent a genuine need for flexibility in international adjudication, which could be accommodated in the formalisation of this area of procedure through the identification of alternative 'objective' standards of proof.[226] However, the most appropriate standard to adopt for general application in most situations would be a standard reflecting the common law standard for civil cases: the balance of probabilities or 'preponderance of the evidence' test.[227]

Commentators are in accord that this test captures best the current practice of international judges and arbitrators, even though for many adjudicators the question of whether they are convinced of a point or not may be the fulcrum around which their evaluation has tended to focus. If a formal standard or standards of proof were adopted, a distinct shift would be involved in terms of how a Court approached the question of proof. In assessing the evidence before it, a Court would be required always to bear in mind the need to justify its decision against the identified standard of proof. The exercise of judicial discretion in the appreciation of evidence would become more apparent.

As mentioned above, the absence of a formal standard of proof is one respect in which international adjudication more closely resembles civil law proceedings than common law proceedings.[228] The common

[224] *Ibid.*, *Methanex*, Part IV, Chapter E, para. 19, referring to the proposition that the Californian science on MTBE was so faulty that the Tribunal might reasonably infer it merely provided a convenient excuse for regulation.

[225] Kazazi, *Burden of Proof*, pp. 347–50; Brown, *A Common Law*, p. 98; Amerasinghe, *Evidence*, p. 234. On conclusive proof, see the judgment of the International Court of Justice in the *Oil Platforms* case, above n. 125, paras. 71, 72.

[226] Green, 'Fluctuating evidentiary standards', 167.

[227] Brown, *A Common Law*, p. 19. Indeed this formulation was adopted by Judge Greenwood in the *Case concerning Pulp Mills*: 'I believe that Argentina was required to establish the facts which it asserted only on the balance of probabilities (sometimes described as the balance of the evidence).' *Case concerning Pulp Mills*, Separate Opinion of Judge Greenwood, para. 26. In relation to the WTO, see also Grando, *Evidence*, pp. 132, 149, 356–7. Grando still contemplates a higher standard of proof in cases concerning the protection of human, animal and plant life or health in the territory of the respondent, on the basis that more is at stake in these cases. *Ibid.*, p. 141.

[228] Riddell and Plant, *Evidence*, p. 125.

lawyer regards the use of an objective standard of proof as a logical aspect of judicial decision-making,[229] bringing to the application of the law an element of standardisation and transparency. The standard of proof applied in civil cases in common law jurisdictions is whether a court considers a fact to be established 'on the balance of probabilities' or on the preponderance of the evidence.[230] There may be different degrees of proof within one standard of proof, depending on the subject matter.[231] For example, in an instance of alleged fraud a court may require more probative evidence than would be needed in the case involving allegations of negligence.[232] This has been described as involving an 'enhanced standard of proof'.[233]

Civil lawyers have expressed the contrasting view that judicial appraisal of facts is a subjective exercise.[234] As in Roman law,[235] the approach of the civil law judge is to decide whether he or she, personally, is persuaded by the evidence before the court. The *conviction intime du juge*[236] or *freie richterliche Überzeugung*[237] is the basis for findings of fact, that is to say a *preuve morale*,[238] or *ce qui persuade l'esprit d'une vérité*.[239] At present, the situation would seem to be that international courts and tribunals are either persuaded by parties' dossiers, or they are not. In the

229 O'Connell, *International Law*, p. 1098.

230 Tapper, *Cross and Tapper on Evidence*, pp. 169, 174. See also Zuckerman, *Civil Procedure*, pp. 756–79.

231 *Ibid.*, p. 185, although see *Re B (Children)* (FC) [2008] UKHL 35.

232 In the United States, an additional category of proof has been created, according to which 'clear and convincing' evidence is required. Anderson *et al.*, *Analysis of Evidence*, 243. This approach was adopted by the Iran–US Claims Tribunal in cases where forgery was alleged. Amerasinghe, *Evidence*, pp. 373–5.

233 Amerasinghe, *Evidence*, pp. 373–5.

234 Kazazi, *Burden of Proof*, pp. 325 and 377. Another argument is that a standard of proof cannot be a fixed concept because it is not realistically possible to specify meaningfully and objectively a particular point in the spectrum of 'degrees of belief to which human minds may be susceptible'. *Ibid.*, p. 343.

235 Fergusson, 'A day in court', 766.

236 Lalive, '*Quelques remarques*', 78; Damaška, *Evidence*, pp. 20–1. See also Taruffo, 'Rethinking', 666.

237 Frowein, 'Fact-finding', 248. Kazazi, *Burden of Proof*, p. 324; Kokott, *Burden of Proof*, pp. 1, 18, 196.

238 Taruffo, 'Rethinking', 667.

239 Cheng regards the standard of proof in international tribunals as 'the truth'. Cheng, *General Principles of Law*, p. 329; Sandifer, *Evidence*, p. 173. The notion of moral certainty is also part of common law thinking: the standard of proof beyond reasonable doubt in criminal cases derives from the notion of 'moral certainty, to the exclusion of reasonable doubt'. Twining, *Theories of Evidence*, p. 95, citing T. Starkie, *Practical Treatise on the Law of Evidence*, 4th edn (1853).

European Court of Justice, where the civil law tradition may be at its strongest, there is an implicit reliance on the continental European test that the conviction of the judge determines proof.[240]

The relationship between the concept of a standard of proof and the presumption of compliance underlying the rule of burden of proof is one of compatibility, and need not stand in the way of the adoption of a formalised standard or standards of proof. The presumption of compliance that is employed in the allocation of the burden of proof assumes that most actors comply with their legal obligations most of the time. A standard of proof, such as proof on the balance of probabilities, is applied in any particular case where non-compliance is asserted as a gauge against which the presumption of compliance may be overcome. Both the presumption of compliance and the standard of proof are creatures of a legal system designed to produce findings either of compliance or non-compliance.

However, for the meantime there is no agreement among international judges and arbitrators on the application of consistent rules on standard of proof. Minimal discipline applies, although there have been efforts towards greater articulation of courts' and tribunals' reasoning with reference to standards of proof to bring about greater transparency and to generate open discussion of the matter.

The prima facie case approach and the weighing of the evidence

Scope for the exercise of judicial discretion is seen also where the prima facie case rule is used as a decision-making tool. The origins of the prima facie case may be found in Roman law, with reference to the understanding of *probatio*. An actor was considered to have presented *probatio* by furnishing evidence at the outset of a case, although in the face of counter-evidence it was necessary to keep up the *probatio*.[241] In the context of international adjudication, a prima facie case has been

[240] Hanotiau, 'Satisfying the burden', 341, 346. This is seen in the various phrases that have been employed to refer to the standard of proof. There has been reference to: '*une preuve complète*', 'convincing proof' and '*preuve intégrale*', a 'reasonable degree of certainty', '*des indices graves établissant un haut degré de probabilité*', 'sufficiently precise and coherent proof', 'sufficiently clear evidence', 'specific and concrete evidence', and 'a firm, precise and concordant body of evidence'. Lasok, *The European Court*, pp. 429–30; Plender, 'Procedure', 171.

[241] Thayer, 'Burden of proof', 67.

described as evidence 'which, unexplained or uncontradicted is sufficient to maintain the proposition affirmed'.[242]

The concept of the prima facie case has provided a vehicle for exercising judicial discretion in favour of considerations of fairness. In decisions by the Iran–US Claims Tribunal,[243] and other claims commissions,[244] the establishment of a prima facie case has been considered sufficient basis for a decision in favour of a claimant in circumstances where evidence to substantiate a fuller case may be especially difficult to obtain,[245] or where a litigant is put in the position of attempting to furnish an impossible proof or *probatio diabolica*.[246] The extent to which the necessary evidence for a fuller case is genuinely unobtainable will be relevant.[247] The prima facie case rule is also regarded as being of potential assistance in cases where an actor must prove a negative proposition.[248] However, it is understood that 'mere suspicions can never be a basic element of juridical findings'.[249]

Commentators have argued that a prima facie case must meet the usual standard of proof applying to a case,[250] and urged care in the use of the prima facie case, given the absence of appeal from the decisions

[242] See the decisions of the USA–Mexico General Claims Commission in *Lillie S. Kling (USA* v. *United Mexican States)*, 8 October 1930, 4 UNRIAA, 585 and the *Parker* case *(USA* v. *Mexico)*, 31 March 1926, 4 UNRIAA (hereafter the *Parker* case) at 39–40. See also Grando's discussion of the claims commission decisions. Grando, *Evidence*, pp. 142–6.

[243] See e.g. *Lockheed Corporation* v. *The Government of Iran, the Iranian Airforce and others*, 9 June 1988, 18 Iran–US CTR 292, 95–7; *Rockwell International Systems* v. *The Government of the Islamic Republic of Iran (The Ministry of National Defence)*, 5 September 1989, 23 Iran–US CTR 150 at 188.

[244] Sandifer, *Evidence*, pp. 129–30, discussing the decision of the US–Mexican General Claims Commission in the *Parker* case.

[245] Kazazi, *Burden of Proof*, pp. 332–40. *International Technical Products Corp.* v. *Iran*, Award of 19 August 1985, 9 Iran–US CTR 10, 28; *Time Inc.* v. *The Islamic Republic of Iran*, Award of 22 June 1984, 7 Iran–US CTR 8, 11.

[246] Cheng, *General Principles of Law*, p. 323.

[247] Amerasinghe, *Evidence*, pp. 139–40, discussing the decision of the British–Mexican Claims Commission *In re Odell* (1931) 13 May 1931, 6 ILR 423. Also see e.g. *Sola Tiles Inc.* v. *The Government of the Islamic Republic of Iran*, 22 April 1987, 14 Iran–US CTR 223, 232–3. See also the 1956 decision of the Permanent Court of Arbitration in the *Lighthouses Arbitration*, Claim No. 6, 678.

[248] For example in the *Mexico City Bombardment Claims*, the British–Mexican Claims Commission was prepared to take the view that there was strong prima facie evidence of Mexico's failure to respond to revolutionary forces' occupation and looting of a YMCA hostel where the British Agent demonstrated that the circumstances were known to the Mexican authorities at the time. *Mexico City Bombardment Claims*, 1930, 15 February 1930, 5 ILR 166. Amerasinghe, *Evidence*, p. 249. Kolb, 'General principles', 825.

[249] Amerasinghe, *Evidence*, p. 249. [250] *Ibid.*, p. 256.

of most international courts and tribunals.[251] When it is taken into account that the 'usual' standard of proof remains unelaborated in international adjudication, the scope for judicial discretion where a prima facie case approach is expressly adopted seems particularly ample.

The question of the standard of proof arose in *Request for an Examination of the Situation*. Judge Weeramantry took the view that where danger could be shown prima facie to exist the burden of proof shifted to those claiming that the activity in question was safe, and a judicial tribunal was entitled to act on such a prima facie case.[252] He found that a prima facie case had been made out of the possible 'release into the ocean of the pent-up radioactive debris of around 127 nuclear explosions'.[253] However, these remarks were made in the context of a decision dealing with whether New Zealand's earlier case against France could be reopened in connection with a request for provisional measures. A prima facie test would usually be applicable for determining jurisdiction in a request for provisional measures.

In the WTO, a 'prima facie case' rule is a central and established feature of judicial decision-making,[254] used in all cases and not merely in cases where evidence is difficult to obtain. For example, *US – Wool Shirts*, in which the prima facie case approach was laid down, concerned a complaint by India that the US had not acted consistently with its obligations under the Agreement on Textiles and Clothing in adopting a safeguard action that affected India.[255] The Appellate Body said that a party claiming that a WTO Agreement had been violated by another member had to assert and prove its claim. This meant that India had to put forward sufficient evidence and legal argument to provide a prima facie case demonstrating that the United States' safeguard action was unjustified under the Agreement. When India had done this, the onus then shifted to the United States, which had to bring forward evidence and argument in order to disprove India's claim. The United States was not able to do so, and therefore the Panel had been correct in finding that the US action violated the Agreement.[256] Although the language of

[251] *Ibid.*, p. 253.

[252] *Request for an Examination of the Situation*, Dissenting Opinion of Judge Weeramantry, 345–8. See also Dissenting Opinion of Judge Koroma, 373–4.

[253] *Ibid.*, 361. [254] For history and critique, Pauwelyn, 'Evidence', 243 f.

[255] *United States – Measure Affecting Imports of Woven Wool Shirts and Blouses from India*, Complaint by India (WT/DS33), Report of the Appellate Body DSR 1997: I, 323, Report of the Panel DSR 1997: I, 343 (hereafter *US – Wool Shirts* ABR).

[256] *US – Wool Shirts* ABR, 16–17.

a shift in the burden of proof has been used inconsistently in WTO dispute resolution, as noted above,[257] the application of the prima facie case rule remains standard practice. For example, in the *EC – Hormones* case the Panel recalled the rule laid down in *US – Wool Shirts*.[258] Accordingly, in this case Canada and the US bore the burden of establishing a prima facie case that the EC's ban on meat from cattle treated with growth-promotion hormones was inconsistent with the SPS Agreement. Once a prima facie case was established, the EC had to rebut the case established by Canada and the US, which the EC failed to do.

WTO practice also applies the prima facie case rule in relation to defences.[259] In *United States – Measures Affecting the Cross-Border Supply of Gambling and Betting Services*, the US unsuccessfully invoked Article XIV of GATS, which is a general exceptions provision that parallels Article XX of GATT. The US asserted that its measures restricting internet gambling were 'necessary to protect public morals' and so were justified under Article XIV(a). The US was found to have raised an unrebutted prima facie case that its measures were necessary under paragraph (a) of Article XIV, but the US case was unsuccessful due to failure to prove that its measures were applied in accordance with the chapeau to Article XIV in a way that did not involve arbitrary or unjustifiable discrimination.

Does the use of the prima facie case rule as applied in the WTO involve a potential lowering of the standard of proof? May only a low level of proof be required from a claimant, provided that an adequate case has been presented and that no evidence is presented by the other party that might rebut this case?[260] There is still a clear bottom line. In *EC – Hormones* the Appellate Body commented that:

[257] See pp. 205–6.

[258] *EC – Hormones* PR, para. 8.58; *EC – Hormones* ABR, para. 98: 'we consider that, as is the case in most legal proceedings, the initial burden of proof rests on the complaining party in the sense that it bears the burden of presenting a *prima facie* case of inconsistency with the SPS Agreement. It is, indeed, for the party that initiated the dispute settlement proceedings to put forward factual and legal arguments in order to substantiate its claim that a sanitary measure is inconsistent with the SPS Agreement . . . Once such a *prima facie* case is made, however, we consider that, at least with respect to the obligations imposed by the SPS Agreement that are relevant to this case, the burden of proof shifts to the responding party.'

[259] Appellate Body Report, *United States – Measures Affecting the Cross-Border Supply of Gambling and Betting Services*, paras. 309–11, also 358 *et seq.*

[260] Pauwelyn, 'Evidence', 246, 256. Canvassing authorities, Grando notes that the prima facie case standard in the WTO would seem to be a low one. Grando, *Evidence*, pp. 106, 131. She considers there is no justification for applying a lower standard of proof in the WTO, although reliance on inference may be necessary in some cases. *Ibid.*, p. 147.

It is also well to remember that a *prima facie* case is one which, in the absence of effective refutation by the defending party, requires a panel, as a matter of law, to rule in favour of the complaining party presenting the *prima facie* case.[261]

However, again this bottom line remains a flexible one. Rather than articulating a standard of proof to guide panels in working out when a prima facie case has been established, in *US – Wool Shirts* the Appellate Body said only that:

precisely how much and precisely what kind of evidence will be required to establish such a presumption will necessarily vary from measure to measure, provision to provision, and case to case.[262]

Thus, it seems, in practice the prima facie case approach operates through the exercise of judicial discretion, both in the WTO and elsewhere. The standard involved in establishing a prima facie case may tend in practice to be lower than usual. The standard remains unarticulated and susceptible to variation. A claimant need only discharge its initial burden of proof as measured by the particular, and tacit, prima facie standard that the members of courts or tribunals choose to apply.[263] It may even be that higher standards of proof may still be applied in relation to the other party's response to a prima facie case.[264] Concern about low standards of proof was expressed by Judge Warioba in his Dissenting Opinion in the *M/V Saiga No. 2*,[265] where the International Tribunal for the Law of the Sea applied an approach similar to that seen in the WTO.

In the absence of a recognised and generally applicable standard of proof in international adjudication, it is unlikely that a specific standard of proof for the establishment and rebuttal of a prima facie case will be developed. At present, there seems little distinction between the undisciplined use of prima facie case approaches and the exercise of discretion in the weighing of evidence. Indeed the exercise

[261] *EC – Hormones* ABR, para. 104.

[262] *US – Wool Shirts* ABR, 14. The WTO Appellate Body has here used the term 'presumption' to refer to a prima facie case. This contrasts with the more specific use of the term 'presumption' in the context of factual and legal presumptions discussed below.

[263] 'The standard for presenting a prima facie case is, under virtually any definition, relatively low.' Cameron and Orava, 'GATT/WTO Panels', 237.

[264] Christoforou, 'WTO Panels', 243–65, 644, and note 60. Pauwelyn considered that a party rebutting a prima facie case should be required only to cast reasonable doubt on it. Pauwelyn, 'Evidence', 257.

[265] *M/V Saiga (No. 2)*, paras. 72–3; Dissenting Opinion of Judge R. Warioba, para. 33.

of discretion in the weighing of evidence will sometimes be a more flexible and less cumbersome method to give effect to the need for fairness in the application of the rules on burden of proof, although international courts and tribunals will want to bear in mind that such discretion is only to be exercised in especial circumstances. For example, reference might be made to the comment of the International Court of Justice in the *Nicaragua* case that Nicaragua's evidence in response to US allegations over the supply of arms was to be assessed bearing in mind that Nicaragua had to prove a negative.[266] There is also the possibility that a court or tribunal might be prepared to rely on factual inferences where evidence is scarce, as seen in the *Corfu Channel* case, discussed below, which some may consider amounts to relying on a prima facie case.

Presumptions

In addressing the subject of the burden of proof, it is important also to consider the concept of presumptions, known both to the common law and the civil law.[267] Reference has already been made to the 'presumption of compliance'. However, when the term 'presumption' is used by an international court or tribunal, it usually takes a different meaning. The designation 'presumption' applies where one fact is deemed to be proved on the basis of another.[268] The application of presumptions is an accepted aspect of international adjudication, and is considered a legitimate judicial method for the evaluation of evidence.[269] Presumptions, indicia and circumstantial evidence may all be relied upon by international courts and tribunals, in addition to direct evidence.[270]

Reliance upon inference is seen quite clearly in the work of a number of international tribunals,[271] including not only the International Court

[266] Judgment of 27 June 1986, ICJ Reports 1986 14, 80.

[267] Malaurie and Morvan, *Droit Civil*, pp. 128–30, Larroumet, *Droit Civil*, pp. 339, 342–4; Ghestin *et al.*, pp. 699–702; Prieto-Castro y Ferrandiz, *Derecho Procesal*, pp. 151–2 and 192–4. Indeed, the active use made of presumptions has been described as an outstanding feature of the main categories of civil suit. Ngwasiri, 'The role', 167. See also Beardsley, 'Proof of fact', 472–4.

[268] Amerasinghe, *Evidence*, p. 211; Amerasinghe, 'Presumptions', 395; Tapper, *Cross and Tapper on Evidence*, p. 146.

[269] As agreed by the parties in *Islamic Republic of Iran* v. *United States of America*, Case A/20, Decision of 10 July 1986, 11 Iran–US CTR 271, 276.

[270] *Velásquez-Rodríguez* case, above n. 200, para. 130.

[271] Cheng, *General Principles of Law*, pp. 322 f.

of Justice,[272] but also the Iran–US Claims Tribunal,[273] the human rights courts,[274] the WTO[275] and the European Court of Justice.[276] Inferences have also been drawn on the basis of failure to deny an alleged point of fact. In the *Nicaragua* case, at the merits stage, the International Court of Justice drew the inference that undenied US overflights above foreign territory had indeed taken place.[277] The Court adopted the same approach in respect of the supply of arms by Nicaragua to the Salvadorean opposition. The *Corfu Channel* case is often cited as the classic illustration of reliance upon inference and circumstantial evidence.[278] In *Corfu Channel* the Court agreed that, given the difficulties involved in gathering evidence, 'a more liberal recourse to inferences of fact and circumstantial evidence' was permissible in concluding that Albania must have known of the minelaying that had taken place in the Corfu Channel.[279] The circumstantial and indirect evidence relied upon included the geographical configuration of the relevant territory, the estimated time required for minelaying, the distance of the minefield from the coast, the absence of an Albanian investigation into certain events and notes kept by the Albanian government.[280] The Court also took into account the 'exclusive territorial control exercised by a state within its frontiers'.[281] The Court found that:

> In cases where proof of fact presents extreme difficulty, a tribunal may [thus] be satisfied with less conclusive proof i.e. *prima facie* evidence . . . *the inference in every case must, however, be one which can reasonably be drawn.*[282]

272 Highet, 'Evidence and proof of facts', 363–5.

273 Holtzmann, 'Fact-finding by the Iran–United States Claims Tribunal', 270, 354.

274 Pasqualucci, *The Practice and Procedure*, p. 209; *Velásquez-Rodríguez* case, paras. 124, 126.

275 Waincymer, *WTO Litigation*, p. 619.

276 The European Court of Human Rights has indicated that 'proof may follow from the co-existence of sufficiently strong, clear and concordant inferences or of similar unrebutted presumptions of fact.' *Ireland* v. *United Kingdom*, 65, para. 161. See also *Nachova and others* v. *Bulgaria*, ECHR, 6 July 2005, para. 147.

277 *Case concerning Military and Paramilitary Activities in and against Nicaragua (Nicaragua* v. *United States of America) (Merits)* ICJ Reports 1986 14, 51–2; Amerasinghe 'Presumptions', 406.

278 Amerasinghe, *Evidence*, pp. 139, 204–8; Cheng, *General Principles of Law*, pp. 323 and 325, as cited by Sandifer, *Evidence*, at 173; see also Highet, 'Evidence', p. 364.

279 *Corfu Channel* case, 18. Judge Azevedo also agreed on this point in his Dissenting Opinion at 90–1: 'it would be going too far for an international court to insist on direct and visual evidence and refuse to admit, after reflection, a reasonable amount of human presumptions with a view to reaching that state of moral, human certainty with which, despite the risk of occasional errors, a court of justice must be content'.

280 Kazazi, *Burden of Proof*, pp. 86–9 and 261.

281 *Corfu Channel* case, 18.

282 Emphasis added.

In the WTO context, reference might be made to the assumptions relied on by the Panel in *Australia – Measures Affecting Importation of Salmon.*[283] Assumption was also employed, in quite different circumstances, by the UNCC when faced with particular difficulties obtaining evidence in relation to claims for mental suffering consequent upon Iraq's invasion of Kuwait.[284] On the basis of a commissioned expert report, particular policies were adopted to guide the level of awards made, in an attempt to mitigate difficulties with proof and to streamline the processing of claims. As a general point the UNCC decided to 'lower the levels of evidence required',[285] and held that the level of evidence required for Category C Claims was 'the reasonable minimum appropriate under the circumstances involved'.[286] More specifically, once the fact of injury was proven, mental suffering was assumed.[287]

Judicial presumptions have their roots in the judicial capacity for inference,[288] which is linked with judicial freedom in relation to the evaluation of evidence. A judicial presumption is an inference that is commonly applied in a recurring situation.[289] This distinction between presumptions and inferences has not always been clearly maintained, and the two terms are often used interchangeably.[290] The presumption

283 *Australia – Measures Affecting Importation of Salmon*, Complaint by Canada (WT/DS18), Report of the Panel DSR 1998: VIII, 3407 (hereafter *Australia – Salmon* PR), paras. 8.124 and 8.135, see also at 8.159.

284 *Claims against Iraq (Category 'C' Claims) (Report and Recommendations Made by the Panel of Commissioners concerning the First Instalment of Individual Claims up to US $100 000)* 2 September 1994 109 ILR 205.

285 *Ibid.*, 243, citing Sandifer, *Evidence*, p. 22, on the practice of claims commissions dealing with complex questions of fact relating to hundreds and thousands of individuals' claims, and noting that such claims may arise out of circumstances of conflict where evidence is not retained.

286 *Ibid.*, 243. 287 *Ibid.*, 440.

288 Rosenne, *The Law and Practice*, p. 1046. See also Kolb, 'General principles', 824 on inferences or presumptions of fact *(praesumptiones hominis)*.

289 Amerasinghe, 'Presumptions', 405.

290 Kazazi, *Burden of Proof*, pp. 240 and 260; Amerasinghe, *Evidence*, pp. 224, 405. For example, in *Argentina – Footwear* the Panel consulted a number of dictionaries and concluded that a presumption was an inference in favour of a particular fact, or a conclusion reached in the absence of direct evidence. *Argentina – Measures Affecting Imports of Footwear, Textiles, Apparel and Other Items*, Complaint by the United States, WT/DS56, Report of the Panel DSR 1998: III, 1033, 253. The *Iran National Airlines Co.* case also provides an example. In this case, the Iran–US Claims Tribunal rejected US arguments for the application of a 'presumption' that the US Air Force had already made payment on a number of invoices from Iran on the basis that past practice showed a pattern of prompt payment. As it happened, the Tribunal did not doubt US practice, but did not consider there was adequate evidence to justify drawing such an inference. *Iran*

most frequently invoked in international legal proceedings is a judicial presumption, the presumption of the regularity of government activity: *omnia acta rite esse praesumuntur*.[291] This presumption is applied, for example, with respect to the validity of nationalisation and consular certificates as evidence of citizenship,[292] and the validity of municipal court decisions.[293] A range of other presumptions have been applied in international courts and tribunals, most notably by the Inter-American Court of Human Rights. These include a presumption of death in relation to individuals who have disappeared in violent situations and have not reappeared for many years, a presumption that victims' relatives pay for their funeral and a presumption that impunity causes anguish, pain and sadness to victims and their families.[294] To take another example, the Iran–US Claims Tribunal has consistently applied a presumption that invoices are correct and are evidence of a debt.[295]

Whereas a judicial presumption reflects a repeated practice of drawing a particular conclusion regarding one type of fact on the basis of another, a legal presumption is a presumption requiring a certain conclusion to be drawn as a matter of law.[296] This distinction holds true across both the civil and common law systems.[297] An example of a legal presumption is found in Article 2.5 of the WTO TBT Agreement. The first sentence of Article 2.2 of the TBT Agreement provides that 'Whenever a technical regulation is prepared, adopted or applied for one of the legitimate objectives explicitly mentioned in paragraph 2, and is in accordance with relevant international standards, *it shall be* rebuttably

National Airlines Company and The Government of the United States of America, Award of 30 November 1987, 17 Iran–US CTR 187, 193; Amerasinghe, 'Presumptions', 402.

291 Mani, *International Adjudication*, p. 208; cf. Cheng, *General Principles of Law*, pp. 305 f. Amerasinghe, 'Presumptions', 397; Witenberg, '*Onus probandi*', 329. This presumption was regarded as a 'universally accepted rule of law' by the German–Venezuelan Mixed Claims Commission in the *Valentiner* case (1903), X UNRIAA 403, 564, as cited by Amerasinghe, *Evidence*, pp. 26 and 214.

292 Sandifer, *Evidence*, p. 145; Simpson and Fox, *International Arbitration*, p. 199.

293 Sandifer, *Evidence*, pp. 143, 144; Ralston, *The Law and Procedure*, p. 217.

294 Pasqualucci, *The Practice and Procedure*, pp. 209–10, referring also to a number of additional examples. In the *Velásquez-Rodríguez* case, the IACHR found that, where government support for or toleration of a policy of forced disappearances had been established, the disappearance of an individual could be proved through presumptive, circumstantial or indirect evidence, as a matter of logical inference. *Velásquez-Rodríguez* case, paras. 124 and 131.

295 Amerasinghe, *Evidence*, pp. 375–6.

296 *Ibid.*, pp. 211–12. See also Kolb, 'General principles', p. 823 on ordinary presumptions of law *(praesumptiones juris)*.

297 Amerasinghe, 'Presumptions', 395, note 1. Amerasinghe, *Evidence*, p. 212.

presumed not to create an unnecessary obstacle to international trade.'[298] In domestic law, legal presumptions may derive from statute, although common lawyers are also comfortable with the notion of presumptions finding their origin in the judgments of the courts. In international law, legal presumptions have been recognised as deriving from general principles of law, treaty law and customary international law.[299] Whether legal presumptions can be created through the implied or inherent powers of international courts and tribunals is an open question.

All presumptions have a certain effect in relation to the discharge of the burden of proof. When weighing the evidence in a case, a tribunal will take into account any presumptions that may favour one party or the other and consider the extent to which they have been rebutted.[300] The effect of presumptions has been described by one writer, adopting the terminology of the Roman law, as providing a *levamen probationis*.[301] However, it has been observed in relation to most presumptions that the burden of proof does not shift; that is, the burden of proof in the sense corresponding to the first aspect of the burden of proof, relating to the proof of legal claims, referred to above.[302] However, where the result of applying a presumption is that a legal claim is considered to be proved, then there has arguably been a reversal in the burden of proof in the sense of the first aspect of the rule on burden of proof described above.

There have been cases in which the adoption of relatively powerful presumptions has been contemplated within the International Court of Justice. In both *Corfu Channel*[303] and *DRC* v. *Uganda*[304] the issue arose as to whether a respondent state should be allocated the burden of proof by virtue of states' obligations to exercise vigilance and be aware of illegal acts in their own territories.[305] The Court rejected the idea of a reversed burden of proof in the *Corfu Channel* case.

[298] Emphasis added. See also Article 3.2 of the SPS Agreement, as referred to above. As to rebuttable presumptions in international law, see Kolb, 'General principles', at 824 (*praesumptiones juris et de jure*).

[299] Kazazi, *Burden of Proof*, p. 245. Amerasinghe, *Evidence*, pp. 214, 218; Witenberg, '*Onus probandi*', 329–31; Sandifer, *Evidence*, p. 141.

[300] Amerasinghe, *Evidence*, pp. 219, 227–8; Amerasinghe, 'Presumptions', p. 401.

[301] Thayer, 'Burden of proof', 63.

[302] See above, pp. 200–1 and 219. Amerasinghe, *Evidence*, pp. 219 and 223; Kazazi, *Burden of Proof*, pp. 251 and 253, but see also at p. 258.

[303] Individual Opinion of Judge Alvarez, 44.

[304] Separate Opinion of Judge Kooijmans, 15.

[305] Riddell and Plant, *Evidence*, pp. 88, 92.

Conclusion

The purpose of this chapter has been to ascertain the sources, rationale and scope of the rules on burden of proof, standard of proof and presumptions in international adjudication. The rules on burden of proof were found to be derived from combined international legal sources, including the inherent powers of international courts and tribunals. The rules as applied in disputes involving state responsibility are consistent with a presumption of compliance by states with their international legal obligations, and their development has been guided by principles of fairness. There also remains significant scope for considerations of fairness within the application of the rules on burden of proof. Of special importance is the capacity of international courts and tribunals to apply a prima facie case approach where necessary in order to accommodate fairness in international adjudication.

This is the landscape in which we must consider the potential to reverse the burden of proof in order to accommodate the precautionary principle in the adjudication of international disputes involving scientific uncertainty. The argument for greater certainty in the articulation of the rules on burden of proof may generate a sense that an exceptional approach should not be taken. Yet a new approach may be a matter of imperative, and it may be possible to develop a clearly defined rule or practice which can become known by all.

6 Reversing the burden of proof to give effect to the precautionary principle

Initially it would seem that applying the precautionary principle to reverse the burden of proof in international adjudication would be inconsistent with the need for certainty within the articulation and application of the rules on burden of proof, and would run counter to the presumption that states are in compliance with their international legal obligations. However, in the type of dispute under consideration in this book, justification for reversing the burden of proof can be found at both the legal and theoretical levels.

As a matter of law, the inherent powers of international courts and tribunals may include the capacity to reverse the burden of proof to accommodate the need for precaution in order to ensure the sound administration of justice. As a matter of theory, reversal of the burden of proof is consistent with the principles of fairness underlying the rules on burden of proof, and with an extended rationalist conception of adjudication. Within the extended rationalist tradition rectitude of decision (through the 'correct application of valid law to true facts')[1] is an important social value, but it is not an absolute requirement for rationalist adjudication. Other values may sometimes be overriding.[2]

[1] See above, Ch. 1, p. 5.

[2] Twining refers not only to values related to the adjudicatory process, but also independent values such as state security and the protection of family relationships. Twining, *Rethinking Evidence*, p. 76, point 7. See also Postema, 'The principle of utility and the law of procedure', 1408–9, on Bentham's intention to allow for ends additional to rectitude of decision, such as minimisation of delay and complications. Bentham's ultimate appeal was to the principle of utility. In pursuit of that end, rules should be flexible where necessary provided that steps were taken to enhance the moral aptitude of judges, including giving adequate publicity to judicial decisions. Postema, 'The principle of utility and the law of procedure', 1419–24. See also Grando, *Evidence*, pp. 12–13, 41.

In this instance, these other values would include both procedural fairness and the proper protection of human health and the environment.

Rules relating to the burden and standard of proof and the application of presumptions in any event do not fit well into the rationalist category of rules that are purely procedural.[3] In this they differ from other adjectival rules. Decisions about the burden's allocation are partially substantive and partially procedural, and this becomes especially obvious in a dispute involving scientific uncertainties.[4] International courts and tribunals cannot maintain a rigid approach that turns a blind eye to the substantive effects of applying the rules on burden of proof where fairness requires a specific modification to the rules, or to the way in which they are applied.[5]

For international courts and tribunals to contemplate reversal of the burden of proof in order to accommodate the precautionary principle, there are a number of issues that would need to be addressed. In particular, it would be necessary to determine and apply a consistent legal test for identifying when the threshold for the application of precaution is reached.

The precautionary principle

International courts and tribunals have expressed the understanding that there is a vital role to be played by precaution in decision-making about risks faced in the context of scientific uncertainty. In the *Southern Bluefin Tuna* cases the International Tribunal for the Law of the Sea took the view that:

[3] Cf. Witenberg, '*Onus probandi*', 327. On the distinction between procedural and substantive rules within the rationalist tradition see above, Ch. 1.

[4] Risinger, '"Substance" and "procedure" revisited', 206, refers to 'procedural rules stemming from what is essentially a substantive decision'. Kazazi, *Burden of Proof*, p. 30, has referred to the rule on burden of proof 'both as a procedural presumption and as an instance of substantive law'. See also Kokott, *Burden of Proof*, p. 3. 'The rules governing the burden of proof . . ., though belonging to international procedure, affect the substance of the case.' Amerasinghe, *Evidence*, pp. 42–3. For discussion on the difficulty in categorising the rules on burden of proof as substantive or procedural for the purposes of private international law, see North and Fawcett, *Cheshire and North's Private International Law*, pp. 88–9.

[5] As international law becomes more interdisciplinary 'the virtual impossibility of separating substantive and adjectival law' generally becomes more apparent. Rosenne, 'Fact-finding', 249.

> the parties should in the circumstances act with prudence and caution to ensure that effective conservation measures are taken to prevent serious harm to the stock of southern bluefin tuna.[6]

As noted earlier, in this case the Tribunal issued a provisional measures order requiring the parties to abide by existing quota limits.

In the *Dispute concerning the MOX Plant, International Movements of Radioactive Materials and the Protection of the Marine Environment of the Irish Sea (Ireland* v. *United Kingdom)* Ireland requested provisional measures to suspend immediately the authorisation of the MOX nuclear reprocessing plant at the Sellafield nuclear power station in Cumbria. Although the International Tribunal for the Law of the Sea did not find that the urgency of the situation required prescribing the provisional measures requested by Ireland, the Tribunal considered that:[7]

> prudence and caution require that Ireland and the United Kingdom cooperate in exchanging information concerning risks or effects of the operation of the MOX Plant and in devising ways to deal with them, as appropriate.

In the *Case concerning the Gabčíkovo-Nagymaros Project (Hungary/Slovakia)*, the International Court of Justice was asked by Hungary to consider the application of new norms of international environmental law relating to the prevention of damage to the environment pursuant to the precautionary principle. The Court did not explicitly identify the precautionary principle as one of these recently developed norms, but recognised the significance of such developments as the precautionary principle, in observing that:[8]

> in the field of environmental protection . . . new norms and standards have been developed, set forth in a great number of instruments during the last two decades. Such new norms have to be taken into consideration, and such new standards given proper weight . . .

[6] *Southern Bluefin Tuna cases (New Zealand* v. *Japan; Australia* v. *Japan)*, Order of 27 August 1999, 38 ILM 1624 (hereafter *Southern Bluefin Tuna*, Provisional Measures), paras. 77, and 90(1)(c), (d).

[7] *Dispute concerning the MOX Plant, International Movements of Radioactive Materials and the Protection of the Marine Environment of the Irish Sea (Ireland* v. *United Kingdom)*, Request for Provisional Measures, Order of 3 December 2001, 41 ILM 405 (hereafter *MOX Plant* Provisional Measures Order), para. 84.

[8] *Case concerning the Gabčíkovo-Nagymaros Project (Hungary/Slovakia)*, Judgment of 25 September 1997, ICJ Reports 1997 7 (hereafter *Gabčíkovo-Nagymaros* case), para. 140, and see paras. 111–14.

As noted above, the Court found that developments in environmental knowledge and environmental law could not be said to have been completely unforeseen by the parties.[9]

The WTO Appellate Body has also acknowledged the importance of the precautionary principle and the scope for its accommodation within international trade law, citing the *Gabčíkovo-Nagymaros* case and commenting in 1998 in *European Communities – Measures Concerning Meat and Meat Products (Hormones)* that:

> a panel charged with determining, for instance, whether 'sufficient scientific evidence' exists to warrant the maintenance by a Member of a particular SPS measure may, of course, and should, bear in mind that responsible, representative governments commonly act from perspectives of prudence and precaution where risks of irreversible, e.g. life-terminating, damage to human health are concerned.[10]

The Appellate Body noted the view that the principle had 'crystallised into a general principle of customary international environmental law', but refrained from adopting this view.[11] Views continue to differ on the status of the precautionary principle in international law. International courts and tribunals have not recognised the precautionary principle as a rule of law, although in the *Arbitration regarding the Iron Rhine Railway (Belgium/Netherlands)* the imperative to prevent potential harm was regarded as a principle of general international law.[12] Litigants have expressed widely diverging views on the principle's status.[13] Certain commentators suggest there is a 'good argument' that the precautionary

[9] *Gabčíkovo-Nagymaros* case, para. 104.

[10] *European Communities – Measures Concerning Meat and Meat Products (Hormones)* Complaint by Canada (WT/DS48), Complaint by the United States (WT/DS26), Report of the Appellate Body DSR 1998: I, 135 (hereafter *EC – Hormones* ABR), para. 124.

[11] *Ibid.*, para. 123.

[12] *Arbitration Regarding the Iron Rhine ('IJZEREN RIJN') Railway (Belgium/Netherlands)*, Award of 24 May 2005, www.pca-cpa.org, para. 59.

[13] Cf. Australia's Statement of Claim in the *Southern Bluefin Tuna* case, paras. 63–6, with the Response of the Government of Japan to Request for Provisional Measures and Counter-Request for Provisional Measures, 28–9. Also compare EC arguments in *EC – Hormones* with US and Canadian arguments. *European Communities – Measures Concerning Meat and Meat Products (Hormones)*, Complaint by Canada (WT/DS48), Complaint by the United States (WT/DS26). Two identically constituted WTO dispute settlement Panels (the Panel) circulated parallel reports in this case: Report of the Panel (Canada) DSR 1998: II, 235 (hereafter *EC – Hormones*, Complaint by Canada, PR), Report of the Panel (United States) DSR 1998: III, 699 (hereafter *EC – Hormones*, Complaint by the US, PR). In the Complaint by Canada, PR, paras. 4.210–4.213, 8.160; in the Complaint by the US, PR, paras. 4.202–4.207, 8.157. In the Appellate Body's report, see paras. 121 and 122.

principle has 'emerged as'[14] or 'reflects'[15] a principle of customary international law.[16] Others have viewed uncertainties about the application of the principle as detracting from its potential to become a general principle of international law in the sense of Article 38(1)(c) of the Statute of the International Court of Justice.[17] The principle clearly does appear to have some legal effect in the sense that it has attracted an international consensus, increasingly informs states' approaches to environmental issues, and may be relied upon in the reasoning of international tribunals on substantive points.[18] Principles of international environmental law, including the precautionary principle, are frequently recognised indirectly in legal provisions.[19]

The idea of reversing the adjudicative burden of proof with reference to the precautionary principle does not require that the principle has attained the status of a legally binding rule of international law. It is not proposed that the principle be applied directly to constrain the action of states in the absence of scientific certainty or to require them to take preventive measures to avoid serious and irreversible harm. Rather, the principle would be applied as part of the decision-making process. By virtue of the precautionary principle, a decision might be made that a party was out of compliance with international legal obligations relating to protection of human health or the environment if that party could not establish that it was in compliance with the applicable obligations. Alternatively, a decision might be made that a party could rely on environmental exceptions to protect its population or ecology where a challenging party was unable to prove that these exceptions did not apply.

[14] Freestone, 'Caution or precaution', p. 137. Cameron considers the precautionary principle has evolved into a general principle of international law. Cameron, 'The precautionary principle: Core meaning', 30. Cameron and Abouchar consider the precautionary principle 'a kind of constitutional principle for international society', 23–5, asserting it involves a duty which 'is owed to international society as a whole'. Cameron and Abouchar, 'The precautionary principle: A fundamental principle', 22. Cameron, 'The precautionary principle in international law', 113.

[15] Sands, *Principles*, p. 279; Cameron and Abouchar 'The status of the precautionary principle', 30.

[16] Hey took the view in 1992 'that the concept has at least approached the status of a rule of customary international law, and that the support expressed by states for documents containing the concept is not without legal significance', although 'the precise content and implications of this development remain . . . unclear and "elusive"'. Hey, 'The precautionary concept', 307, citing Gündling, 'The status', 25.

[17] Freestone, 'Caution or precaution', 136.

[18] Birnie *et al.*, *International Law*, pp. 159–64.

[19] de Sadeleer, *Environmental Principles*, pp. 230–31. Trouwborst, *Evolution*, Ch. 3, including at pp. 51–3, 260–84 and 285–6.

International courts may take into account the growing international legal status of the precautionary principle in considering whether the rules on burden of proof should be modified to allow reversal of the burden in disputes involving scientific uncertainty. Indeed, a new approach among international courts and tribunals on the precautionary reversal of the burden of proof would feed into the increasing status of the precautionary principle.

'Administrative' and 'adjudicative' burdens of proof

The application of the precautionary principle in an administrative setting is often referred to as involving 'reversal of the burden of proof'.[20] For example, when applying for the approval of a new pharmaceutical product under domestic law a commercial enterprise is required to establish the safety of the product before approval is granted. The same approach is commonly applied in domestic law in many fields of environmental and consumer protection regulation, including in relation to resource consents and food safety. 'Burden of proof' in the administrative sense is generally distinct from the burden of proof in the context of adjudication or the 'adjudicative' burden of proof.[21] It would be altogether incorrect to suggest that it is accepted as yet that the application of the precautionary principle may involve the reversal of the burden of proof in the adjudicative setting.

The distinction between administrative and adjudicative burdens of proof was recognised by a dispute settlement panel of the World Trade Organization (WTO) in *Japan – Measures Affecting Agricultural Products*. In response to a comment from Japan on the Panel's interim report,[22] the Panel stressed 'that the issue of burden of proof in a WTO dispute settlement proceeding set out above is different and should be distinguished from what a Member requires from an exporting country

[20] On the use of the concept of a burden of proof in this setting, see Fisher, *Risk Regulation and Administrative Constitutionalism*, pp. 44–6.

[21] Although where a national court is tasked with carrying out the judicial review of an administrative decision on the merits, a challenging party may bear both administrative and adjudicative burdens of proof. For discussion, see Fisher, *Risk Regulation and Administrative Constitutionalism*, Ch. 4, pp. 125–61. Alternatively in jurisdictions where a *de novo* appeal in the courts is available in resource management matters, an applicant's initial administrative burden of proof converts into an adjudicative burden of proof.

[22] On interim reports, see above, Ch. 3, p. 120.

before it will approve the import of that country's products'.[23] In this case dispute arose over which party should prove whether or not variety made a difference to the efficacy of treatment of fruit against codling moth. Japanese practice required exporting governments to demonstrate, for each variety of the exported product, that the treatment they used against codling moth would achieve the level of protection required by Japan.[24] This burden, imposed on exporters under Japanese law, is an 'administrative' burden of proof. Then there was the burden of proof placed on the US in the context of its legal proceedings in the WTO against Japan, which is an 'adjudicative' burden of proof. The US bore the adjudicative burden of proving that Japan had not complied with its obligations under the WTO Agreement on Sanitary and Phytosanitary Measures (SPS Agreement).[25] For example, it fell to the US to establish that Japan's varietal testing practices were not based on scientific principles, and were being maintained without sufficient scientific evidence, and were therefore inconsistent with Article 2.2 of the Agreement.[26]

In disputes arising under the SPS Agreement, the allocation of the adjudicative burden of proof favours a party that has imposed risk-response measures. This is because of the way the Agreement is structured and drafted. However, in cases arising in other international legal contexts a party seeking to protect itself against a risk may be less fortunate, and may be required to discharge the adjudicative burden of proof when a precautionary reversal of the burden of proof is applied.

[23] *Japan – Measures Affecting Agricultural Products*, Complaint by the United States (WT/DS76), Report of the Panel DSR 1999: I, 315 (hereafter *Japan – Agricultural Products* PR), para. 8.13. The distinction between administrative and adjudicative burdens of proof was also explicitly recognised by the US: 'it was important not to confuse the fact that the exporter would typically assume the burden of meeting the importing country's concerns with the question of the burden of proof for dispute settlement purposes'. *Ibid.*, para. 4.49. See also *Japan – Measures Affecting the Importation of Apples*, Complaint by the United States (WT/DS245), Report of the Panel DSR 2003: IX, 4481, para. 8.41.

[24] *Japan – Agricultural Products* PR, paras. 4.165, 8.3.

[25] Agreement on the Application of Sanitary and Phytosanitary Measures, WTO, *The Legal Texts: The results of the Uruguay round of multilateral trade negotiations*, p. 59.

[26] See also Waincymer, *WTO Litigation*, p. 557. The language of the burden of proof is employed from time to time in the ECJ to refer to legal obligations imposing administrative burdens of proof. For example, in the *Monsanto* case the ECJ explained in terms of the burden of proof Member States' substantive legal obligations under Regulation No. 258/97 concerning novel foods and food ingredients, including the obligation to show specific grounds for considering a novel food endangered human health or the environment. Case C-236/01, *Monsanto Agricoltura Italia SpA and others and Presidenza del Consiglio dei Ministri and others* [2003] ECR I-8105, paras. 108–9.

As Malaysia's advocate in the *Case concerning Land Reclamation by Singapore in and around the Straits of Johor (Malaysia* v. *Singapore)*, Sir Elihu Lauterpacht pointed out the 'role reversal' that takes place where a party likely to be affected by another actor's risk-bearing activities is obliged to institute legal proceedings in order to protect its interests. The result is that the allegedly affected party must bear an adjudicative burden of proof when the natural order of things would otherwise have been for the allegedly offending party to bear an administrative burden of proof in accordance with the precautionary principle. Malaysia said:

> One may argue about the status of the precautionary principle, but Malaysia submits that this Tribunal should not reject the widely-held view that it is for the State that proposes action that may detrimentally affect the environment to show, not to itself, but to those that may be affected by it, that there is no real likelihood of harm to the environment.[27]

Further examples are readily identifiable. As noted earlier, in the *MOX Plant* case counsel for Ireland argued that the precautionary principle required the UK to demonstrate that no harm would arise from discharges from MOX operations. In *Request for an Examination of the Situation in Accordance with Paragraph 63 of the Court's Judgment of 20 December 1974 in the Nuclear Tests (New Zealand* v. *France)*, New Zealand's legal team argued that under the precautionary principle 'the burden of proof fell on a State wishing to engage in potentially damaging environmental conduct to show in advance that its activities would not cause contamination'.[28] New Zealand argued that France was required to prove the safety of its activities. The precautionary principle was spoken of as a rule to guide French conduct or a rule that had been breached by France,[29] and to support the argument that France should carry out an environmental impact assessment.[30] New Zealand seems to have been

[27] *Case concerning Land Reclamation by Singapore in and around the Straits of Johor (Malaysia* v. *Singapore) (Provisional Measures)*, Order of 8 October 2003 (hereafter *Land Reclamation (Provisional Measures)*), decision available at www.itlos.org, Sir Elihu Lauterpacht, advocate for Malaysia, Verbatim Record, Saturday, 27 September 2003, 9.30 am, 23, lines 13 *et seq.*

[28] *Request for an Examination of the Situation*, para. 34. See also Dissenting Opinion of Judge *ad hoc* Palmer at para. 89. Aide-Mémoire of New Zealand of 5 September 1995, para. 38.

[29] New Zealand's Request, paras. 105, 110; Aide-Mémoire of New Zealand of 5 September 1995, paras. 37–8. See also the Dissenting Opinion of Judge *ad hoc* Palmer, 412.

[30] Argument by Mr Elihu Lauterpacht for New Zealand, Verbatim Record, Monday 11 September 1995, 62, para. 49; argument of Sir Kenneth Keith QC for New Zealand, Verbatim Record, Tuesday 12 September 1995, 10.00 am; argument of Mr Don MacKay for New Zealand, Verbatim Record, Tuesday 12 September 1995, 10.00 am, 20–1.

inviting the Court to consider a shift in the adjudicative burden of proof by virtue of the precautionary principle.[31] France, at least, understood New Zealand to be inferring that the Court should consider reversing the adjudicative burden of proof in the circumstances of the case. France took the view that New Zealand bore the burden of proof,[32] but had been unable to adduce evidence of damage or serious risk and was for this reason advocating a reversal of the burden.[33] France said 'it still remains that international law recognizes no ecological exception in the law of evidence. Environmental law, like the other fields of law, obeys the well-known principle of *actori incumbit probatio* ...'.[34]

It is clear that 'burden of proof' is generally used in connection with the precautionary principle in the sense of an administrative burden of proof, rather than an adjudicative burden of proof.[35] To suggest that a basis may exist on which the precautionary principle may reverse the adjudicative burden of proof raises new questions. As is apparent from the arguments of the various advocates referred to just above, the idea is one that international courts and tribunals should be invited to consider further. Commentators have already raised the issue in the context of the common law.[36] However, there has been no investigation

[31] Argument of Mr John McGrath for New Zealand, Verbatim Record, Monday 11 September 1995, 46–9, para. 64; Aide-Mémoire of New Zealand of 5 September 1995, paras. 38 and 41(v); Argument of Mr John McGrath for New Zealand, Verbatim Record, Tuesday 12 September 1995, 2.30 pm, 55–6, 59–60.

[32] Argument of Sir Arthur Watts QC for France, Verbatim Record, Tuesday 12 September 1995, 2.30 pm, 38.

[33] Opening argument for France, M. Marc Perrin de Brichambaut, Verbatim Record, Tuesday 12 September 1995, 10.00 am, 62, translation in Watts, *New Zealand at the International Court*, 207.

[34] Opening argument for France, M. Marc Perrin de Brichambaut, Verbatim Record, Tuesday 12 September 1995, 10.00 am, 62, translation in Watts, *New Zealand at the International Court*, pp. 207–8.

[35] See above, Ch. 1, pp. 18–19.

[36] For example, Peel remarks: 'In legal settings, a major concern remains the interaction of the precautionary principle with notions of proof, including whether precaution should lead to 'reversal' of the onus of proof or lowering of the standard of proof and if so, how these mechanisms might be given effect in light of competing considerations of environmental protection and socially beneficial development.' Peel, *The Precautionary Principle*, p. 149. See also at pp. 141 and 154–5; Fisher, 'Is the precautionary principle justiciable?', 330; Verhoosel, 'Gabčíkovo-Nagymaros', 250; Olson, 'Shifting the burden', 899; See also Kokott, *The Burden of Proof*, pp. 24–5 and 209–11. Kokott's arguments that the rules on the burden of proof should be modified in favour of complainants in human rights cases rest on the observation that the balance of power between the parties is unequal in these cases, yet, at a deeper level, the underlying interests of the parties coincide.

of whether it may be a valid exercise of international judicial authority to reverse the burden of proof in order to give effect to the precautionary principle.

The inherent powers of international courts and tribunals

Chapter 5 identified the sources of the rules on proof in international courts and tribunals. The rules on proof were found to constitute a unique category of international rule, deriving their authority from several different sources. These sources include international courts' inherent powers to determine procedural issues as necessary to ensure the fulfilment of the judicial function, including framing rules of procedure and making procedural orders.[37] The best known of the inherent powers is the power of international courts to determine the extent of their own jurisdiction, *la compétence de la compétence*.[38] The practice of hearing preliminary objections to a case separately from the merits is likewise considered an exercise of inherent powers,[39] and inherent powers also extend to comprehensive powers in relation to the management of proceedings.[40] It has also been suggested that the awarding of remedies involves the exercise of an inherent power.[41]

International courts and tribunals have also invoked their inherent powers on many other occasions. The adoption of practice directions by the International Court of Justice has been identified as an example of the exercise of inherent powers.[42] Additional significant examples of the exercise of international courts' and tribunals' inherent powers include the invocation by the Iran–US Claims Tribunal of a power to order interim measures[43] and the invocation by the International

[37] Although international courts will often be endowed with express powers for these purposes, they will in any event possess such powers 'as a necessary incident of their judicial functions'. Brown, *A Common Law*, p. 63; Hudson, *The Permanent Court*, p. 86; Ralston, *The Law and Procedure*, p. 197. Indeed, even where international courts enjoy express powers, they have from time to time stated that they are exercising inherent powers. Brown, *A Common Law*, p. 61.

[38] Brown, *A Common Law*, p. 63. [39] *Ibid.*, p. 63.

[40] *Ibid.*, p. 65; Watts, 'New practice directions', 255. Rosenne describes the International Court of Justice's 'inherent jurisdiction to control all aspects of the proceedings themselves'. Rosenne, *The Law and Practice*, p. 584.

[41] Brown, *A Common Law*, p. 66. [42] *Ibid.*, p. 33.

[43] *United Technologies International, Inc.* v. *Iran*, Decision of 10 December 1986, 13 Iran–US CTR 254, 257, cited by Brown, *A Common Law*, p. 36.

Tribunal for the former Yugoslavia of a power to deal with contempt.[44] Reference has also been made to the adoption by the Permanent Court of International Justice of a power to rule on counterclaims,[45] and to the Permanent Court's adoption of a procedure for dealing with preliminary objections to its jurisdiction, again in order to ensure the sound administration of justice and the execution of the Court's functions in a manner best suited to procedure before an international tribunal.[46] Tribunals dealing with investment disputes have also found it necessary from time to time to exercise inherent powers.

The International Court of Justice has not publicly discussed the origin or the extent of its inherent powers.[47] The Court's dictum in the *Nuclear Tests cases (New Zealand* v. *France) (Australia* v. *France)* provides a starting point. As discussed above, in these cases the Court rendered a judgment declining either to determine the question of its own jurisdiction or to proceed to the merits, on the basis that the applications submitted by Australia and New Zealand had been rendered moot or '*sans objet*' by the French unilateral declaration that testing was to cease. Grounding this decision in its inherent jurisdiction, the Court said:

> Such inherent jurisdiction, on the basis of which the Court is fully empowered to make whatever findings may be necessary for the purposes just indicated, *derives from the mere existence of the Court as a judicial organ* established by the consent of states, and is conferred upon it *in order that its basic judicial functions may be safeguarded.*[48]

The Court has thus accentuated the concept that such powers inhere automatically in international judicial bodies, and that their purpose

[44] *Prosecutor* v. *Simic, Judgment in the Matter of Contempt Allegations Against an Accused and his Counsel*, Case No. IT-95-9-R77, 30 June 2000, para. 91, cited by Brown, *A Common Law*, p. 38.

[45] Brown, *A Common Law*, p. 29.

[46] *Mavromattis Palestine Concessions*, Judgment of 30 August 1924, PCIJ Series A (No. 2), 6–93 at 16; Gaeta, 'Inherent Powers', p. 371; Brown, *A Common Law*, p. 29. In 1999 the International Court of Justice exercised an inherent power to remove a case from its list where the Court was 'manifestly not competent in the case'. *Case concerning Legality of Use of Force (Serbia and Montenegro* v. *United Kingdom) (Serbia and Montenegro* v. *Belgium) (Serbia and Montenegro* v. *Canada) (Serbia and Montenegro* v. *France) (Serbia and Montenegro* v. *Germany) (Serbia and Montenegro* v. *Italy) (Serbia and Montenegro* v. *Netherlands) (Serbia and Montenegro* v. *Portugal) (Yugoslavia* v. *Spain) (Yugoslavia* v. *United States of America)*, ICJ Reports 1999 761, 773–4; [1999] ICJ Rep 916, 925–6.

[47] Lauterpacht, 'Partial judgments', 477.

[48] *Nuclear Tests case (Australia* v. *France)*, Judgment of 20 December 1974, ICJ Reports 1974 253, 259–60; *Nuclear Tests case (New Zealand* v. *France)*, Judgment of 20 December 1974, ICJ Reports 1974 457, 463.

is to protect the basic functions of international judicial bodies. This approach has won support,[49] and probably represents the best way to understand the inherent powers of international courts and tribunals.[50] The idea of the exercise of inherent powers or inherent jurisdiction is familiar for legal scholars from common law jurisdictions,[51] and is known also to civil law.[52]

The alternative view is that these powers are not inherent, but rather are to be implied from the constituent documents of international courts and tribunals in much the same way as international organisations' powers can be implied from their constituent documents.[53] On this view, international judicial organs are attributed the powers necessary to carry out their role on the same basis as other international institutions established by states.[54] Here, the principle of effectiveness permits or requires the interpretation of tribunals' governing instruments in such a way that judicial bodies are impliedly endowed with certain powers.[55] However, examples of where international courts have adopted the language of implied powers are very rare.[56] The appeal of the view that inherent powers are in reality implied powers is that these powers are then more clearly grounded in the consent of states – albeit that this consent is more obvious in the case of express powers specifically conferred under tribunals' governing documents.[57] The

[49] Brown, *A Common Law*, p. 71; Gaeta, 'Inherent powers', 364–8.

[50] See e.g. Thirlway, 'The law and procedure', Part Nine, 41.

[51] Brown, *A Common Law*, pp. 18–19 and 23. [52] Gaeta, 'Inherent Powers', 365.

[53] For discussion, Brown, *A Common Law*, p. 69; Gaeta, 'Inherent powers', p. 362.

[54] Lauterpacht, 'Partial judgments', 477. See *Reparation for Injuries suffered in the service of the United Nations, Advisory Opinion*, 11 April 1949, ICJ Reports 174, 182.

[55] See the *La Grand* case, confirming the binding nature of the Court's provisional measures orders in light of the object and purpose of the Court's Statute. *La Grand case (Germany* v. *United States of America)*, Judgment of 27 June 2001, ICJ Reports 2001, 466, 494.

[56] Brown, *A Common Law*, p. 69. Gaeta refers to the phrasing used by the Trial Chamber of the International Criminal Tribunal for the Former Yugoslavia in 1997 in *Prosecutor* v. *Blaskic*, 110 ILR 608, but notes that the Appeals Chamber preferred the language of 'inherent powers', considering that 'the International Tribunal must possess the power to make all those judicial determinations that are necessary for the exercise of its primary jurisdiction'. Gaeta, 'Inherent powers', 704. In *Mexico – Taxes on Soft Drinks*, WT/DS308/AB/R, the WTO Appellate Body indicated the same preference, disregarding the appellant's use of the term 'implied powers' in stating 'We agree with Mexico that WTO panels have certain powers that are inherent in their adjudicative function'. *Mexico – Tax Measures on Soft Drinks and Other Beverages*, Complaint by the United States (WT/DS308), Report of the Appellate Body, DSR 2006: I, para. 45.

[57] Even if inherent powers are in reality implied powers, states' implied consent to the creation of a power does not of course equate to their agreement with its exercise in any given case. Thirlway, 'The law and procedure', 4.

attractions of an approach based on consent may explain the reference to states' consent in the remarks of the International Court of Justice in the *Nuclear Tests* cases, quoted above, and the Court's reference to 'conferral' of powers (by states) upon international judicial bodies. Of course, even if the term 'inherent powers' is used, international courts enjoy no power to override the express terms of their constituent instruments.[58]

A third alternative source of international courts' inherent powers has also been suggested: that international courts have inherent powers under general principles of international law common across the major national legal systems.[59] However, international courts and tribunals have not applied the methodologies that would have been expected in order to justify the powers as derivations from general principles of law.[60] Further, the paucity of sufficiently universal general principles means this potential source is too narrow to support the range of inherent powers exercised by international tribunals.[61]

For present purposes, it is not ultimately necessary to determine whether international courts' inherent powers are technically 'inherent' or 'implied'. In either case, such powers exist in order to safeguard the judicial function. However, 'inherent' powers is the term preferred. The reason is essentially rhetorical. At this stage in their development it may be more conducive to the realisation of a strengthened international rule of law to choose terminology that emphasises the autonomy of international courts. The concept of inherent powers more distinctly affirms an independence for international courts that is helpful for their performance of the international judicial function.

58 Brown, *A Common Law*, p. 80.

59 *Ibid.*, 67; Gaeta, 'Inherent powers', 354. See also at 367 and 368–71, on the notion that there has gradually taken shape a general principle of international law in accordance with which international judicial bodies exercise powers necessary to guarantee the sound administration of justice and protect their own judicial character. Gaeta cites Rosenne, *The Law and Practice of the International Court of Justice 1920–1996* (1997), II, pp. 600–1, explaining the assumption of inherent jurisdiction by inferring that in exercising such jurisdiction the Court is applying 'general principles of international procedural law' 'in its designated capacity of juridical organ'. See also the comments of Judge Cançado Trindade in his dissent in *Genie Lacayo (Request for Review of the Judgment of 29 January 1997)*, Annual Report of the Inter-American Court of Human Rights 1997, 177, 180. Another alternative explanation that has been noted, but for which no supporting evidence or authority has been indicated, is that a rule of customary international law gives international courts all the powers necessary to fulfil their functions. Gaeta, 'Inherent powers', 355.

60 Brown, *A Common Law*, p. 69. 61 *Ibid.*, p. 68.

As international courts and tribunals take on a workload that increasingly corresponds to a central role in the international legal order, it is important that they should release themselves from a sometimes overdeveloped sense of deference to sovereign states that may impede their work.[62] This is not to suggest that international courts' inherent powers are unbounded.[63] In practice international courts will be fully aware of the need to operate in a way that is consistent with both the needs and the expectations of the international community.[64] Most importantly, from the legal point of view, the breadth of international courts' inherent powers will always be determined with reference to what is necessary to fulfil the international judicial function.

The view has consistently been taken that the judicial function involves the settlement of disputes and the sound administration of justice.[65] A core component in both must be the need to ensure procedural fairness as between the parties.[66] A situation of scientific uncertainty is likely to prejudice the ability of one of the parties to establish its claims, and in the appropriate circumstances this may need to be rectified in order to fulfil the judicial task. The situation may also threaten important substantive interests, including important community interests.[67] Thus there are many reasons why a new approach allowing the precautionary reversal of the burden of proof might be considered necessary to the sound administration of justice. In deciding whether to adopt a new approach involving the precautionary reversal of the burden of proof, international courts and tribunals will need to assess whether, on balance, the integrity of the judicial function will be enhanced, rather than diminished.

The need to protect the judicial function may provide a strong justification for the reversal of the burden of proof in cases where it is clear

[62] Higgins, 'Respecting sovereign states' discussing the ICJ's working methods in relation to pleadings and evidence; also Abi-Saab, 'De l'Évolution', 282.

[63] Brown, *A Common Law*, p. 78: 'International courts cannot simply assert the existence of inherent powers to do whatever they choose.'

[64] As Judge Shahabuddeen has observed in relation to the International Court of Justice, it will be necessary to balance an awareness of the international judicial function with an awareness of the voluntary basis on which international law and international courts are established. Shahabuddeen, 'The International Court'.

[65] Brown, *A Common Law*, pp. 72–8; Gaeta, 'Inherent powers', 354–5.

[66] Gaeta, 'Inherent powers', 368, refers to the necessity of ensuring the fair administration of justice as one of the grounds on which inherent powers have been asserted.

[67] Benzing contemplates the burden's reversal by virtue of the substantive community interests involved. Benzing, 'Community interests'.

that the purposes of dispute settlement and the administration of justice will be most appropriately served by doing so. In applying a new approach, it may be appropriate for a court or tribunal to provide some indication to the parties that the reversal of the burden of proof is under contemplation. This might best be done through a direct question to the parties indicating that a new approach may be applicable and asking about their views on the general issue of whether and when the burden of proof should be reversed or lightened in response to scientific uncertainty. Such a question would serve the purposes of notification and consultation, consistent with traditions of co-operation between disputants and international courts and tribunals.[68] Inviting the parties to express their views on the issue should help ensure a thoughtful approach to any actual reversal of the burden of proof, although initially the notion may be a new one of which litigants are wary. In order to allow time for the parties to accustom themselves to the idea, consultation should take place at an early stage in the proceedings. Indeed, a pre-hearing phase in the proceedings of the International Court of Justice has been advocated to provide a forum in which the parties may clarify their factual allegations and how they intend to prove them, while the Court might indicate applicable standards of proof and also assess whether it may need to appoint its own experts to help it deal with the case.[69]

The threshold for the reversal of the burden of proof

At the same time as enquiring whether international courts and tribunals may have the inherent power to adopt a new approach reversing the allocation of the burden of proof through the application of the precautionary principle, it is important to enquire into the mechanics of their doing so. In relation to which legal provisions might the precautionary principle be brought into effect in this way? What would be the thresholds or triggers for the application of the precautionary principle? How appropriately does the formulation in the 1992 Rio Declaration[70] encapsulate the precautionary principle? How exceptional would the circumstances have to be for a reversal of the burden of proof to be applied?

[68] Riddell and Plant, *Evidence*, p. 21.
[69] *Ibid.*, pp. 75, 418–19; Amerasinghe, *Evidence*, p. 155. [70] See p. 19.

The way in which the proposal for reversal of the burden of proof would work in practice in international adjudication would depend on the interplay between the concept of precaution and the particular substantive legal rule that was being applied. An intersection between the substantive rules invoked by the parties and the precautionary principle would be essential. For example, one party might assert that another party was causing pollution or was failing to fulfil an obligation to manage a resource in a sustainable way. The party putting forward such a claim or allegation would usually bear the burden of proof. Such legal rules prohibiting pollution and unsustainable use of resources are strong candidates for a marriage with the precautionary principle, because they involve obligations to take or desist from certain actions in order to avoid potential harm. Depending on the state of scientific knowledge, a sufficiently well-supported assertion that the alleged pollution or overuse of resources was serious, and might have potentially irreversible consequences, could render that party's claims eligible to benefit from a reversal of the burden of proof by virtue of the precautionary principle. Alternatively, a party might complain that another party was refusing to allow it to continue to carry out a risk-creating activity, such as the export of products that were environmentally unfriendly. Environmental exceptions to free trade on which an importing party might rely to defend itself are also closely connected with precaution in terms of their subject matter.

Once it is established that the subject matter of a claim or defence is such that the reversal of the burden of proof might be called for, the question would be whether the reversal would automatically apply, or whether an evaluation of the level of scientific uncertainty and the potential seriousness of the situation was a prerequisite. The radical approach would be to reject any potential requirement that the party who will benefit from the reversal must demonstrate that a threshold for the application of the precautionary principle has been crossed. This would mean that any claim that could be aligned with the notion of precaution would automatically benefit from a presumption of validity so far as the establishment of the supporting facts was concerned. However, the value to be obtained from the application of the precautionary principle in this way could not exceed the detriment that would be experienced by international actors who might find themselves brought before international courts and tribunals on the simple 'say so' of offended parties and required to discharge the burden of proof in order to continue to engage in various activities of economic significance.

An alternative approach clearly requires to be developed, one that is calibrated to the seriousness of the risks involved in a situation.

In order to obtain the benefit of a reversal, a party would therefore first need to establish the actual applicability of the precautionary principle. The threshold for the precautionary principle's application has two dimensions: the existence and degree of scientific uncertainty and the scale of the harm that might be experienced if a threat remains unaddressed. How much scientific uncertainty would there have to be for the precautionary principle to apply? Determining an objective and precise level of scientific certainty or uncertainty in relation to any piece of scientific knowledge is not possible. Indeed, a central point emerging in relation to scientific uncertainty in the social sciences has been that subconscious and other perceptions of the role of knowledge will influence the extent to which any piece of scientific knowledge is viewed as uncertain.[71] International law presently provides only a number of rather broad formulations, to which reference might be made depending on the context, representing different degrees of scientific uncertainty. For example, the United Nations Agreement relating to the Conservation and Management of Straddling Fish Stocks and Highly Migratory Fish Stocks invokes a precautionary approach 'where adequate scientific information is lacking'.[72] The Cartagena Protocol on Biosafety uses the phrase 'where relevant scientific evidence is insufficient'.[73] The Convention for the Protection of the Marine Environment of the North-East Atlantic refers to circumstances where there 'is no conclusive evidence of a causal relationship'.[74] The Bamako Convention on the Ban of the Import into Africa and the Control of Transboundary Movement and Management of Hazardous Wastes within Africa says that action should be taken 'without waiting for scientific proof regarding such harm'.[75]

[71] Wynne, 'Uncertainty and environmental learning', 119.

[72] United Nations Agreement for the Implementation of the Provisions of the United Nations Convention on the Law of the Sea of 10 December 1982 Relating to the Conservation and Management of Straddling Fish Stocks and Highly Migratory Fish Stocks 1995, New York, 4 August 1995, in force 11 December 2001, 34 ILM 1542, Article 6(2).

[73] Cartagena Protocol on Biosafety to the Convention on Biological Diversity, Cartagena, 29 January 2000, in force 11 September 2003, 39 ILM 1027, Articles 10(6) and 11(6).

[74] Convention for the Protection of the Marine Environment of the North-East Atlantic, Paris, 22 September 1992, in force 25 March 1998, 32 ILM 1069, Article 2.

[75] Bamako Convention on the Ban of the Import into Africa and the Control of Transboundary Movement and Management of Hazardous Wastes within Africa, Bamako, 30 January 1991, in force 22 April 1998, 30 ILM 773, Article 4(3)(f).

There have been attempts to identify a generically applicable formulation of the scientific uncertainty that would trigger precaution. These include the potentially flexible concept of 'reasonable scientific plausibility', a criterion that would be demonstrated where 'empirical scientific data (as opposed to simple hypothesis, speculation, or intuition) make it reasonable to envisage a scenario, even if it does not enjoy unanimous support'.[76] However, this proposal has been subject to the critique that a criterion of 'reasonable scientific plausibility' might not allow sufficiently for cases raising issues falling nearer the limits of scientific knowledge, where there may be a high level of ignorance or indeterminacy in relation to the factual scenario before a court.[77] Other formulae for the application of the precautionary principle include whether there is: 'reason to believe' there is a risk or 'reasonable grounds for concern';[78] 'reasonable belief in the cause'[79] or 'plausible' risk[80] of harm; 'likelihood of' or a 'reasonable concern for' harm;[81] 'reasonable possibility' of damage;[82] 'credible' threat;[83] 'plausible' risk;[84] or a 'non-negligible' environmental risk.[85]

The conclusion that can be reached for present purposes is that there must clearly be some minimum threshold of scientific uncertainty in order for the precautionary principle to be applied. However, this threshold remains to be identified in practice. It is important to reject the assumption that precaution would be mandated in every situation where there is a lack of full scientific certainty. This version of precaution has been criticised for producing decisions that are irrational, protectionist, or overly risk-averse.[86] Such an 'extreme' notion of precaution can be tracked to a misaligned appreciation of the Rio formulation of the precautionary principle.[87] The Rio formulation needs rather to be seen as a broad articulation of the principle, and as only one among many articulations of how the precautionary principle may function, each of which is context-dependent. In different formulations and reflections of the principle there are differently tailored

[76] de Sadeleer, *Environmental Principles*, p. 160; Peel, *The Precautionary Principle*, p. 50.
[77] Peel, *The Precautionary Principle*, p. 51. [78] Birnie *et al.*, *International Law*, p. 156.
[79] Hohmann, *Precautionary Legal Duties*, p. 303. [80] *Ibid.*, p. 334.
[81] Nollkaemper, 'What you risk', 75.
[82] Harding and Fisher (eds.), *Perspectives*, pp. 2, 14; Hickey and Walker refer to 'reasonable scientific possibility' and 'reasonable scientific probability' confidence levels in scientific information. Hickey and Walker, 'Refining the precautionary principle'.
[83] O'Riordan, 'The politics', 283. [84] Hohmann, *Precautionary Legal Duties*, p. 334.
[85] Cameron, 'The precautionary principle: Core meaning', 30.
[86] Peel, *The Precautionary Principle*, p. 49. [87] *Ibid.*, p. 49.

commitments to the adoption of precautionary approaches, which combine different expressions of the level of uncertainty and the seriousness of the potential harm that together will activate the principle's application. The Rio articulation itself is a broadly crafted call for states to take action in relation to global environmental challenges where there is a lack of full scientific certainty *and* there are threats of serious or irreversible effects if action is delayed.[88] The second dimension of the threshold for the application of the precautionary principle is thus also an important part of assessing the situation.

The 'threshold' for application of the precautionary principle in terms of its second dimension, the harm that might be experienced in the case of inaction, has also been expressed in a variety of different ways in different contexts outside the adjudicatory framework. The Rio Declaration and the Framework Convention on Climate Change both refer to 'threats of serious or irreversible damage',[89] while the Convention on Biological Diversity refers to the 'threat of significant reduction or loss of biological diversity'.[90] The Cartagena Protocol on Biosafety to the Convention on Biological Diversity of 2000 refers only to 'potential adverse effects'.[91] The EC Communication on the Precautionary Principle refers to 'indications that the possible effects ... may be potentially dangerous and inconsistent with the chosen level of protection'. International courts and tribunals contemplating the application of a precautionary presumption will need to take into account both dimensions of the principle's threshold in the context of the factual and legal situation before them.

Judicial interest in the reversal of the burden of proof

How likely is it that an international tribunal might look to novel applications of the precautionary principle to help with the task of adjudicating a dispute involving scientific uncertainty? There have

88 Declaration of the UN Conference on Environment and Development, adopted by the UN Conference on Environment and Development at Rio de Janeiro, 14 June 1992, UN Doc. A/CONF.48/14, 11 ILM 1416, Principle 15.

89 *Ibid*; Framework Convention on Climate Change, Rio de Janeiro, 9 May 1992, in force 21 March 1994, 31 ILM 851, Article 3(3).

90 Convention on Biological Diversity, Rio de Janeiro, 5 June 1992, in force 29 December 1993, 31 ILM 818, preamble.

91 Cartagena Protocol on Biosafety to the Convention on Biological Diversity, Cartagena, 29 January 2000, in force 11 September 2003, 39 ILM 1027, Articles 10(6) and 11(8).

been dicta indicating judicial thinking on the possible application of the precautionary principle to moderate the burden of proof, in particular in the *Southern Bluefin Tuna* case, in *Request for an Examination* and in the *MOX Plant* case.

In the provisional measures phase of the *Southern Bluefin Tuna* case we find a hint of the idea that the precautionary principle could be applied to reverse the burden of proof. In his separate opinion Judge Laing referred to the precautionary principle as a way to counter 'forensic or proof difficulties'.[92] Judge Laing implied that he considered that applying the principle would involve a reversal of the burden of proof:

> However, in my view, while the Tribunal has drawn its conclusions and based its prescriptions in the face of scientific uncertainty, it has not, per se, engaged in an explicit reversal of the burden of proof. I believe that, where possible, such matters are best reserved for the stage of the merits, i.e. for the arbitral tribunal.[93]

The judge did not elaborate on what he viewed as involved in such a reversal of the burden of proof, except to say in a footnote that:

> In fact, in the area of fisheries management, such a decision should be made with great care, because of its possible impact on fishermen which, prima facie, could be unfair and unrealistic, unless the level of scientific certainty about probable damage increases.[94]

In *Request for an Examination* the majority did not discuss the allocation of the burden of proof, but in his Dissenting Opinion Judge Weeramantry discussed burden of proof with respect to environmental damage. He said:

> There are two ways of approaching this question. The first is to place the burden of proof fairly and squarely upon New Zealand, and to ask whether a *prima facie* case has been made out of the presence of such dangers as New Zealand complains of.
>
> The second approach is to apply the principle of environmental law under which, where environmental damage of any sort is threatened, the burden of proving that it will not produce the damaging consequences complained of is placed upon the author of that damage … the second approach is sufficiently well established in international law for the Court to act upon it. Yet, it is sufficient for present purposes to act upon the first approach, throwing the burden of proof upon New Zealand.[95]

92 *Southern Bluefin Tuna*, Provisional Measures, Separate Opinion of Judge Laing, para. 14.

93 *Ibid.*, para. 21, emphasis added. 94 *Ibid.*, note 8.

95 *Request for an Examination of the Situation*, Dissenting Opinion of Judge Weeramantry, 48.

Although he did not explicitly refer to the practice of drawing adverse inferences from the non-production of evidence, Judge Weeramantry bolstered his argument on the precautionary principle with reference to the underlying rationale of that practice:

> New Zealand has placed materials before the Court to the best of its ability, but France is in possession of the actual information. The [precautionary] principle then springs into operation to give the Court the basic rationale for considering New Zealand's request and not postponing the application of such means that there are available to the Court to prevent, on a provisional basis, the threatened environmental degradation, until such time as the full scientific evidence becomes available in refutation of the New Zealand contention.[96]

In his Dissenting Opinion in the *MOX OSPAR* case, arbitrator Gavan Griffith QC stated strongly that:

> In my opinion the majority also is in error to assume, and to apply, the burden of proof as falling on Ireland. In this regard, I maintain that the obvious application of the precautionary principle (not considered by the majority) must shift the burden to the United Kingdom.[97]

In his view, the United Kingdom bore responsibility for proving that future damage was insignificant and that there was no likelihood of adverse effect.[98] Indeed, Griffith considered that a finding adverse to Ireland could only be made on the basis that there was in fact no such potentially adverse effect.[99] Griffith considered the principle to be an established principle of customary international law, and called in support also the incorporation of the principle in Article 2(2)(a) of the Convention for the Protection of the Marine Environment of the North-East Atlantic, 1992 (the OSPAR Convention).[100]

In *Prohibition of the Importation of Retreaded Tyres from Uruguay* the burden of proof was reversed by a Mercosur tribunal on the basis of the precautionary principle, but without detailed analysis.[101] That decision was overridden at the appeal stage by the Mercosur Permanent Review

[96] *Ibid.*, 343. See also 348.

[97] *Dispute concerning Access to Information under Article 9 of the OSPAR Convention (Ireland* v. *United Kingdom of Great Britain and Northern Ireland)*, Award of 2 July 2003, 42 ILM 1116 (hereafter *MOX OSPAR* case). Dissenting Opinion of Gavan Griffith QC, para. 72.

[98] *Ibid.*, para. 74. [99] *Ibid.*, para. 75.

[100] Convention for the Protection of the Marine Environment of the North-East Atlantic, Paris, 22 September 1992, in force 25 March 1998, 32 ILM 1069, Article 32.

[101] Laudo del Tribunal *Ad Hoc* del Mercosur constituido para entender en la controversia presentada por la República Oriental del Uruguay a la República Argentina sobre 'Prohibición de Importación de Neumáticos Remoldeados', paras. 69–70.

Tribunal, holding that a party relying on an exception to the rules of free trade should always bear the burden of proof. The Permanent Review Tribunal was concerned about the potential for arbitrary decision-making associated with accommodating scientific uncertainty, 'for which there is no justification in this case'.[102]

How might a reversal of the burden of proof work in practice?

The new approach would cater for situations where the level of scientific uncertainty and the interests at issue in a dispute are such that the administration of justice may be vitiated if the burden is left to lie where it would usually fall. If international courts and tribunals were to adopt the view that it is open to them to reverse the burden of proof, the primary effect of this would be to refocus the pleadings and evidence in disputes involving scientific uncertainty on the subject of the appropriate thresholds for the application of precaution and whether those thresholds have been crossed.

(a) Cases that proceed to the merits

The concept of a reversal of the burden of proof is likely to be most instrumental in cases that proceed to the merits. The circumstances of the *Gabčíkovo-Nagymaros* case may be considered. It will be recalled that Hungary bore the burden of establishing the defence of ecological necessity that was asserted in justification of the Hungarian suspension of works at Nagymaros. This required Hungary to prove that the environmental peril engendered by the Gabčíkovo-Nagymaros project was 'grave and imminent'. The Court found that the asserted dangers to water quality in the Gabčíkovo sector were uncertain, and was prepared to reject the Hungarian defence on the basis that an uncertain peril could not have been an imminent peril.[103] Hungary thus lost the dispute for failure to prove the defence of ecological necessity, despite Hungary's

[102] Laudo del Tribunal Permanente de Revisión Constituido para entender el Recurso de Revisión Presentado por la República Oriental del Uruguay contra el Laudo Arbitral del Tribunal Arbitral *Ad Hoc* de fecha 25 de Octubre de 2005 en la Controversia 'Prohibición de Importación de Neumáticos Remoldeados Procedentes del Uruguay', paras. 19–20. For an English translation, www.siel.org.

[103] See above, Ch. 2. pp. 37–41. The Court's interpretation of the substantive law on ecological necessity is open to question where the uncertainty that is involved is scientific and technical in character See, inter alia, Foster, 'Necessity and precaution'.

reminder that 'the court has itself the vocation to act in a precautionary mode, confronted with a degree of scientific uncertainty'.[104]

Seeking to move beyond the inertia seen in the *Gabčíkovo-Nagymaros* case, Argentina encouraged the Court in the *Case concerning Pulp Mills on the River Uruguay (Argentina* v. *Uruguay)* to take into account 'the power of modern forensic science to identify the beginnings of long-term damage, as well as the immediate gross effects of pollution'.[105] In the *Case concerning Pulp Mills* the merits of the complaint lodged by Argentina concerned allegations that Uruguay was in breach of obligations that Argentina asserted were owed by Uruguay to Argentina under the 1975 Statute of the River Uruguay and other rules of international law, including the international law relating to watercourses. As noted earlier, these included the obligation to take all necessary measures for the optimum and rational utilisation of the River Uruguay, the obligation to take all necessary measures to preserve the aquatic environment and prevent pollution and the obligation to protect biodiversity and fisheries, as well as associated procedural obligations relating to environmental impact assessment, notification and co-operation.[106] The precautionary principle could have been of distinct relevance as part of the equation in determining whether these obligations had been fulfilled.

The Court rejected Argentina's arguments that there should be a reversal of the burden of proof, or at least an equal sharing of the burden.[107] Argentina argued that the 1975 Statute transferred the burden of proof to Uruguay.[108] This was based on the argument that the Statute's adoption of an approach shaped around preventing deterioration in the river's water quality necessitated that Uruguay prove that its actions would not prejudice the waterway.[109] Argentina took into account various identifiable scientific uncertainties including in

[104] Verbatim Record, Thursday 10 April, 16.

[105] Verbatim Record, Thursday, 17 September 2009, 22.

[106] *Case concerning Pulp Mills on the River Uruguay (Argentina* v. *Uruguay)*, Judgment of 20 April 2010, ICJ Reports 2010 (hereafter *Case concerning Pulp Mills*).

[107] *Case concerning Pulp Mills*, para. 164. Although Judge Cançado Trindade remarked that the principles of prevention and precaution and related factors should be kept in mind in 'the judicial determination of the facts'. Separate Opinion of Judge Cançado Trindade, para. 6. See also Separate Opinion of Judge *ad hoc* Vinuesa, who was persuaded by Argentina's arguments that there should be an equal distribution of the burden, paras. 41–3.

[108] *Case concerning Pulp Mills*, Memorial of the Republic of Argentina, para. 5.15.

[109] *Ibid.*, para. 5.18; Reply of the Republic of Argentina, para. 4.55.

relation to the implications of reverse flow for the concentration of pollutants, wind direction, climatic changes and the probable effects of pollutants on fish.[110]

In the event, the case turned on Argentina's inability to demonstrate that the Botnia Mill had harmful effects contravening the Statute. The Court concluded that there was 'no conclusive evidence in the record' that Uruguay had failed to act with due diligence or that the mill's discharges had been having deleterious effects.[111] Argentina's allegations regarding dissolved oxygen remained unproven;[112] it had 'not been established to the satisfaction of the Court' that a recent algal bloom episode had been caused by discharges from the mill;[113] there was 'insufficient evidence' to attribute an alleged increase in concentrations of phenolic substances in the river to the mill;[114] Argentina had not 'in the view of the Court, adduced clear evidence' establishing a link between the mill and nonylphenols found in the river and the evidence in the record did not 'substantiate the claims made by Argentina on this matter';[115] the Court considered there was 'no clear evidence' showing a link between dioxins and furans in the river and the mill;[116] nor had the Court found sufficient evidence to establish a clear relationship between the mill's discharges and specific effects on flora and fauna (including loss of fat in clams, the finding of dioxin in the sábalo fish and the malformation of rotifers).[117]

On the particular facts of the case the Court appears to have considered that the scientific uncertainty attaching to the evidence before it was relatively minimal. As expressed by Judge Keith, 'For my part, I think that the resolution of those matters which the Court did have to decide, based on the raw data, is relatively straightforward.'[118] It remains an open question whether, with another fifteen years or more of data and research, the situation will look any different. However, the *Case concerning Pulp Mills* does demonstrate that, if it were called for on the facts, a precautionary reversal of the burden of proof could make all the difference. There are likely to be similar cases in future where the

[110] Memorial of the Republic of Argentina, para. 5.17.
[111] *Ibid.*, para. 265. See also para. 264. [112] *Case concerning Pulp Mills*, para. 239.
[113] *Ibid.*, para. 250. [114] *Ibid.*, para. 254. [115] *Ibid.*, para. 257.
[116] *Ibid.*, para. 259. [117] *Ibid.*, para. 262.
[118] Separate Opinion of Judge Keith, para. 11. Judges Al-Khasawneh and Simma were strongly critical of the Court's overall approach. *Ibid.*, Joint Dissenting Opinion of Judges Al-Khasawneh and Simma, para. 5.

scientific available information requires an international court or tribunal seriously to consider a reversal of the burden of proof.

Environmental and health cases that have arisen in the WTO may also be considered. In disputes decided through the application of the environmental exceptions in Article XX of the General Agreement on Tariffs and Trade (GATT) and Article XIV of the General Agreement on Trade in Services (GATS), the burden of proof will lie on the party invoking these provisions. Whether this will be appropriate in all circumstances calls for careful consideration. If the *EC – Asbestos* case is considered, it would seem appropriate that the EC was required to establish that the French ban on chrysotile asbestos was a measure necessary to the protection of human health in terms of Article XX(b) of GATT. However, the situation could have been different if the dispute had arisen some years earlier, in circumstances where a WTO member had decided to ban chrysotile at a point in time when there was less evidence that it was to be classed as a dangerous substance alongside the serpentine forms of asbestos. In the light of our knowledge today, it is an uncomfortable thought that a member might conceivably have lost its case for failure to discharge the burden of proof, and have been obliged to continue to import and market asbestos. It would be preferable if it were possible to contemplate that a WTO panel or the Appellate Body might be prepared to consider in such a case the application of a new approach to burden of proof that takes account of the precautionary principle.

In contrast with Article XX of GATT, it is a strength of the design and jurisprudence of the SPS Agreement that the burden of proof lies with a WTO member seeking to challenge risk-response measures. This is in alignment with the result that would be produced through a reversal of the burden of proof to accommodate the precautionary principle in meritorious cases under Article XX. Occasionally the dynamics of an Article XX case may approximate those of an SPS case. Although it was an Article XX case, an unusual feature of *United States – Import Prohibition of Certain Shrimp and Shrimp Products* is that it was as though a precautionary reversal of the burden of proof were at work.[119] A significant proportion of the complainants' argument went to showing that US actions were discriminatory, contrary to the chapeau to Article XX, even

[119] *United States – Import Prohibition of Certain Shrimp and Shrimp Products*, Complaint by India (WT/DS58); Complaint by Malaysia (WT/DS58); Complaint by Pakistan (WT/DS58); Complaint by Thailand (WT/DS58), Report of the Appellate Body, DSR 1998: VII, 2755.

though the US bore the burden of showing that it was entitled to rely on Article XX. Ultimately the complainants were successful. As discussed earlier, it was found that the US could not rely on Article XX because, inter alia, the US was treating various shrimp-exporting members alike, even though different conditions prevailed in those members in terms of the prominence of different threats posed to sea turtles.

Proceedings on the merits did not take place in either the *Southern Bluefin Tuna* case or the *MOX Plant* case. The *Southern Bluefin Tuna* case was the stronger of the two. If the *Southern Bluefin Tuna* case had gone to the merits, there might have been call for reversal of the burden of proof in relation to Japan's alleged breach of obligations intersected by the precautionary principle. If it had been interested in taking this approach, the Annex VII Tribunal that would have considered the merits would have needed to address two matters. The first matter is whether the Tribunal had the inherent power to adopt a modification to the rules on burden of proof allowing for reversal of the burden of proof; and the second is whether the subject matter, the potential seriousness of the situation and the level of uncertainty involved would have taken the case across the thresholds of the precautionary principle such that this new approach was applicable.

The precautionary principle might have been considered to intersect with all, or at least nearly all, of Japan's alleged breaches of its obligations. However, the precautionary principle's interplay with obligations directly relating to conservation is stronger than its interconnection with procedural obligations requiring co-operation among the parties to the United Nations Convention on the Law of the Sea (LOSC) in the sustainable management of marine resources. Articles 117 and 119 of the LOSC incorporate obligations where there is a relatively direct interplay with the precautionary principle. This is because the factual questions relating to the status of the stock and the effect of taking an additional catch could determine whether Japan was in compliance with these obligations. Fulfilment of states' obligation in Article 117 to take such measures for their nationals as may be necessary for the conservation of the living resources of the high seas is determinable with reference to the scientific questions associated with identifying the necessary conservation measures. Fulfilment of states' obligation under Article 119(1)(a) to take measures designed to maintain or restore populations of harvested species at levels which can produce the maximum sustainable yield is determinable with reference to the scientific questions associated with assessing a stock's maximum sustainable yield and how it can be maintained.

In contrast, the claims lodged against Japan under Articles 64 and 118 of the LOSC reflected the Convention's emphasis on the procedural duties of states party in this field. Relating specifically to highly migratory species, Article 64 requires coastal states' and fishing states' co-operation, directly or through international organisations, with a view to species conservation and optimum utilisation. Article 118 contains a more general obligation to co-operate in and to negotiate necessary measures for the conservation of living resources, including co-operating in the establishment of regional and subregional fisheries organisations. The precautionary principle is certainly also of significance here, but its relevance is likely to be more direct and more obvious in relation to obligations that focus more closely on the status of the stocks.

Much of the emphasis in the *Southern Bluefin Tuna* case fell on questions relating to the need for co-operation. However, in the circumstances of the case it is conceivable that the precautionary principle could have been applied to modify the allocation of the burden of proof, in respect at least of the conservation-related claims. Levels of uncertainty were high in relation to the potential for the southern bluefin tuna parental biomass to recover to 1980 levels, and the threat to southern bluefin tuna was serious in that the potential outcome of continuing unrestrained fishing was a catastrophic collapse of the stock. In this situation, it would have seemed inconsistent with the purposes of adjudication to reject the claimed breach of obligations including those found in Articles 117 and 119(1)(a) on the grounds simply that the claimants had not substantiated their case. This outcome would not have helped to settle the parties' dispute, and, in terms of the unfairness involved would not have conformed well to conceptions of the administration of justice. This example demonstrates why it may be helpful to modify the allocation of the burden of proof in international courts and tribunals in order to make better allowance for the precautionary principle.

(b) Provisional measures requests

Requests for provisional measures are frequently lodged with international courts and tribunals in scientific disputes. As noted earlier, examples include the *Nuclear Tests* cases, the *Southern Bluefin Tuna* case, the *MOX Plant* case, the *Case concerning Land Reclamation* and the *Case concerning Pulp Mills*. The provisional measures jurisdiction exercised by most international courts and tribunals is a valuable feature of their operations when it comes to the settlement of disputes involving scientific uncertainty. So far as our present enquiry is concerned, the point that emerges from the cases is that the potential reversal of the burden of proof may be a degree less significant in the context of requests for provisional measures than it may come to be in cases that proceed directly to the merits. This is because the powers of international courts and tribunals to order provisional measures may to some degree eclipse the potential need for them to exercise their inherent powers in order to modify the allocation of the burden of proof to give effect to the precautionary principle. However, this does not mean that the precautionary principle should be lost sight of in the application of the rules about proof at the provisional measures stage. The issue is a live one:

> Provisional measures were thus refused in the *MOX Plant Case* and the *Pulp Mills Case* because the applicants failed to establish a serious risk, despite their reliance on the precautionary principle, but granted in *Land Reclamation* and *Southern Bluefin Tuna* because they could do so.[120]

In the *Southern Bluefin Tuna* case, New Zealand and Australia requested a number of provisional measures, including that Japan be required immediately to cease unilateral experimental fishing for southern bluefin tuna and to restrict its catch to the total allowable catch most recently agreed in the Commission for the Conservation of Southern Bluefin Tuna (CCSBT) (subject to a reduction reflecting the catch taken during Japan's experimental fishing in 1998 and 1999), and that the parties act consistently with the precautionary principle pending final settlement of the dispute.[121] For its part, Japan requested that the Tribunal make a provisional measures order under which Australia and New Zealand would be required to recommence negotiations with Japan for a six-month period, and if consensus were not reached within that period remaining disagreement would be referred for resolution to the panel of independent scientists referred to in the terms of reference for the parties' Experimental Fishing Programme Working Group.[122] The Tribunal declined to grant these requests, but prescribed provisional measures requiring all three parties to ensure that their annual catches did not exceed the levels agreed through the CCSBT, as modified to take account of Japan's 1999 experimental fishing catch, and

[120] Birnie et al., *International Law*, p. 158.

[121] *Southern Bluefin Tuna*, Provisional Measures, paras. 31, 32 and 34.

[122] *Ibid.*, paras. 33 and 35.

requiring all three parties to refrain from conducting an experimental fishing programme without the agreement of the other parties.[123] Negotiations on the management of southern bluefin tuna were to be resumed without delay, and further efforts made to include other states and fishing entities engaged in fishing for southern bluefin tuna.[124]

The Tribunal's decision at the provisional measures stage in the *Southern Bluefin Tuna* case was thoroughly infused with precaution. There was little doubt of the urgency of the situation or that provisional measures should be taken both to preserve the parties' rights and to prevent further damage to southern bluefin tuna stock levels.[125] The power to order provisional measures in order to prevent serious harm to the environment pending a final decision, expressly bestowed on courts and tribunals operating under the LOSC,[126] enhances the precautionary aspect of their provisional measures jurisdiction. The Tribunal recorded the parties' agreement that southern bluefin tuna stocks were severely depleted, were at their lowest historical levels, and that this was cause for serious concern.[127] Although there was scientific uncertainty,[128] and the Tribunal could not conclusively assess the parties' scientific evidence,[129] the Tribunal had little doubt of the need for provisional measures. The question of reversing the burden of proof did not require consideration. It is of course entirely possible that the same threat and the same uncertainty that encourage the indication of provisional measures could found a reversal of the burden of proof at the merits.

In considering a request for provisional measures, a court or tribunal is consciously seeking to prevent irreparable prejudice to the rights of the parties. This preventative function is precautionary in essence. The intention is to preserve the status quo, where the evidence provides a sufficiently solid foundation for reading the view that judicial intervention to that end is necessary. As observed by Judge Tullio Treves in the *Southern Bluefin Tuna* case, a precautionary approach is inherent in the notion of provisional measures:

> The precautionary principle can be seen as a logical consequence of the need to ensure that, when the arbitral tribunal decides on the merits, the factual situation has not changed.[130]

[123] *Ibid.*, para. 90(1)(c) and (d). [124] *Ibid.*, para. 90(1)(e) and (f). [125] *Ibid.*, para. 80.

[126] United Nations Convention on the Law of the Sea, Montego Bay, 10 December 1982, in force 16 November 1994, 21 ILM 1261, Article 290(1).

[127] *Southern Bluefin Tuna*, Provisional Measures, para. 71. [128] *Ibid.*, para. 79.

[129] *Ibid.*, para. 80. [130] Separate Opinion of Judge Treves.

The *MOX Plant* case underlines that judicial responses to scientific uncertainty at the provisional measures stage may tend to take the form of findings as to whether or not the conditions for a grant of provisional measures have been met, rather than a decision to reverse the burden of proof. In the *MOX Plant* case it was clear that under the ordinary rules the burden of proof fell on Ireland to establish the case for a provisional measures order.[131] The International Tribunal for the Law of the Sea did record Ireland's argument that it would be consistent with the precautionary principle for the burden of proof to fall on the United Kingdom, but at the same time the Tribunal noted the United Kingdom's contention that it had produced evidence that the risks from the MOX Plant would be very low indeed.[132] The Tribunal's decision to record these two points one after the other hints that, if there were to have been a reversed burden of proof, the United Kingdom could have been considered to have discharged it. On the other hand, the Tribunal also recorded the United Kingdom's argument that Ireland had failed to supply proof that there would be irreparable damage to Ireland's rights or serious harm to the natural environment and that the precautionary principle had no application.[133]

During oral submissions, Ireland made a number of comments which seemed designed to encourage a reversal of the burden of proof in the light of the precautionary principle. Ireland noted that the precautionary principle placed the burden on the United Kingdom to demonstrate that no harm would arise from the operation of the plant,[134] and observed the approach taken by the International Court of Justice at the provisional measures stage of the *Nuclear Tests* cases gave the benefit of doubt to the complainants. As noted earlier, the Court had commented that the information before it *did not exclude the possibility* that damage to Australia and New Zealand might be shown to be caused by the deposit on their territory of radioactive fallout from the French tests, and might be shown to be irreparable.[135] In relation to this comment, Ireland argued:

[131] Separate Opinion of Judge Anderson, point 3, final paragraph.

[132] *Mox Plant Provisional Measures Order*, paras. 71 and 72. [133] *Ibid.*, para. 75.

[134] Verbatim Record, Monday 19 November 2001, 10.00 am.

[135] *Nuclear Tests case (Australia* v. *France)*, Request for the Indication of Interim Measures of Protection, Order of 22 June 1973, ICJ Reports 1973 99, 105; *Nuclear Tests case (New Zealand* v. *France)*, Request for the Indication of Interim Measures of Protection, Order of 22 June 1973, ICJ Reports 1973 135, 141. Judge Koroma commented that although certain evidence was not conclusive, nevertheless it was sufficient to show the risk of marine contamination from France's underground nuclear tests. Dissenting Opinion of Judge Koroma, 379.

That is a shift of burden on to that side of the room.[136]

For its part, the United Kingdom appeared to suggest that the standard of proof applying to a provisional measures request was particularly high, commenting that an applicant had to make a compelling case, as there was a presumption against the grant of such measures. The United Kingdom characterised provisional measures as an exception to the usual rules relating to burden of proof because they allowed a remedy to be granted without an applicant fully proving its case.[137]

In his Separate Opinion, Judge Wolfrum considered Ireland's argument that the precautionary principle applied, and noted that it was generally agreed that the consequences flowing from the principle included the reversal of the burden of proof concerning the possible impact of a given activity:

> A State interested in undertaking or continuing a particular activity has to prove that it will result in no harm, rather than the other side having to prove that it will result in harm.[138]

However, Judge Wolfrum considered that Ireland could not rely on the precautionary principle to reverse the burden of proof in the proceedings because this would have required the Tribunal to assess matters that had to be dealt with on the merits by the Annex VII Tribunal, including assessing the radioactivity of the Irish Sea, the potential impact of the plant, and whether the impact prejudiced Ireland's rights. The judge also considered that Ireland's arguments were problematic because they could result in an automatic grant of provisional measures wherever an applicant argued with some plausibility that its rights might be prejudiced or that there was serious risk to the marine environment. Provisional measures were exceptional in character, and were limited by the requirement that they not anticipate a judgment on the merits. This limitation could not be bypassed by invoking the precautionary principle.[139]

However, Judges Treves[140] and Wolfrum[141] appear to have considered that, had more evidence been introduced by Ireland, it might have been possible for the International Tribunal for the Law of the Sea to apply

[136] Verbatim Record, Monday, 19 November 2001, 10.00 am, 33, line 5.
[137] Written Response of the United Kingdom, Request for Provisional Measures, paras. 128–9; Verbatim Record, Tuesday 20 November 2001, 9.30 am, 13–14.
[138] *MOX Plant* Provisional Measures Order, Separate Opinion of Judge Wolfrum, 5.
[139] *Ibid.*, 5. [140] Separate Opinion of Judge Treves, para. 8.
[141] Separate Opinion of Judge Wolfrum, 5.

the precautionary principle in relation to Ireland's substantive rights, rather than referring to prudence and caution in respect only of the need for the parties to co-operate.[142] Judge ad hoc Székely believed that the Tribunal ought to have been more responsive to the uncertainty in the *MOX Plant* case,[143] and that Ireland should have been given the benefit of the doubt.[144] The judge considered that the British assertions about the low impact of the plant were unilateral and unproven,[145] and that the Tribunal should, in response to the uncertainty in the case, have applied the precautionary principle expressly.[146] Commentators have also addressed the issue. The suggestion has explicitly been made that if the Annex VII Tribunal dealing with the *MOX Plant* case had applied the precautionary principle, its perspective on the allocation of the burden of proof might have been different.[147]

The request for provisional measures in the *Case concerning Pulp Mills* may also be considered. The provisional measures requested by Argentina were that the Court order Uruguay to suspend all authorisations for the construction of the two mills on the River Uruguay and ensure the prolonged suspension of building work, as well as to conduct itself in certain ways, including co-operating with Argentina on the optimum and rational utilisation of the river in order to protect and preserve the aquatic environment and to prevent pollution.[148]

The Court reiterated that the Court's power to indicate provisional measures could be exercised only where there was an urgent need to prevent irreparable prejudice to the rights of the parties that were the subject of the dispute.[149] It is interesting to note that, in arguing that provisional measures should not be granted, Uruguay expressly imported the concept of imminent harm seen in the *Gabčíkovo-Nagymaros* case, and equated urgency with imminence.[150] Uruguay apparently

[142] *MOX Plant* Provisional Measures Order, para. 84.

[143] Separate Opinion of Judge ad hoc Székely, para. 22.

[144] *Ibid.*, para. 18. [145] *Ibid.*, para. 20. [146] *Ibid.*, paras. 22 and 24.

[147] Churchill and Scott, 'The MOX Plant litigation', p. 651. Churchill and Scott make the same point in relation to the OSPAR Tribunal's decision in the *MOX OSPAR* case. See also the views of dissenting arbitrator Gavan Griffith in the *MOX OSPAR* case. See p. 260.

[148] *Case concerning Pulp Mills on the River Uruguay (Argentina* v. *Uruguay), Request for the Indication of Provisional Measures*, Order of 13 July 2006 ICJ Reports 2006, 11 (hereafter *Case concerning Pulp Mills (Provisional Measures)*), para. 20.

[149] *Ibid.*, para. 35; Verbatim Record, Thursday 8 June 2006, 3.00 pm, translation, 57.

[150] *Case concerning Pulp Mills (Provisional Measures)*, paras. 44, 46; Verbatim Record, Thursday 8 June 2006, 3.00 pm, 49. The same use of the concept of imminence was made by counsel for the United Kingdom in the *Mox Plant* case.

sought to rely on the Court's view in the *Gabčíkovo-Nagymaros* case that uncertainty could preclude a finding of imminence. The Court did employ the language of 'imminence' in making findings that the record revealed nothing to demonstrate that authorisation of the mills' construction posed an imminent threat of irreparable damage to the river's aquatic environment or the interests of the Argentines who lived alongside the river,[151] and that the threat of any pollution was not imminent because the mills were not expected to be operational before August 2007 (the Orion Mill) and June 2008 (the CMB Mill) respectively.[152] However, these uses of the concept of imminence by the Court are clearly without prejudice to the question of whether uncertainty may preclude imminence.

In reaching the overall conclusion that the circumstances of the case did not require a provisional measures order directing Uruguay to suspend authorisation of construction, or construction itself,[153] the Court made several references to the effect that Argentina had failed to discharge the burden of establishing grounds for the ordering of provisional measures.[154] The burden of proof would appear to have rested firmly in its place in the provisional measures proceedings in the *Case concerning Pulp Mills*.

Technical methods for reversing the burden of proof

Throughout the discussions above, the suggestion has been, in general terms, that a new approach be developed allowing for the burden of proof to be reversed to accommodate the precautionary principle. For common lawyers, the proposition of a differing allocation of the burden of proof in disputes involving the precautionary principle is not altogether unnatural. The allocation of the burden of proof in the common law depends on moral and political decisions including the need for parties to be given special consideration in some categories of case. These decisions are embodied not only in legislation but also in the common law. That is to say, occasionally a Court will 'step in to decide the burden of proof as a matter of policy'.[155] However, as explained in

[151] *Case concerning Pulp Mills (Provisional Measures)*, para. 73.
[152] *Ibid.*, para. 75. [153] *Ibid.*, para. 77.
[154] 'Whereas Argentina has not provided evidence at present that suggests that any pollution resulting from the commissioning of the mills would be of a character to cause irreparable damage to the River Uruguay'; *ibid.*, para. 75; see also para. 74.
[155] Zuckerman, *Civil Procedure*, pp. 755–6.

Chapter 5, the allocation of the burden of proof in international law follows more fixed rules. Various alternative ways of achieving a precautionary reversal of the burden of proof in international law include developing a precautionary presumption, lightening the standard of proof or applying a prima facie case approach.

It would not be altogether satisfactory for international courts and tribunals to develop a precautionary presumption, or rely on inferences as a means to reverse the burden of proof. The situations in cases involving reliance on inference and presumptions have differed from those where scientific uncertainty is involved. As Judge Badawi remarked in the *Corfu Channel case (United Kingdom* v. *Albania)*, 'in international law, circumstantial evidence means facts which, while not supplying immediate proof of the charge, yet make the charge probable with the assistance of reasoning'.[156] It is a different matter where the science is lacking and no amount of judicial reasoning can fill the gap. Perhaps more problematically, it could be difficult in practice to identify the specific basic fact on which a precautionary presumption was based. As noted in Chapter 5, both judicial and legal presumptions involve drawing a conclusion regarding a factual issue on the basis of another fact.[157] In situations calling for a precautionary reversal of the burden of proof there is not likely to be a single basic fact on which to base a presumption. Rather, it is a constellation of facts that together create the need to look beyond the usual approach to burden of proof. It has been observed that 'Presumptions without a basic fact are rules of substantive law whose only function is to allocate the burden of proof.'[158] Indeed, it is entirely true that an appreciation of the potential substantive effects of a court or tribunal's decision would underpin any steps taken to ensure that the adjudicatory process can effectively accommodate the precautionary principle.

For similar reasons, the option of a lightening of the standard of proof lacks appeal.[159] On the civil law approach the idea of a lightened standard of proof presumably makes little sense at all. How can a judge or arbitrator be personally 'convinced' of a matter in the acknowledged absence of scientific proof? From the common law perspective, the notion of altered standards of proof also sits awkwardly, probably

156 *Corfu Channel* case, 59 per Judge Badawi. 157 See above, Ch. 5.

158 Grando, *Evidence*, p. 94; Tapper, *Cross and Tapper on Evidence*, p. 148. An example is the presumption of innocence in domestic criminal law.

159 Cf. Benzing, 'Community interests', 391.

because standards of proof are often conceptualised as governing proof of facts rather than proof of legal claims. The purpose of applying the precautionary principle to the allocation of the burden of proof in an international scientific dispute is not to alleviate the burden that may lie upon a party to prove the factual dimensions of its claims, so much as to rebalance the litigation, allowing certain claims to be accepted where the high thresholds of the precautionary principle have been met. Therefore, it is more appropriate for the precautionary principle's effects on the burden of proof to operate directly on that burden, rather than indirectly via the standard of proof. The facts themselves ought not to be regarded as proven: they are acknowledged to be uncertain. Providing a dispensation from the need to prove a bevy of such facts is not fundamentally what is sought from a reversal of the burden of proof in cases involving the precautionary principle. The purpose is to look beyond the need to prove unobtainable facts, and focus on the matter of which party should have to establish its legal claim in order to prevail. Thus, a reversal of the burden itself is the more appropriate course.

For a wide variety of reasons, the prospects in the near future of general international agreement between states on a formal rule permitting reversal of the adjudicatory burden of proof in circumstances of scientific uncertainty on the matter are less than minimal. Most basically, there is presently no forum in which the matter falls to be addressed. This leaves international courts and tribunals in the position of having to address the issue as a matter of procedural fairness. In these circumstances, the best option would be to reverse the burden of proof through the application of a form of prima facie case approach. This would be consistent with the application of the prima facie case approach generally in international adjudication in circumstances where evidence is hard to obtain or a disputant is required to prove a negative assertion. In terms of its connection with the principles underlying the rules on burden of proof, the approach thus rests on the need for fairness. Such an approach would provide a softer, and potentially more flexible approach than an outright reversal of the burden.[160]

[160] For this reason, domestic commentators have favoured a lowering of the standard of proof instead of a reversal of the burden of proof. Peel, *The Precautionary Principle*, p. 155. Hesitation has also been expressed about the proposition of reversing the burden of proof outright because a 'bipolar' approach fails to recognise the complexities of decision-making in situations that may call for precaution. *Ibid.*, p. 155, citing Fisher, 'Is the precautionary principle justiciable?', 331 ff.

Further, the precautionary prima facie case approach would be more easily applied without contravening the requirement sometimes specified in international courts' and tribunals' governing documents that each party has the burden of proving the facts relied on to support its claim.[161]

The precautionary prima facie case approach would operate through the adoption of a new practice that recognises the licence of courts and tribunals to find in favour of a party on the basis of a prima facie case where the thresholds for the application of the precautionary principle are met. The question of whether there is a prima facie case in any given instance will depend on a judicial appreciation of the circumstances in the particular dispute. The prima facie case option would mean that reversals are only made where, setting aside the issues on which there is scientific uncertainty, a party's case looks capable of amounting to a relatively strong one. Thus the burden will only be reversed where it would actually be useful to do so. This might provide some comfort to litigants who are concerned about the impact of international courts' and tribunals' adoption of a practice of precautionary reversal of the burden of proof. However, relative to an outright reversal of the burden, the element of judicial discretion would be enlarged under a prima facie case approach, and correspondingly it would be important that international courts and tribunals explained their reasoning in each case where they applied the new precautionary prima facie case approach.

Ideally, the new practice would be recognised over time as applicable generally in international adjudication and arbitration across the range of international courts and tribunals presently operating. The precautionary prima facie case approach could come to form an established and appropriate method for the application of the rule on burden of proof articulated by international courts and tribunals. Judicial discretion would still be involved in the application of the new approach, and undeniably this would be grounded in a judicial sense

[161] See e.g. the rules of procedure in the *MOX OSPAR* case and in the *Mox Plant case (Ireland* v. *United Kingdom) (Suspension of Proceedings on Jurisdiction and Merits and Request for Further Provisional Measures)*, Order of 24 June 2003, 42 ILM 1187. Rules of Procedure for the Arbitral Tribunal constituted under the Ospar Convention pursuant to the Request of Ireland dated 15 June 2001, Article 12(1); Rules of Procedure for the Tribunal constituted under Annex VII to the United Nations Convention on the Law of the Sea pursuant to the notification of Ireland dated 25 October 2001, Article 12(1). Both sets of rules are available at www.pca-cpa.org.

of the broader policy considerations, but as discussed above there would remain serious constraints on the discretion because of the strictly defined circumstances in which it could be exercised. Given the underlying normative problem, the prima facie case approach is not completely fitted as a response to cases involving scientific uncertainties, but it may be the best option available within the constraints of the rationalist tradition.

Conclusion

As international environmental law commentators have observed, 'Determining what the standard of proof should be ... or who bears the burden of proof of risk, are questions of immense practical importance.'[162] States are already comfortable with the notion of a reversal of the burden of proof to give effect to the precautionary principle in the administrative context. Reversal of the adjudicatory burden of proof in international cases offers a way to ensure that proper account is taken of the risks faced by complainants and by the international community in many disputes involving scientific uncertainty. There is potential scope for a new approach allowing for reversal of the burden of proof in disputes involving scientific uncertainty through the exercise of international courts' and tribunals' inherent powers. Reversal would be an option in relation to claims made under legal rules that intersected sufficiently with the precautionary principle in terms of their content, provided that scientific uncertainty and the risk of harm in the case concerned lay above certain thresholds. A clear set of defined legal tests for the application of the new approach could readily be developed, and the discussion in this chapter is intended to provide a starting point for that process.

Discussion of the potential reversal of the burden of proof in trade disputes has had a relatively low profile in this chapter. Depending on the cases that arise, the first steps towards establishing a modification of the rules on burden of proof in public international law to accommodate the precautionary principle are more likely to be taken in other adjudicatory fora. However, the same logic and the same principles would apply to reversal of the burden in the trade context as in other disputes. The day-to-day use of the terminology of the prima facie case approach to the allocation of the burden of proof in WTO dispute

[162] Birnie *et al.*, *International Law*, p. 154.

settlement means that the prima facie case technique for precautionary reversal of the burden might be susceptible of ready application in a WTO dispute. Transparency would be of notable importance politically in the multilateral trade context. A thorough and reasoned assessment of whether the high thresholds for the application of the precautionary principle had been reached would be essential. In practice, it would most likely be in cases arising under the environmental exceptions to the GATT or GATS that a reversal of the burden was usefully to be contemplated, rather than the SPS Agreement, as the burden of proof under the GATT or GATS exceptions usually falls on the responding party. As noted earlier, this contrasts with the SPS and TBT Agreements where the burden of proof already falls on complainants to establish the inconsistency with WTO law of a responding party's environmental or health related measures.

In contemplating the reversal of the burden of proof it must be borne in mind that this will cut across the presumption of compliance operating in international adjudication. Further, it is likely to result in decisions that could curtail economic activities in situations of scientific uncertainty. The overarching question will be whether, on balance, and taking into account the importance in principle of normative neutrality in judicial decision-making, the sound administration of justice is best served by adopting a new approach that allows international courts and tribunals to reverse the burden of proof.

PART IV

The finality of adjudication

7 Finality, revision and nullity in scientific cases

The judgments and awards of international courts and tribunals provide points of stability in international politics, permanently allocating resources and responsibility according to law. They offer disputing parties a decision that will enable them to close down their disputes and move on.[1] They also reinforce the status of the law and help to clarify and develop its content.[2] The finality of international adjudication is important in enabling international courts' and tribunals' decisions to fulfil these systemic functions. For judgments and awards dependent on continually advancing scientific research there is thus an awkward problem. Within a relatively short period of time it is always possible that new scientific evidence could show a judgment or award to have been based on erroneous factual foundations.

The principle of finality should not be seen as an end in itself. Appropriately circumscribed processes of review are also an essential aspect of international adjudication. International law has always readily accommodated the need for procedures allowing the rectification, interpretation and even the revision of judgments and awards. On rare occasions, express provision is also made by an international court or tribunal for a decision to be revisited, as in the *Nuclear Tests cases (Australia* v. *France) (New Zealand* v. *France)*.[3] There are also other case-specific rubrics under which the parties might return to the courtroom.

[1] Reisman, *Nullity and Revision*, p. 246.

[2] Lauterpacht, *The Development of International Law by the International Court*.

[3] *Nuclear Tests case (Australia* v. *France)*, 20 December 1974, ICJ Reports 1974 253, para. 60; *Nuclear Tests case (New Zealand* v. *France)*, 20 December 1974, ICJ Reports 1974 457, para. 63; *Request for an Examination of the Situation in Accordance with Paragraph 63 of the Court's Judgment of 20 December 1974 in the Nuclear Tests case (New Zealand* v. *France)*, Judgment of 22 September 1995, ICJ Reports 1995 288 (hereafter *Request for an Examination of the Situation*).

In the *Case concerning the Gabčíkovo-Nagymaros Project (Hungary/Slovakia)*, Slovakia invoked Article 5(3) of its Special Agreement with Slovakia in 1998.[4] This paragraph provided that, although the parties would accept the Court's judgment as final and binding, either party could return to the Court if necessary for an additional judgment to determine the modalities for executing its judgment, should negotiations fail. The ways in which catering for developments in scientific research might affect these modalities is an open question, and this makes it difficult to assess the ways in which any revisitation of the case might potentially accommodate new scientific information or the precautionary principle. Slovakia asked the Court to declare that the parties must resume their negotiations in good faith and conclude as a next step a binding framework agreement, and that in default of this the parties were obliged to comply with the 1977 Treaty. However, over a decade later it is possible that a different approach might be taken if the parties were to take the case back to the Court.[5]

In the World Trade Organization (WTO), use may be made of the institutional provision for proceedings to determine whether a WTO member previously found to be out of compliance with its WTO obligations has since come into compliance.[6] Ultimately the availability of these review processes strengthens the authority of judicial and arbitral decisions.[7] Continued respect for international judicial and arbitral decision-making depends on the availability of such review processes as 'safety valves' for disposing of difficulties that will otherwise undermine their authority. An absolutist view that an award must be accepted even if it is unjust will not help maintain international stability.[8]

The discussions that follow focus on the generic forms of review that may be available for dealing with situations where new scientific developments affect the basis of an international adjudicatory decision. In relation to all the forms of review that are canvassed, a central point

4 *Case concerning the Gabčíkovo-Nagymaros Project (Hungary/Slovakia)* Judgment of 25 September 1997, ICJ Reports 1997 7 (hereafter *Gabčíkovo-Nagymaros* case). See above, Ch. 2, pp. 37–41.

5 See above, Ch. 2, p. 41.

6 Understanding on Rules and Procedures Governing the Settlement of Disputes, WTO, *The Legal Texts: The results of the Uruguay round of multilateral trade negotiations*, p. 354, Article 21.5. For further discussion of the use of Article 21.5 see below, Ch. 8, pp. 321–2.

7 Reisman, *Nullity and Revision*, pp. 423–4; Bowett, 'Res judicata', 577.

8 For discussion, Reisman, *Nullity and Revision*, pp. 22–9, examining the views of Hugo Grotius, Samuel Pufendorf and Emmerich de Vattel. See also Carlston, *The Process of International Arbitration*, pp. 187–9 and 193; Lauterpacht, *Private Law Sources*, p. 209.

must be borne in mind. In many cases even a subsequent scientific discovery of considerable magnitude would not be relevant in the context of the legal obligations applying to the dispute, because these obligations are often temporally conditioned. For example, there will be obligations governing the legality of risk-generating activity that are based on the state of scientific knowledge at the time of the activity that gives rise to a dispute, such as a requirement that the parties act on the basis of the best scientific evidence available. By way of illustration, in the *Southern Bluefin Tuna case (Australia and New Zealand* v. *Japan)* Australia and New Zealand alleged that Japan had breached Article 119(1)(a) of the United Nations Convention for the Law of the Sea (LOSC), which requires parties to take measures designed on the best scientific evidence available to maintain stocks at or restore stocks to a level which can produce the maximum sustainable yield.[9] Under the existing generic forms of review in general international law, subsequent scientific discoveries would be irrelevant to the question of compliance with obligations of this type, at least so far as compliance with a party's obligations at the time of the original proceedings is concerned.

There will also be procedural obligations that may require impact assessment or risk assessment before an activity begins, as well as requirements of notification and co-operation in certain circumstances, as seen for example in the *Case concerning Pulp Mills on the River Uruguay (Argentina* v. *Uruguay).*[10] In most cases, these rules are likely to be regarded as having been complied with where due consideration was given to the science available at the time. Additionally, international scientific disputes may involve obligations governing how the parties should have acted in the light of scientific uncertainties, for example requiring the application of a precautionary approach. These rules would probably be regarded as heavily temporally conditioned: a party can only be expected to have made decisions at the time in question in the light of the scientific evidence then available. However all the examples of legal rules here could be considered to incorporate a requirement for the exercise of reasonable diligence in gathering and applying scientific and technical knowledge.[11] This requirement could be found to have been breached if reasonable diligence would have revealed

[9] United Nations Convention on the Law of the Sea, Montego Bay, 10 December 1982, in force 16 November 1994, 21 ILM 1261.

[10] *Case concerning Pulp Mills on the River Uruguay (Argentina* v. *Uruguay), Request for the Indication of Provisional Measures*, Order of 13 July 2006, ICJ Reports 2006.

[11] ILC Report (2001) GALR A/55/10 394, para. 11; Birnie *et al.*, *International Law*, p. 148.

important scientific evidence. Arguably in some circumstances this might even require a state to engage in scientific research itself.

In assessing each of the alternative options for dealing with the problem of subsequent scientific developments the same point needs to be recalled: in what ways are the obligations at issue temporally conditioned and does this limit the utility of the form of review under consideration? There will be instances where the obligations at issue are not temporally conditioned at all, and scientific developments are directly relevant. For example, the question whether risk-response measures are necessary to protect human health or the environment is an objective one that does not depend on the state of scientific knowledge at any given point in time.

This chapter explores first the limitations of the revision process. On a thorough assessment of the features of the revision process it is found that revision is not likely to be the procedure of most assistance. Revision has always been intended as a restricted process, where rehearing should be kept to a minimum. The alternative to revision that is canvassed in this chapter is the potential for a judicial decision to be declared a nullity. The doctrine of nullity is not usually considered to extend to decisions based on erroneous facts, but could potentially apply where an award cannot stand in light of the scale and significance of an error.

The following chapter considers a further procedural avenue that might permit the review of a judicial decision in the light of subsequently emerging scientific evidence. The chapter contemplates that on occasion international courts and tribunals may decide to 'future-proof' their judgments and awards by making provision for the reassessment of a case where necessary in the light of subsequent scientific developments. This would involve the use of clauses akin to the review clause built into the judgment in the *Nuclear Tests* cases and possibly the return-to-court provision built into the Special Agreement in the *Gabčíkovo-Nagymaros* case. For ad hoc tribunals, general institutional provision for reassessment in exceptional cases is advocated, as the tribunal is likely to be *functus officio* by the time that any new scientific evidence comes to light. The reassessment proceedings envisaged in Chapter 8 would be similar, regardless of the type of tribunal. Either party could institute such proceedings. There would be a 'special circumstances' exception to the doctrine of res judicata where new material is submitted that could not have been provided at the time of the prior proceedings, as seen in English jurisprudence. New claims would be permitted where they deal with issues inseparably linked with the claims in the original case by the scientific developments in question, provided that they do not fall into the category of claims that might properly have been raised at the time of the original proceedings. Certain potential features of the envisaged reassessment proceedings could be drawn from experience in relation to compliance proceedings in the WTO. For example, so far as the allocation of the burden of proof is concerned, the original claimant could be allocated the burden of proof in relation to any new claims, while for other claims the burden of proof would lie with the original respondent.

There is also the possibility that an original respondent may lodge a challenge to countermeasures that have been imposed with the intention of pressuring a respondent to come into compliance with its obligations. This was effectively the route chosen by the EC in the *Continued Suspension of Obligations* cases in the WTO.[12] The Appellate Body considered this an inappropriate approach in the WTO context. However, it is also a strategy that could be pursued in public international law outside the WTO. This avenue for review is therefore also discussed in Chapter 8.

The principle of finality

In international law, as in national legal systems, the public interest dictates that there be an end to litigation.[13] The principle of finality is recognised widely as a general principle of law,[14] and there are strong arguments for recognising a rule of customary international law regarding international adjudicatory decisions as final and binding.[15]

[12] *Canada - Continued Suspension of Obligations in the EC - Hormones Dispute*, Complaint by the EC (WT/DS321) Report of the Panel, Report of the Appellate Body, adopted 14 November 2008; *US - Continued Suspension of Obligations in the EC - Hormones Dispute*, Complaint by the EC (WT/DS320) Report of the Panel, Report of the Appellate Body, adopted 14 November 2008 (hereafter respectively *Canada - Continued Suspension* PR, *US - Continued Suspension* PR, and, to refer to the identical paragraphs of the two Appellate Body reports, *Continued Suspension* ABR).

[13] *Interest reipublicae ut sit finis litium*. Rosenne, *Interpretation, Revision and Other Recourse*, p. 20; Brown, *A Common Law*, p. 153.

[14] Scobbie, 'Res judicata', 299; Shany, *The Competing Jurisdictions of International Courts and Tribunals*, p. 246; Brown, *A Common Law*, p. 155. The principle has been recognised, for example, in the Hindu, Greek and Roman traditions, as well as in the civil and common law. Cheng, *General Principles*, p. 336 and see note 16 at p. 340. Barnett, *Res Judicata*, p. 455. For further comment, Rosenne, *The Law and Practice*, p. 1599, note 230.

[15] Shany, *The Competing Jurisdictions of International Courts and Tribunals*, p. 245.

Finality is frequently also attributed to international judicial decisions on the basis of convention, as seen most notably in Article 60 of the Statute of the International Court of Justice, providing that a judgment of the Court is final and without appeal.[16] Likewise, Article 296 of the LOSC provides that a decision rendered by any court or tribunal having compulsory jurisdiction under the Convention shall be final and shall be complied with by the parties.[17] Article 81 of the 1907 Convention for the Peaceful Settlement of Disputes provides that an award of the Permanent Court of Arbitration settles a dispute definitively and without appeal.[18] There is no such express provision in the WTO Dispute Settlement Understanding (DSU), but finality is certainly envisaged.[19]

In international adjudication the principle of finality takes the classic form of res judicata.[20] The res judicata rule was recognised clearly in the award of the Arbitral Tribunal constituted under an agreement between the parties in *Pious Fund of the Californias*[21] in 1902 and described in the following way by the French–Venezuelan Mixed Claims Commission in 1905 in *Company General of the Orinoco*:

> The general principle announced in numerous cases is that a right, question or fact *distinctly put in issue and directly determined* by a court of competent jurisdiction, as a ground of recovery, cannot be disputed.[22]

The Dissenting Opinion of Judge Anzilotti in the *Chorzów Factory (Interpretation)* case, decided by the Permanent Court of International Justice in 1927, is commonly regarded as encapsulating the res judicata

[16] For discussion, Rosenne, *The Law and Practice*, p. 1598; Rosenne, *Interpretation, Revision and Other Recourse*, pp. 43–7.

[17] See similarly Article 33(1) of the Statute of the International Tribunal for the Law of the Sea, 1833 UNTS 3, providing that an award by a tribunal 'shall be final and without appeal, unless the parties to the dispute have agreed in advance to an appellate procedure'. See also the provision on the finality of the awards of tribunals operating under Annex VII of the United Nations Convention for the Law of the Sea, Annex VII, Article 11.

[18] This provision is based on Article 54 of the Convention for the Pacific Settlement of International Disputes, 18 October 1907, in force 26 January 1910, 1 Bevans 577.

[19] Note, in particular, Articles 17(14), 22(7) and 25(3) of the DSU. For discussion in light of the cases, Grando, *Evidence*, p. 40.

[20] For an overview of res judicata see Cheng, *General Principles*, Ch. 17. The res judicata rule has been regarded as an *exceptio*, according to one writer. Grisel, 'Res judicata',143.

[21] *Pious Fund of the Californias (US* v. *Mexico)*, 14 October 1902, 9 UNRIAA 11 (hereafter *Pious Fund* case), 12–13. For comment, Lauterpacht, *Private Law Sources*, pp. 244–5.

[22] *Company General of the Orinoco*, French–Venezuelan Mixed Claims Commission, 31 July 1905, 10 UNRIAA 184 (hereafter *Company General of the Orinoco)*, 276, adopting the remarks of the US Supreme Court in *Southern Pacific R. Co.* v. *US.*, 168 Sup. Ct. Rep., 1.

rule, determining that res judicata will apply in respect of earlier decisions where there is (a) identity of the parties, (b) identity of object (*petitum*) and (c) identity of grounds (*causa petendi*).[23] Despite the broad remarks of the French–Venezuelan Mixed Claims Commission, it has been held that the res judicata rule may not apply to findings of fact, only to findings of law.[24] In later proceedings, previous factual findings may be relied upon only as a probable or provisional truth.[25] The res judicata rule has changed little over the last century.[26] The International Court of Justice recognised the status of the res judicata rule as a well-established and generally recognised principle of law in its 1954 Advisory Opinion on the *Effect of Awards of Compensation made by the United Nations Administrative Tribunal*,[27] in the *Barcelona Traction (New Application) (Belgium* v. *Spain) (Preliminary Objections)* case[28] and in the *Corfu Channel (United Kingdom of Great Britain and Northern Ireland* v. *Albania)*[29] and *Haya de la Torre (Colombia* v. *Peru)* cases.[30]

The principle of finality is subject to certain recognised procedural exceptions in international adjudication, specifically rectification, interpretation and revision.[31] Interpretation and rectification are both

[23] *Interpretation of Judgments Nos. 7 and 8 Concerning the Case of the Factory at Chorzów*, Judgment of 16 December 1927, PCIJ Series A, No. 13, 20 (hereafter *Chorzów Factory (Interpretation)*), 23, 24, 27. See similarly the second arbitral award in the *Trail Smelter* case *(US* v. *Canada)*, 11 March 1941, 3 UNRIAA 1938, 1952. Professor Cheng has queried the accuracy of requiring identity of object (*petitum*) as a distinct matter from identity of grounds (*causa petendi*), preferring to group the two together by simply asking whether the same question or matter is at issue. Cheng, *General Principles*, p. 346. Requiring only identity of the parties and of subject matter, see the *Pious Fund* case, p. 5, as well as the Advisory Opinion of the Permanent Court of International Justice in *Polish Postal Service in Danzig*, 16 May 1925, PCIJ Series B, No. 11, 30.

[24] Kolb, 'General principles', 826–7. [25] *Ibid.*, 827.

[26] As seen for example in the ICSID arbitral tribunal award in *AMCO* v. *Indonesia*, Resubmitted Case, Decision on Jurisdiction, 10 May 1988, 5 ICSID Reports 543 (hereafter *AMCO* v. *Indonesia*, Resubmitted Case, Decision on Jurisdiction), or the discussion in the proceedings under the UNCITRAL Rules in *CME Czech Republic B.V. (The Netherlands* v. *The Czech Republic*), Final Award, 14 March 2003, paras. 432–7, decision available at http://ita.law.vic.ca.

[27] *Effect of Awards of Compensation made by the United Nations Administrative Tribunal*, Advisory Opinion of 13 July 1954, ICJ Reports 1954 49, 53.

[28] When a matter is res judicata, it 'is finally disposed of for good'. *Barcelona Traction, Light and Power Company Limited, (New Application) (Belgium* v. *Spain) (Preliminary Objections)*, Judgment of 24 July 1964, ICJ Reports 1964 6, 20.

[29] *The Corfu Channel case (United Kingdom of Great Britain and Northern Ireland* v. *Albania)*, Judgment of 15 December 1949, ICJ Reports 1949 244, 248.

[30] *Haya de la Torre case (Colombia* v. *Peru)*, Judgment of 13 June, ICJ Reports 1951, 71.

[31] For a comprehensive commentary, Rosenne, *Interpretation, Revision and Other Recourse*.

tightly limited procedures.[32] In situations where scientific developments reveal new and sanguine information subsequent to a judgment or award, revision is the review procedure with the most potential for providing a resolution of the situation. Rectification or correction procedures will only enable a tribunal to rectify minor errors such as clerical, typographical and arithmetical errors.[33] Nor is great assistance to be gained from the power of interpretation often expressly conferred on international tribunals.[34] In interpreting a judgment, a court or tribunal must refrain from examining new facts arising subsequent to the judgment.[35] An interpretation of a judgment cannot go beyond the limits of that judgment,[36] nor may such a request 'concern the reasons for the judgment except in so far as these are inseparable from the operative part'.[37] The power of interpretation is essentially intended for situations where the parties are in dispute over the meaning or scope of a judgment.[38] Interpretation and rectification thus have relatively minimal impact on the principle of finality and offer minimal potential for addressing the problems arising out of judgments and awards involving scientific uncertainty. However the procedure of revision deserves further attention.

[32] Although Professor Reisman notes the potential kinship of interpretation with revision. Reisman, *Nullity and Revision*, pp. 186, 203–4. See *Application for Revision and Interpretation of the Judgment of 24 February 1982 in the Case concerning the Continental Shelf (Tunisia/Libyan Arab Jamahiriya) (Tunisia* v. *Libyan Arab Jamahiriya)*, Judgment of 10 December 1985, ICJ Reports 1985 192 (hereafter *Case concerning the Continental Shelf (Tunisia/Libyan Arab Jamahiriya) (Revision)*), 198.

[33] For an example of provision for correction by a panel of the Permanent Court of Arbitration, Article 94 of the Rules of Procedure adopted in the *Iron Rhine* case. Article 94 was applied after the award at Belgium's request. The power of rectification may also be inherent to international courts. Bowett, 'Res judicata', 580.

[34] See e.g. the Statute of the International Court of Justice, 26 June 1945, in force 24 October 1945, 3 Bevans 1153 (hereafter Statute of the International Court of Justice), Article 60, together with Article 98 of the Rules of Court of the International Court of Justice. The power of interpretation may also be inherent. Bowett, 'Res judicata', 581; Rosenne, *The Law and Practice*, pp. 1611–12; Brown, *A Common Law*, pp. 161–6, Reisman, *Nullity and Revision*, pp. 192–4.

[35] *Chorzów Factory (Interpretation)*, 21.

[36] *Treaty of Neuilly (Interpretation)*, Judgment of 26 March 1925, PCIJ Series A, No. 4, 7; Reisman, *Nullity and Revision*, p. 206.

[37] *Request for Interpretation of the Judgment of 11 June 1998 in the Case concerning the Land and Maritime Boundary between Cameroon and Nigeria (Cameroon* v. *Nigeria), (Preliminary Objections) (Nigeria* v. *Cameroon)*, Judgment of 25 March 1999, ICJ Reports 1999, 31, 36.

[38] Bowett, 'Res judicata', 582; Rosenne, *The Law and Practice*, pp. 1621–2; Rosenne, *Interpretation, Revision and Other Recourse*, pp. 93–7; *Chorzów Factory (Interpretation)*, 10–11.

Revision

As seen in Article 61 of the Statute of the International Court of Justice, an application for revision may be made based on the discovery of a fact of such a nature as to be a decisive factor, where this fact was unknown to the Court and to the party claiming revision at the time of the judgment,[39] provided this ignorance was not due to that party's negligence.[40] These same criteria apply across all international courts and tribunals.[41] The same provision was found in the Statute of the Permanent Court of International Justice,[42] itself reflecting the terms of Article 83 of the 1907 Hague Convention,[43] although the Hague Convention does require the parties to have reserved in their *compromis* the right to demand revision of an award.[44] Provision for revision is incorporated likewise in the constitutive instruments of other international courts and tribunals, including the European Court of Justice[45] and ICSID tribunals.[46] Revision is altogether distinct from the reopening of proceedings to accommodate decisive new evidence before an award has been rendered.

Differing views have been expressed as to whether the power of revision is an inherent power.[47] There is some strength to the argument

[39] For discussion of the precise point of time involved, see Brown, *A Common Law*, p. 182.

[40] For details of the procedures that apply, see the Rules of Court of the International Court of Justice, www.icj-cij.org, Article 99.

[41] Cheng, *General Principles*, pp. 365–70. For an overview of the evolution of the revision procedure see the Commentary on the draft Convention on Arbitral Procedure adopted by the International Law Commission at its Fifth Session, prepared by the Secretariat, A/CN.4/92.1955.

[42] Statute of the Permanent Court of International Justice, Article 61.

[43] Convention for the Pacific Settlement of International Disputes, 29 July 1907, in force 4 September 1900, 1 Bevans 577, Article 83.

[44] For the predecessor of Article 83 see Convention for the Pacific Settlement of International Disputes 1899, 1 Bevans 230, Article 55.

[45] Statute of the European Court of Justice, Article 44. For discussion on revision in the European courts, Di Bucci, 'Revision'.

[46] Convention for the Settlement of Investment Disputes between States and Nationals of other States, Washington, 18 March 1965, in force 14 October 1966, 575 UNTS 159, Article 51(1). Also Rule 80, Rules of Court of the European Court of Human Rights, in force 1 June 2010, www.echr.coe.int; Rules of the International Tribunal for the Law of the Sea, www.itlos.org (hereafter Rules of the International Tribunal for the Law of the Sea), Article 127. For discussion, Rosenne, *Interpretation, Revision and Other Recourse*, pp. 74–80.

[47] Bowett, 'Res judicata', 590; Advisory Opinion on the *Polish – Czechoslovakian (Jaworzina Frontier)* case, 6 December 1923, PCIJ, Series B, No. 8, 38. The position taken in *Jaworzina* has been contrasted with the perspective adopted in the PCIJ's subsequent advisory opinion, *Monastery at Saint Naoum*, 4 September 1924, 1924 Series B, No. 9, 21–2. Brown, *A Common Law*, pp. 163–5 and 166–71; Reisman, *Nullity and Revision*, p. 210. Also

that a power of revision should be regarded as an inherent power because of its importance in helping ensure the fulfilment of the international judicial function, viz. the settlement of disputes and the proper administration of international justice.[48] On this basis it has been suggested that the power of revision may inhere even in WTO panels and the Appellate Body, although not directly contemplated in the DSU.[49]

Applications for revision must be made within limited timeframes. Under Article 61(4) and (5) of the Statute of the International Court of Justice, an application must be made within six months of the discovery of the new fact, and no application for revision may be made after the lapse of ten years from the date of the judgment.[50] The same timeframes apply for applications to the International Tribunal for the Law of the Sea.[51] ICSID timeframes are shorter, with an application to be made within ninety days of the discovery of a fact and within three years of an award.[52] No timeframes are specified in the Hague Conventions.[53]

A tribunal's authority to revise its earlier decision is a concomitant of its jurisdiction over the merits of a case,[54] as for rectification and interpretation, and an application for revision may be made *ex parte*. The revision procedure does not apply in respect of provisional measures orders, but these orders do not in any event have the status of a final judgment.[55] They may be superceded by subsequent provisional measures orders, and by a decision on the merits.

supporting an inherent power, see the Advisory Opinion on *Effect of Awards of Compensation made by the United Nations Administrative Tribunal*, Advisory Opinion of 13 July 1954, ICJ Reports 1954, 47, 55. See also *Trail Smelter* at 1954. For a discussion of the cases in the Iran–US Claims Tribunal see Brower and Brueschke, *The Iran–United States Claims Tribunal*, 242–60. The doctrine of inherent powers may have a more natural appeal here for common lawyers, but seem constitutionally questionable to the civil lawyer. Herzog and Karlen, 'Attacks', 9.

48 Brown, *A Common Law*, p. 171; Carlston, *The Process of International Arbitration*, p. 240; Gaeta, 'Inherent powers', 359, discussing the remarks of Judge Cançado Trindade in his Dissenting Opinion in the *Genie Lacayo* case, Request for Review of the Judgment of January 29 1997, Annual Report of the Inter-American Court of Human Rights, 177 (hereafter *Genie Lacayo* case), 183.

49 Brown, *A Common Law*, pp. 172–3. Nor is there any provision for revision in the UNCITRAL or ICC arbitration rules.

50 On the negotiation of the predecessor provisions in the Statute of the Permanent Court of International Justice see Rosenne, *Interpretation, Revision and Other Recourse*, pp. 31–3.

51 Rules of the International Tribunal for the Law of the Sea, Article 127(1).

52 ICSID Convention, Article 51(2).

53 Convention for the Pacific Settlement of International Disputes 1899, Article 55 and Convention for the Pacific Settlement of International Disputes 1907, Article 83.

54 Brown, *A Common Law*, p. 176.

55 Rosenne, *The Law and Practice*, p. 206.

A two-stage procedure is employed for dealing with applications for revision. Initially a preliminary decision is taken by the court on the admissibility of the request. If the application is admissible, the court will issue a judgment recording the existence of the new fact, recognising that it is of such a character as to lay the case open to revision, and declaring the application's admissibility.[56] Substantive proceedings for revision can then go ahead. The practice of adopting a two-stage revision procedure is relatively uniform across international courts and tribunals,[57] and has been adopted by the International Court of Justice,[58] the International Tribunal for the Law of the Sea[59] and tribunals of the Permanent Court of Arbitration,[60] as well as the European Court of Justice.[61] During the negotiation of the ICSID Convention there were proposals for the Secretary-General to play a greater role in determining admissibility, and for a procedure requiring leave to review a prior decision, but these were not carried forward.[62] In scientific disputes it may make sense to combine the two stages of the revision procedure, especially if scientific expertise is needed to assist the court at both stages.[63] In reality a decision on jurisdiction at the first stage of the procedure will inevitably involve the partial assessment of the merits of a request for revision.[64]

56 Statute of the International Court of Justice, San Francisco, 26 June 1945, 3 Bevans 1153, in force 24 October 1945, Article 61(2); Brown, *A Common Law*, p. 179.

57 Brown, *A Common Law*, p. 179; Cheng, *General Principles*, p. 370. For an early example, see the decision of the US–German Mixed Claims Commission in *Lehigh Valley Railroad Company, Agency of Canadian Car and Foundry Company, Limited, and Various Underwriters (United States* v. *Germany)*, 15 December 1933, 8 UNRIAA 160 (hereafter *Lehigh Valley Railroad Company*), 185.

58 Statute of the International Court of Justice, Article 61(2); Rosenne, *The Law and Practice*, pp. 264, 1625.

59 Rules of the International Tribunal for the Law of the Sea, Article 127(2).

60 Convention for the Pacific Settlement of International Disputes 1907, Article 83; Convention for the Pacific Settlement of International Disputes 1899, Article 55.

61 Protocol on the Statute of the Court of Justice of the European Union, OJ C 310/210, Article 44. See also Rules of the European Court of Human Rights, www.echr.coe.int, Rule 80.

62 Schreuer, The *ICSID Convention*, p. 873. An application for revision under the ICSID Convention must address in detail the required elements of the application. The Secretary-General may require an applicant to address further such elements as the discovery of the new fact and the explanation of the applicant's previous ignorance of the fact, but is unlikely to refuse to register the application. *Ibid.*, pp. 882 and 929 ff.

63 In *Lehigh Valley Railroad Company*, difficulties in appointing an impartial expert to help the Commission appraise the new evidence resulted in the relevant expert's evidence being submitted by affidavit by one of the parties. *Lehigh Valley Railroad Company*, 183.

64 Tsagourias, 'Application for revision of the judgment of 11 July 1996', 737.

Revision has often been viewed primarily as a way to deal with decisions induced by fraud, including forgery and perjury.[65] However, mistake induced by fraud is merely one of the problems that could lead a tribunal into error and require revision of an award.[66] Requests for revision are not commonplace. The Permanent Court of International Justice received no applications. The International Court of Justice has received three applications. The first was the *Application for Revision and Interpretation of the Judgment of 1982 in the Case concerning the Libya/Tunisia Continental Shelf (Tunisia/Libyan Arab Jamahiriya) (Tunisia* v. *Libyan Arab Jamahiriya)*;[67] the second was the *Application for Revision of the Judgment of 11 July 1996 in the Case concerning the Convention on the Prevention and Punishment of the Crime of Genocide (Bosnia and Herzegovina* v. *Yugoslavia) (Preliminary Objections) (Yugoslavia v. Bosnia)*;[68] the third was the *Application for Revision of the Judgment of 11 September 1992 in the Case concerning the Land, Island and Maritime Frontier Dispute (El Salvador/Honduras: Nicaragua intervening) (El Salvador* v. *Honduras)*.[69] In all three cases these applications for revision were rejected at the admissibility stage. In only one of the cases was the request for revision based on new scientific evidence. El Salvador's request for revision in the *Land, Island and Maritime Frontier Dispute (Revision)*, was put forward on the basis of new scientific evidence concerning a change in the course of the Goascorán river, asserted to have been due to a cyclone. However, the Court concluded that the decision of its Chamber had been taken on wholly different grounds.[70]

[65] *Dames and Moore* v. *Islamic Republic of Iran and others*, 23 April 1985, 8, 107; *Ram International Industries, Inc.* v. *Air Force of Iran*, 28 December 1993, 29 Iran-US CTR 383 (hereafter *Ram Industries*); Brower and Brueschke, *The Iran-United States Claims Tribunal*, pp. 254–9; Brown, *A Common Law*, p. 169. See also the UNCITRAL tribunal award in *Biloune and Marine Drive Complex Ltd* v. *Ghana Investments Centre and the Government of Ghana* (Award on Damages and Costs) 95 ILR 184, 222 (1990).

[66] See *Lehigh Valley Railroad Company*, 188, 190.

[67] *Case concerning the Continental Shelf (Tunisia/Libyan Arab Jamahiriya) (Revision)*.

[68] *Application for Revision of the Judgment of 11 July 1996 in the Case concerning Application of the Convention on the Prevention and Punishment of the Crime of Genocide (Bosnia and Herzegovina* v. *Yugoslavia), (Preliminary Objections) (Yugoslavia* v. *Bosnia and Herzegovina)*, Judgment of 3 February 2003, ICJ Reports 2003, 7 (hereafter *Application of the Convention on the Prevention and Punishment of the Crime of Genocide (Revision)*.

[69] *Application for Revision of the Judgment of 11 September 1992 in the Case concerning the Land, Island and Maritime Frontier Dispute (El Salvador/Honduras: Nicaragua intervening) (El Salvador* v. *Honduras)*, Judgment of 18 December 2003, ICJ Reports 2003 392 (hereafter *Land, Island and Maritime Frontier Dispute (Revision)*).

[70] *Ibid.*, paras. 26–9, 38–40, see also paras. 41 and 52–5.

Revision has a controversial history.[71] At the Hague Peace Conference of 1899 negotiations on Article 55 of the Act for Pacific Settlement of International Disputes were intense.[72] Holls, secretary to the US delegation, proposed that every litigant before an international tribunal should have the right to seek the re-examination of a case within three months upon presentation of evidence that a judgment contained a substantial error of fact or law. This suggestion was implacably opposed in the committee of examination by Russian delegate de Martens, pursuing resolutely the view that the final award of a tribunal should decide definitely the points in dispute and finally close all proceedings. In due course the resistance was overcome.[73] The concerns expressed by de Martens should not be overlooked. Especially significant may be the potential situation where a dispute over an award engendering widespread public dissatisfaction is considerably prolonged because of the possibility of revision, or of establishing the nullity of an award.[74] On the other hand, as Holls insisted, continued international respect for the institution of adjudication required that there be provision for dealing with an otherwise irreparably unjust award.[75] The importance of a balance between the principle of finality and the need for revision in certain circumstances was reflected subsequently in the report of the Advisory Committee of Jurists responsible for preparation of a draft statute for the Permanent Court of International Justice. The Committee noted that the right of revision had adverse effects in relation to the rule of res judicata, but considered the right of revision very important, given the legitimate requirements of justice.[76]

Will the process of revision readily accommodate the situation where new scientific evidence that would have had a significant bearing on the case comes to light after a judgment or award has been

[71] See e.g. the remarks of the Tribunal in *Battus* v. *Bulgarian State*, Franco-Bulgarian Mixed Arbitral Tribunal, 6 June 1929, 5 ILR 458, emphasising the extraordinary character of the revision procedure and the need for rigour to prevent its use merely as a way to resubmit for discussion questions that have previously been determined.

[72] Wetter, *The International Arbitral Process*, pp. 542–52; Reisman, *Nullity and Revision*, pp. 34–8; Rosenne, *Interpretation, Revision and Other Recourse*, pp. 9–12; Carlston, *The Process of International Arbitration*, pp. 233–5.

[73] Reisman, *Nullity and Revision*, p. 43.

[74] *Ibid.*, p. 39, referring to the situation in England after the Alabama Claims Commission Award.

[75] *Ibid.*, p. 40.

[76] Report of the Committee, Annex No. 1, Advisory Committee of Jurists, Procès Verbaux of the Proceedings of the Committee 693, 744 (1920); Reisman, *Nullity and Revision*, pp. 46–7; Rosenne, *Interpretation, Revision and Other Recourse*, pp. 28–31.

rendered? The essential criteria for revision require there to have been the discovery of a fact, that this fact has been unknown to the court and to the party claiming revision at the time of the award and that the fact be of such a nature as to be a decisive factor. In addition it has been suggested that the new fact ought to have already been in existence at the time of the original proceedings, although the fact is required to have been unknown. In all of this it is presupposed that the new fact is a relevant one within the legal matrix of the case as discussed at the outset of this chapter. Each of these requirements may be examined in turn. Procedural issues will then be addressed.

(a) Discovery of a fact

A distinction between questions of fact and law has been maintained throughout the development of revision.[77] Accordingly, the expectation has been that there will be no re-argument of legal points or questioning of the legal reasoning on which a previous award was based.[78] Re-argument would be expected in the context of appeal, but not revision.[79] The Secretariat's Commentary to the ILC draft Convention on Arbitral Procedure describes the task of a tribunal considering a request for revision as placing the newly discovered fact in conjunction with the facts that previously had formed the basis of the tribunal's decision and determining whether the new facts materially modify the significance of the earlier facts and the conclusions drawn from them.[80]

Disputes involving scientific uncertainty may raise issues where the relationship between fact and law is closer than in other disputes, and

[77] See e.g. the *Laguna del Desierto Arbitration, Dispute concerning the Course of the Frontier between BP62 and Mount Fitzroy (Argentina/Chile)* 13 October 1995, 113 ILR 194, para. 27. As Judge Koroma noted in his Separate Opinion in response to the Federal Republic of Yugoslavia's request for revision in the *Application of the Genocide Convention* case, '[t]he revision procedure is [thus] essentially *about newly discovered facts or arguments*, and *not a legal challenge*, as such, *to the conclusion reached earlier* by the Court based on the facts as then known'. Para. 2, p. 33. Emphasis original. On the drafting of the Court's Rules of Procedure see also Rosenne, *Interpretation, Revision and Other Recourse*, p. 60.

[78] Commentary on the draft Convention on Arbitral Procedure, 102; *Ventense Epoux v. Etat Autrichien S.H.S.*, German-Yugoslavia Mixed Tribunal, 24 October 1923 RDTAM 1928 79. Bowett, 'Res judicata', 591. A suggestion during the drafting of the ICSID Convention that revision be allowed in a case of manifest error of law was not pursued. Schreuer, *The ICSID Convention*, p. 873.

[79] Reisman, *Nullity and Revision*, p. 212.

[80] Commentary on the draft Convention on Arbitral Procedure adopted by the International Law Commission at its Fifth Session: prepared by the Secretariat. A/CN.4/92 1955 (hereafter Secretariat's Commentary), 102.

where the possibility of maintaining a clear-cut distinction between fact and law is challenged.[81] In *Laguna del Desierto Arbitration, Dispute concerning the Course of the Frontier between BP62 and Mount Fitzroy (Argentina/Chile)*, a boundary dispute, the tribunal took the strict view that 'In international law there are two types of error: errors of fact and errors of law . . . *Tertium non datur*.' These remarks will be inapposite in many cases involving scientific uncertainty. For example, a new scientific development achieved with relatively little effort might reveal that a disputing party had earlier failed to meet a legal test requiring a thorough evaluation of all risks posed to another party by a given activity, or a legal test requiring best available efforts to ensure minimal risk to another party. To take another example, new scientific research might show that a respondent's risk-response measures were, after all, necessary to protect the environment, when this argument had been rejected in the original proceedings. As always, the new fact will need to be evaluated alongside the pre-existing factual evidence, and consideration given to how the relevant legal rules will now apply. In a dispute involving scientific uncertainty the relationships between the new fact, pre-existing evidence, and the legal consequences may be particularly complex. It is the overall analysis of these factors operating together on which revision will hinge, more than on the isolable effect of the new fact. Accordingly, for a proper evaluation of a case at the revision stage it would be helpful to admit also any other new scientific evidence that has been generated since the original judgment was rendered, and not just the new evidence concerning this specific discovery triggering the applicability of the revision process.

Whether it will be appropriate for a court or tribunal to revise its views without inviting argument from the parties will depend on how simple or complex the point at hand may be. In many cases, the procedure that would necessarily evolve might have more in common with a limited appeal to the original tribunal or with various other forms of proceeding than with a classic instance of revision. If such a procedure is to be made available an emphasis on the need for the new 'fact' to be both new and potentially decisive would be important in order to maintain respect for the finality of international adjudication, and to avoid prolonging disputes, tying up valuable legal resources and causing unnecessary expenditure.

[81] On mixed questions of fact and law, see above, Ch. 4, pp. 137–48.

(b) That the fact be unknown

In the *Libya/Tunisia Continental Shelf* case Libya failed to meet the requirement that a fact asserted in a request for revision must have been unknown at the time of the judgment, and that this should not be due to the negligence of the claimant, although the Court noted that in any event its reasoning had been unaffected by Tunisia's failure to assert the relevant co-ordinates during the original proceedings.[82] In a request for revision based on scientific developments, when can it be said that a new fact was previously 'unknown'? This question could raise several issues in connection with scientific developments. For example, we could consider a situation where particular scientific arguments were being asserted by only a minority of the scientific community at the time that a case was originally heard and judgment given, and they subsequently come instead to be asserted by a majority of scientists. Could such a development clothe the arguments with the legal status of a fact previously 'unknown'?

There is also the requirement that ignorance of the new fact was not due to negligence. This is quite distinct from the question of whether a requirement for diligence is to be read into the applicable legal obligation,[83] although the evidentiary basis for addressing the two questions might overlap. For example, a party might need to ensure there were records reflecting that they had exercised due diligence in consulting with scientists at the time of the original proceedings, and in conducting requisite scientific research themselves, if appropriate, to establish the facts of a case before it was first considered. An assessment of whether a party's ignorance of a fact was due to negligence may depend on whether a limited timeframe applied for the researching of a case, such as to foreclose exhaustion of all sources of information and evidence.[84] It seems reasonable that 'If careful preparation would have avoided the situation leading to the request for revision, this would give rise at least to the presumption of negligence'.[85] Diligence would seem to be lacking in particular where the relevant science had already been conducted and the results were accessible at the time of the earlier

[82] The co-ordinates of the petroleum concession of which Tunisia claimed to be previously unaware had been fixed by resolution of the Libyan Council of Ministers in 1968, and published in the Libyan Official Gazette and elsewhere. *Case concerning the Continental Shelf (Tunisia/Libyan Arab Jamahiriya) (Revision)*, 205–7.

[83] See above, pp. 283–4.

[84] Cheng, *General Principles*, pp. 367–8, citing *Lehigh Valley Railroad Company*, 188.

[85] Rao and Gautier (eds.), *The Rules of the International Tribunal for the Law of the Sea*, p. 363.

proceedings, even if they had not come to the notice of a party's public authorities.

(c) That the fact be a pre-existing one

The decision of the International Court of Justice on the request by the Federal Republic of Yugoslavia (FRY) for revision in the *Case concerning the Convention on the Prevention and Punishment of the Crime of Genocide* is based on the requirement that a fact already be in existence at the time of a judgment. In these proceedings, the FRY argued that its admission to the United Nations in 2000 implied facts that had existed in 1996 at the time of the original judgment but had been unknown at that time: notably that the FRY had not been party to the Court's Statute or the Genocide Convention when the case was decided.[86] If this were so, it would mean that the Court had not had jurisdiction over the case at the time it was originally heard. The Court rejected the FRY's request for revision, taking the view that the FRY was not in reality basing its request for revision on facts that existed in 1996 at the time of the earlier proceedings, but on the legal consequences of subsequent facts.[87] The *sui generis* legal position of the FRY over the period from 1992 to 2000, and its position in relation to the Statute and the Genocide Convention, were known to the Court and to the FRY at the time of the original proceedings, and were not retroactively converted into a different position by virtue of the events of 2000.[88]

The reasoning in the *Genocide* case derives the requirement that a fact be a pre-existing one from the requirement that a fact be 'unknown' at the time of the judgment, taking this to infer that the fact be 'knowable'. Alternatively, it has been suggested that the requirement that a fact be a pre-existing one could be derived from the requirement for a new fact to be 'of a decisive nature',[89] or from the requirement for 'discovery' of a fact.[90] The underlying consideration is the same: to accept that revision may be available in order to take account of facts that come into being subsequent to a judgment would pose a particular challenge to finality. At the time of a judgment, participants would

[86] Paras. 19, 69. [87] Paras. 67, 69.

[88] Paras. 70, 71. See also *Battus* v. *Bulgarian State*, Franco-Bulgarian Mixed Arbitral Tribunal, 6 June 1929, 1929 9 RDTAM 284. In this case the Tribunal rejected Bulgaria's invocation of a new fact in the form of a judicial decision revealing Battus's title to a disputed forest to be false, on the basis that the judgment was a subsequent fact rather than a pre-existing one.

[89] Bowett, 'Res judicata', 589. [90] Cheng, *General Principles*, p. 365.

become obliged to accept that unforeseeable new developments might yet alter the apparently final outcome of their case. Judgments would in effect be liable to be adapted at a later point in order to take account of subsequent events.[91] Nevertheless, it is desirable to allow for revision in case of scientific developments subsequent to a judgment, and for the purposes of revision new scientific evidence, while a fact in itself, should be regarded as new evidence of a pre-existing unknown fact.[92] In the *Land, Island and Maritime Frontier Dispute (Revision)*, the Court was prepared to suppose that the scientific and technical studies produced by El Salvador were new evidence of a pre-existing unknown fact and met the requirement for a new fact.[93] Thus, 'If a fact can be proven, for example, due to new scientific developments only after the delivery of the judgment, such a fact may become relevant in a revision case.'[94]

However, even if situations involving scientific developments may potentially qualify as involving pre-existing 'new facts', will subsequent scientific developments have to provide something amounting to definitive proof of a pre-existing fact before they do qualify? As a matter of law, what can constitute a new fact will depend in large measure on the legal rules that were applicable in the parties' dispute. On consulting the legal rules applying to scientific disputes it becomes apparent that the parties' obligations to one another in circumstances of scientific uncertainty are often crafted not in terms contingent upon absolute or certain scientific knowledge or 'facts' about the physical world, but in terms more accepting of science as an ongoing endeavour gradually accumulating increased knowledge. Accordingly, it will seldom

[91] Tsagourias, 'Application', 735. However, under ICSID revision may also be sought, exceptionally, on the basis of a fact arising after an award. For example, where payments made after the date of an award have not been included in the calculation of costs in the award. Schreuer, *The ICSID Convention*, p. 884.

[92] Highlighting the distinction between a new means of proving a fact, which may itself constitute a fact, and the pre-existing fact itself, see Di Bucci, 'Revision', 708; also Tsagourias, 'Application', 735; and *Heim and Charmant* v. *Germany*, 7 and 25 September 1922, 3 RDTAM 50, 55, Franco-German Mixed Arbitral Tribunal, rejecting a strict delineation between points of law and facts going to the interpretation of the law, in the context of an unsuccessful German request for revision in the light of new evidence that the provisions of the Treaty of Versailles concerning reparation should be interpreted in such as way as to recognise citizens of Alsace-Lorraine as having German rather than French nationality during the First World War.

[93] *Land, Island and Maritime Frontier Dispute (Revision)*, paras. 36, 40. See also the arguments of the parties at paras. 26–33 and 42. See also the Dissenting Opinion of Judge Cançado Trindade in the *Genie Lacayo* case, para. 16.

[94] Rao and Gautier (eds.), *The Rules of the International Tribunal for the Law of the Sea*, p. 362.

be necessary even to consider whether or not subsequent scientific evidence constitutes definitive proof of the fact it supports. The potential relevance of the new scientific evidence will rather be that it changes the factual picture that was before the Court in the original proceedings. Further, as indicated earlier there will be times when new facts will have an impact not only on judicial assessment of matters 'which bear empirical scrutiny, such as maps or geographical features such as the course of a deep water channel or the size of a particular fish stock or the environmental damage caused by an oil spill'[95] but also on the assessment of mixed questions of fact and law.

(d) That the fact be relevant

As discussed at the beginning of this chapter, determining the relevance of subsequent scientific developments will be important for assessing whether any form of review is appropriate. Revision may be more appropriate in cases concerning the legality of risk-response measures rather than the legality of risk-generating activity. Depending on the context, the way in which the applicable rules are crafted may be less tightly temporally conditioned. Notably, WTO members' obligations under Article XX of the General Agreement on Tariffs and Trade (GATT), and Article XIV of the General Agreement on Trade in Services, could be interpreted as leaving considerable scope for the re-evaluation of compliance with these obligations in the light of subsequent scientific developments. For example, new scientific evidence could justify the setting aside of WTO findings on whether a risk-response measure was '*necessary* to protect human, animal or plant life and health' under Article XX(b) of GATT, or was a measure '*relating to* the conservation of exhaustible natural resources' under Article XX(g) of GATT. Similarly, a conclusion as to whether or not a measure was directed to a 'legitimate objective' under Article 2.2 of the Agreement on Technical Barriers to Trade (TBT Agreement) could change in the light of new scientific evidence.[96] These provisions embody objective and substantive tests of a measure's legality. In contrast, most of the obligations in the Agreement on the Application of Sanitary and Phytosanitary Measures (SPS Agreement) are procedural in character and/or are relatively strongly

[95] *Ibid.*, p. 362.

[96] Agreement on Technical Barriers to Trade 1995, WTO, *The Legal Texts: The results of the Uruguay round of multilateral trade negotiations*, p. 121.

temporally conditioned.[97] For example, Article 2.2 of the SPS Agreement requires that an SPS measure 'is based on scientific principles and is not maintained without sufficient scientific evidence', with Article 5.1 requiring measures to be based on a risk assessment. Subsequent scientific discoveries will probably not be relevant to the question whether a member was in compliance with these obligations at the time of the original proceedings. In any event, although these provisions provide helpful examples, WTO dispute resolution processes do not, to date, encompass revision, instead relying on the availability of the compliance proceedings found in the DSU as referred to below.

(e) *That the fact be of such a nature as to be a decisive factor*

Assuming that the threshold of relevance can be crossed, the 'decisive factor' test must still be met. This is a demanding test. As described by ILC rapporteur, Georges Scelle, the test is whether the new fact that has come to light 'makes it appear that, had the judges known it, they would have made a different award'.[98] Applications for revision have failed the 'decisive factor' test in the past.[99] In a dispute where it has been understood at the time of the original judgment that the relevant science is uncertain, assessing the decisiveness of a new fact may be a particularly complex task. New scientific 'facts' will generally take the form of new scientific evidence or research, and so the importance of the new fact will usually be a matter of degree. Such new facts are unlikely to be determinative of the propositions they support but they may still be of such a nature as to be decisive factors in a legal dispute.

A related question is whether a Court may revisit and extend its interpretations of legal rules in the light of subsequent facts. Discoveries of radical importance could alter the extent to which a court viewed a legal rule as one that was tightly temporally conditioned. For example, an obligation to conduct resource exploitation in accordance with the principle of sustainable development could be interpreted in such a way that a party was regarded as being in compliance with the obligation provided

[97] Agreement on the Application of Sanitary and Phytosanitary Measures, WTO, *The Legal Texts: The results of the Uruguay round of multilateral trade negotiations*, p. 59

[98] Arbitral Procedure, Draft on Arbitral Procedure adopted by the Commission at its Fifth Session, Report by Georges Scelle, Special Rapporteur, UN Doc. A/CN.4/113, (1958) II *Yearbook of the International Law Commission* 1, 12.

[99] Bowett, 'Res judicata', 589. See *Case concerning the Continental Shelf (Tunisia/Libyan Arab Jamahiriya) (Revision)*, paras. 28–40. See also the decision of the Iran–US Claims Tribunal in *Ram Industries*.

that account had been taken of the science as it stood at the time that the exploitation was conducted. However, a court might take a different approach if scientific discovery subsequent to the award made it clear that a valuable global ecosystem was likely to collapse and that, objectively, resource exploitation had not been conducted in accordance with the principle of sustainable development.

(f) Procedural considerations

The adjudication of disputes involving scientific uncertainty may give rise to new questions about the procedures employed for dealing with requests for revision. Although revision is intended to be a streamlined process, it may be necessary for a court to seek expert advice on the status and significance of an asserted new fact. Under Article 99 of the Rules of the International Court of Justice, the application procedure for revision is to be conducted in writing, with the opportunity for the other party also to make written observations. This precludes the receipt of oral input from scientists by the Court and forces it to rely on written evidence. This procedure might need reassessing, especially given the benefit of oral consultation with experts in cases involving scientific uncertainty. As noted earlier, where experts are to be consulted, it will probably then be particularly helpful to join proceedings on the question of admissibility with proceedings on the substance. However, together with the potential need to allow re-argument on mixed questions of fact and law, it has to be accepted that a meaningful consultation with experts that includes party participation will result in revision proceedings that may come close to full-blown substantive proceedings. Is revision the most appropriate procedure for dealing with a case of these dimensions? In addressing this question, further factors also call for consideration.

Courts' rules of procedure may specify that an application for revision, as with a request for interpretation, be dealt with by the same body as the original proceedings. Under the Rules of the International Court of Justice, if the original judgment was given by the full court, a request for revision is to be heard by the full Court. If the original judgment was given by a chamber, a request is to be heard by the chamber if at all possible.[100] In the case of decisions made by the International Court of Justice or the International Tribunal for the Law of the Sea, which are

[100] Rules of Procedure of the International Court of Justice, Article 100(1); Rules of the International Tribunal for the Law of the Sea, Article 129(1) and (2).

large, standing bodies, the electoral system should help ensure that a proportion of the original members remain at the time when an application or revision is received. While it would be most desirable for the membership of the body hearing the request for revision to be identical with the membership of the body that made the original decision, a partial overlap in membership will be more helpful than none at all. For decisions made by chambers of the International Court of Justice or the International Tribunal for the Law of the Sea, the situation may be more difficult. For example, at the time of revision proceedings in the *Land, Island and Maritime Frontier Dispute* only one member of the original chamber of the International Court of Justice still survived, and his term of office was due to terminate.[101] At the request of the parties, a new chamber was formed.[102] Even in such circumstances, the principle of the secrecy of a court's deliberations would prevent judges from examining the records of the deliberations at the time of the original proceedings.[103] For a decision by a tribunal that is not a standing body, revision may not be possible after the point in time where the tribunal has become *functus officio*. A new tribunal may have to be constituted.[104] The new body may or may not include any members of the original tribunal. The inclusion of original members is desirable, but depends on their availability.[105] In ICSID arbitration it has proved possible to reconstitute the original tribunal on a number of occasions.[106]

As a result of these problems with the membership of bodies tasked with handling requests for revision, it has been asked whether the ten-year period within which parties may lodge a request for revision by the International Court of Justice may be too long.[107] In addressing the question of the appropriate timeframe within which to permit revision, the desirability of revision in case of subsequent scientific

101 Rosenne, *Interpretation, Revision and Other Recourse*, p. 181.

102 *Land, Island and Maritime Frontier Dispute (Revision)*, Order of 27 November 2002, ICJ Reports 2002 618.

103 Statute of the International Court of Justice, Article 54(3); Rosenne, *Interpretation, Revision and Other Recourse*, p. 182.

104 ICSID Convention, Article 50(2). See also ICSID Rules of Procedure for Arbitration Proceedings, *ICSID Convention, Regulations and Rules* (Washington: International Centre for the Settlement of Investment Disputes 2006), Rule 51(3), permitting a new tribunal to be appointed if necessary.

105 Schreuer, *The ICSID Convention*, pp. 875–6, 886.

106 *Ibid.*, p. 886.

107 Rosenne, *The Law and Practice*, p. 1629. See also Rosenne, *Interpretation, Revision and Other Recourse*, pp. 13–14; Brown, *A Common Law*, p. 183.

developments needs to be taken into account, as well as the pace of scientific research, while taking into account also the parties' need for closure and the international legal need for finality in adjudicatory decision-making. If revision is to be retained as an option for dealing with scientific developments subsequent to a case, it would be better on balance to retain the ten-year period. A timeframe that was too short would decrease international courts' capacity to revise their decisions and could remove their capacity to do so in circumstances where an apparently incorrect decision was still relatively recent. The credibility of international adjudication might suffer, and injustice result. New proceedings might have to be instituted that otherwise would not have been required.

(g) *Assessing the utility of revision in scientific cases*

An overall assessment of the utility and appropriateness of using the revision procedure to deal with subsequent scientific developments in disputes involving scientific uncertainty suggests there will be a role for revision only in a limited number of cases. As discussed above, there will be many cases where subsequent scientific developments are not likely to be relevant within the framework of the legal obligations that apply to the parties' dispute, particularly where these are heavily temporally conditioned obligations.[108] Even if a court or tribunal, had it been better informed, might have been inspired to interpret the parties' legal obligations differently, it may be too late to revisit such issues. Even where subsequent scientific developments are relevant, in many cases a proper consideration of the new facts would require hearing argument from the parties and consultation with scientific experts. Depending on the time that has elapsed, this may have to take place before a differently constituted tribunal. If a further judicial contribution to resolving a dispute is to be sought, other procedures might be more suitable than revision proceedings.

[108] See pp. 283–4. Although see, in a different context, Dissenting Opinion of Judge Weeramantry, *Request for an Examination of the Situation*, 339–41. Concerned that it would be 'an exercise in unreality' to address the issues before the Court in 1995 on the basis of the scientific knowledge of 1974, Judge Weeramantry considered that the question of whether the basis of the earlier judgment had been affected had to be approached in the light of all that was known scientifically at the time of the later proceedings.

Nullity

The vital contribution made to international stability of habitual acceptance of judicial and arbitral awards can readily be accepted. However, as a general principle and a matter of basic logic, surely there will be circumstances where the validity of an arbitral award is vitiated, and such an award simply does not constitute an international legal award at all?[109] Insisting on the implementation of all awards, including invalid awards, might not help ensure stability and orderliness as effectively as making allowance for invalidity in the rare cases where this is warranted. At the same time, it has to be recognised that a proliferation of unilateral declarations of nullity would be unhelpful. Argentina's unilateral declaration of the nullity of the unanimous *Beagle Channel* award, in which the five arbitrators were all members of the International Court of Justice, may be considered.[110]

The problem of unilateral determinations of nullity has long provoked deep-seated concerns about admitting the concept of nullity.[111] However, the potential for unilateral declarations of nullity can be curbed through the development of institutionalised procedures for dealing with claims of nullity and validity.[112] Indeed, the view presently prevails that a party is entitled to continue to rely on an award until such time as its nullity has been declared by an independent judicial authority.[113] Processes for determining nullity require the identification of a suitable body to investigate and pronounce upon a claim. In relation to disputes involving uncertain science, it is clear that considerable legal expertise may be necessary, particularly in cases involving issues where there are mixed questions of fact and law.

[109] As Judge Winiarski remarked in his individual opinion in *Awards of the Administrative Tribunal*, where an award is subject to defects that render it void 'it is a natural and inevitable application of a general principle existing in all law ... [that it] ... is incapable of producing legal effects ...'. *Effect of Awards of Compensation made by the United Nations Administrative Tribunal, Advisory Opinion of 13 July 1954*, ICJ Reports 1954 47, Individual Opinion of Judge Winiarski, 65. See also Carlston, *The Process of International Arbitration*, 223.

[110] Paulsson, 'ICSID's achievements', 387. *Beagle Channel Arbitration (Argentina* v. *Chile)* Award of 18 February 1977, 52 ILR 93.

[111] Reisman, *Nullity and Revision*, pp. 29–30, 35, 41–2. Brierly, 'The Hague Conventions', 116.

[112] Of course, a unilateral declaration of nullity can be effective only if consistent with the substantive legal rules relating to nullity. Carlston, *The Process of International Arbitration*, pp. 213–19.

[113] Whether this is by virtue of any legal rule is unclear, but among the governing principles is the rule that no one should be a judge in their own cause. Cheng, *General Principles*, p. 372.

(a) The process for determining nullity under the ICSID Convention

Awards under the ICSID Convention are subject to a specialised annulment regime. In this scheme any complaint about nullity will have to be determined through annulment proceedings before the complainant may regard an award as null. Even though the logic of the Convention's grounds for annulment indicate that an award that is null is a nullity *ab initio*, parties to the ICSID Convention regard the moment of annulment as the point when nullification takes place.[114] The allocation of the burden of proof in annulment proceedings is seldom addressed, but there has been some reference to the notion that doubts about whether a ground for annulment has been established should be resolved in favour of the validity of the previous award: *in favorem validitatis sententiae*.[115] The notion has been criticised as unfounded, but with little discussion of alternative approaches to the allocation of the burden.[116] In a case that is resubmitted following an annulment, the burden of proof will be allocated according to the usual rules.

Annulment under the ICSID Convention may be sought on the grounds that a tribunal was not properly constituted, that it manifestly exceeded its powers, that there was corruption on the part of a member of the tribunal, that there has been a departure from a fundamental rule of procedure (including the rules on burden of proof)[117] or that the award has failed to state the reasons on which it is based.[118] An application for annulment is to be made within 120 days of the rendering of

[114] Note the terms of the ICSID Convention, Article 52(5).

[115] *Klöckner* v. *Republic of Cameroon*, Decision on Annulment, 3 May 1985, 2 ICSID Reports 95 (hereafter *Klöckner* v. *Republic of Cameroon*, Decision on Annulment), 116; Reisman, 'The breakdown', 761, 795.

[116] For criticism of the notion *in favorem validitatis sententiae*, Schreuer, *The ICSID Convention*, p. 905; *Soufraki* v. *UAE*, Decision on Annulment, 5 June 2007 (hereafter *Soufraki* v. *UAE*, Decision on Annulment), para. 22, decision available at http://ita.law.uvic.ca/. See also Gaillard, 'Centre international', 188, considering this notion essentially a rhetorical one and open to question, both within and beyond ICSID arbitration, but not addressing the matter of identifying an appropriate basis on which to allocate the burden.

[117] See Schreuer's discussion on the Decision on Annulment of the award in the resubmitted case in *Klöckner* v. *Cameroon*. *Klöckner* v. *Cameroon*, Resubmitted Case: Decision on Annulment, 17 May 1990 (hereafter *Klöckner* v. *Republic of Cameroon*, Resubmitted Case: Decision on Annulment), para. 6.80. Schreuer, *The ICSID Convention*, pp. 992–4.

[118] ICSID Convention, Article 52(1). Although the Convention's list of grounds for annulment is understood to be exhaustive, the interchangeability of the grounds in practice demonstrates that their boundaries are somewhat blurred. Schreuer, *The ICSID Convention*, pp. 1047 and 1048.

the award, with a longer timeframe in case of alleged corruption,[119] and will be considered by an ad hoc Committee appointed from the Panel of Arbitrators by the Chairman of the ICSID Administrative Council,[120] in practice on the recommendation of the Centre's Secretary-General.[121] The ad hoc Committee has the authority to annul the award,[122] but arguably may refuse to do so where the defect has insufficient material impact.[123] A prior award is not to be impeached for failing to address arguments or evidence that were not put before the original tribunal.[124] Nor are annulment proceedings an opportunity merely for raising new arguments against the other party's case. When an award is annulled, in whole or in part, resubmission may be sought by one or both parties. New claims may not be introduced when a case is resubmitted, nor new counterclaims.[125] The new tribunal may consider claims and arguments that had been put before the original tribunal but on which there had been no ruling.[126]

New facts that emerge during ICSID annulment proceedings may serve as the basis for annulment provided that a party so requests, and that such facts warrant annulment.[127] If new facts were to emerge after a successful application for annulment they could be taken into account by a new tribunal hearing the resubmitted case,[128] but decisions on annulment are not subject to the Convention's provisions for revision. Nor is a decision on annulment subject to annulment under the scheme in the ICSID Convention,[129] as the Convention is designed to avoid the consequences of such an ongoing chain of review.[130] However there are instances where a request for annulment is made in relation to an award in a resubmitted case.[131] Where the ground of error is not

[119] ICSID Convention, Article 52(2). [120] *Ibid.*, Article 52(3).

[121] Paulsson, 'ICSID's achievements', 392. [122] ICSID Convention, Article 52(3).

[123] Schreuer, *The ICSID Convention*, pp. 1035–40; Reisman, 'The breakdown', 792.

[124] *Patrick Mitchell* v. *Democratic Republic of the Congo*, Decision on Annulment of 1 November 2006 (hereafter *Mitchell* v. *Democratic Republic of the Congo*, Decision on Annulment), paras. 58, 62. Decision available at http://ita.law.uvic.ca.

[125] *AMCO* v. *Indonesia*, Resubmitted Case, Decision on Jurisdiction, 567.

[126] Schreuer, *The ICSID Convention*, pp. 1093; *AMCO* v. *Indonesia*, Resubmitted Case, Decision on Jurisdiction, 555.

[127] Schreuer, *The ICSID Convention*, pp. 1053–4. [128] *Ibid.*, pp. 209, 1056, 1093.

[129] *Ibid.*, pp. 1056. Supplementation and rectification remain possible.

[130] Reisman, 'The breakdown', 797–8.

[131] For early examples, see *Klöckner* v. *Republic of Cameroon*, Resubmitted Case: Decision on Annulment; *AMCO* v. *Indonesia*, Resubmitted Case: Decision on Annulment, 3 December 1992, 9 ICSID Reports 9 (hereafter *AMCO* v. *Indonesia*, Resubmitted Case: Decision on Annulment).

invoked at all in an application for annulment, it has been held that an ad hoc committee has no independent or inherent jurisdiction to inquire into factual dimensions of a case, even where these may be of concern as a matter of principle.[132]

(b) Bases of nullity in international arbitration and adjudication more generally

The true foundation of the nullity of international judicial and arbitral awards lies arguably in the concept of *excès de pouvoir*,[133] a term borrowed from French law of the revolutionary period accompanying the introduction of Montesquieu's separation of powers.[134] *Excès de pouvoir*, or excess of powers, has long been recognised in international arbitral and judicial practice as a basis for nullity. The underlying logic is that wherever a decision-making body has gone beyond exercising the role entrusted to it, its actions have no validity. A decision-making body may have exceeded its mandate in various ways, but they all boil down to a failure to execute the task at hand with respect for the limits of this task. As Reisman observes 'a purported award which is accomplished in ways inconsistent with the shared contractual expectations of the parties is something to which they had not agreed'.[135] Arguably, an error of fact or law of sufficient significance to vitiate the validity of an award or judgment is an instance of *excès de pouvoir*.[136]

Alternatively, error of fact and error of law have been identified as potentially specific and independent bases of nullity.[137] Of the two, error of fact is less frequently referred to, particularly within the continental European tradition, and there is a greater lack of consensus about whether it constitutes a basis of nullity.[138] Yet both continental and common law writers have often considered 'unjust', 'inequitable' or 'unconscionable' awards to be subject to nullification, and such

[132] *RSM Production Corporation* v. *Granada*, Decision on RSM Production Corporation's Application for a Preliminary Ruling of 29 October 2009, para. 26. Decision available at http://ita.law.uvic.ca.

[133] Reisman, *Nullity and Revision*, p. 247.

[134] Balasko, 'Causes de nullité', 151.

[135] Reisman, 'The breakdown', 745.

[136] Reisman, *Nullity and Revision*, p. 424; Castberg, 'L'Excès de pouvoir', 361; Vattel, 'The law of nations', p. 223, suggesting that arbitrators divest themselves of their character as such when they render a decision that is evidently unjust and unreasonable. Cf. *Soufraki* v. *UAE*, Decision on Annulment, para. 87.

[137] Cheng, *General Principles*, p. 361.

[138] Reisman, *Nullity and Revision*, pp. 424, 430. Cheng, *General Principles*, p. 363.

awards could readily include awards based on serious factual errors.[139] In 1877 the Institute of International Law took the view that an arbitral award was null in case of 'essential' error.[140]

One early draft set of rules for arbitral proceedings did also include express provision for nullification in case of error of fact, the *Projet Corsi*.[141] This provision specifically envisaged that there may be facts that cannot be proved until after the publication of an award. Reisman points out that the *Corsi* provision as a whole relates to unknown facts, rather than misappreciation, or misinterpretation, of facts.[142] A serious misappreciation of fact, serious enough to vitiate an award, might raise complex difficulties. Legal reasoning built on fundamentally misappreciated facts might be distorted,[143] and it might be necessary for the tribunal reviewing the case to look closely into mixed questions of fact and law in order to assess the situation. There is a concern that what will eventuate is a trial *de novo*.[144] Mistake of fact

[139] Reisman, *Nullity and Revision*, pp. 424–5. See also Carlston, *The Process of International Arbitration*, p. 189. Cf. Cheng, *General Principles*, pp. 357–61, taking the view that manifest and essential error, error through lack of essential evidence, or fraud of the parties and collusion of witnesses, provide only a cause for the voidability of an award. In contrast, he says, the nullity of an award results automatically from lack or excess of competence, non-observance of vital procedural principles, or fraud and corruption on the part of a tribunal.

[140] Article 27, *Projet de Réglement pour la Procédure Arbitrale Internationale*, Institut de Droit International, 7 *Revue de Droit International et Législation Comparé* (1875) 277, at 282. What was intended by 'essential error' remained vague, however. Balasko, 'Causes de nullité', 133. See also Dissenting Opinion of Judge Urrutia Holguin in *King of Spain* (details from footnote 164), 234 and 238.

[141] Article 40 of the *Projet Corsi* read:

> c) erreur de fait – à condition que la sentence soit fondée expressément sur l'existence ou sur le défaut d'un acte ou d'un fait, dont l'existence ou le défaut n'ait pas été observé avant le tribunal ou n'ait pu être prouvé tandis qu'après la publication de l'arrêt on réussit à en donner de telles preuves que toutes les parties doivent les admettre comme décisives.

Article 40, *Rules for International Arbitration*, Professor the Marquis Corsi, in Evans Darby, William *International Tribunals: A collection of the various schemes which have been propounded and of instances since 1815*, 1897; Reisman, *Nullity and Revision*, p. 425.

[142] Reisman, *Nullity and Revision*, p. 425. A distinction also drawn by Cheng, *General Principles*, p. 364.

[143] Reisman, *Nullity and Revision*, p. 425.

[144] *Ibid.*, p. 426. In the 1910 *Orinoco Steamship Company* case President Lammasch stated that 'if an arbitral decision could be disputed on the ground of erroneous appreciation, appeal and revision, which the Conventions of the Hague of 1899 and 1907 made it their object to avert, would be the general rule'. *Award of the Tribunal of Arbitration, Constituted under an Agreement signed at Caracas February 13th 1909 between the United States*

is not generally recognised in national arbitral laws even as a ground for appeal.[145]

Determining the reach of 'error of fact' as a basis for nullity is indeed awkward. This may help explain why it has achieved relatively little recognition. Where error of fact *is* identified as a basis of nullity, in the *Corsi* draft, there is a requirement that subsequent proof of a point of fact must be such that the parties agree that this proof is decisive. This clause is probably intended to try to ensure the better workability of the provision as a whole and to remove the need for a full investigation by a judicial body. Whether such a clause would function well in practice is open to question, as the parties might not agree that the fact has been decisively proved. Yet it seems that tribunals will nevertheless recognise and respond to significant factual error in line with the remarks of the Permanent Court of International Justice in its 1924 Advisory Opinion, *Monastery of Saint Naoum*[146] and the approach taken by the German–United States Mixed Claim Commission.[147]

Error of law is even less established than error of fact as a basis of nullity.[148] Occasionally, error of law has been accepted as a basis for revision where there is a 'manifest error of law', for example if a relevant treaty were overlooked.[149] As with error of fact, hesitation in accepting error of law as a basis of nullity has been due partly to concern that this could require an investigation into an original tribunal's reasons for its award, precipitating 'a new examination of the case on the merits'.[150] Yet there is clearly scope for international adjudicatory error

of America and the United States of Venezuela, 25 October 1910, 11 UNRIAA 237 (hereafter *Orinoco Steamship Company*), 238–9.

145 Bishop *et al.*, *Foreign Investment Disputes*, p. 505.

146 *Question of the Monastery at St Naoum (Albanian Frontier)* Advisory Opinion, PCIJ Series B, No. 9, 1924, 21–2.

147 *Lehigh Valley Railroad Company*, 188.

148 Reisman, *Nullity and Revision*, p. 430.

149 Lowe, 'Res judicata', 40. *Trail Smelter Arbitration (US* v. *Canada)*, 3 UNRIAA 1938, 1955 and 1957; *Klöckner* v. *Republic of Cameroon*, Decision on Annulment, para. 61; see also *Lehigh Valley Railroad Company* and *George Moore* v. *Mexico*, No. 701, 26 July 1871, 2 Moore, *International Arbitrations*, 1357. Cf. Commentary to the draft Convention on Arbitral Procedure stating clearly that '[r]evision may not be justified by an allegation of material error of law', p. 102; also the practice of the Mixed Arbitral Tribunals established after the First World War: '[o]nly the insufficiency of the information as to the facts of a case would give rise to [revision], not that the decision was illy judged in failing to consider a doctrine of law or to appreciate in an exact manner the facts presented . . .'. Carlston, *The Process of International Arbitration*, pp. 239–40.

150 Carlston, *The Process of International Arbitration*, p. 192. The occurrence of 'serious errors in the application of substantive law' was rejected for this reason as a ground for annulment during the drafting of the ICSID Convention.

of a scale or complexity that cannot be satisfactorily addressed through the mere modification of an award by process of revision. A distinction might be drawn between an erroneous legal proposition that forms the foundation of a decision and an error on a lesser scale that can be addressed without undermining the award as a whole.[151]

There have been various instances since early in arbitral history where awards have been set aside or remained unimplemented due to error of law. For example, in a review of the award in the *Pelletier* case before the US Senate Committee on Foreign Relations it was recommended that the award should not be executed. The *Pelletier* case concerned the attempted abduction and enslavement of Haitian citizens in Haitian waters. The umpire had erred in viewing the direction in the *compromis* to decide the case according to international law as rendering Haitian criminal law irrelevant.[152] Haiti had jurisdiction over a US ship in Haitian waters regardless of whether *Pelletier* had committed piracy *jure gentium* as defined at international law, or had only intended and made preparations to do so. Also in the 1910 *Orinoco Steamship Company* case the Tribunal found to be null that part of the umpire's decision based on an error of law. Transfer of a debt arising due to an extinguished concession granted by the Venezuelan government for navigation of the *Orinoco* had to be distinguished from transfer of the concession itself and did not require formal notice to Venezuela.[153]

In neither of these cases, however, was the error of law clearly identified as such.[154] Indeed, in *Orinoco* the parties' agreement required the original award to have been based on 'absolute equity', and the finding at the review stage was that the umpire's legal mistake as to what it was that had been transferred had produced a decision that was not based on absolute equity.[155] Accordingly, the tribunal had acted outside its jurisdiction. In the *Pelletier* case, US Secretary of State Bayard, who carried out the review, explained that the US could not have intended, under the terms of the request for arbitration, to have

[151] Fiore, *Nouveau Droit International Public*, p. 644; *Soufraki* v. *UAE*, Decision on Annulment, para. 86, also 99, 101. See also the *Drier* case, US–Germany Mixed Claims Commission, 29 July 1935, VIII UNRIAA 127, 140–58 and reference to 'palpable error' by the umpire of the same Commission in *Lehigh Valley Railroad Company*, 188.

[152] *Pelletier's case*, 1887–8, Foreign Relations of the United States, 593.

[153] *Orinoco Steamship Company*, 239–40.

[154] Reisman, *Nullity and Revision*, p. 435.

[155] As emphasised by Feldman, 'The annulment proceedings', 102.

deprived Haiti of territorial jurisdiction in connection with slave-trading or piracy.[156]

Successive ad hoc committees considering applications for annulment under the ICSID Convention have emphasised that annulment is intended as a review only of the legitimacy of the process of a tribunal's decision-making, and not as an appeal on matters of substance.[157] On this basis neither errors of fact nor errors of law will lead to annulment. The view has been taken that error of fact cannot even give rise to a manifest excess of powers,[158] and a proposal to include a ground of 'manifestly incorrect application of the law' was defeated by seventeen votes to eight in the Legal Committee advising the Executive Directors of the World Bank during the preparation of the draft Convention.[159] Misapplication or erroneous application of the law, '*error in judicando*', is distinguished from failure to apply the proper law.[160] While error of law has not been considered within ICSID to constitute an independent basis for annulment, there is general agreement that failure to apply the proper law may amount to an excess of powers constituting a ground for annulment.[161] A clear distinction between failure to apply the proper law and its erroneous application will not always be easy to sustain.[162] It does seem that, if it is serious enough, an error in the application of the law can amount to a manifest excess of powers. The threshold has not yet been identified,[163] but will potentially be crossed where the misapplication or

[156] *Pelletier's case*, 605–6. Further early instances of nullity based on error of law are referred to by Professor Reisman. Reisman, *Nullity and Revision*, pp. 440–1.

[157] Schreuer, *The ICSID Convention*, pp. 901, 902, 913–15. See, inter alia, *M.C.I. Power Group L.C. and New Turbine Inc.* v. *Republic of Ecuador*, Decision on Annulment of 19 October 2009, decision available at ita.law.uvic.ca (hereafter *M.C.I. Power Group*), para. 24; *MINE* v. *Guinea*, Decision on Annulment 22 December 1989, 4 ICSID Reports 85, para. 4.04. *CDC Group plc* v. *Republic of Seychelles*, Decision on Annulment, 29 June 2005, 11 ICSID Reports 237, paras. 34–5; *Empresas Lucchetti S. A. and Lucchetti Peru, S. A.* v. *Republic of Peru*, Decision on Annulment, 5 September 2007, para. 97, decision available at http://ita.law.uvic.ca.

[158] *Soufraki* v. *UAE*, Decision on Annulment, para. 87, decision available at http://ita.law.uvic.ca.

[159] Broches, 'Observations', 329. [160] *M.C.I. Power Group*, paras. 42, 54.

[161] Schreuer, *The ICSID Convention*, pp. 955–64. Cf. Feldman, 'The annulment proceedings'. For an antecedent, see Balasko, 'Causes de nullité', 135.

[162] Schreuer, *The ICSID Convention*, p. 964. *AMCO* v. *Indonesia*, Decision on Annulment, 16 May 1986, 1 ICSID Reports 509; Broches, 'Observations on the finality of ICSID awards', 362.

[163] '... une grande incertitude demeure sur le seuil à partir duquel l'erreur commise dans l'application du droit deviant un excès de pouvoir'. Rambaud, 'L'Annulation', 264.

error of law is 'of such a magnitude as to amount to a veritable non-application of the proper law as a whole'.[164]

However, the question is a delicate one. The early decisions on requests for annulment in *Klöckner* v. *Cameroon* and *AMCO* v. *Indonesia* were criticised for not maintaining that distinction, and for engaging in the substance of the law. The 2006 decision in *Mitchell* v. *DR Congo* was likewise criticised.[165] In the 2007 case of *CMS Gas* v. *Argentina* even the manifest error of law that had occurred was not regarded as a manifest excess of powers.[166] The ad hoc Committee was very clear that its mandate under the ICSID Convention was constrained, and that it was not tasked with deciding an appeal from the original award.

Applying international law in such a way as to violate certain fundamental rules of substance (including peremptory norms such as the prohibitions on slavery and genocide) or certain important structural rules (such as the principles of *pacta sunt servanda* or the rules on state responsibility) might constitute an excess of powers.[167] A particular light is also arguably cast on the issue where the subject matter of a judgment or award concerns globally shared interests, such as interests in ecological protection or the conservation of migratory species. A restrictive approach to review may be inappropriate here.[168] By way of analogy it might be noted that under English arbitral law the right of appeal in case of serious error applies where, inter alia, the legal question involved is one of 'general public importance'.[169] Indeed, Professor Reisman has argued that delineation of the grounds for nullity should

[164] Schreuer, *The ICSID Convention*, p. 965, citing *AMCO* v. *Indonesia*, Resubmitted Case: Decision on Annulment, para. 7.19. See also *Soufraki* v. *UAE*, Decision on Annulment, para. 86. However, see the position taken in *MTD* v. *Chile*, Decision on Annulment of 21 March 2007, 13 ICSID Reports 500, para. 47.

[165] *Mitchell* v. *Democratic Republic of the Congo*, Decision on Annulment; Walid, 'Two nebulous ICSID features', 302–4.

[166] *CMS Gas Transmission Company* v. *Argentine Republic*, Decision on Annulment, 25 September 2007, decision available at http://ita.law.uvic.ca.

[167] Schreuer, *The ICSID Convention*, pp. 566–7, 975–6. Cf. proposal of the International Law Association's Committee on International Commercial Arbitration that the public policy bar to enforcement of arbitral awards, as seen in the UNCITRAL Model Law on Arbitration, should incorporate international public policy including peremptory norms of international law. ILA Committee on International Commercial Arbitration's Interim Report on Public Policy as a Bar to Enforcement of International Arbitral Awards (London Conference, 2000), as referred to by Redfern *et al.*, *Law and Practice*, p. 498. Simpson and Fox, *International Arbitration*, p. 257.

[168] Reisman, 'The supervisory jurisdiction', 231.

[169] s. 69(3)(c)(ii) Arbitration Act 1996 (UK).

be informed not by a contractual, but rather by an institutional view of international adjudication.[170]

(c) *The possibility of developing new processes for determining nullity beyond the ICSID system*

The International Law Commission expended some effort in its work on arbitral procedure towards establishing a general conception of international arbitration in which it was understood that authoritative declarations of nullity could be made through a process involving objective assessment by a disinterested third party.[171] However, no automatic general jurisdiction of this sort has been adopted, and procedures for determining nullity are still not incorporated routinely in documents governing international dispute resolution, apart from under the ICSID Convention. On limited occasions states have requested the International Court of Justice to consider the validity of an arbitral award,[172] and discussion continues over the idea of an international court of arbitral awards dealing with disputes about the validity of awards.[173]

Historically, the League of Nations had some involvement in the review of arbitral awards. A proposal drawn up by Colonel House in 1918 envisaged the appeal of arbitral awards to the League, with the setting aside of such awards to be determined by the League. Where this

[170] Reisman, *Nullity and Revision*, pp. 65–6, 226.

[171] Arbitral Procedure, Draft on Arbitral Procedure adopted by the Commission at its Fifth Session, Report by Georges Scelle, Special Rapporteur, UN Doc. A/CN.4/109, (1957) II *Yearbook of the International Law Commission* 1, Articles 29–31; Arbitral Procedure, Draft on Arbitral Procedure adopted by the Commission at its Fifth Session, Report by Georges Scelle, Special Rapporteur, UN Doc. A/CN.4/113, (1958) II *Yearbook of the International Law Commission* 1, Article 35. An early draft of the provision on annulment in the ICSID Convention was based on Article 35.

[172] *Arbitral Award made by the King of Spain on 23 December 1906 (Hondura* v. *Nicaragua)*, Judgment of 18 November 1960, ICJ Rep 1960, 192; *Case concerning the Arbitral Award of 31 July 1989 (Guinea-Bissau* v. *Senegal)*, Judgment of 12 November 1991, ICJ Rep 1991 53. Rosenne, *Interpretation, Revision and Other Recourse*, pp. 145–54. Also, provision for review by the ICJ was earlier incorporated in the statute of the UN Administrative Tribunal. Reisman, *Nullity and Revision*, pp. 69–72. However, this provision was removed in 1995 on the basis it had not proved to be a constructive or useful aspect of the statute.

[173] See e.g. the proposal by Schwebel, 'The creation', 115–23. See also Rosenne, 'The International Court' and Reisman 'The supervisory jurisdiction'. In a context such as applications for annulment of investment disputes under ICSID, there is scope for creation of a type of 'super' annulment body through the consistent appointment by the Secretary-General of the same individuals to serve on the ad hoc committees that handle the applications. Reisman, 'The breakdown', 804–5.

occurred, the draft provided for submission of the same legal dispute to a new arbitral tribunal for a final and binding decision with no further right of appeal.[174] The same provision was included in President Wilson's draft Covenant.[175] In 1927 in the *Hungarian–Rumanian Land Dispute* (the *Optants* case) the Council of the League reviewed a preliminary ruling of the Rumanian-Hungarian Mixed Arbitral Tribunal. A Committee of Three, comprising the representatives of the United Kingdom, Chile and Japan, was appointed by the Council to make a report on the issues raised.[176] The Committee of Three consulted the jurists of six delegations present in Geneva.[177] The Council's action was heavily criticised, and the reasons behind it remain unclear.[178] The question of the competence of the Rumanian–Hungarian Mixed Arbitral Tribunal would have gone to the Permanent Court of International Justice but that Rumania rejected Hungary's proposal that this be done[179] and the Council failed to refer the case for an advisory opinion due to an assumption that this could not be done without the parties' agreement.[180]

Following the *Optants* case, the Polish member of a committee of jurists appointed by the League of Nations to consider the revision of the Statute of the Permanent Court proposed in 1928 that the Permanent Court be endowed with appeal jurisdiction in relation to international arbitral awards, including in relation to claims that arbitral tribunals had exceeded their jurisdiction,[181] a proposal taken forward by Finland the following year.[182] The Finnish proposal was referred to the Council by the Assembly, and thence to a committee of jurists who proposed a draft protocol to invest the Permanent Court with such jurisdiction. However, the proposal did not progress because

[174] Reisman, *Nullity and Revision*, p. 48, citing Miller, D. H., *The Drafting of the Covenant* (1928), I, p. 12; II, pp. 7, 9.

[175] *Ibid.*, p. 50, citing S. Doc. No. 106; 66th Cong., 1st Sess., *Hearings before the Senate Committee on Foreign Relations*, at 1167 (1919).

[176] Report of the Committee of Three (1927) 8 *League of Nations Official Journal* 1379 at 1382.

[177] Reisman, *Nullity and Revision*, pp. 691. [178] For discussion, *ibid.*, pp. 686–97.

[179] (1927) 8 *League of Nations Official Journal* 1379 at 1384.

[180] Reisman, *Nullity and Revision*, pp. 53.

[181] (1929) 10 *League of Nations Official Journal* 1125. Reisman, 'The breakdown', 752; Carlston, *The Process of International Arbitration*, pp. 247–8. Rosenne, *Interpretation, Revision and Other Recourse*, pp. 70, 83–5, 145–61.

[182] Secretariat's Commentary, 112–3. In 1929 the *Institut de Droit International* also recommended such a role for the Permanent Court of International Justice. Resolutions Votées par l'Institut au Cours de la XXXVI Session, Annuaire de L'Institut de Droit International (Brussels, 1929), vol. 2, 304.

of deep concerns that establishing such a procedure might overly encourage claims of nullity.[183]

As mentioned above, the proposal for a general review jurisdiction was picked up again by the International Law Commission, and incorporated in Article 31 of the Commission's Draft Convention on Arbitral Procedure, providing that the International Court of Justice would determine an assertion of nullity, upon the application of either party.[184] This attempt to institutionalise procedures for the determination of nullity did not succeed either. Indeed, of the five permanent members of the Security Council only China supported the proposal,[185] and the General Assembly decided against adopting the International Law Commission's draft Convention. Thus any procedure for determining the alleged nullity of an international court's or tribunal's judgment or award would have to be considered under special ad hoc arrangements.

(d) Procedural considerations

If proceedings seeking a determination of nullity were to be launched, there would be some efficiency in combining these proceedings with proceedings to determine a resubmitted case. This would especially be so where expert assistance is needed for both sets of proceedings. An example of a case where the tasks of determining nullity and of re-examining the merits were entrusted to the same body is found in the *Orinoco* arbitration.[186] Combined proceedings will not be possible for disputes addressed under the ICSID Convention. Under ICSID, annulment proceedings are entirely distinct from a subsequent rehearing of an annulled case, being heard by an entirely separate and differently constituted body, in the form of an ad hoc committee.[187] Formally, it is

[183] Reisman, *Nullity and Revision*, pp 53–60.

[184] Arbitral Procedure, Draft on Arbitral Procedure adopted by the Commission at its Fifth Session, Report by Georges Scelle, Special Rapporteur, UN Doc. A/CN.4/109, (1957) II *Yearbook of the International Law Commission* 1, Articles 29–31.

[185] Reisman, 'The supervisory jurisdiction', 223.

[186] In the *Orinoco* case the tribunal was requested by the parties to address whether the previous award was void, and then, if so, to reassess the merits of the case and to substitute its own findings for those of the previous umpire. *Orinoco Steamship Company*, 234.

[187] Similarly, under Article 31 of the ILC draft Convention, the role of the International Court of Justice was limited to that of cassation, and no power was envisaged to adjudicate the case *de novo* on the merits. Limiting the Court's role in this way was expected to help overcome objections that a hierarchy of courts was being established, and that the independence of arbitral tribunals would be affected. Secretariat's Commentary, 115. Note, however, the provision in the draft Protocol seen in the 1931

of course necessary to decide to set aside an award before re-deciding a case. However, if an agreement between the parties could be reached, both written and oral proceedings could be structured in such a way as to allow the tribunal a natural progression from one task into the next.

Who will bear the burden of proof in nullity proceedings? In general arbitral and judicial practice under public international law, the notion of the presumed validity of an original decision may have slightly less power than it does within the ICSID system,[188] where the annulment process is accepted as the sole authoritative determinant of nullity. However, arguably the notion *in favorem validitatis sententiae* still provides the best anchor for the allocation of the burden of proof, recognising the significant authority of international courts' and tribunals' existing awards. Accordingly the burden of proof would lie with the party challenging the validity of the judgment or award. An analogy might be drawn with the presumptions applied in relation to the validity of administrative acts at the national level, *omnia acta rite esse praesumuntur*,[189] although administrative acts at the national level take place within a complex gridwork of accountability under domestic administrative and constitutional law that helps guarantee their correctness. The notion *in favorem validitatis sententiae* operates at a more foundational level, taking the place of the presumption of compliance that undergirds the rules on the allocation of the burden of proof in original proceedings in disputes involving state responsibility.[190]

(e) Assessing the utility of the doctrine of nullity in scientific cases

The doctrine of nullity could potentially be of use in a case where subsequent scientific developments have revealed especially significant previous factual error, particularly if this is closely connected with the court's or tribunal's legal determinations in the original case. As with revision, the crafting of the legal provisions applied in the original case would need to be considered, especially the extent to which they were temporally conditioned.[191] Depending on the relevance of the scientific facts within these legal rules, a decision might not be null at all, but

report of the First Committee, in which the substance of a case might be brought before the Permanent Court of International Justice if the parties did not agree on its resubmission to arbitration within three months of a determination of nullity by the Permanent Court. *Ibid.*, 114.

188 Reisman, *Nullity and Revision*, p. 372. 189 See above, Ch.5, p. 237, note 291.

190 On the role of the presumption of compliance, see above, Ch. 5, pp. 189–90.

191 See above pp. 283–4.

merely outmoded. However, in an appropriate case, seeking a determination of nullity could be an appropriate way to proceed if an award cannot be fixed up through the revision procedure and new proceedings are required. There is, though, a vital difference between employing the revision process and employing the doctrine of nullity. If a claim for nullity were successful, but the dispute was not automatically resubmitted for adjudication, the result would potentially be to leave the parties' legal dispute unresolved unless fresh proceedings were instituted. In either case, whether it is revision or nullity that is relied upon, the scope of the process will depend on the scope of the legal provisions that were applicable in the original proceedings, including their temporal scope.

Conclusion

Neither revision proceedings nor requests for a determination of nullity cater well for the envisaged problem of a judgment in a complex scientific case that requires revisiting because of subsequent scientific developments. The revision process would require adaptation to allow for a reasonably full rehearing more closely resembling an appeal. The doctrine of nullity has not traditionally extended to error of fact. Further, turning to this doctrine might tend to undermine the institution of international adjudicatory dispute settlement rather than reinforce its authority, although this difficulty could perhaps be ameliorated if resubmission of a case were expected as a matter of course. In addition the lack of a forum for authoritative determinations of nullity might prove insuperable. As discussed in the Chapter 8, an alternative solution might be for international courts' and tribunals' to incorporate in their decisions a provision for reassessment proceedings in cases where the basis of a prior judgment or award was affected by subsequent scientific developments, and to make institutional provision for reassessment in the case of decisions by ad hoc tribunals.

8 Reassessment proceedings and res judicata

The previous chapter dealt with two procedural avenues that could be helpful in dealing with situations where it is asserted that new scientific evidence requires an international adjudicatory decision to be reconsidered. However, it was found that neither the revision procedure nor the doctrine of nullity offers the type of process that may be needed. This final chapter therefore proposes the institutionalisation of reassessment proceedings for disputes involving scientific uncertainty, drawing on experience in the WTO in the *Continued Suspension of Obligations* cases. Additionally the chapter addresses the application of the rules on res judicata in subsequent proceedings in scientific cases.

'Reassessment' proceedings would be concentrated on assessing an original respondent's compliance with its international legal obligations at the point in time after new scientific research has been invoked. A number of factors point to the need to treat the idea of reassessment with caution. There are obvious problems in providing what would be an opportunity for a reasonably full rehearing. Making use of such a procedure would consume considerable resources, and the procedure is open to abuse. The issues lying behind ongoing litigation in disputes involving potential future harm may in some instances be social and political, and ongoing litigation may not be the best way to resolve them. Further, for all concerned it is most desirable to make an enduring decision at the time of the original proceedings. For example, if investment and clean technology are to be required, this needs to be clear from early on in a commercial venture. Requiring investors to change technology may not be economically feasible at a later stage. However, despite all these factors, it is clear in principle that the possibility of subsequent scientific developments must be accommodated within international legal procedure.

'Reassessment' proceedings

'Reassessment' proceedings would need to assess the parties' compliance with their international legal obligations at the time that the proceedings took place, rather than at the time of the earlier decision. Nor should they be limited to assessing compliance with a prior ruling but rather incorporate assessment of the parties' compliance with all the relevant legal obligations at the time of the reassessment proceedings, based on the facts as they stand at that time. These proceedings would potentially thus encompass a range of new issues. At the same time, some limitations on the scope of the proceedings would be helpful in order to avoid extensive ongoing litigation. Counterclaims ought not to be permissible, although a respondent should be able to put forward arguments and factual allegations distinct from those advanced by a claimant, provided they are relevant.[1] New claims should only be permissible provided they deal with issues inseparably linked, by virtue of the science, with the claims in the original case. Argument in such proceedings should be heard in the usual way, and scientific experts fully consulted as necessary. There should be no time bar. It would be up to the parties to determine the desirability of having the same body decide the case as previously, and to take this into account in deciding how soon to launch proceedings. A hearing by the same body would be more efficient, given the complex questions of fact and law likely to arise and their overlap with the issues addressed in the previous case.

Arguably the best vehicle for ensuring that an international court or tribunal will have jurisdiction to hear a case for reassessment would be a clause to this effect inserted in the original judgment or award. As in the *Nuclear Tests cases (New Zealand* v. *France) (Australia* v. *France)*,[2] a court or tribunal might specify that it would entertain a subsequent request for an examination of the situation in circumstances affecting the basis of the judgment or award. Preferably, this avenue of access to the court or tribunal would be one of last resort. Such a clause should direct the parties in the event of subsequent scientific developments to co-operate with

[1] This is the usual practice in WTO compliance proceedings under Article 21.5 of the DSU, as discussed below. See *Japan – Measures Affecting the Importation of Apples*, Complaint by the United States (WT/DS245), Report of the Appellate Body DSR 2003: IX, 4391 (hereafter *Japan – Apples* ABR), 135–6.

[2] *Nuclear Tests case (Australia* v. *France)*, 20 December 1974, ICJ Reports 1974 253; *Nuclear Tests case (New Zealand* v. *France)*, 20 December 1974, ICJ Reports 1974 457. For an explanation of the cases, see Ch. 2, pp. 54–9.

one another at a technical level and to negotiate with one another on the implementation of their international legal obligations. In this respect, reassessment clauses might resemble the provision on negotiation in the parties' Special Agreement in the *Case concerning the Gabčíkovo-Nagymaros Project (Hungary/Slovakia)*.[3] Where efforts at co-operation and negotiation failed, the court or tribunal would retain adjudicatory authority if the subsequent scientific developments were sufficiently significant to trigger the application of the clause.

As an alternative to provision by international courts and tribunals for reassessment in individual cases, institutionalised provision for such proceedings would be possible. This would be akin to the provision that is made for revision in the Hague Convention and in the governing documents of many international courts and tribunals. A template or model clause could be developed for inclusion in special agreements and other documents including bilateral treaties. This would be especially helpful in relation to the decisions of ad hoc tribunals, who may not themselves be in a position to provide for a revisitation of their awards if they are likely to become *functus officio* and disband in the interim before any reassessment might become necessary.

The advantages and disadvantages of making institutionalised provision for reassessment proceedings in cases involving subsequent scientific developments are similar to those applying to the question of nullity discussed in the previous chapter. In relation to nullity, states have avoided institutionalisation because of concerns that making express provision for determinations of nullity would signal tolerance towards the non-fulfilment of judgments and awards. There is also the problem of the inefficiencies engendered in asking new bodies to acquaint themselves with all the details of cases put forward for reassessment, as discussed in relation to revision proceedings. However, it should be possible to limit institutional provision for reassessment proceedings relatively tightly to instances or categories of case where there is scope for significant scientific developments.

(a) Preliminary proceedings

Where a reassessment clause was invoked, it might be helpful for a court or tribunal to hold preliminary proceedings in order to determine

[3] *Case concerning the Gabčíkovo-Nagymaros Project (Hungary/Slovakia)* Judgment of 25 September 1997, ICJ Reports 1997 7 (hereafter *Gabčíkovo-Nagymaros* case).

whether the science had developed sufficiently such that reassessment proceedings were warranted. These proceedings could be considered as a jurisdictional phase. Alternatively, preliminary proceedings under a reassessment clause could be considered akin to the admissibility procedures that operate in relation to requests for revision. In any event, the preliminary question will be whether the reassessment clause applies in the circumstances of the case. The scientific developments at issue will have to be sufficiently significant to trigger its application.

Would it be valuable to have an expert investigation at the preliminary stage that would determine whether a case should proceed? The idea is attractive, as it would divest international courts and tribunals of the need to reconsider themselves any requests for reassessment that did not survive this investigation. However, such a procedure would potentially suffer from many of the same problems discussed in relation to the two-stage adjudicatory proceedings considered in Chapter 4.[4] The closeness of fact and law would still require a relatively high level of engagement on the part of lawyers and the adjudicators who were to decide the merits of the case, and scientists' appreciations of the normative dimensions of their advice would have to be open to scrutiny. Further, even if the preliminary decision on jurisdiction or admissibility were considered a distinct question, in practice such decisions would probably be closely bound up with the merits. Accordingly, it might be most efficient to adopt one streamlined procedure for dealing with both the preliminary question and the merits.

(b) The WTO approach

The idea of reassessment proceedings draws on the provision seen in Article 21.5 of the WTO Dispute Settlement Understanding (DSU)[5] and elaborated by the Appellate Body in the *Continued Suspension of Obligations* cases. Article 21.5 provides that where there is disagreement as to whether measures taken to comply with recommendations and rulings of the DSB have been adopted or are consistent with the relevant WTO obligations, this dispute is to be decided through recourse to the dispute settlement procedures in the DSU. Usually, compliance proceedings

[4] Ch. 4, pp. 158–65.

[5] Understanding on Rules and Procedures Governing the Settlement of Disputes, WTO, *The Legal Texts: The results of the Uruguay round of multilateral trade negotiations*, p. 354.

under Article 21.5 are taken by an original claimant, but the Appellate Body has made it clear that an original respondent may also take proceedings under Article 21.5.

Article 21.5 has been invoked in scientific disputes in the past. For example, there were compliance proceedings in *Australia - Measures Affecting Importation of Salmon* and *Japan - Measures Affecting the Importation of Apples*. In both these cases, the Article 21.5 proceedings involved a full consultation with scientific experts, with the same written and oral phases seen in the original proceedings.[6] In *Japan - Apples* the same experts were consulted as in the original proceedings, and neither party objected. In *Australia - Salmon* new experts were appointed at the compliance stage. In *Japan - Apples*,[7] Japan submitted four new scientific studies, which, together with the original evidence, were assessed by the compliance panel to determine whether they constituted sufficient scientific evidence to legitimise the Japanese phytosanitary requirements on US apples under Article 2.2 of the WTO Agreement on Sanitary and Phytosanitary Measures (SPS Agreement).[8] Japan's defence was unsuccessful.

(c) The Continued Suspension of Obligations cases

In the growth-promotion hormones dispute the EC, the original respondent, chose initially not to launch Article 21.5 compliance proceedings itself. Instead the EC launched the *Continued Suspension of Obligations* cases, directly challenging the action taken by the US and Canada in suspending trade obligations towards the EC in order to pressure the EC into compliance with the original ruling in *European Communities - Measures Concerning Meat and Meat Products (Hormones)*.[9]

[6] *Japan - Measures Affecting the Importation of Apples*, Complaint by the United States (WT/DS245), Report of the Panel, Recourse to Article 21.5 of the DSU DSR 2005: XVI, 7911 (hereafter *Japan - Apples* Article 21.5 PR); *Australia - Measures Affecting Importation of Salmon*, Complaint by Canada (WT/DS18), Report of the Panel, Recourse to Article 21.5 of the DSU DSR 2000: IV, 2031.

[7] *Japan - Apples* Article 21.5 PR, para. 8.45.

[8] See above, Introduction, p. 13.

[9] *Canada - Continued Suspension of Obligations in the EC - Hormones Dispute*, Complaint by the EC (WT/DS321), Report of the Panel, Report of the Appellate Body, adopted 14 November 2008; *US - Continued Suspension of Obligations in the EC - Hormones Dispute*, Complaint by the EC (WT/DS320), Report of the Panel, Report of the Appellate Body, adopted 14 November 2008 (hereafter respectively *Canada - Continued Suspension* PR, *US - Continued Suspension* PR, and, to refer to the identical paragraphs of the two Appellate Body reports, *Continued Suspension* ABR).

Indeed, the EC argued that the US and Canada were obliged to take compliance proceedings under Article 21.5 against the EC, and that as they had not done so their suspension of concessions to the EC was illegal.

Why did the EC initially choose not to attempt proceedings itself under Article 21.5 to establish its own compliance with the SPS Agreement? The EC's reason was partly connected with the allocation of the burden of proof.[10] In mounting its challenge to the US and Canadian suspension of concessions, the EC argued that it was entitled afresh to the full benefit of a presumption of compliance, despite having been found to be out of compliance with its WTO obligations previously in the original *EC – Hormones* proceedings. The EC argued that it had adopted a new policy, expressed in new instruments, and had done so in good faith.[11] According to the EC, this meant that the original complainants now had to bring an end to their suspension of trade concessions.[12]

In the *Continued Suspension of Obligations* cases the Appellate Body found that it would be more appropriate for both parties to pursue Article 21.5 proceedings, indicating that the EC's direct challenge to the US and Canadian suspension of obligations was inappropriate.[13] The Appellate Body's view on how compliance proceedings might progress in the *Continued Suspension of Obligations* cases involved two sets of proceedings under Article 21.5 of the WTO DSU. In the first set of proceedings the original respondent, the EC, initiating the proceedings, was expected to put forward claims that it had rectified the specific inconsistencies with WTO law identified in the prior ruling.[14] In the second set of proceedings the original complainants were expected to put forward claims concerning the ways in which the original respondent's implementing measures were allegedly inconsistent with provisions of the WTO agreements not covered by the original respondent's

[10] See above, Ch. 5, p. 188. [11] See above, Ch. 2, p. 65.

[12] On this argument, see the summary of the main arguments of the parties on the second series of EC claims. *Canada – Continued Suspension* PR, paras. 7.245–7.825; *US – Continued Suspension* PR, paras. 7.252–7.269.

[13] Responses to the Appellate Body's Report have raised a number of concerns, including questioning the Appellate Body's authority to make recommendations to the parties in this regard. Minutes of Meeting held in the Centre William Rappard on 14 November 2008, Dispute Settlement Body, 4 February 2009, WT/DSB/M/258; Minutes of Meeting held in the Centre William Rappard on 11 December 2008, Dispute Settlement Body, 3 March 2009, WT/DSB/M/260.

[14] *Continued Suspension* ABR, para. 353.

request for a panel in the first set of proceedings, or violated the WTO agreements in ways different from the original measure.[15] Previous WTO jurisprudence has established that if a WTO member has replaced a WTO-inconsistent measure by another measure that is allegedly inconsistent with a different WTO provision, there could be good reason to allow new claims to be raised in Article 21.5 proceedings.[16]

The Appellate Body report may have helped unblock the growth-promotion hormones dispute between the EC and the US, who subsequently reached a provisional settlement of their dispute.[17] The EC requested consultations with Canada under Article 21.5 of the DSU shortly after the Appellate Body's report in the *Continued Suspension of Obligations* cases.[18]

From a practical point of view, the two sets of WTO compliance proceedings envisaged by the Appellate Body in the growth-promotion hormones dispute would ideally be combined, as indeed the Appellate Body envisaged.[19] If such proceedings are structured into two, it might become impracticable to recombine them, if the party responsible for initiating the second set of proceedings does not do so promptly.[20] Further, structuring compliance proceedings into two sets of proceedings could generate falsely simplified perceptions of the complex relationships between the claims and issues to be addressed in the litigation and imply an overstated degree of party control over the scope of what is to be addressed in each of the two sets of proceedings.

[15] *Ibid.*, para. 354.

[16] *United States – Subsidies on Upland Cotton*, Complaint by Brazil (WT/DS267), Report of the Appellate Body – Recourse to Article 21.5 of the DSU WT/DS267/AB/RW, adopted on 20 June 2008, para. 211. See also *Canada – Measures Affecting the Export of Civilian Aircraft*, Report of the Appellate Body – Recourse to Article 21.5 of the DSU DSR 2000: IX, 4299. Although the jurisprudence has also established that a complaining party will not ordinarily be allowed to raise claims at the compliance stage that it could have pursued in the original proceedings.

[17] See above, Ch. 2, p. 68. Under the terms of deal, the EC could maintain its prohibition on beef from cattle treated with growth-promotion hormones, but would pay the price for this by granting greater market access for 'premium' beef. Other beef exporters have been anxious to ensure that this new market access is granted to all on a genuinely non-discriminatory basis. See Minutes of Meeting held in the Centre William Rappard on 23 October 2009, Dispute Settlement Body, WT/DSB/M/275, 22 December 2009.

[18] See, above, Ch. 2, p. 68. *European Communities – Measures Concerning Meat and Meat Products (Hormones)*, Complaint by Canada WT/DS48/21, Recourse to Article 21.5 of the DSU by the European Communities, Request for Consultations, 8 January 2009 (hereafter *EC – Hormones*, Request for Consultations, 2009)

[19] *Canada – Continued Suspension* ABR, 354. [20] *Ibid.*, 151, n. 772.

(d) Allocation of the burden of proof in the proposed reassessment proceedings

Writing on the problem of non-compliance with decisions of the International Court of Justice, Rosenne has observed that, 'An approach to the problem of the post-adjudication phase of judicial settlement cannot be based on any presumption of law that States observe their treaty obligations, because the problem arises when the conduct of a State does not follow the pattern of conduct prescribed in the binding statement of what its legal obligations are.'[21] Considering non-compliance to be a wrong of a special kind, Rosenne expresses the view that the original complainant's burden of proof is lightened so that if an original complainant can establish a prima facie case of non-compliance then the original complainant ought to be able to rely on inferences.[22]

In many cases the reassessment proceedings proposed in this chapter would take place in a context of alleged non-compliance, and adoption of Rosenne's approach would provide a way for dealing with the allocation of the burden of proof. However, scientific disputes where new scientific evidence has come to light may differ from the classic non-compliance dispute, where the dispute over non-compliance with a judgment or award will usually be a distinct legal dispute from the dispute that was the subject of the original proceedings.[23] This discrete non-compliance dispute will generally involve the alleged breach of the recalcitrant state's obligation to abide by the original judgment as a matter of general international law,[24] and in the case of decisions of the International Court of Justice, a breach of the United Nations Charter obligation to comply with judgments in cases to which it is party.[25] In contrast, reassessment proceedings involving subsequent scientific discoveries are likely to involve a greater legal focus on the merits of the original case. They may also generate a range of additional new legal issues at the reassessment stage that were not on the table during the original proceedings but would have gone to the merits of that decision.

There is a good argument that an allegedly non-complying party should not necessarily bear the burden of proof at the post non-compliance stage in relation to a dispute that has involved scientific uncertainty. Where more evidence has emerged on significant scientific points, the

[21] Rosenne, *The Law and Practice*, p. 202. [22] *Ibid.*, p. 224. [23] *Ibid.*, p. 211.
[24] *Ibid.*, p. 210. [25] *Ibid.*, pp. 202, 220.

allegedly non-complying party should surely be permitted the full benefit of these developments in scientific knowledge. It seems unfair in principle that this party be put at a disadvantage simply because science was not sufficiently advanced at the time of the original proceedings to permit a solid defence. In this respect, the situation could be considered to differ from other types of non-compliance cases.

Returning to the example of the *Continued Suspension of Obligations* cases may be helpful here. One of the specific incentives for the EC's initial decision not to pursue Article 21.5 proceedings in the *Continued Suspension of Obligations* cases appears to have been the potential for the allocation of the burden of proof under Article 5.7 of the SPS Agreement to the EC instead of to the original complainants. It will be recalled that Article 5.1 provides that members are to ensure that their sanitary or phytosanitary measures are based on a risk assessment. Article 5.7 provides that, where relevant scientific evidence is insufficient, a member may instead adopt sanitary or phytosanitary measures on a provisional basis. Much could turn on Article 5.7. The EC argues that it has:

> initiated and funded a number of specific studies and research projects, requested third countries ... for any scientific data and information in their possession, reviewed the findings of independent expert bodies, taking into account information from relevant international organisations, and performed an extensive review of the available scientific evidence and of available pertinent information concerning the six substances at issue.[26]

As a result, the EC relied on Article 5.7 to justify its ban on five of the six growth-promotion hormones, arguing that, having regard to its appropriate level of protection, the relevant scientific evidence was insufficient for performing a risk assessment within the meaning of Article 5.1.[27]

Given the central place of Article 5.7 at this stage in the growth-promotion hormones dispute, a compliance decision under Article 21.5 could have hinged on establishing that there was or was not 'insufficient' scientific evidence for a risk assessment to be carried out on the five hormones covered by the EC's new provisional ban. This would have been a decidedly awkward issue for a compliance panel, and the decision could have turned on the allocation of the burden of proof. If the EC had initially taken Article 21.5 proceedings, it was likely that the burden of proof could have been expected to lie with the EC in respect of all the legal claims arising. A party initiating proceedings

[26] *EC – Hormones*, Request for Consultations, 2009, 2. [27] *Ibid.*, 2.

under Article 21.5 traditionally bears the burden of proof.[28] If allocated the burden of proof, the EC would have had to show that there was insufficient evidence for a risk assessment – a negative assertion, and one that could have been difficult to establish to the satisfaction of the compliance panel.

The Appellate Body recognised that the parties harboured significant apprehensions about the allocation of the burden of proof in respect of the EC's compliance with the rulings in the original *EC – Hormones* case.[29] The Appellate Body addressed the allocation of the burden of proof in the dual compliance proceedings that it envisaged.[30] In the first set of proceedings, the original respondent, the EC, would bear the burden of proof in relation to the assertions it was putting forward, and would not benefit from a presumption of compliance.[31] In the second set of proceedings, the original respondent would benefit in the usual way from a presumption of compliance in relation to any new claims raised against it.[32]

The approach to burden of proof proposed for compliance proceedings in the *Continued Suspension of Obligations* cases could be adopted for use in reassessment proceedings in general international law. Under this schema, the original respondent would carry the burden of proof for old claims where there had already been a ruling against it, while for new claims the original respondent would benefit from a presumption of compliance and would not have to carry the burden of proof. The question of real significance in reassessment proceedings would then be how to determine which issues traversed in the reassessment litigation formed part of the original proceedings, and which do not.

[28] See e.g. *Canada – Measures Affecting the Importation of Milk and the Exportation of Dairy Products*, Complaint by New Zealand (WT/DS113), Recourse to Article 21.5 of the DSU DSR 2001: XIII, 6865, Report of the Appellate Body, para. 66; *European Communities – Regime for the Importation, Sale and Distribution of Bananas*, Report of the Panel, Recourse to Article 21.5 of the DSU (European Communities) DSR 1999: II, 783, para. 4.13; *Chile – Taxes on Alcoholic Beverages*, Complaint by the European Communities (WT/DS87), (WT/DS110), Report of the Appellate Body DSR 2000: I, 281, para. 74. At the same time, it has been made clear that a respondent relying on an exception with WTO law who has not taken steps to come into compliance cannot expect successfully to defend itself in compliance proceedings merely by re-arguing its case in an effort better to discharge the burden of proof. *United States – Measures Affecting the Cross-Border Supply of Gambling and Betting Services*, Complaint by Antigua (WT/DS285), Recourse to Article 21.5 of the DSU by Antigua and Barbuda, Report of the Panel DSR 2007: VIII, 3105, paras. 6.15–6.28.

[29] *Continued Suspension* ABR, para. 359. See above, Ch. 5, p. 188. [30] *Ibid.*, paras. 359–65.

[31] *Ibid.*, para. 362. [32] *Ibid.*, para. 363.

The growth-promotion hormones litigation again provides a practical example of the challenges potentially arising. In this case the matter of the allocation of the burden of proof had the potential to become highly technical. What would the EC be expected to prove, if the growth-promotion hormones dispute did come before a compliance panel under Article 21.5? The EC would have to show that it has cured the defects identified in the original *EC – Hormones* ruling in relation to consistency with the requirement in Article 5.1 of the SPS Agreement that SPS measures be based on a risk assessment. However, the EC now claims consistency with Article 5.1 only in relation to one of the six offending hormones. In relation to the remaining five hormones, the EC is instead relying on the provision in Article 5.7 of the SPS Agreement allowing WTO members to adopt provisional measures that are not based on a risk assessment in situations where 'relevant scientific evidence is insufficient'. The EC's initial caution about taking Article 21.5 proceedings was vindicated in the *Continued Suspension of Obligations* cases. The Appellate Body indicated that the issue of 'insufficiency' could be regarded as going to the question of compliance with Article 5.1.[33] This would mean that the burden of proof on the question of 'insufficiency' falls on the EC. According to the Appellate Body in the *Continued Suspension of Obligations* cases:

> the EC had to provide an adequate explanation of how the new provisional ban taken under Article 5.7 rectifies the inconsistencies found in *EC – Hormones*. Such explanation had to include, inter alia, an identification of the insufficiencies in the relevant scientific evidence that precluded the European Communities from performing a sufficiently objective risk assessment.[34]

The EC could develop various arguments to try and avert assumption of the burden of proof in relation to 'insufficiency'. To begin with there is the foundational point that it has now been established that it is consistent with the nature of Article 5.7, as an exemption from the requirement in Article 5.1, for the original complainant to bear the burden of proof in relation to any assertion that is integral to its new claim of reliance on Article 5.7.[35] Arguably, it is beside the point that the question of sufficiency is also integral to the question of the applicability of Article 5.1. In *European Communities – Measures Affecting the Approval and Marketing of Biotech Products* the burden of proof was allocated to the

[33] *Ibid.*, para. 716. [34] *Ibid.*, para. 716.
[35] On the status of Article 5.7 as an exemption, see above, Ch. 5, p. 217.

complaining parties under both Article 5.1 and 5.7 in relation to the individual EC Member State safeguard measures. This was consistent with the status of Article 5.7 as an exemption. The *EC – Biotech* Panel addressed the question of insufficiency as part of a distinct assessment of whether Article 5.7 could apply, although this assessment was nested within an analysis of compliance with Article 5.1.[36] In addition, the EC could potentially put forward the arguments concerning the reversal of the burden of proof in response to the need to take into account the precautionary principle as set out in Chapter 6, above.[37]

However, the Appellate Body's approach to the allocation of the burden of proof in relation to 'insufficiency' may be the one that is sustained in the WTO in the long run. The Appellate Body's approach will discourage WTO members who might be tempted to adopt a long-running strategy, keeping Article 5.7 in their 'back pocket', unused during original proceedings, mustering further scientific evidence if they should lose the original case and hoping that proving the non-applicability of Article 5.7 on the basis of 'insufficiency' will fall to the original complainants at the compliance stage. This is not to detract from the seriousness of the EC's position in the specific instance of the growth-promotion hormones dispute. The EC itself has said that 'WTO Members are not excessively litigious and do not gaily engage in endless loops of litigation.'[38]

The level of technicality seen in these discussions about the delineation of Article 5.1 and 5.7 of the SPS Agreement would, hopefully, not be reached in most reassessment cases. Certainly, if the proposed notion of special compliance proceedings in general public international law were to progress, it would be better if there were only one set of compliance proceedings. More generally, in a complex scientific case a court

[36] The *EC – Biotech* Panel first carried out an initial assessment of the EC's compliance with Article 5.1. *EC – Biotech* Panel Report 7.3015. The Panel found that the EC had not based its measures on a risk assessment as required in Article 5.1. The Panel then moved on to assess whether the EC could rely on Article 5.7, but found that the complainants had established an unrebutted case that the relevant scientific evidence was not 'insufficient' for a risk assessment and so Article 5.7 could not be applied. It followed that in the final assessment the EC was in breach of Article 5.1. *European Communities – Measures Affecting the Approval and Marketing of Biotech Products*, Complaint by United States, Canada, Argentina (WT/DS291, WT/DS292, WT/DS293), Report of the Panel DSR 2006: III, 847, paras. 7.3260, 7.3262.

[37] See above, Ch. 5, pp. 231–3 on prima facie cases in the WTO.

[38] Closing Statement of the European Communities, *Continued Suspension of Obligations cases*.

or tribunal would not necessarily be in a position to assess how the burden of proof was to be allocated until all the evidence had been received. Only once a case had been fully presented and the tribunal had heard from its appointed experts would the tribunal be in a position to assess properly which issues were integral to a curing of the defects identified in an original ruling and which issues rightly fell into the category of 'other issues'. This means that the parties would have to argue their cases as fully as possible.

Challenges to countermeasures

As a practical matter, an original respondent being subjected to countermeasures may also have the option of taking proceedings challenging the legality of such countermeasures. This would require an international court or tribunal to assess the original respondent's compliance with its international legal obligations at the time of the challenge in light of the scientific developments that had occurred since original proceedings had taken place. In general public international law this procedural avenue presently lies open for any state affected by countermeasures.

Under general international law the burden of proof will lie with a party seeking to rely on any exceptional justification for a breach of international law, including the justification that the breach is a countermeasure.[39] Countermeasures must be deployed with the aim of inducing a state to come into compliance with its obligations, and may remain in place only so long as the other party's illegal conduct continues.[40] If challenged, a party imposing countermeasures may have to prove that its countermeasures are consistent with these conditions. This could be expected to include proving that the original respondent remains out of compliance with its international legal obligations, although this onus might be softened in appropriate cases by applying the prima facie case approach identified by Rosenne in

[39] 'Where conduct in conflict with an international obligation is attributable to a State and that State seeks to avoid its responsibility by relying on a circumstance under Chapter V . . . the onus lies on that State to justify or excuse its conduct.' ILC Articles on State Responsibility, above n. 78, Commentary on Chapter V. Circumstances Precluding Wrongfulness, para. 8. See above, Ch. 5.

[40] Draft Articles on the Responsibility of States for Internationally Wrongful Acts, Articles 49 and 53, (2001) II *Yearbook of the International Law Commission* 26, also published as Crawford, *The International Law Commission's Articles.*

non-compliance cases.[41] The arguments in Chapter 6, above, concerning the reversal of the burden of proof in order to give effect to the precautionary principle might also be helpful.

(a) The Continued Suspension of Obligations *cases and Article 22.8 of the DSU*

The situation in relation to countermeasures is a little different in the WTO, due to the provision found in Article 22.8 of the DSU. Article 22.8 of the DSU specifically provides that a suspension of concessions shall only be applied until such time as a measure found to be inconsistent with a WTO agreement has been removed. Thus, as seen in the *Continued Suspension of Obligations* cases, there is scope for a suit arguing that an original complainant has breached Article 22.8 by continuing to maintain a suspension of concessions even once the original respondent has come into compliance. The scope for such challenges may soon be eliminated. During discussions on the amendment of the DSU a number of WTO members have suggested altering the sequencing of post-adjudicatory proceedings so that a member will be obliged to have recourse to Article 21.5 before seeking authorisation to suspend concessions against another member.[42] Further, as discussed above, in the *Continued Suspension of Obligations* cases the Appellate Body appears to have considered it inappropriate for a WTO member to pursue another member for an alleged breach of Article 22.8. This was reflected in how the Appellate Body dealt with the allocation of the burden of proof in relation to the EC's Article 22.8 claim.

The Panel in the *Continued Suspension of Obligations* cases considered the allocation of the burden of proof in a rather complicated way. In relation both to Article 5.1 and the pivotal question of the insufficiency of relevant scientific evidence under Article 5.7 the Panel allocated the

[41] See above, p. 235.

[42] For a helpful discussion of the sequencing debate and the issues as they have arisen in the litigation over importation of bananas into the EC, see Lester *et al.*, *World Trade Law: Text, materials and commentary*, pp. 172–4. Article 32 of the Mercosur Olivos Protocol provides explicitly for challenges to compensatory measures in cases where the party that has been targeted considers it has already taken satisfactory measures to bring itself into compliance with its obligations. *The Olivos Protocol for the Settlement of Disputes in Mercosur* (Translation) UNTS, vol. 2251, A-37341. However, there is only a short window for such challenges, of fifteen days from the adoption of the compensatory measures.

burden of proof to the EC.[43] However, the Panel then had the EC's initial burden of proof swing promptly to the original complainants, supposedly on the basis that the EC enjoyed a presumption of compliance.[44] Here the Panel misunderstood the fundamental nature of the presumption of compliance. Rather than viewing the presumption of compliance as a foundational principle that underlies the framework of international law and dispute resolution,[45] and determines the allocation of the burden of proof *ab initio*, the Panel applied the presumption as an ordinary evidential presumption that helped discharge the EC's burden of proof. The Panel also suggested that both parties enjoyed presumptions based on good faith, which would neutralise one another.[46]

The Panel's approach seemed arbitrary, suggesting that the panel saw no real purpose to allocating the burden of proof, as, in any event, a panel will weigh all the evidence together and determine in the round whether the parties have proven their various allegations against one another.[47] The Panel cited the remarks of the Appellate Body in *Japan – Apples* (demonstrating how an emphasis on the proof of factual allegations alone, as discussed earlier in Chapter 5, can be unhelpful).[48] In relation to Article 5.7, the Panel also seems to have perpetuated to some degree the error by the panel in the original *EC – Hormones* case by taking the view that one of the reasons why the EC should bear the burden of proof in relation to the insufficiency of relevant scientific evidence was that the EC had chosen not to rely on international standards and so did not benefit from the presumption of consistency under Article 3.2 of the SPS Agreement.[49]

The Appellate Body found that the Panel had erred in its allocation of the burden of proof.[50] Indeed, this was one of the bases on which the Appellate Body reversed the Panel's findings that the EC had acted inconsistently with the requirements of both Article 5.1 and Article

43 *Canada – Continued Suspension* PR, paras. 7.382, 7.629; *US – Continued Suspension* PR, paras. 7.375, 7.652.

44 *Canada – Continued Suspension* PR, para. 7.382; *US – Continued Suspension* PR, para. 7.375.

45 On the presumption of compliance, see above, Ch. 5, pp. 189–91.

46 *Canada – Continued Suspension* PR, para. 7.383; *US – Continued Suspension* PR, para. 7.386.

47 *Canada – Continued Suspension* PR, para. 7.383; *US – Continued Suspension* PR, para. 7.386. For discussion of the Panel's use of the notion of good faith, see also Ch. 5, pp. 190–1.

48 Above, Ch. 5, pp. 200–4.

49 *Canada – Continued Suspension* PR, para. 7.629 although see para. 7.624; *US – Continued Suspension* PR, paras. 7.652 and 7.646.

50 *Continued Suspension* ABR, paras. 580, 584, 717–18.

5.7 of the SPS Agreement.[51] However, the approach to burden of proof adopted by the Appellate Body was also out of the ordinary. The Appellate Body took the view that the allocation of the burden in relation to claims arising under Article 22.8 should be a function of three considerations: first, the nature of the cause of action being taken under Article 22.8; secondly, which party may be expected to be in a position to prove an issue; thirdly, the requirements of procedural fairness.[52] Taking into account that 'the suspension of concessions is a remedy of last resort imposed after an elaborate multilateral dispute settlement process', the Appellate Body considered that an original respondent should bear the burden of showing that its implementing measure had cured the defects identified in the original proceedings.[53] The Appellate Body treated the burden of proof as though the *Continued Suspension of Obligations* cases were themselves compliance proceedings. Indeed, the Appellate Body said that this approach would equally apply in cases where an original respondent initiates Article 21.5 proceedings.[54] The Appellate Body also elaborated the 'quantum of proof' required. An original respondent had to provide 'a clear description of its implementing measure, and an adequate explanation regarding how this measure rectifies the inconsistencies found in the original proceedings, so as to place the Article 21.5 panel in a position to make an objective assessment of the matter'.[55]

Clearly, the Appellate Body's main consideration was the belief that WTO members in the EC's position should take Article 21.5 proceedings rather than pursuing proceedings against other members for breach of Article 22.8, with the burden of proof to be allocated as set out above.[56] Envisaging a dual set of Article 21.5 compliance proceedings, or at least a split allocation of the burden of proof in these proceedings, the Appellate Body also intended to help ensure the full participation in these proceedings of the original complainants. Parties in the position of the US and Canada would have to establish any new claims concerning the new ways in which an original respondent's conduct was allegedly inconsistent with its WTO obligations. The idea is that original complainants in such a case will not be able to maintain a suspension of concessions in relation to an earlier decision without participating in compliance litigation. This would make for sounder dispute settlement, and better trade and political relations.

51 *Ibid.*, paras. 617–18, 733–4. 52 *Continued Suspension* ABR, para. 361.
53 *Ibid.*, para. 362. 54 *Ibid.*, para. 363. 55 *Ibid.*, paras. 362, 363. 56 See above, p. 327.

(b) Assessing the situation in relation to challenges to countermeasures

The adoption of countermeasures involves a breach of public international legal obligations and should not be commonplace. A party who adopts countermeasures must stand ready to defend itself, although benefiting perhaps from a judicial lightening of the burden of proof in relation to the specific issue of the other party's compliance with its adjudicated obligations. Preferably, the imposition of countermeasures should not be necessary at all, if a dispute over compliance can be disposed of before things reach such a pass. As discussed in the first part of this chapter, reassessment proceedings based on the model seen in the WTO under Article 21.5 of the DSU may provide a procedure for dealing with legal disputes arising out of scientific developments subsequent to a judgment or award.

Res judicata in subsequent proceedings

Chapter 7 and the earlier parts of this chapter have addressed the problem of how to deal with the discovery of important new scientific information after a judgment or award has already been rendered. The possibilities of revision and nullification proceedings have been discussed, and in the case of nullification it was suggested that consideration be given to hearing a resubmitted case in association with the request for nullification or annulment. In this chapter, two additional forms of action have been identified in which scientific developments subsequent to a judgment or award might be addressed: proposed 'reassessment' proceedings, and challenges to countermeasures. All of these forms of proceedings may involve application of the rule of res judicata in relation to the issues already decided in the previous proceedings.

As reflected in the dictum in *Company General of the Orinoco* referred to in Chapter 7,[57] a right, question or fact distinctly put in issue and directly determined by a court of competent jurisdiction may not later be called into question.[58] The doctrine of res judicata is accordingly

[57] *Company General of the Orinoco*, French-Venezuelan Mixed Claims Commission, 31 July 1905, 10 UNRIAA 184. See above, Ch. 7, p. 286.

[58] In *AMCO* an ICSID tribunal replaced 'directly determined' with 'distinctly determined', adopting language used in a legal opinion by Professor Reisman that was submitted by Indonesia. *AMCO* v. *Indonesia*, Resubmitted Case, Decision on Jurisdiction, 10 May

understood to apply to points distinctly argued in earlier proceedings and essential to an earlier decision.[59] Consistent with this, the doctrine of res judicata does not bar judicial consideration of new questions. This is clear from the *Haya de la Torre* case.[60] In the Court's decision on the admissibility of Cuba's application to intervene in the new proceedings, the Court rejected Peru's objections to Cuba's application, and admitted Cuba as an intervenor. Despite Cuba's interest in pursuing matters already decided in the *Asylum* case, the fact remained that the subject matter of the new proceedings related to a new question that had not been decided in that case. At the merits stage of the *Haya de la Torre* case, the Court made the same point: 'the question of the surrender of the refugee was not decided by the judgment of November 20th. This question is new ... There is consequently no res judicata upon the question of surrender.'[61]

Generally, the question of a state's compliance with a prior judgment will be a new issue. However, the situation may be different in the case of the reassessment proceedings proposed earlier in this chapter. In these reassessment proceedings what would be taking place is instead a re-litigation of the question of the state's compliance with the legal obligations that were at issue in the prior case. The legal issues will not all be new, and arguably the doctrine of res judicata would preclude the

1988 (hereafter *AMCO* v. *Indonesia*, Resubmitted Case, Decision on Jurisdiction) 10 May 1988, 1 ICSID Reports 543, 560. Doubts arise as to whether WTO panels will consider themselves authorised by the DSU to apply the rule of res judicata in relation to decisions from outside the WTO, such as a decision by a *Mercosur* tribunal as seen in *Argentina – Definitive Anti-Dumping Duties on Poultry from Brazil*, Complaint by Brazil (WT/DS241), Report of the Panel, DSR 2003: V, 1727, paras. 7.33–7.42.

59 Lowe, 'Res judicata', 39. For discussion, Cheng, *General Principles*, pp. 348–350.

60 Proceedings in the *Haya de la Torre* case were lodged by Colombia following the decision of the International Court of Justice in the *Asylum* case in 1950. *Columbian – Peruvian Asylum* case, Judgment of 29 November 1950, ICJ Reports 1950 266. The *Asylum* case dealt with the status as a refugee of the Peruvian, Victor Raúl Haya de la Torre, who had been granted diplomatic asylum in the Colombian Embassy in Lima. The judgment in the *Asylum* case did not deal with the matter of whether or not Colombia was required to surrender de la Torre to the Peruvian authorities. Colombia's request for an interpretation of the judgment failed to elucidate this matter, as the Court was unable to address in the context of a request for interpretation a matter that had fallen altogether outside the scope of its original judgment. Later the same year, Colombia lodged the new proceedings in the *Haya de la Torre* case in order to resolve the issue. *Haya de la Torre case (Colombia* v. *Peru)*, Judgment of 13 June, ICJ Reports 1951 71 (hereafter *Haya de la Torre* case).

61 *Haya de la Torre* case, 80. See also the Court's remarks in the *Request for Interpretation of the Judgment of November 20th, 1950, in the Asylum case*, Judgment of 27 November 1950, ICJ Reports 1950 395, 403.

reconsideration of complaints. In the *Continued Suspension of Obligations* cases, the Appellate Body observed that it would be open to a compliance panel to determine that certain claims could not be addressed within Article 21.5 proceedings, for example where the operation of the principle of res judicata precluded a complainant from taking a second opportunity merely to make out the same claim that had already failed in the original proceedings.[62]

However, what is the position where the circumstances have allegedly changed due to scientific advances? In such disputes there should arguably be a modification to the res judicata rule that allows for re-litigation in special circumstances where further material becomes available that could not have been provided in the prior proceedings even with the exercise of reasonable diligence.[63] If it could be established that scientific research has been so fluid as to create a 'changing situation' there might even be scope to argue that the doctrine of res judicata is not applicable at all.[64] In assessing the state of the factual dimension of a case at the time of subsequent proceedings, including whether there are special circumstances or even a 'changing situation', it will be important that the later case is viewed as a whole and previous evidence on relevant points is reheard together with new evidence.[65]

[62] Citing a number of its earlier reports in cases involving compliance proceedings in the WTO, the Appellate Body specified clearly that a complainant who had failed to make out a prima facie case in original proceedings could not re-litigate an unchanged element of the same claim. Nor could a complainant reassert the same claim against an unchanged aspect of a measure previously found to be WTO-consistent. *Continued Suspension* ABR, para. 354, note 771, referring to *United States – Import Prohibition of Certain Shrimp and Shrimp Products*, Report of the Panel, Recourse to Article 21.5 of the DSU (Malaysia) DSR 2001: XIII, 6529, para. 96.

[63] An exception to the res judicata rule to this effect is found in English law. *Arnold* v. *National Westminster Bank Plc* [1991] 2 AC 93, HL per Lord Keith of Kinkel at 109. Spencer Bower *et al.*, *Res Judicata*, p. 94; Barnett, *Res Judicata*, pp. 176–8. The exception is also built into the extended doctrine of res judicata as recognised in *Henderson* v. *Henderson* (1843) [1843–60] All ER Rep 378.

[64] For substantial authority to this effect in English law, see Spencer Bower *et al.*, *Res Judicata*, p. 382.

[65] Spencer Bower *et al.*, Res Judicata, p. 382; *O'Donel* v. *Comr for Road Transport and Tramways*, High Court of Australia, (1939] AC 1, per Evatt J. at 20. An analogy might be drawn with the circumstances in *Canada – Measures Affecting the Export of Civilian Aircraft*, where there were difficulties obtaining evidence from the respondent and the Appellate Body stated that in upholding the Panel's finding that Brazil had not proven its claim it was not intended that Brazil would be precluded from initiating fresh proceedings in the same dispute. *Canada – Measures Affecting the Export of Civilian Aircraft*, Complaint by Brazil (WT/DS70), Report of the Appellate Body, DSR 1999: III 1377, para. 205–6.

In all of this it is important to remain aware of the temporal scope of the legal rules applying to a case. Arguing the inapplicability of res judicata will only be necessary where the court must determine in the later proceedings any legal issues that are temporally conditioned by the applicable law such that they are in fact the same legal issues that were determined in the earlier case. In Roman law the point was made explicit: a valid plea of res judicata required proof 'that the point, or period, of time with which the judicial decision dealt was identical with that to which the subsequent proceedings related, and not prior, or subsequent thereto'.[66]

An additional problem also arises. In disputes where there have been significant scientific developments since the time of an original judgment or award, new claims and defences in relation to a state's ongoing conduct may be put forward. Can an international court readily regard these claims and defences as raising new issues? In English law, under the extended doctrine of res judicata such claims or defences would not be permitted if they might properly have been raised at the time of the original proceedings.[67] A similar rule already applies in WTO compliance proceedings.[68] Such a test could likewise be imposed in public international law in order to help limit the extent of subsequent proceedings, for example in the context of an award that is resubmitted following annulment or in the context of compliance proceedings.

In determining the scope of the res judicata in an earlier judgment or award it may be important to refer to the reasoning of a court or tribunal and not merely to the terms of its decision. This may be important in scientific cases, where there is a possibility that a court's or tribunal's intentions regarding the law may not always carry all the way through to

[66] Spencer Bower *et al.*, *Res Judicata*, p. 460.

[67] Under the extended doctrine of res judicata in English law the rule of res judicata applies to every point which 'properly belonged' to the subject of litigation but was not brought forward due to negligence, inadvertence or accident. *Henderson* v. *Henderson* (1843) [1843–60] All ER Rep 378, 381–2. A litigant is precluded from raising in subsequent proceedings any subject matter that the litigant had a duty to raise in the exercise of due diligence and that could have been raised without detriment to his or her interests, including erroneous assumptions as to fundamental facts. Spencer Bower *et al.*, *Res Judicata*, p. 189. According to Somervell LJ in *Greenhalgh* v. *Mallard* [1947] 2 All E.R. 255, 257, a point properly belongs to the subject of litigation if it is an issue of fact that is 'so clearly part of the subject matter of the litigation and so clearly could have been raised that it would be an abuse of the process of the court to allow a new proceeding to be started'. See also Scobbie, 'Res judicata', 301; Dallal v. *Bank Mellat* (High Court, England) (1985) 75 ILR 151, 162.

[68] See above, p. xx.

the factual level. The importance of determining the res judicata with reference to a court's reasoning is underlined in the decision on the United Kingdom's request for interpretation in *Delimitation of the Continental Shelf (United Kingdom of Great Britain and Northern Ireland and the French Republic)*.[69] In relation to the Channel Islands section of the Continental Shelf boundary, the original decision in the case incorporated a discrepancy between the legal reasoning of the Court of Arbitration charged with deciding the case on the one hand, and, on the other hand, the co-ordinates included in the *dispositif* and used in the boundary chart appended to the Court's decision. Despite the Court's intention that a twelve-mile enclave be drawn from established baselines, the Court's technical expert, a hydrographer, had (as disclosed in his own report, annexed to the decision) omitted seven established base-points (five low-tide elevations and two dry-land features). In these circumstances, the relevant part of the *dispositif* did not constitute res judicata, and the Court rectified the material error in the exercise of its inherent powers.[70]

The same point has been made in decisions in other fora. In the *Pious Fund* arbitration a tribunal of the Permanent Court of Arbitration observed that the precise meaning and bearing of the *dispositif* or operative part of a judgment was rendered through reference to the other parts of the judgment, and it was through consulting all of the different parts of the judgment that the points on which there was res judicata could be determined: 'all parts of the judgment or the decree concerning the points debated in the litigation enlighten and mutually supplement each other'.[71] Commentators, too, have remarked that the

[69] *Delimitation of the Continental Shelf (United Kingdom of Great Britain and Northern Ireland and the French Republic): Interpretation of the Decision of 30 June 1977*, 14 March 1978, 54 ILR 139 (hereafter *Delimitation of the Continental Shelf (United Kingdom/French Republic)*), 170, para. 28; Bowett, 'Res judicata'.

[70] The United Kingdom fared less well in its request for interpretation in relation to the Atlantic sector. Here the Court's reasoning required adoption of a median line between an equidistance line drawn using the Scilly Islands as basepoints and another equidistance line drawn without reference to the Scillies. In drawing these equidistance lines the Court's expert applied a system that did not allow for the curvature of the Earth, using a straight line on a Mercator projection to produce a 'loxodrome' rather than a geodesic or true equidistance line. However, the Court did not consider this technique so outmoded as to be incompatible with its reasoning, and considered the determination of the boundary in this sector to be res judicata.

[71] *Pious Fund*, Hague Court Reports (1916) 1, 5. For discussion, Lauterpacht, *Private Law Sources*, pp. 245–6. This was endorsed by the Permanent Court of International Justice in its Advisory Opinion on the *Polish Postal Service in Danzig*, 16 May 1925, PCIJ Series B, No. 11, 30, although the Permanent Court took the view here that in so far as they went beyond the scope of the operative part of a judgment the reasons contained in a

res judicata derives from the Court's reasoning, rather than from the operative clause of a judgment per se.[72]

Conclusion

The finality of international adjudication is important for international dispute settlement. On occasion, a scientific dispute will be ongoing and attempts will be made to have an earlier judgment set aside on the basis of scientific advances that are argued to have removed the basis of the judgment. Such a challenge could take various forms, although none of the existing review procedures is well-designed to deal with the problem. The limitations of the revision process and the doctrine of nullity were seen in Chapter 7.

In this chapter provision for reassessment proceedings has been proposed. These reassessment proceedings would allow for a proper hearing, with a shared allocation of the burden of proof depending on whether a claim was an original claim or a new claim. Although reasonably full proceedings are envisaged, there would still be certain restrictions on jurisdiction, consistent with the status of the proceedings as a form of review. Making allowance for such proceedings would be

decision would have no binding force. An umpire's expression of views irrelevant to the point actually decided were not res judicata, 29–30. See also the debate in *AMCO* v. *Indonesia*, Resubmitted Case, Decision on Jurisdiction where the tribunal hearing the resubmitted case rejected Amco's argument that the ad hoc Committee's reasoning in relation to the annulled parts of the original award was res judicata. The Tribunal found that what had been put in issue and determined by the ad hoc Committee was only whether the original tribunal had manifestly exceeded its powers, failed to state the reasons for its award, or seriously departed from a fundamental procedural rule. *AMCO* v. *Indonesia*, Resubmitted Case, Decision on Jurisdiction, 555, 560, citing Spencer Bower *et al.*, *Res Judicata*, para. 63. For commentary, Reisman, 'The breakdown', 783, 800; Schreuer, *The ICSID Convention*, pp. 1090.

72 Rosenne, *The Law and Practice*, p. 1603. Cf. 'L'autorité de la chose jugée ne s'attache qu'au dispositif de la sentence à l'exclusion des motifs', states de Visscher, *Aspects récents*, p. 17. See also, allowing recourse to a court's reasoning 'in order to elucidate the meaning and scope of the *dispositif*', Dissenting Opinion of Judge Anzilotti, *Interpretation of Judgments Nos. 7 and 8 Concerning the Case of the Factory at Chorzów*, Judgment of 16 December 1927, PCIJ Series A, No. 13, 20 (hereafter *Chorzów Factory (Interpretation)*), 24; *Delimitation of the Continental Shelf (United Kingdom/French Republic)*, 170 para. 28. In addition, a finding constituting a condition essential to a decision will be considered to have been included in the points decided by the court with binding force. *Delimitation of the Continental Shelf (United Kingdom/French Republic)*, para. 30; *Chorzów Factory (Interpretation)*, 20. Simpson and Fox, *International Arbitration*, pp. 229–30, 234. This approach parallels the concept of 'res judicata by implication' seen in English law, according to which the rule of res judicata will extend to determinations that must have been integral to a decision. Spencer Bower *et al.*, *Res Judicata*, pp. 184, 443.

preferable to a more laissez-faire approach. Left to run their course, scientific disputes may be ongoing, possibly even with counter-measures imposed and then challenged by an original respondent. Such situations become untidy, and costly in both economic and political terms. Prior recourse to reassessment proceedings might well be preferable.

9 Conclusion

Scientific disputes pose new challenges within the rationalist conception of adjudication in the international setting. Important factual elements of such disputes are acknowledged as unknowable, and so it becomes difficult to maintain a strict traditional rationalist conception of adjudication as a process where the law is applied to the facts. As a result, scientific disputes are generating renewed attention to rules about evidence and proof in international courts and tribunals.

The scientific disputes discussed in this book are 'live' policy cases where complainants want respondents to change their conduct. These cases differ from other disputes where complainants are seeking only compensation or the restoration of their dignity. At the national level it has been suggested that policy disputes call for a modification to traditional adversarial procedure. This is precisely what is taking place in international courts and tribunals, as they increasingly experiment with a wide range of methods for investigating central aspects of these scientific disputes.

Among the results of this experimentation is a greater reliance on expert evidence. Here, complex problems begin to arise. Many of the legal rules that are applicable will have been crafted with scientific uncertainty in mind. They may incorporate tests according to which a state is required to conduct itself as 'necessary' in the circumstances, or take steps based on 'sufficient' scientific evidence, for example. International courts and tribunals will need the close assistance of experts to interpret and apply these tests in different contexts. The legal and the factual dimensions of the case may become intertwined. Experts' views on what is in *general* 'necessary' or 'sufficient' will contribute to legal interpretations of these terms that may be perpetuated through successive adjudicatory decisions.

This subtle erosion of the operative distinction between fact and law could generate a concern in relation to the ongoing authority of international courts and tribunals and the integrity of the international adjudicatory decision-making process. To address this concern, it will be important that transparency is accorded to the intellectual contribution made by experts, and the reasoning of the international court or tribunal, as well as that international courts and tribunals continue to assume full responsibility for their decisions. The adjudication of scientific disputes may be a demanding task, but it must be remembered that the court or tribunal is not required to take a position on each and every scientific issue arising. A thorough appreciation of the science is necessary, but a court or tribunal only has to reach a view on the science in so far as this is required in order to reach its legal findings.

Provided these guidelines are observed, the trend towards greater use of a variety of evidence-gathering mechanisms is welcome. More judicial interaction with experts should facilitate in-depth understanding of the science. Structured dialogue, both written and oral, is to be encouraged. International adjudicatory bodies may wish to look to one another's practice in order to reflect on possible developments in their own. The model developed in World Trade Organization (WTO) dispute settlement has proved beneficial, as has the practice of expert witness-conferencing in investment arbitration. The ICJ's site visit in the *Gabčíkovo-Nagymaros* case was regarded as extremely useful. In contrast, the step taken by the parties of incorporating scientists into their delegations to speak as advocates subsequently proved controversial with the Court in the *Case concerning Pulp Mills*. Consultation with international organisations and reliance on their reports has assisted various international courts and tribunals.

Experts' expressions of the need for precaution will be found within all of these procedures for the taking of expert evidence, and indeed even where scientific evidence is presented by the parties' own experts. The recommendation made in this book is that we should welcome such expressions of precaution. Where well-researched, well-reasoned, credible high-quality scientific evidence indicates that a precautionary approach is important, international courts and tribunals should not hesitate to take this fully into account. Consistent with the overall approach to be taken to expert testimony, it would be best if transparency can be given to experts' value judgments about the appropriate course of action in the circumstances, and the court or tribunal will need to make sure that it still assumes overall responsibility for the decision.

Scientific disputes also pose a challenge within the rationalist tradition in relation to the application of the rules about burden of proof, by highlighting their potentially substantive effects. If ever these rules could have been considered essentially adjectival, they can no longer. The unfairness of applying the usual rules on burden of proof in a scientific dispute may be entirely apparent. The science may indicate a good chance that a case is justified, yet there may not be enough scientific evidence to enable a party to discharge the burden of proof. The resulting unfairness will take several forms. There may be a strong element of procedural unfairness because one of the parties is disadvantaged in pursuing its case. There is also the real danger of substantive unfairness in the judgment. Then there is the risk of significant harm to broader unrepresented interests, such as the environment.

Addressing this problem within the rationalist tradition should be possible. There is recognised scope within the rationalist approach to accommodate important values other than rectitude of decision. Further, the principle of fairness is an important undergirding principle in relation to the burden of proof. This suggests that the usual rules should be adapted where necessary in order to try and achieve ongoing fairness. The pump is already primed in the sense that states are accustomed to a reversal of the burden of proof in the administrative setting at the national level in order to give effect to the precautionary principle. Indeed, there has already been a degree of judicial interest in the idea of a reversal of the adjudicative burden of proof in international law.

Among the sources of the rule on burden of proof, attention should be paid especially to the inherent powers of international courts and tribunals. By virtue of their own existence, international courts and tribunals have the powers necessary to exercise the international judicial function: the settlement of disputes and the sound administration of justice. International courts and tribunals have the inherent power to modify the rules regarding burden of proof if it is necessary to do so in order to fulfil this dual function. Accordingly this book recommends that a new precautionary prima facie case approach be adopted by international courts and tribunals. This approach would apply in cases where the precautionary principle is applicable, and would lighten the load of the party whose case relies on the precautionary principle.

The new approach would be based on specified and explicit requirements. What would these requirements be? Most obviously, there would need to be interconnection between the substantive legal rules being applied and the concept of precaution. In addition, to trigger the application of the precautionary principle, the potential harm at issue would need to be serious enough and there would need to be enough scientific uncertainty. The practice of a precautionary reversal of the burden of proof would thus be subject to considerable discipline, requiring a series of careful judgments to be made in each case about whether these thresholds had been crossed. Further, the technical means for reversal of the burden of proof that is advocated in this book would further narrow down the instances in which a reversal of the burden would actually take place. Under a precautionary prima facie case approach, reversal should only take place where, setting aside the elements on which there is scientific uncertainty, a party's case looks like a strong case. Where the thresholds for precaution were met, a court or tribunal might then find in favour of a party on the basis of a prima facie case.

Scientific disputes also pose a challenge to the international institution of adjudication because of the possibility that subsequent scientific development could undermine a prior judgment or award. This possibility is one reason why scientific disputes may tend to become prolonged, politicised, and hard to settle. In the face of this dynamic, one of the most troublesome matters in relation to scientific disputes is to reach a view on the extent to which inroads should be made on the usual principle of finality. Existing review mechanisms are ill-fitted for dealing with the problem of subsequent scientific development. Revision is a restricted procedure, and the doctrine of nullity is regarded with caution in case it should undermine the effectiveness of international dispute settlement. This book has recommended that international courts and tribunals dealing with scientific cases consider making provision in their judgments and awards for a return to the court or tribunal in circumstances where subsequent scientific developments affect the basis of their decisions. In this way, allowance could be made to help ensure the authority and integrity of the international adjudicatory process while still protecting its finality. Institutional provision for reassessment is proposed for ad hoc tribunals and other bodies that may become *functus officio* in the interim before new scientific evidence comes to light.

International disputes involving scientific issues will continue to arise. In 2008, Ecuador submitted an application to the International Court of Justice in relation to aerial spraying by Colombia of herbicides at its border with Ecuador, as part of Colombia's coca eradication programme. Ecuador has reported serious adverse health reactions as well as negative effects on crops and biodiversity.[1] In the WTO there are ongoing issues in relation to European requirements for the labelling of biotech products, while New Zealand has entered into dispute settlement proceedings against Australia over long-standing phytosanitary restrictions on the importation of New Zealand apples,[2] and Mexico is suing the US over the required labelling of tuna as having been caught using 'dolphin-friendly' methods.[3] The Dispute Settlement Body has established a panel to consider the United States' complaint in *European Communities – Certain Measures Affecting Poultry Meat and Poultry Meat Products from the United States*, concerning the EC prohibition on poultry processed with pathogen reduction treatments.[4] Disputes may also arise in relation to climate change, both in the WTO, where non-discrimination disciplines are under considerable pressure, and in other fora.[5] Regional fisheries organisations are giving serious consideration to adopting trade sanctions in order to enforce stock management and conservation measures, and this may give rise to further scientifically oriented trade disputes. Australia is contemplating legal action before the International Court of Justice in relation to Japan's scientific whaling programme.

Scientific issues will also be to the fore in a number of North American Free Trade Agreement cases that are already underway. In September 2009, argument on the merits was heard in *Crompton (Chemtura) Corp.* v. *Government of Canada*, regarding a prohibition on the use of lindane-based seed treatment for canola.[6] In *Dow AgroSciences*

1 Application Instituting Proceedings, 31 March 2008.

2 *Australia – Measures Affecting the Importation of Apples from New Zealand*, Complaint by New Zealand, DS 367.

3 *United States – Measures Concerning the Importation, Marketing and Sale of Tuna and Tuna Products*, DS 381.

4 For further information, www.wto.org.

5 Drawing attention to the plight of the Inuit, we have already seen the *Petition to the Inter-American Commission on Human Rights Seeking Relief from Violations Resulting from Global Warning Caused by Acts and Omissions of the United States*, submitted by Sheila Watt-Cloutier, with the support of the Inuit Circumpolar Conference, on Behalf of All Inuit of the Arctic Regions of the United States and Canada, 7 December 2005. The Commission was unable to process the petition because it included insufficient information about a possible violation of rights, but a hearing of a general nature was convened on the relationship between global warming and human rights.

6 *Crompton (Chemtura) Corp.* v. *Government of Canada*, Notice of intent to submit a claim to arbitration under Section B of Chapter 11 of the North American Free Trade Agreement, 6 November 2001, www.international.gc.ca.

LLC v. *Government of Canada*, a case concerning a precautionary ban by the government of Quebec on pesticides, consideration will need to be given to the thresholds for the invocation of the precautionary principle.[7] In *Vito G. Gallo* v. *The Government of Canada* the Canadian government is subject again to challenge, in relation to legislative intervention to prevent the use of a decommissioned iron ore mine in northern Ontario as a waste disposal site.[8] *Bilcon of Delaware* v. *Canada* concerns an allegedly unduly lengthy environmental-assessment review process in relation to a proposed quarry and marine terminal in Nova Scotia.[9] Disputes are also arising in other investment fora. For example in the investment dispute *Marion Unglaube* v. *Republic of Costa Rica*[10] a German couple are bringing a suit against the Republic of Costa Rica regarding legislation interfering with their tourist project in Playa Grande through the establishment of a national park for the protection of leatherback turtle nesting grounds. Tobacco company Philip Morris is pursuing Uruguay under the bilateral investment treaty between Uruguay and Switzerland following an Uruguayan decision to require extensive health warnings on cigarette boxes.

Arguably, international law today requires international courts and tribunals to deal with situations for which the institution of international adjudication is not constitutionally ideally equipped and which should be dealt with *ex ante* through the exercise of other forms of legal authority. Yet the world frequently lacks the legal rules and structures needed to create shared and effective responsibility for taking executive decisions on issues that cross physical and jurisdictional boundaries. This increases the importance attaching to sound adjudicatory decision-making in scientific cases. The various pathways forward discussed in the chapters of this book will reduce in different ways the

[7] *Dow AgroSciences LLC* v. *The Government of Canada*, Notice of intent to submit a claim to arbitration under Chapter 11 of the North American Free Trade Agreement, 25 August 2008. Issues arising in this case will include whether, in light of all the circumstances of the case, reliance on the precautionary principle was sufficiently appropriate that the treatment accorded to the investor could be considered fair and equitable, and sufficiently appropriate that the actions of the host state could be classified as being for a public purpose such that the ban would not be regarded as an expropriation.

[8] *Vito G. Gallo* v. *The Government of Canada*, Statement of Claim, 23 June 2008, www.pca-cpa.org.

[9] *Bilcon of Delaware* v. *Canada*, Statement of Claim, 30 January 2009, www.pca-cpa.org. See also www.international.gc.ca.

[10] *Marion Unglaube* v. *Republic of Costa Rica*, Tribunal constituted 12 June 2008, icsid.worldbank.org; see also *Reinhard Hans Unglaube* v. *Republic of Costa Rica*, Tribunal constituted 29 December 2009, icsid.worldbank.org.

pressures faced by international courts and tribunals. Effective processes for expert input should reduce the need to rely on the rules relating to the allocation of the burden of proof, as will the availability of appropriate processes of review for any cases where there are genuinely significant subsequent developments in scientific knowledge.

Overall, the best way to deal with disputes involving scientific uncertainty may lie in an ongoing awareness of the alternatives to litigation, or at least the processes that can be combined with adjudication. Especially in interstate disputes, why should the parties need to go head to head on issues where the science is uncertain, when the best outcome would involve the selective application of what science there is to protect the interests held most dear by each side? Preferably disputes will be resolved by co-operative means before they reach the stage of adjudication. Alternatively, where adjudication becomes necessary, the most desirable dispute settlement outcomes may revolve around constructive use of a platform for ongoing co-operation. This is likely to be most productive and appropriate in situations involving the ongoing activities of the parties, where there is scope for agreement on the future management of these activities. The methods employed will need to incorporate mechanisms to facilitate the establishment of a sound, shared knowledge base, the adjustment of the parties' expectations, and the rebalancing of their interests. The settlement reached between Chile and the European Union in the *Case concerning the Conservation and Sustainable Exploitation of Swordfish Stocks in the South-Eastern Pacific Ocean* provides a good example.[11]

Many factors will make the experience of dealing with fact-intensive issues in disputes involving scientific uncertainty more challenging for an international court or tribunal than for a national court. Generally, the substantive legal rules being applied in a scientific dispute before an international court or tribunal may differ from those applying in a national legal context. As seen in the disputes discussed in the course of this book, seldom will a case turn directly on a simple question of whether an activity passes a certain threshold of likely harmfulness. Seldom can an international court or tribunal decide a case by

[11] *Case concerning the Conservation and Sustainable Exploitation of Swordfish Stocks in the South-Eastern Pacific Ocean (Chile/European Union)*, International Tribunal for the Law of the Sea, Order of 16 December 2009. Chile and the EU agreed on a 'more structured framework of fisheries cooperation' and a commitment to co-operation for long-term stock management, also establishing a Bilateral Scientific and Technical Committee. *Ibid.*, para. 12.

preferring the view of the majority of the experts appearing before it. In addition, domestic courts deal with a higher volume of cases, and those domestic courts whose role incorporates the finding of fact have long experience in the handling of evidence. Generally, they have smaller benches and longer hearings than international courts and tribunals. Further, there is no appeal from the decisions of many international courts and tribunals.

The burden on an international court becomes considerable: one and the same body must fulfil the functions of a 'Court of first instance and as a court of last resort'.[12] Most significantly of all, there is an institutional gulf in international law between processes of lawmaking and processes for the peaceful resolution of disputes. For domestic courts the prospect that the legislature will make new laws that provide a firmer basis for addressing problematic and unresolved situations provides a supportive backstop to the judicial process. In international law, lawmaking machinery operates slowly and in a decentralised and often reactive fashion. This means that international courts and tribunals must consider most attentively the implications of their procedural decisions, including their normative dimensions as well as their practical outcomes.

[12] Rosenne, *The Law and Practice*, p. 1340.

Bibliography

Abi-Saab, Georges. 'De l'Évolution de la Cour Internationale: Reflexions sur quelques tendances recentes' (1992) 2 *Revue Générale De Droit International Public* 273–96

Alford, Neill H. Jr. 'Fact finding by the World Court' (1958) 4 *Villanova Law Review* 37–91

Allison, J. W. F. 'Fuller's analysis of polycentric disputes and the limits of adjudication' (1994) *Cambridge Law Journal* 367–83

'The procedural reason for judicial restraint' (1994) *Public Law* 452–73

A Continental Distinction in the Common Law: A historical and comparative perspective on English public law (Oxford: Clarendon Press, 1996)

Allison, Richard C. and Holtzmann, Howard M. 'The Tribunal's use of experts' in David D. Caren and John R. Crock (eds.), *The Iran–United States Claims Tribunal and the Process of International Claims Resolution* (New York: Transnational Publishers, 2000), p. 275

Alvarez, Jose E. 'Burdens of proof' (1993) 14 *Michigan Journal of International Law* 399–427

Amerasinghe C. F. 'Presumptions and inferences in evidence in international litigation' (2004) 3(3) *Law and Practice of International Courts and Tribunals* 395–410

Evidence in International Litigation (Leiden; Boston: Martinus Nijhoff, 2005)

Anderson, Terrence, Schum, David and Twining, William. *Analysis of Evidence*, 2nd edn (Cambridge University Press, 2005)

Balasko, A. *Causes de nullité de la sentence arbitrale en droit international public* (Paris: Pedone, 1938)

Barnett, Peter. *Res Judicata, Estoppel, and Foreign Judgments* (Oxford; New York: Oxford University Press, 2001)

Bartels, Lorand. 'Commentary', in Federico Ortino and Sergey Ripinsky (eds.), *WTO Law and Process: The proceedings of the 2005 and 2006 Annual WTO Conferences* (London: British Institute of International and Comparative Law, 2007), p. 220.

Bar-Yaacov, N. *The Handling of International Disputes by Means of Inquiry* (Oxford University Press, 1974)

Beardsley, James. 'Proof of fact in French civil procedure' (1986) 34 *American Journal of Comparative Law* 459–86

Beck, Ulrich. *Risk Society: Towards a new modernity* (London; Thousand Oaks; New Delhi: Sage Publications, 1992)

'Risk society revisited: Theory, politics and research programmes' in Barbara Adam, Ulrich Beck and Joost Van Loon, *The Risk Society and Beyond* (London; California; New Delhi: Sage Publications, 2000)

Bedjaoui, Mohammed. 'La "Descente sur les lieux" dans la pratique de la Cour International de Justice et de sa devancière' in Gerhard Hafner, Gerhard Loibl and Ignaz Seidlhohenveldern (eds.), *Liber Amicorum: Professor Ignaz Seidl-Hohenveldern in honour of his 80th birthday* (The Hague: Kluwer Law International, 1998), p. 1

Bell, J., Boyron, S. and Whittaker, S. *Principles of French Law* (Oxford University Press, 1998)

Bentham, J. *Rationale of Judicial Evidence: Specially applied to English practice: From the manuscripts of Jeremy Bentham* (London: Hunt and Clarke, 1827)

'Principles of judicial procedure with the outlines of a procedural code' in John Bowring (ed.), *The Works of Jeremy Bentham* 11 vols. (Edinburgh: William Tait, 1843), II

Benzing, Markus. 'Community interests in the procedure of international courts and tribunals' (2006) 5 *The Law and Practice of International Courts and Tribunals* 369–408

Berger, Adolf. *Encylopedic Dictionary of Roman Law* (1953) 43(2) *Transactions of the American Philosophical Society*

Bilder, Richard. 'Some limitations of adjudication as an international dispute settlement technique' (1983) 23 *Virginia Journal of International Law* 1–12

'The fact/law distinction in international adjudication' in R. B. Lillich (ed.), *Fact-Finding before International Tribunals: Eleventh Sokol Colloquium* (Ardsley-on-Hudson, NY: Transnational Publishers, 1991), p. 95

Birnie, P., Boyle, A. and Redgwell, C. *International Law and the Environment*, 3rd edn (Oxford University Press, 2009)

Bishop, R. D., Crawford, J., and Reisman, W. M. *Foreign Investment Disputes: Cases, materials and commentary* (The Hague: Kluwer Law International, 2005)

Bodansky, Daniel. 'The legitimacy of international governance: A coming challenge for international environmental law?' (1999) 93 *American Journal of International Law* 596–623

Bohlander, Michael. 'The German advantage revisited: An inside view of German civil procedure in the nineties' (1998) 13 *Tulane European and Civil Law Forum* 25–46

Bone, Robert G. 'Lon Fuller's theory of adjudication and the false dichotomy between dispute resolution and public law models of litigation' (1995) 75 *Boston University Law Review* 1273–324

Bostian, Ida L. 'Flushing the Danube: The World Court's decision concerning the Gabčíkovo Dam' (1998) 9 *Colorado Journal of International Environmental Law and Policy* 401–27.

Bowett, D. 'Res judicata and the limits of rectification of decisions by international tribunals' (1996) 8 *African Journal of International and Comparative Law* 577–91

et al., *The International Court of Justice: Process, practice and procedure* (London: British Institute for International and Comparative Law, 1997)

Brealey, Mark. 'The burden of proof before the European Court' (1985) 10 *European Law Review* 250–62

Brierly, J. L. 'The Hague Conventions and the nullity of international arbitral awards' (1928) 9 *British Yearbook of International Law* 114–17

Broches, Aron. 'Observations on the finality of ICSID awards' (1991) 6 *ICSID Review – Foreign Investment Law Journal* 321–78

Broude, Tomer. 'Genetically modified rules: The awkward rule-exception-right distinction in *EC – Biotech*' (2007) 6(2) *World Trade Review* 215–31

Brower, Charles N. 'Evidence before international tribunals: The need for some standard rules' (1994) 28 *International Law* 47–58

Brower, Charles N. and Brueschke, Jason D. *The Iran – United States Claims Tribunal* (The Hague; Boston: M. Nijhoff Publishers, 1998)

Brown, Chester. *A Common Law of International Adjudication* (Oxford; New York: Oxford University Press, 2007)

Brown, David. 'Oral evidence and experts in arbitration', *Dossier of the ICC Institute of World Business Law: Arbitration and oral evidence* (www.iccdrl.com: 2005), p. 77

Brown Weiss, Edith. *In Fairness to Future Generations: International law, common patrimony and international equity* (Hotei Publishing, 1989)

Brownlie, Ian. *Principles of Public International Law*, 7th edn (Oxford University Press, 2008)

Bucci, Vittorio Di. 'Revision' in Richard Plender (ed.), *European Courts: Practice and Precedents* (London: Sweet and Maxwell, 1997), p. 699.

Button, Catherine. *The Power to Protect: Trade, health and uncertainty in the WTO* (Oxford: Hart Publishing, 2004)

Cameron, James. 'The precautionary principle: Core meaning, constitutional framework and procedures for implementation' in Ronnie Harding and Elizabeth Fisher (eds.), *Perspectives on the Precautionary Principle* (Leichhardt, New South Wales: The Federation Press, 1999), p. 29

'The precautionary principle in international law' in Tim O'Riordan, James Cameron and Andrew Jordan (eds.), *Re-Interpreting the Precautionary Principle* (London: Cameron, 2001), p. 113

Cameron, James and Abouchar, Juli. 'The precautionary principle: A fundamental principle of law and policy for the protection of the global environment' (1991) 14 *Boston College International and Comparative Law Review* 1–28

'The status of the precautionary principle in international law' in David Freestone and Ellen Hey (eds.), *The Precautionary Principle and International Law: The challenge of implementation* (The Hague; London; Boston: Kluwer Law International, 1996) p. 29

Cameron, James and Orava, Stephen J. 'GATT/WTO Panels between recording and finding facts: Issues of due process, evidence, burden of proof, and standard of review in GATT/WTO dispute settlement' in Friedl Weiss (ed.), *Improving WTO Dispute Settlement Procedures: Issues and lessons from the practice of other international courts and tribunals* (London: Cameron May, 2000), p. 195

Cappelletti, Mauro and Garth, Bryant G. 'Introduction: Policies, trends and ideas in civil procedure' in *International Encyclopedia of Comparative Law*, XVI: *Civil Procedure* (Tübingen, Dordrecht, Boston, Lancaster: J. C. B. Mohr (Paul Siebeck) and Martinus Nijhoff Publishers, 1988)

Cappelletti, Mauro and Jolowicz, J. A. *Public Interest Parties and the Active Role of the Judge in Civil Litigation* (Milan: Dott. A. Giuffrè Editore; and New York: Oceana Publications, Inc., 1975)

Carlston, Kenneth S. *The Process of International Arbitration* (New York: Columbia University Press, 1946)

Castberg, F. 'L'excès de pouvoir dans la justice internationale' (1931) 35 *Recueil des cours* 353–472

Charnovitz, S., Bartels, L., Howse, R., Bradley, J., Pauwelyn, J. and Regan, D. 'Internet roundtable: The Appellate Body's GSP decision' (2004) 3(2) *World Trade Review* 239–65

Chayes, A. 'The role of the judge in public law litigation' (1976) 89 *Harvard Law Review* 1281–316

Cheng, Bin *General Principles of Law as Applied by International Courts and Tribunals* (Cambridge: Grotius Publications Ltd, 1987)

Christoforou, Theofanis. 'WTO Panels in the face of scientific uncertainty' in Friedl Weiss (ed.), *Improving WTO Dispute Settlement Procedures: Issues and lessons from the practice of other international courts and tribunals* (London: Cameron May, 2000), p. 243

Churchill, Robin and Scott, Joanne. 'The *MOX Plant* litigation: The first half-life' (2004) 53 *International and Comparative Law Quarterly* 643–76

Corti Varela, Justo. 'The EU "coexistence" policy under WTO law: Problems and solutions', paper presented at *Changing Futures? Science and International Law*, ESIL-ASIL Research Forum, University of Helsinki, Finland, 2–3 October 2009

Crawford, James. *The International Law Commission's Articles on State Responsibility: Introduction, text and commentaries* (Cambridge University Press, 2002)

Croley, Stephen P. and Jackson, John H. 'WTO dispute procedures, standard of review, and deference to national governments' (1996) 90 *American Journal of International Law* 193–213

Damaška, Mirjan. *The Faces of Justice and State Authority: A comparative approach to the legal process* (New Haven; London: Yale University Press, 1986)

Evidence Law Adrift (New Haven: Yale University Press, 1997)

'The uncertain fate of evidentiary transplants: Anglo-American and Continental experiments' (1997) 45 *American Journal of Comparative Law* 839–52

Eijsvoogel, Peter V. (ed.), *Evidence in International Arbitration Proceedings* (London: Graham and Trotman / Martinus Nijhoff and Association Internationale de Jeunes Avocats, 1994)

Erichson, Howard M. 'Mass tort litigation and inquisitorial justice' (1999) 87 *The Georgetown Law Journal* 1983–2024

Feldman, Mark B. 'The annulment proceedings and the finality of ICSID arbitral awards' (1987) 2 *ICSID Review – Foreign Investment Law Journal* 85–110

Fergusson, M. Carr. 'A day in court in Justinian's Rome: Some problems of evidence, proof and justice in Roman law' (1961) 46 *Iowa Law Review* 732–72

Fiore, Pasquale. *Nouveau droit international public*, 2nd edn (Paris: Durand and Pedone, 1885), II

Fisher, Elizabeth. 'Is the precautionary principle justiciable?' (2001) 13(3) *Journal of Environmental Law* 315–34

Risk Regulation and Administrative Constitutionalism (Oxford; Portland: Hart Publishing, 2007)

Fisher, Elizabeth and Harding, Ronnie. 'The precautionary principle: Towards a deliberative, trans-disciplinary problem-solving process' in Ronnie Harding and Elizabeth Fisher (eds.), *Perspectives on the Precautionary Principle* (Leichhardt, New South Wales: The Federation Press, 1999), p. 290

Fitzmaurice, Malgosia. 'Equipping the Court to deal with developing areas of international law: Environmental law' in Connie Peck and Roy S. Lee (eds.), *Increasing the Effectiveness of the International Court of Justice* (The Hague: Martinus Nijhoff Publishers, 1997), pp. 397–417.

Foster, Caroline E. 'The "real dispute" in the *Southern Bluefin Tuna* case: A scientific dispute?' (2001) 16(4) *International Journal of Marine and Coastal Law* 571–601

'Social science experts and amicus curiae briefs in international courts and tribunals: The WTO *Biotech* Case' (2005) 52 *Netherlands International Law Review* 433–59

'Necessity and precaution in international law: Responding to oblique forms of urgency' (2008) 32(2) *New Zealand Universities Law Review* 265–83

'Prior approval systems and the substance-procedure dichotomy under the WTO SPS Agreement' (2008) 42(6) *Journal of World Trade* 1203–17

'Public opinion and the interpretation of the World Trade Organization's Agreement on Sanitary and Phytosanitary Measures' (2008) 11(2) *Journal of International Economic Law* 427–58

'Precaution, scientific development and scientific uncertainty under the WTO Agreement on Sanitary and Phytosanitary Measures' (2009) 18(1) *Review of European Community and International Environmental Law* 50–8

'The consultation of independent experts by international courts and tribunals', *Finnish Yearbook of International Law*, Volume 20, 2009 (Oxford: Hart Publishing, 2011)

'Burden of proof in international courts and tribunals' (2010) 29 *Australian Yearbook of International Law* (forthcoming)

Foster, Kenneth R. and Huber, Peter W. *Judging Science: Scientific knowledge and the Federal Courts* (Cambridge, MA: MIT Press, 1997)

Fraiberg, Jeremy D. and Trebilcock, Michael J. 'Risk regulation: Technocratic and democratic tools for regulatory reform' (1998) 43 *McGill Law Journal* 835–87

Franck, Thomas M. *Fairness in International Law and Institutions* (New York: Clarendon Press, 1995)

Freestone, David. 'Caution or precaution: "A rose by any other name"?' (1999) 10 *Yearbook of International Environmental Law*, 25–32

Freestone, David and Hey, Ellen. 'Origins and development of the precautionary principle' in David Freestone and Ellen Hey (eds.), *The Precautionary Principle and International Law: The challenge of implementation* (The Hague; London; Boston: Kluwer Law International, 1996), p. 3

Freyer, Dana. 'Assessing expert evidence' in Lawrence W. Newman and Richard D. Hill (eds.), *The Leading Arbitrators' Guide to International Arbitration*, 2nd edn (New York: Juris Publishing Inc., 2008), p. 429

Frowein, Jochen A. 'Fact-finding by the European Commission of Human Rights' in Richard B. Lillich (ed.), *Fact-Finding before International Tribunals: Eleventh Sokol Colloquium* (Ardsley-on-Hudson, NY: Transnational Publishers, 1991), p. 237

Fuller, Lon L. 'The forms and limits of adjudication' (1978) 292 *Harvard Law Review* 353–409

Gaeta, Paola. 'Inherent powers of international courts and tribunals' in Lal Chand Vohrah, Fausto Pocar, Yvonne Featherstone *et al.* (eds.), *Man's Inhumanity to Man: Essays on international law in honour of Antonio Cassese* (The Hague; New York: Kluwer Law International, 2003), p. 353

Gaillard, Emmanuel. 'Centre International pour le Réglement des Différends Relatifs aux Investissements' (1987) 114 *Journal du Droit International* 135–91

Garapon, Antoine. 'Incertitude et expertise: l'expertise française sous le regard international' in *Séminaire risques, assurances, responsabilités 2004–2005: le traitement juridique et judiciaire de l'incertitude*, Cour de Cassation, colloques et activités de formation, www.courdecassation.fr

Ghestin, J., Goubeaux, G. and Fabre-Magnan, M. *Traité de Droit Civil* (Paris: Librairie Générale de Droit et de Jurisprudence, Editions Juridiques Associées, 1994)

Gordon, Edward. 'The World Court and the interpretation of constitutive treaties: Some observations on the development of an international constitutional law' (1965) 59 *American Journal of Interational Law* 794–833

Grando, Michelle T. 'Allocating the burden of proof in WTO disputes: A critical analysis (2006) 9(3) *Journal of International Economic Law* 615–56

Evidence, Proof, and Fact-Finding in WTO Dispute Settlement (Oxford University Press, 2009)

Green, James A. 'Fluctuating evidentiary standards for self-defence in the International Court of Justice' (2009) 58(1) *International and Comparative Law Quarterly* 163–79

Griffith, J. A. G. 'Judicial decision-making in public law' (1985) *Public Law* 564–82

Grisel, Étienne. 'Res judicata: l'autorité de la chose jugée en droit international' in Bernard Dutoit and Étienne Grisel (eds.), *Melanges Georges Perrin: recueil de travaux offerts à M. Georges Perrin* (Lausanne: Payot, 1984) p. 136

Gündling, Lothar. 'The status in international law of the principle of precautionary action' (1990) 5 *International Journal of Estuarine and Coastal Law* 23–30

Hand, Learned. 'Historical and practical considerations regarding expert testimony' (1901) 15 *Harvard Law Review* 40–58

Handl, Günter. 'Environmental security and global change: The challenge to international law' in W. Lang, H. Neuhold and K. Zemanek (eds), *Environmental Protection and International Law* (London; Dordrecht; Boston: Graham and Trotman / Martinus Nijhoff, 1991)

Hanotiau, Bernard. 'Satisfying the burden of proof: The viewpoint of a "civil law" lawyer' (1994) 10(3) *Arbitration International* 341–53

Harremoës, P., Gee, D., MacGarvin, M. *et al.* 'Twelve late lessons' in Poul Harremoës, D. Gee, M. MacGarvin *et al.* (eds.), *The Precautionary Principle in the 20th Century: Late lessons from early warnings* (London; Sterling, VA: Earthscan Pub. Ltd, 2002), p. 185

Hautecloque, Jean de. 'French judicial expertise procedure and international arbitration' (1987) 4 *Journal of International Arbitration* 77–101

Helfer, Lawrence R. and Slaughter, Anne-Marie. 'Toward a theory of effective supranational adjudication' (1997) 107 *Yale Law Journal* 273–392

Herzog, Peter E. and Karlen, Delmar. 'Attacks on judicial decisions' in *International Encyclopedia of Comparative Law*, XVI: *Civil Procedure* (Tübingen, The Hague: J. C. B. Mohr (Paul Siebeck), Martinus Nijhoff Publishers, 1982)

Hey, Ellen. 'The precautionary concept in environmental policy and law: Institutionalizing caution' (1991–1992) 4 *Georgetown International Environmental Law Review* 303–18

Hickey, James E. Jr and Walker, Vern R. 'Refining the precautionary principle in international environmental law' (1995) 14 *Virginia Environmental Law Journal* Spring, 423–54

Higgins, Rosalyn. 'Respecting sovereign states and running a tight courtroom' (2001) 50 *International and Comparative Law Quarterly* 121–32

Highet, Keith. 'Evidence and proof of facts' in Lori F. Damrosch (ed.), *The International Court of Justice at a Crossroads* (Dobbs Ferry, NY: Transnational Publishers Inc., 1987), pp. 355–75

Hodgkinson, Tristram and James, Mark. *Expert Evidence: Law and practice*, 3rd edn (London: Sweet and Maxwell, 2010)

Hof, Jacomijn J. van. *Commentary on the UNCITRAL Arbitration Rules: The application by the Iran–U.S. Claims Tribunal* (Deventer, The Netherlands: Kluwer Law and Taxation Publishers, 1991)

Hohmann, Harold. *Precautionary Legal Duties and Principles of Modern International Environmental Law: The precautionary principle: International environmental law between exploitation and protection* (London; Boston: Graham and Trotman / Martinus Nijhoff, 1994)

Holtzmann, Howard M. 'Fact-finding by the Iran–United States Claims Tribunal' in Richard B. Lillich (ed.), *Fact-Finding Before International Tribunals: Eleventh Sokol Colloquium* (Ardsley-on-Hudson, NY: Transnational Publishers, 1991), p. 101

Holtzmann, Howard, Judge of the Iran–United States Claims Tribunal, 'Streamlining arbitral proceedings: Some techniques of the Iran–United States Claims Tribunal' (1995) 11 *Arbitration International* 39–50.

Hooper, Laural L., Cecil, Joe S. and Willging, Thomas E. 'Assessing causation in breast implant litigation: The role of science panels' (2001) 64(4) *Law and Contemporary Problems* 139–89

Howse, Robert. 'Democracy, science, and free trade: Risk regulation on trial at the World Trade Organization' (2000) 98 *Michigan Law Review* 2329–57

Huber, Peter. *Galileo's Revenge: Junk science in the courtroom* (New York: Basic Books, 1991)

Hudson, Manley O. *The Permanent Court of International Justice: A treatise* (New York: Macmillan, 1934)

'Visits by international tribunals to places concerned in proceedings' (1937) 31 *American Journal of International Law* 696–7

Hunter, Martin. 'Expert conferencing and new methods' in Albert Jan Van Den Berg (ed.), *International Arbitration 2006: Back to Basics?* (Alphen aan den Rijn: Kluwer Law International, 2006), pp. 820–5

Hunter, William A. *Introduction to Roman Law* (London: Sweet and Maxwell, 1908)

Hwang, M. 'Witness conferencing,' in Jamie McKay (ed.), *Guide to the World's Leading Experts in Commercial Arbitration* (Legal Media Group, www.legalmediagroup.com, 2008), pp. 3–5

'Witness conferencing and party autonomy' *Transnational Dispute Management* (October 2009 provisional issue) 19–27

Iynedjian, Marc. 'The case for incorporating scientists and technicians into WTO Panels' (2008) 42(2) *Journal of World Trade* 279–97

Jasanoff, Sheila. 'What judges should know about the sociology of science' (1992) 32 *Jurimetrics Journal* 345–60

Jenks, Wilfred. *The Prospects of International Adjudication* (London: Stevens & Sons Limited, 1964)

Jolowicz, J. A. 'The active role of the court in civil litigation' in Mauro Cappelletti and J. A. Jolowicz (eds.), *Public Interest Parties and the Active Role of the Judge in Civil Litigation* (Dobbs Ferry, NY: Oceana Publications Inc., 1975), pp. 157–278

On Civil Procedure (Cambridge; New York: Cambridge University Press, 2000)

Jones, Doug. 'Party appointed expert witnesses in international arbitration: A protocol at last' (2008) 24(1) *Arbitration International* 137–55

Kazazi, Mojtaba. *Burden of Proof and Related Issues: A study on evidence before international tribunals* (The Hague; Boston: Kluwer Law International, 1996)

Kokott, Juliane. *The Burden of Proof in Comparative and International Human Rights Law: Civil and common law approaches with special reference to the American and German legal systems* (The Hague; Boston: Kluwer Law International, 1998)

Kolb, Robert. 'General principles of procedural law' in Andreas Zimmerman, Christian Tomuschat and Karin Oellers-Frahm (eds.), *The Statute of the International Court of Justice: A commentary* (Oxford; New York: Oxford University Press, 2006), pp. 793–835

Koskenniemi, Martti. 'Peaceful settlement of environmental disputes' (1991) 60 *Nordic Journal of International Law* 73–92

Kuhn, Thomas S. *The Structure of Scientific Revolutions*, 3rd edn (Chicago: University of Chicago Press, 1996)

Kwast, Patricia Jimenez. 'Cooperating on the law of UNCLOS Article 76 and the science of the outer limits: The normativity of the institutional dimension', paper presented at *Changing Futures? Science and International Law*, ESIL-ASIL Research Forum, University of Helsinki, Finland, 2–3 October 2009

Lachs, Manfred. 'Evidence in the procedure of the International Court of Justice: Role of the Court' in Emmanuel G. Bello and Bola A. Ajibola (eds.), *Essays in Honour of Judge Taslim Olawale Elias*, 2 vols., I: *Contemporary International Law and Human Rights* (Dordrecht: Kluwer, 1992), p. 265

Lalive, J. F. 'Quelques remarques sur la preuve devant la Cour Permanente et La Cour Internationale de Justice' (1950) 7 *Annuaire Suisse de Droit International* 77–103

Langbein, John H. 'The German advantage in civil procedure' (1985) 52 *The University of Chicago Law Review* 823–66

Larroumet, Christian. *Droit Civil I* (Paris: Economica, 1998)

Lasok, K. P. E. *The European Court of Justice: Practice and procedure*, 2nd edn (London: Butterworths, 1994)

Law and Institutions of the European Union, 7th edn (London: Butterworths, 2001)

Lauterpacht, Elihu. 'Partial judgments and the inherent jurisdiction of the International Court of Justice' in Vaughan Lowe and Malgosia Fitzmaurice (eds.), *Fifty Years of the International Court of Justice* (Cambridge University Press 1996), pp. 465–86

Lauterpacht, Hersch *Private Law Sources and Analogies of International Law* (New York: Longmans, Green and Co., 1927)

The Development of International Law by the International Court (London: Stevens and Sons Limited, 1958)

Lester, Simon *et al. World Trade Law: Text, materials and cases* (Oxford; Portland, OR: Hart Publishing, 2008)

Lévesque, Céline. 'Science in the hands of international investment tribunals: A case for "scientific due process"', *Finnish Yearbook of International Law*, Volume 20, 2009 (Oxford: Hart Publishing, 2011)

Lind, E. Allan and Tyler, Tom R. *The Social Psychology of Procedural Justice* (New York: Plenum Press, 1988)

Loughlin, Paula and Gerlis, Stephen. *Civil Procedure*, 2nd edn (London: Cavendish Publishing, 2004)

Lowe, Vaughan. 'Res judicata and the rule of law in international arbitration' (1996) 8 *African Journal of International and Comparative Law* 38–50

MacDonald, John M. 'Appreciating the precautionary principle as an ethical evolution in ocean management' (1995) 26 *Ocean Development and International Law* 255–86

MacLennan, Jacquelyn. 'Evidence, standard and burden of proof in the use of experts in procedure before the Luxembourg Courts' in Friedl Weiss (ed.), *Improving WTO Dispute Settlement Procedures: Issues and lessons from the practice of other international courts and tribunals* (London: Cameron May, 2000), p. 265

Malaurie, Philippe and Morvan, Patrick. *Droit civil: introduction générale* (Paris: Editions Juridiques Associés, 2005)

Mani, V. S. *International Adjudication: Procedural aspects* (The Hague: Martinus Nijhoff Publishers, 1980)

Mansfield, Bill. 'The *Southern Bluefin Tuna* Arbitration: Comments on Professor Barbara Kwiatkowska's article' (2001) 16 *The International Journal of Marine and Coastal Law* 361–6.

'Compulsory dispute settlement after the *Southern Bluefin Tuna* Award' in Alex G. Oude Elferink and Donald R. Rothwell (eds.), *Oceans Management in the 21st Century: Institutional frameworks and responses* (Leiden: Brill Academic Publishers, 2004), p. 255.

Martha, Rutsel Silvestre J. 'Presumptions and burden of proof in world trade law' (1997) 14 *Journal of International Arbitration* 67–98

Matet, Patrick. 'Propositions du groupe de travail', in *Séminaire risques, assurances, responsabilités 2004–2005: le traitement juridique et judiciaire de l'incertitude* Cour de Cassation colloques et activités de formation (www.courdecassation.fr)

McDonell, Gavan. 'Risk management, reality and the precautionary principle: Coping with decisions' in Ronnie Harding and Elizabeth Fisher (eds.), *Perspectives on the Precautionary Principle* (Leichhardt, New South Wales: The Federation Press, 1999), p. 190

Mueller, Christopher B. and Kirkpatrick, Laird C. *Evidence*, 4th edn (Alphen aan den Rijn: Wolters Kluwer, 2003)

Nance, Dale A. 'Civility and the burden of proof' (1994) 17 *Harvard Journal of Law and Public Policy* 647–90

Ngwasiri C. N. 'Some problems of expertise in French civil proceedings' (1989) 10 *Civil Justice Quarterly* 168–83

'The role of the judge in French civil proceedings' (1990) 9 *Civil Justice Quarterly* 167–85

Nollkaemper, André. '"What you risk reveals what you value" and other dilemmas encountered in the legal assaults on risks' in David Freestone and Ellen Hey (eds.), *The Precautionary Principle and International Law: The challenge of implementation* (The Hague; London; Boston: Kluwer Law International, 1996), p. 73

North, Sir Peter and Fawcett, J. J. *Cheshire and North's Private International Law*, 14th edn (Oxford University Press, 2008)

O'Connell, D. P. *International Law*, 2nd edn (London: Stevens and Sons, 1970)

Oesch, Matthias. *Standards of Review in WTO Dispute Resolution* (Oxford University Press, 2003)

Okowa, Phoebe N. 'Procedural obligations in international environmental agreements' (1996) 67 *British Yearbook of International Law* 275–336

'*Case concerning the Gabčíkovo-Nagymaros Project (Hungary/Slovakia)*' 47 (1998) *International and Comparative Law Quarterly* 688–98.

'Environmental dispute settlement: Some reflections on recent developments' in Malcolm D. Evans (ed.), *Remedies in International Law: The institutional dilemma* (Oxford: Hart Publishing, 1998), p. 157

Olson, James M. 'Shifting the burden of proof: How the common law can safeguard nature and promote an earth ethic' (1990) 20 *Environmental Law* 891–915

Orellana, Marcos A. 'The role of science in investment arbitrations concerning public health and the environment' (2006) 17 *Yearbook of International Environmental Law* 48–72

O'Riordan, Tim. 'The politics of the precautionary principle' in Ronnie Harding and Elizabeth Fisher (eds.), *Perspectives on the Precautionary Principle* (Leichhardt, N.S.W.: The Federation Press, 1999), p. 283

Orrego Vicuña, Francisco. *The Changing International Law of High Seas Fisheries* (Cambridge University Press, 1999)

Pasqualucci, Jo M. *The Practice and Procedure of the Inter-American Court of Human Rights* (Cambridge University Press, 2003)

Paulsson, Jan. 'ICSID's achievements and prospects' (1991) 6 *ICSID Review – Foreign Investment Law Journal* 380–99

Pauwelyn, Joost. 'Evidence, proof and persuasion in WTO dispute settlement: Who bears the burden?' (1998) 1 *Journal of International Economic Law* 227–58

'The WTO Agreement on Sanitary and Phytosanitary (SPS) Measures as applied in the first three SPS disputes: *EC – Hormones, Australia – Salmon* and *Japan – Varietals*' (1999) 2(4) *Journal of International Economic Law* 641–64

'The use of experts in WTO dispute settlement' (2002) 51 *International and Comparative Law Quarterly* 325–64

'Expert advice in WTO dispute settlement' in George A. Bermann and Petros C. Mavroidis (eds.), *Trade and Human Health and Safety* (Cambridge; New York: Cambridge University Press, 2006), p. 235

Peel, Jacqueline. 'Risk regulation under the WTO SPS agreement: Science as an international normative yardstick?' Jean Monnet Working Papers, 2004

The Precautionary Principle in Practice: Environmental decision-making, and scientific uncertainty (Annandale, N.S.W.: Federation Press, 2005)

'International law and the legitimate determination of risk: Is democratising expertise the answer?' (2007) 38 *Victoria University Law Review* 363–80

Peter, Wolfgang. 'Witness conferencing revisited' in *Arbitral Procedure at the Dawn of the New Millennium: Reports of the International Colloquium of CEPANI* (Brussels: Bruylant, 2005), pp. 155–71

Plender, Richard. 'Procedure in the European Courts: Comparisons and proposals' (1997) 267 *Receuil des Cours*

Poli, Sara. 'Continuity and change in the EU Regulatory Framework on Genetically Modified Organisms, after the WTO dispute on "Biotech Products"' (2010) *Legal issues of Economic Integration* (forthcoming)

Popper, K. *The Logic of Scientific Discovery*, 4th edn (London: Hutchinson, 1959)

The Myth of the Framework: In defence of science and rationality (London; New York: Routledge, 1994)

Postema, Gerald J. 'The principle of utility and the law of procedure: Bentham's theory of adjudication' (1977) 11 *Georgia Law Review* 1393–424

Prager, Dietmar W. 'Procedural developments at the International Court of Justice' (2004) 3 *Law and Practice of International Courts and Tribunals* 125–42

Prieto-Castro y Ferrandiz, Leonardo. *Derecho Procesal Civil*, 5th edn (Madrid: Editorial Tecnos, S.A., 1989)

Raeschke-Kessler, H. 'Witness conferencing' in L. W. Newman and R. D. Hill (eds.), *The Leading Arbitrators Guide to International Arbitration*, 2nd edn (New York: Juris Publishing Inc., 2008), pp. 415–28

Ralston, Jackson H. *The Law and Procedure of International Tribunals: Being a resumé of the views of arbitrators upon questions arising under the law of nations and of the procedure and practice of international courts* (Stanford, CA: Stanford University Press, 1926)

Rambaud, Patrick. 'L'Annulation des sentences Klöckner et AMCO' (1986) 32 *Annuaire Français de Droit International* 259–74

Rao, P. Chandrasekhara and Gautier, Ph. (eds). *The Rules of the International Tribunal for the Law of the Sea: A commentary* (Leiden, Boston: Martinus Nijhoff Publishers, 2006)

Redfern, A. *et al. Law and Practice of International Commercial Arbitration* (London: Sweet and Maxwell, 2004)

Reisman, W. Michael. *Nullity and Revision: The review and enforcement of international judgments and awards* (New Haven: Yale University Press, 1971)

'The breakdown of the control mechanism in ICSID arbitration' 1989 (4) *Duke Law Journal* 739–807

'The supervisory jurisdiction of the International Court of Justice: International arbitration and international adjudication (1996) 258 *Recueil des Cours*

Reitz, John C. 'Why we probably cannot adopt the German advantage in civil procedure' (1990) 75 *Iowa Law Review* 975–1009

Ress, Georg. 'Fact-finding at the European Court of Justice' in R. B. Lillich (ed.), *Fact-Finding before International Tribunals: Eleventh Sokol Colloquium* (Ardsley-on-Hudson, NY: Transnational Publishers, 1991), pp. 177–203

Riddell, Anna and Plant, Brendan. *Evidence Before the International Court of Justice* (London: British Institute of International and Comparative Law, 2009)

Ripert, G. 'Les Règles du droit civil applicables aux rapports internationaux' (1933) 44 *Receuil des Cours*, 569–660

Risinger, D. Michael. '"Substance" and "procedure" revisited with some afterthoughts on the constitutional problems of "irrebuttable presumptions"' (1982–83) 30 *University of California at Los Angeles Law Review* 156–88

Rosenne, Shabtai. *Procedure in the International Court: A commentary on the 1978 Rules of the International Court of Justice* (The Hague: Nijhoff, 1983)

'The International Court of Justice and international arbitration' in Sam Muller and Wim Mijs (eds.), *The Flame Rekindled: New hopes for international arbitration: Leiden Journal of International Law*, Special issue on International Arbitration (Dordrecht: Martinus Nijhoff, 1994), p. 297

'Visit to the site by the International Court' in Emile Yakpo and Tahar Boumedra (eds.), *Liber Amicorum – Mohammed Bedjaoui* (The Hague: Kluwer Law International, 1999), pp. 461–73

The Law and Practice of the International Court, 1920–2005, 4th edn (Leiden; Boston: Martinus Nijhoff Publishers, 2006)

Interpretation, Revision and Other Recourse from International Judgments and Awards (Leiden; Boston: Martinus Nijhoff Publishers, 2007)

'Fact-finding before the International Court of Justice' in S. Rosenne, *Essays on International Law and Practice* (Leiden: Martinus Nijhoff Publishers, 2007), p. 235.

Rosenthal, Lloyd L. 'The development of the use of expert testimony' (1935) 2 *Law and Contemporary Problems* 403–18

Sadeleer, Nicolas de. *Environmental Principles: From political slogans to legal rules* (Oxford; New York: Oxford University Press, 2002)

Salmon, Jean J. A. 'Le Fait dans l'application du droit international' (1982) 175 (II) *Recueil des Cours* 257–414

Sanders, Pieter. 'Commentary on UNCITRAL arbitration rules' (1997) II *Yearbook: Commercial Arbitration* 172– 219

Sandifer, Durward V. *Evidence before International Tribunals* (Charlottesville: University Press of Virginia, 1975)

Sands, Philippe. *Principles of International Environmental Law*, 2nd edn (Cambridge University Press, 2003)

Schomberg, René von. 'The precautionary principle and its normative challenges' in Elizabeth Fisher, Judith Jones and René von Schomberg (eds.), *Implementing the Precautionary Principle: Perspectives and prospects* (Cheltenham, UK; Northampton, MA: Edward Elgar, 2006), p. 19

Schreuer, Christoph H. *The ICSID Convention: A commentary*, 2nd edn (Cambridge University Press, 2009)

Schwarzenberger, Georg. *International Law as Applied by International Courts and Tribunals* (London: Stevens and Sons Ltd, 1986)

Schwebel, S. M. 'The creation and operation of an International Court of Arbitral Awards' in M. Hunter, A Marriott and V. V. Veeder (eds.), *The Internationalisation of International Arbitration* (London; Dordrecht; Boston: Graham and Trotman / Martinus Nijhoff, 1995)

Scobbie, Iain. 'Res judicata, precedent and the International Court: A preliminary sketch' (1999) 20 *Australian Yearbook of International Law* 299–317

Scott, Joanne. *The WTO Agreement on Sanitary and Phytosanitary Measures: A commentary* (Oxford University Press, 2007)

Shahabuddeen, Mohamed. 'The International Court of Justice: The integrity of an idea' in R. S. Pathak and R. P. Dhokalia (eds.), *International Law in Transition, Essays in Honour of Judge Nagendra Singh* (Dordrecht; Boston: Martinus Nijhoff 1992) p. 341

Precedent in the World Court (Cambridge; New York: Cambridge University Press 1996)

Shany, Yuval. *The Competing Jurisdictions of International Courts and Tribunals* (Oxford University Press, 2003)

Shaw, Malcolm N. *International Law*, 6th edn (Cambridge University Press, 2008)

Simpson, J. L. and Fox, Hazel. *International Arbitration: Law and practice* (London: Stevens and Sons Ltd, 1959)

Sivakumaran, Sandesh. 'Application of the Convention on the Prevention and Punishment of the Crime of Genocide (*Bosnia and Herzogovina* v. *Serbia and Montenegro*)' (2007) 56(3) *International and Comparative Law Quarterly* 695–708

Slaughter, Anne-Marie. 'A global community of courts' (2003) 44 *Harvard International Law Journal* 191–220

Smith, Roger and Wynne, Brian. 'Introduction' in Roger Smith, and Brian Wynne (eds.), *Expert Evidence* (London; New York: Routledge, 1989)

Spencer Bower, G., Turner, A. K. and Handley, K. R. *The Doctrine of Res Judicata*, 2nd edn (London; Edinburgh; Dublin: Butterworths, 1996)

Stein, Alex. *Foundations of Evidence Law* (Oxford; New York: Oxford University Press, 2005)

Stein, P. A. 'Civil procedure' in D. C. Fokkema, J. M. J. Chorus, E. H. Hondius and E. C. Lisser (eds.) *Introduction to Dutch Law for Foreign Lawyers* (Deventer: Kluwer, 1978), p. 231

Stephens, Tim. 'The limits of international adjudication in international environmental law: Another perspective on the Southern Bluefin Tuna case' (2004) 19 *International Journal of Marine and Coastal Law* 173–97

International Courts and Environmental Protection (Cambridge University Press, 2009)

Stirling, Andy. 'The precautionary principle in science and technology' in Tim O'Riordan, James Cameron and Andrew Jordan (eds.), *Re-Interpreting the Precautionary Principle* (London: Cameron May, 2001), p. 61

Sward, Ellen E. 'Values, ideology and the evolution of the adversary system' (1989) 64 *Indiana Law Journal* 301–56

Szabó, Marcel. 'The implementation of the judgment of the ICJ in the Gabčíkovo-Nagymaros dispute' (2009) 39 *Environmental Policy and Law* 97–102

Tams, C. J. 'Article 50' in A. Zimmerman, C. Tomuschat and K. Oellers-Frahm (eds.) *The Statute of the International Court of Justice: A commentary* (Oxford University Press, 2006), p. 1109

Tapper, Colin. *Cross and Tapper on Evidence*, 11th edn (Oxford University Press, 2007)

Taruffo, Michele. 'Rethinking the standards of proof' (2003) 51 *American Journal of Comparative Law* 569–678

Taylor, Robert F. 'A comparative study of expert testimony in France and the United States: Philosophical underpinnings, history, practice and procedure' (1996) 31 *Texas International Law Journal* 181–213

Thayer, James B. 'The burden of proof' (1890–1) 4(2) *Harvard Law Review* 45–70

Thibaut, John and Walker, Laurens. 'A theory of procedure' (1978) 66 *California Law Review* 541–66

Thirlway, Hugh. 'Dilemma or chimera? Admissibility of illegally obtained evidence in international adjudication' (1984) 78 *American Journal of International Law* 622–41

'Procedural law and the International Court of Justice' in Vaughan Lowe and Malgosia Fitzmaurice (eds.), *Fifty Years of the International Court of Justice: Essays in honour of Sir Robert Jennings* (Cambridge University Press, 1996), p. 389

'Procedure of international courts and tribunals' in R. Bernhardt (ed.), *Encyclopaedia of Public International Law*, 12 vols. (Amsterdam: Elsevier Science BV, 1997), III, pp. 1128–31

'The law and procedure of the International Court of Justice 1960–1989: Part Nine' (1999) 69 *British Yearbook of International Law* 1–84

'The law and procedure of the International Court of Justice 1960–1989: Part Ten' (2000) 70 *British Yearbook of International Law* 1–63

Thouvenin, Jean-Marc. 'La Descente de la cour sur les lieux dans l'affaire relative au projet Gabčíkovo-Nagymaros' (1997) XLIII *Annuaire Français de Droit International* 333–40

Tochilovsky, Vladimir. *Jurisprudence of the International Criminal Courts and the European Court of Human Rights: Procedure and evidence* (Leiden; Boston: Martinus Nijhoff Publishers, 2008)

Tomka, Peter and Wordsworth, Samuel S. 'The first site visit of the International Court of Justice in fulfilment of its judicial function' (1998) 92 *American Journal of International Law* 133–40

Trouwborst, Arie. *Evolution and Status of the Precautionary Principle in International Law* (The Hague; New York: Kluwer Law International, 2002)

Tsagourias, N. 'Application for revision of the judgment of 11 July 1996 in the Case concerning Application of the Convention on the Prevention and Punishment of the Crime of Genocide (*Bosnia and Herzegovina* v. *Yugoslavia*), Preliminary Objections (*Yugoslavia* v. *Bosnia and Herzegovina*), Judgment of 3 February 2003' (2004) 53 *International and Comparative Law Quarterly* 731–8

Twining, William. *Theories of Evidence: Bentham and Wigmore* (London: Weidenfield and Nicolson, Handon, 1985)

Rethinking Evidence: Exploratory essays, 2nd edn (Cambridge University Press, 2006)

Usher, John A. *European Court Practice* (London: Sweet and Maxwell, 1983)

Vattel, Emmerich de. 'The law of nations or the principles of natural law' (trans. Charles G. Fenwick) in James Brown Scott (ed.), *The Classics of International Law* (Washington: Carnegie Institution of Washington, 1916), III, pp. 1–398

Verhoosel, Gaetan. 'Gabčíkovo-Nagymaros: The evidentiary regime on environmental degradation and the World Court' (1997) 6 *European Environmental Law Review*, 247–53

Victor, David G. 'The Sanitary and Phytosanitary Agreement of the World Trade Organization: An assessment after five years' (1999–2000) 32 *New York University Journal of International Law and Politics* 865–937

Visscher, Charles de. *Aspects récents de droit procédural* (Paris: Pedone, 1966)

Wagner, Martin J. 'International investment, expropriation and environmental protection' (1999) 29 *Golden Gate University Law Review* 465–538

Waincymer, Jeff. *WTO Litigation: Procedural aspects of formal dispute settlement* (London: Cameron May, 2002)

Walid, Ben Hamida. 'Two nebulous ICSID features: The notion of investment and the scope of annulment control: Ad hoc Committee's decision in *Patrick Mitchell* v. *Democratic Republic of Congo*' (2007) 24 (3) *Journal of International Arbitration* 287–306

Walker, Vern R. 'Keeping the WTO from becoming the "World Trans-Science Organization": Scientific uncertainty, science policy, and factfinding in the growth hormones dispute' (1998) 31 *Cornell International Law Journal* 251–322

'Transforming science into law: Default reasoning in international trade disputes' in Wendy Wagner and Rena Steinzor (eds.), *Rescuing Science from Politics: Regulation and the distortion of scientific research* (Cambridge University Press, 2006), p. 165

Watts, Sir Arthur. *New Zealand at the International Court of Justice: French nuclear testing in the Pacific: Nuclear Tests Case New Zealand v. France, 1995* (Wellington, NZ: New Zealand Ministry of Foreign Affairs and Trade, 1996)

'Burden of proof, and evidence before the ICJ' in Friedl Weiss (ed.), *Improving WTO Dispute Settlement Procedures: Issues and lessons from the practice of other international courts and tribunals* (London: Cameron May, 2000), pp. 289–301

'New practice directions of the International Court of Justice' (2002) 1(2) *Law and Practice of International Courts and Tribunals* 247–56

Watts, Sir Arthur and Jennings, Sir Robert. *Oppenheim's International Law*, 9th edn (London: Longman, 1992)

Wesley, John W. 'Scientific evidence and the question of judicial capacity' (1984) 25 *William and Mary Law Review* 675–703

Wetter, J. Gillis. *The International Arbitral Process: Public and private*, 5 vols. (Dobbs Ferry, NY: Oceana Publications, 1979), II

White, Gillian M. *The Use of Experts by International Tribunals* (Syracuse, NY: Syracuse University Press, 1965)

Winickoff, D., Jasanoff, S., Busch, L., Grove-White, R. and Wynne, B. 'Adjudicating the GM food wars: Science, risk, and democracy in world trade law' (2005) 30 *Yale Journal of International Law* 81–123

Wirth, David. 'The role of science in the Uruguay round and NAFTA trade disciplines' (1994) 27 *Cornell International Law Journal* 817–59

Witenberg, J. C. '*Onus probandi* devant les juridictions arbitrales' (1951) 55 *Revue Generale de Droit International Public* 321–42

Woolf, Right Hon. Lord. *Access to Justice: Final report to the Lord Chancellor on the civil justice system in England and Wales* (London: HMSO, 1996)

World Trade Organization, *The Legal Texts: The results of the Uruguay round of multilateral trade negotiations* (Cambridge University Press, 1999)

Wynne, Brian. 'Uncertainty and environmental learning: Reconceiving science and policy in the preventive paradigm' (1992) 2(2) *Global Environmental Change* 111–27

'Risk and environmental issues as STS themes: Reflexivity on the rocks?' (July 2002) Special Issue *Current Sociology*

Zuckerman, A. A. S. *Zuckerman on Civil Procedure: Principles of practice* (London: Sweet and Maxwell, 2006)

Index